STRENGTHS-BASED SUPERVISION IN CLINICAL PRACTICE

This book is the result of an article I wrote with my colleague Mei Chen (Edwards & Chen, 1999), and presentations I carried out at the First Annual International Interdisciplinary Conference on Clinical Supervision held at SUNY Buffalo (2005), at Oakton College's Continuing Education for Health Professionals Series (2005–2006), at Northeastern Illinois University Department of Counselor Education's Professional Development Institutes (2006), at the Illinois Counseling Association's Continuing Education Series (2006–2010) as well as at their annual conference in Springfield, Illinois (2006, 2009, 2010), and at the Illinois Association of Marriage and Family Therapy (2010). I am indebted to the many seasoned supervisors at these presentations for their robust and hardy encouragement and suggestions.

I am sincerely grateful to my student interns and agency supervisees. You taught me how to look for strengths rather than deficits to help us grow together. My graduate assistant, Stef Standefer, who looked up and gathered huge piles of articles for me to read, was a tremendous help in the early stages of this book. My wife and great encourager, Betsy, is my first editor, and she keeps me from sending in copy that is not readable as the King's English. Read the Epilogue to understand why. And finally, to my editors, Eric Garner, Courtney Munz, and Tina Hardy, and especially to my acquisitions editor, Ms. Kassie Graves, who believed in this book from the very beginning; I cannot thank you enough. This book would still be sitting idle and incomplete in a computer file somewhere without your help and encouragement.

STRENGTHS-BASED SUPERVISION IN CLINICAL PRACTICE

JEFFREY K. EDWARDS

Northeastern Illinois University, Walden University

Los Angeles | London | New Delhi
Singapore | Washington DC

Los Angeles | London | New Delhi
Singapore | Washington DC

FOR INFORMATION:

SAGE Publications, Inc.
2455 Teller Road
Thousand Oaks, California 91320
E-mail: order@sagepub.com

SAGE Publications Ltd.
1 Oliver's Yard
55 City Road
London EC1Y 1SP
United Kingdom

SAGE Publications India Pvt. Ltd.
B 1/I 1 Mohan Cooperative Industrial Area
Mathura Road, New Delhi 110 044
India

SAGE Publications Asia-Pacific Pte. Ltd.
3 Church Street
#10-04 Samsung Hub
Singapore 049483

Acquisitions Editor: Kassie Graves
Editorial Assistant: Courtney Munz
Production Editor: Eric Garner
Copy Editor: Tina Hardy
Typesetter: C&M Digitals (P) Ltd.
Proofreader: Carole Quandt
Indexer: Jean Casalegno
Cover Designer: Anupama Krishnan
Marketing Manager: Lisa Sheldon-Brown
Permissions Editor: Adele Hutchinson

Copyright © 2013 by SAGE Publications, Inc.

Printed in the United States of America

Library of Congress Cataloging-in-Publication Data

Edwards, Jeffrey K.

Strengths-based supervision in clinical practice / Jeffrey K. Edwards.

p. cm.
Includes bibliographical references and index.

ISBN 978-1-4129-8720-2 (pbk.)

1. Counselors—Supervision of. 2. Clinical psychologists—Supervision of. 3. Counseling psychology—Study and teaching. I. Title.

BF636.65.E39 2013
361′.060683—dc23   2012003922

This book is printed on acid-free paper.

12 13 14 15 16 10 9 8 7 6 5 4 3 2 1

CONTENTS

Foreword   ix

Kara Zimmerman

Prologue   xi

PART I. IN THE BEGINNING   1

Chapter 1. The History and Traditions of Clinical Supervision   3

History: Somewhat Briefly   4

Supervision Literature in Historical Context   5

Family Systems Supervision   8

Substance Abuse Counseling Supervision   10

Historical Changes in Models and Modes of Clinical Supervision   10

Models of Supervision   11

Formats of Clinical Supervision   15

Supervision Configurations   22

Strengths-Based Supervision   26

Chapter 2. Executive Skills of Strengths-Based Supervision   27

Cross-Cultural and Multicultural Competencies   29

Cross-Culturalism and Multiculturalism   30

Multiculturalism and Supervision   31

Further Discussion on Multicultural Supervision   37

Focus Areas and Domains of a Supervisor   37

Process Skills   38

Conceptualization Skills   38

Personalization Skills   39

Training   39

Consultation   40

Counseling   41

Ethics   43

Developmental Stages of Counselors   44

   Level 1: The Beginning of the Journey   45

   Level 2: Trials and Tribulations   45

   Level 3: Challenge and Growth   47

Isomorphs and Parallel Processes in Supervision   48

Boundary Issues in Clinical Supervision   52

Interpersonal Relationship Skills   57

   Conflict Resolution: A Beginning   59

   A Synthesis of Basic Strategies   60

   Preventing Conflict   61

Promoting Counselor Self-Efficacy and

Personal Agency: A Core Executive Skill   62

   Thoughts on Self-Efficacy and Personal Agency   64

   Session Management   64

The Relationship Between Supervisor and

Supervisee—Personal and Professional   65

   Reflections   65

PART II. A TIME FOR A CHANGE TO A NEW MODEL   **67**

Chapter 3. A Time for Change   **69**

Too Many Contradictions   71

Best Practices: Who Decides?   73

What Really Makes a Difference?   73

Educating Adults   76

Beyond Clinical Skills   78

A First Glimpse at Strengths-Based Clinical Supervision   80

   Clinical Work   81

Chapter 4. Strengths-Based Clinical Supervision Primer:

Social Constructivism and Postmodern Influences   **87**

Strengths-Based Concepts   88

   Social Constructivist and Postmodernist Informed Models   89

   Social Constructivism   91

   Gleaning Useful Supervisory Concepts   95

Solution-Focused Supervision   96

   Gleaning Useful Supervisory Concepts   98

Narrative Supervision   100

   Gleaning Useful Supervisory Concepts   101

Reflecting Team Supervision   104

   Gleaning Useful Supervisory Concepts   105

A Glasnost Look at Postmodern/Social Constructivist Supervision   106

Chapter 5. Strengths-Based Clinical Supervision Primer:
From the Roots of Psychology   **109**
Positive Psychology   109
Positive Psychology Premises   109
Positive Psychotherapy   111
Gleaning Useful Supervisory Concepts   115
Resiliency   118
Gleaning Useful Supervisory Concepts   121
Enfolding Strengths-Based Supervision   122
The World is Flat and We Are Not   124
Just Try and Make Them   125
Wisdom and Truths: Guiding Principles and Systemic Logic   125

Chapter 6. The Larger Picture:
Strengths-Based Management and Leadership   **127**
Leadership in Practice   129
Servant Leadership   129
Service Leadership   130
Strengths-Based Leadership   131
Organizational Evaluation and Change Using Positives   132
Evaluation   133
360-Degree Evaluation   134
Bell Curves as an Epistemological Framer of Evaluating Success   135
The J-Curve as a New Normal of Evaluation and Success   136
Back to 360-Degree Evaluations   137
Appreciative Inquiry   138
The Tipping Point of Change   141
The Law of the Few   142
Solidifying Change   144

PART III. FACES OF STRENGTH:
PUTTING MY CURRENCY WHERE MY MOUTH IS   **147**

Chapter 7. Supervision Sessions and Personnel Management: Vantage Point,
Point of View, and Perspective: It's All in the Way You See It   **149**
Implementing Strengths-Based Supervision Strategies   151
Vantage Point, Point of View, and Perspective   151
What is Clinical Supervision?   157
Stages of Supervision   157
The Administrative Part: But for All Who are Invested in Helping Others   169
What is Administrative Supervision?   169
Motivation   169
Success: What is It All About Anyway?   171

Chapter 8. Case Examples of Strengths-Based Supervision   **175**

     Case Presentations   176

     Jane Faces Her Self   177

     Melody's Strengths Sing   187

Chapter 9. Lessons Learned and Where to From Here?   **195**

     Wrapping Up   196

     Philosophy   196

     Application   198

     Moving Forward   205

     Where to From Here?   206

     Things to Remember and Things You Can Do   206

Chapter 10. Epilogue: Thanks to Officer Blackwell, Mr. Jones, Coach Canino, and All the Rest   **211**

References   **215**

Index   **233**

About the Author   **245**

FOREWORD

Over 14 years ago, as a new graduate with a master's degree, working as a therapist in a social service agency, I went searching for a clinical supervisor to supervise me toward my marriage and family therapy license. I had seen "Dr. Edwards" at the state marriage and family therapy conferences and he had always seemed friendly, positive, and approachable. I called and asked him if he'd be willing to take me on as a supervisee, and I was happy that he agreed. For over 2 years we met regularly in his home, often with his cat curled up in my lap, talking about my clients, my cases, my adjustment to working in an agency setting, and my formation as a therapist.

I think what I remember most from that time was the feeling that even though I was a brand new and young therapist not always sure of what I was doing, Jeff truly believed in me. Even 14 years later I can vividly recall a time when he burst out, in the middle of a discussion, "You are delightful!" To feel valued, enjoyed, and believed in as a person and as a therapist, especially when I was feeling quite unsure and shaky doing very tough clinical work, helped me much more than any technique he could have taught me. I never felt like he was just trying to flatter me; his affirmation felt genuine and was grounded in his belief in people and their self-efficacy in general. The safe environment he provided for me, where

I did not have to try to impress or please him or become just like him, but could be honest in my struggles, questions, successes, and mistakes, was empowering for me in my early development and sense of competency as a clinician. I believe he helped me find and use my own voice.

I don't remember learning anything specific in my master's program on how to do clinical supervision, and I didn't feel well-prepared when, less than 5 years after graduation, I was asked to begin the important role of supervising the therapists who had been my peers, many older than I, in the counseling program where I was working as a therapist. I wish I had had this book then. Reading it now has greatly stretched me in my practice as a supervisor and therapist, and I am now so much more aware of when I am in the context of a deficit- and pathology-based system or setting. Looking back now, after having served for 6 years as a clinical and administrative supervisor of a counseling program at that same social service agency, and currently providing clinical supervision for a group private practice, I believe that my time in supervision with Jeff was truly formational—in how I see my counseling clients, the therapists I supervise, and myself and my role as a therapist and supervisor. I think I "caught" more than it seems I was "taught" in the strengths-based supervision of the counseling I received from Jeff during those important early years.

I am so glad that Jeff has written this book. I believe it will be of great service to clinical supervisors in all settings—agencies, hospitals, schools, churches, clinics, and group practices. It will challenge and encourage supervisors at any stage of their career, helping them not only in their work with their supervisees but also in how they approach clients, people, and life in general.

Jeff does a wonderful job of using research and citations but also his own personal experience of 44 years in the field. His writing style is refreshing. His case examples are deeply helpful. (I smiled as I read them because I could picture him saying and doing just what he wrote.) The quotations he cites are one of my favorite parts of this book; they greatly highlight the importance of strengths-based ideas in clinical supervision but also in our philosophy of the world. Strengths-based ideas may not be all new—and Jeff does an excellent job of showing their history and synthesizing them for clinical supervision—but unfortunately, they are not the ideas I tend to see very often in the actual practice of supervision. I believe the ideas in this book are crucial and critical as we move forward in this field.

Jeff truly practices what he preaches. I think he is the perfect author for this book. He really is collegial and collaborative and has the attitude of resiliency that he writes about. My hope is that those who read this book will become more intentional in how they see and treat their supervisees—focusing less on problems and deficits and more on strengths, less on pathology and more on what is already there that can be built upon. I hope that there will be less attention on a hierarchical relationship in supervision and instead a focus on a more human aspect of the relationship between supervisor and supervisee. I resonate with his focus on the continued imparting of our belief in our supervisees and the development of their own agency, partly because of how I see the affect of that in my own life through Jeff's early supervision of me. In my career, I have found it to be a deep honor and privilege to be a clinical supervisor, to watch how the therapists I supervise grow and find their own voices by discovering, and leaning into, their personal strengths and gifts. It is high time for the paradigm shift in clinical supervision that Jeff so clearly practices and preaches. I am excited for you to dig in to this book and go forth and do the same.

—*Kara Zimmerman, MS, LMFT, LCPC*
Clinical Supervisor and Therapist

PROLOGUE

We all blossom in the presence of one who sees the good in us and who can coax the best out of us.

—Desmond Tutu (Anglican Bishop,
Human Rights Activist, and
1994 winner of the Nobel Peace Prize)

I am pleased that SAGE has allowed me the opportunity to present an extension of my previous work in order to further a strengths-based model of supervision in clinical practice.

I have been given the luxury and fun of studying and writing about not only the benefits of pure clinical supervision but also addressing the fact that more updated practices are needed to change how our field trains, supervises, and maintains clinicians. Management guru Stephen Covey (2004) stated, "If you want to make *minor,* incremental changes and improvements, work on practices, behaviors or attitude. But if you want to make significant, quantum improvement, work on paradigms" (p. 19). It is my contention that there is enough solid evidence to show that our field is ready for a shift.

Several years ago, being curious about what it was that agencies wanted and looked for in interns, both in my own state of Illinois as well as across the nation and across disciplines, I researched what site supervisors wanted. When finished, I was pleasantly surprised. It was apparent from the data that what site supervisors desire in clinicians is quite different from what

most graduate clinical training and supervision prepares them for in our universities. Not that they didn't want well-heeled clinicians, but they seemed to understand that most interns already had excellent entry-level skills, as they were taught, evaluated, and well instructed by their universities in order to be prepared for the internship experience. Site supervisors indicated that they want clinicians who have the ability to work as a teammate and who have maturity and good character. Site supervisors indicated that they wanted more than just well-trained interns; they look for people who are of good quality, substance, integrity, and who hold a positive attitude. They trust that university programs have done their job and have prepared competent entry-level clinicians. Our students are from the "Knowledge and Information Age," after all.

Based on this research, I became interested in information my MBA-degreed operations manager wife kept talking about, and I began to search the literature for current organizational development, leadership, and management thought. In addition, it seemed to me that the growing movement to work with peoples' strengths rather than problems addresses the gatekeeping need we hear so much about, as well as redirects our love for the diagnosis of pathology (they seem the same to me). I advocate here that expertise in supervision, either clinical or administrative, should move beyond (in addition to) the typical executive skills of boundary making, relationship building, consultation, ethics, and the like, and begin with intentionality and forethought to move to empowerment and strengths-based work with the already very well-trained clinicians we prepare.

Most of the current books on supervision are written as texts for doctoral students who are taking a course in clinical or agency supervision. Yet, it is not clear the extent to which even doctoral students are adequately trained in supervision skills (Scott, Ingram, Vitanza, & Smith, 2000). One of the strengths of this book is that doctoral students may be guided to an alternative way of supervising. This book is really dedicated to those thousands of supervisors and administrators who manage and supervise every day. They do so without university doctoral training and are gratified with their very significant place working in agencies or other practice modes. This is where the brunt of clinical work is done, where supervision is critical and administration key to clinical work of all guilds, stripes, and types. It is for this group, where I spent the better part of my 44 years in this field, that I aim this work, as what these professionals do is important and needed.

Strengths-based supervision presents much more than just another model of clinical supervision. Strengths-based work is also embedded in cutting edge organizational development, management, and leadership thinking and practice (Covey, 2004; Cooperrider, 2000). Strengths-based work brings a new paradigmatic way of thinking and operating—a true second order change—in all clinical settings from agency operations to university settings. What is more, strengths-based work has a foundation of ideologies from multiculturalism and cross-cultural studies (Smith, 2006). A strengths-based practice in clinical settings is something whose time has come. Strengths-based clinical supervision is a

model for the 21st century. No longer can we accept hierarchical and deficit-based supervision models that keep us embedded in pathological one-up thinking. I can only hope that this book is preaching to the choir.

Strengths-based ideas are under fire by the more traditional models, mostly those who have adopted and proselytize the medically modeled problem-focused views of big pharmaceutical companies, and by the American Medical Association and American Psychiatric Association. Deep pockets have a serious stake in maintaining this view. Also, I guess it is no secret to most of us that mental health and clinical work where it is needed most is also under fire. I believe that not only do we need to address and work toward correcting these political issues, but we need to advocate strongly for change in the way we work and the way we interface, research, and politicize what we do. I believe in systems thinking and how we are all connected, but I also believe that small changes can affect larger systems. Not only do I address the use and need for strengths-based supervision, but I show research regarding how these concepts have been around for decades, if not centuries, and that they are being used in other venues besides the clinical fields. Strengths-based ideas have been used with great success in organizational development and leadership. The field of psychology has its own brand of strengths-based work called Positive Psychology that is creating a firestorm in the field as well as in education. Strengths-based ideas have begun to take hold in the high towers of academia, as new, more agentic forms of instructing and learning are being used in campuses across the world, using technology and turning the more traditional pedagogical ideas and classrooms on their heads. We live in a technological world, both personally and in our world of work, and today people are more knowledgeable than they have ever been. The idea of working with peoples' strengths is not a novel idea, and throughout this book you will come across names you know well and have studied on your route to clinical work. But education is a funny thing. We are guided by those we admire and who teach concepts with conviction, and most of our clinical work has been brusquely focused on problems to be fixed. The ideas of Carl Rogers, Abraham Maslow, and more recently Martin Seligman and Froma Walsh, may seem only incidental whims as the medical model, the *Diagnostic and Statistical Manual of Mental Disorders,* and the common vernacular of everyday talk on the street, has been taken over by problem-saturated language. We have become like the local weather person who gives us a report of a 30% chance of showers, rather than the more correct statement that we have a 70% chance of staying dry. And those newer ideas like solution-focused clinical work or Narrative Therapy have become quaint but clueless techniques used to work faster and harder to get the job done, rather than to create a lasting exchange of ideas. Except for a cadre of the faithful, most have been integrated into our curriculum and vernacular without understanding and considering the philosophy from which they arose. The consequences of pathologizing people is briefly thought about, only to be put aside, yet the potential for iatrogenic effects is huge (Boisvert & Faust, 2002).

My experience over some 20 years of teaching and maintaining contacts post graduation is that students learn the strengths-based ideas, love the concepts, and even say they are practicing the models. But the truth is that we all repeatedly succumb to the more politically forced problem-focused mentality, because it is expedited by the use of the DSM, and the mythology that DSM continues. It is, after all, what most older clinicians and supervisors know, and continue to teach, and it is what brings in the cash.

This book sets a different path than other books on clinical supervision, both in what it advocates as well as how it is presented. I really believe that this work will be helpful to site supervisors as well as university supervisors alike. At the place I am in my life, after 44 years in the field, the last 23 in academia, I have tried to make this work accessible and readable to a great number of people, not just academics who seem to speak their own language. I want this to be a book where I converse with you, get you to think and mull over what I say and to make it your own, not to pontificate as in a lecture hall oration. This book, about clinical supervision with a definite bias toward working with peoples' strengths, starts with showing how more traditional clinical supervision works, then sets the agenda in a direction that has been less traveled these days, with the hope that it will make all the difference for you (with great respect for Robert Frost, 1916).

PART I

IN THE BEGINNING

What we call the beginning is often the end. And to make an end is to make a new beginning. The end is where we start from.

T. S. Eliot (1943)

The world must seem upside down to some of those who have been around for a while in our field and also to their prodigies. When I was a newbie counselor, therapist, whatever, studying counseling psychology, and being trained in psychodynamic theory at the mental health clinic where I worked, our historical contexts made the difference of our lives come alive. Those theories stayed around for a long time; in fact, they are still around in one fashion or another. But along the way, they were bumped aside by behavior, cognition, systems, client-centered approaches, gestalts, and such. To many people's dismay, the world of brief therapy focused on simple changes that made a difference, and in came the postmodernists, social constructionists, and Positive Psychologists, all of which vied for favor in a world of medicine that has a stronghold of deep pocketed interest groups. But although I make a case for the new—a strengths-based view of life—and link the financial with the way we have been trained and practice, together we will antithetically begin at the end, with the history of what we are discussing. This book is about much more than supervision, but that is also how I tell the tale.

1

THE HISTORY AND TRADITIONS
OF CLINICAL SUPERVISION

The traditional literature of counselling supervision seems to lack uncertainty and timidity. It is mostly written from the supervisor's, or supervisor trainer's perspective and seems to be full of models, structures, checklists and frameworks. It is not a humble or exploratory literature.

—Jane Speedy (2000, p. 3)

From the early medical models of supervision, such as the psychoanalytic models of learning while being analyzed, to the "study one, watch one, do one, teach one" method that medical schools have used, our early models are still embedded in the supervision and training models of our sisters and brothers in medicine. Even our educational models that teach concepts and then spend time pointing out mistakes for remediation more than praising strengths are solidly in this camp. Linked to a hierarchical arrangement and aimed at problem-focused evaluation and change, our roots have mirrored those early modernist days. Miller, Hubble, and Duncan (2007) stated that the usual focus on what a clinician did wrong, rather than looking for what might be more effective, is a terrible fault of our more traditional thinking (Miller et al., 2007). This chapter looks at what history has provided us as a base for our practice, as well as an assembly of the nuts and bolts of how the field of clinical supervisor practices in its various forms, styles, and models. I also offer

my own second opinions with regard to how they fit with strengths-based supervision. Along the way, I offer that other component—the supervisee's point of view—as a vehicle to fill Jane Speedy's (2000) critique for a more holistic point of view.

Long-time author and a leader in the field of supervision, Janine Bernard (see, e.g., Bernard, 1981, 1989, 1992, 1997, 2004, 2005), retrospectively reviewed one of her earlier works with George Leddick and noted that it was easy to review the literature of professional supervision back then, when compared to today (Leddick & Bernard, 1980). Clinical supervision has become a large and expanding field, as we have seen already. In reviewing the field, however, I have noticed that there is little specific literature about clinical supervision per se, and as with many specific fields, the new branches off the base are growing strong and varied, with offshoots that parallel the growth of our field of clinical work. Today, we have models, methods, and points to remember about clinical supervision, and they all have a synergy to them that keep them in flow. Leddick (1994) addressed the issue of models of supervision, indicating that one could categorize them in three general models: developmental, integrated, and orientation specific. "The systematic manner in which supervision is applied is called a 'model,'" (Leddick, 1994, p. 1) and this indicates that specific knowledge of a model, such as practices, routines, and beliefs (social constructions), are critical to understanding clinical supervision. I want to remind the reader again that from my point of view, the decision to use either a strengths-based meta-model or a problem-focused model is the most important "practice" a supervisor and clinician can make up front. There is a lot to know about before practicing clinical supervision, but I don't think it is daunting. I will take care to walk you through it all.

Methods of supervision include the nuts and bolts of providing supervision, from the initial supervisory contracting, to methods of observation or data gathering such as live, audio, or video tape and interpersonal process recall, utilized in one-on-one, group, cotherapy, or triadic supervision formats, as well as case presentation, modeling, feedback, intervention, and evaluation. These are the day-to-day or session-to-session mechanics that frame supervisory work, and they allow for a smooth process.

There is a fine line, I believe, between what we do with our clients and what we do with our supervisees. This book's manuscript has been sent out to a gaggle of other professionals—all from academia I must add—and many have had difficulty with my grouping clients and supervisors under the term "client." It is my contention that anyone we see in a professional capacity, be they coming for clinical work, supervision, or consultation, are clients. According to Merriam-Webster, a client is "1) one that is under the protection of another, 2) a person who engages the professional advice or services of another" (see http://www.merriam-webster.com/dictionary/client). So I hope that clears up any faulty perceptions. Again, I call anyone we are working with a client, be they a person who comes to see

us for clinical work, consultation, or supervision. Of course there are differences, but they are still clients of ours, regardless. We are about protecting and providing a profession service to both clients who come for clinical work, as well as our supervisees. The term supervisor, as we shall come to see, entails many conflicting as well as complimentary behaviors and social constructs. What a clinically trained cognitive behavioral psychologist may believe about supervision will be different in many ways from what a Narrative Therapy social worker or even psychiatrist may act and think, and a brand new doctoral level counselor educator may have even a different view. These beliefs about how to supervise someone are socially constructed and learned both from their own experience, as well as in their education. What follows is some of the history of clinical supervision and the methods and beliefs attached, followed by, in Chapters 4 and 5, a strengths-based perspective that varies by degrees and also by kilometers.

Finally, points of interest that include adhering to a multicultural context, philosophy of training (pedagogical vs. andragogical and modernist vs. postmodernist), and all the currently applied and researched adjoining components that inform us of what connects with good clinical supervision, are covered.

HISTORY: SOMEWHAT BRIEFLY

Predating many of the deep tomes on supervision are an edited book called *Social Work Supervision* by Munson (1979) and another called *Supervision in Social Work* by Kadushin and Harkness (1976). Kadushin and Harkness point out that, prior to the 1920s, the literature that cited supervision meant something completely different than what we now associate with the noun. The first text about social work supervision was published in 1904. It was called *Supervision and Education in Charity* and was authored by Jeffrey Brackett (as cited by Kadushin & Harkness, 2002). Brackett's book was about the supervision of institutions of welfare organizations and Kadushin and Harkness stated the following: "Supervision referred to the control and coordination function of a State Board of Supervisors, a State Board of Charities, or a State Board of Control" (2002, p. 1). Interestingly, social work apparently had a hand in administrative supervision long before the texts on it were published by the American Counseling Association (Henderson, 2009). Of even more interest to me is the statement that as supervision moved from that of administrative focus to direct supervision, it took on the meaning and action of "helping the social worker develop practice knowledge and skills, and providing emotional support to the person in the social work role" (Kadushin & Harkness, 2002, p. 2). Nowhere is it mentioned that supervision also required or focused on the evaluation of deficits that can be associated with the field today. These days, those who have been gatekeeping the profession have morphed this view to one where "hierarchy and evaluation are so intertwined with supervision that to remove them makes the *intervention* [emphasis added] something other than supervision" (Bernard & Goodyear, 2004, p. 12) and "supervision plays a critical role in maintaining the standards of the profession" (Holloway & Neufeldt, as cited in Bernard and Goodyear, 2004, p. 2). I wonder how it is that supervision became an intervention rather than "providing emotional support" (Kadushin & Harkness, 2002, p. 2).

Social work has a long and proud tradition of providing supervision to those in the trenches rather than doctoral students, with a literature that is equally rich and tracks issues common to every guild. See, for example, the history of social work supervision (Tsui, 1997), a retrospective look from one of the first to study this topic (Kadushin, 1992), along with issues of parallel process in supervision (Kahn, 1979), client satisfaction in supervision (Harkness & Hensley, 1991), the usual regrouping and reporting of social work supervision (Tsui, 2005), the use of team supervision (Shamai, 2004) as leadership (Cohen & Rhodes, 1978), and finally, way back in 1999, strengths-based social work practices (Cohen, 1999).

Allen Hess wrote his "seminal" book, *Psychotherapy Supervision,* in 1980, 1 year after Munson (1979) and 4 years after Kadushin and Harkness (1976) published their works on supervision in social work. To those of us outside the field of social work, Hess's volume was a gift that put some sense to what we were doing; some of us went for years without any solid thought, other than the commonsense. Heath and Storm (1985) later pointed out, that most supervisors, at some level, use their own favorite clinical model to inform their clinical supervision practice.

Hess (2008) suggested that the very first clinical supervision occurred after the first therapy session, with a lone clinician observing the feedback, either positive or negative, from the interventions he provided, and correcting his work so that it was more effective—a self-reflective personal supervision, if you will. He also pointed to Breuer and Freud, as they worked on their ideas of hysteria and how it led to breakthroughs in their work as the first documented peer supervision, as well as the Wednesday evening group meetings in Freud's home, where theories as well as case consultations were held (Breuer & Freud, as cited by Hess, 2008, pp. 3–4).

According to Goodyear and Bernard (1998), the literature on the practice of mental health supervision places its beginnings over 120 years ago, when social work was involved early on with supervision (Harkness & Poertner, as cited by Goodyear & Bernard, 1998, p. 6), in addition to the process and swell of psychoanalysis.

Supervision Literature in Historical Context

The literature on clinical supervision began to blossom with the advent of two major journals devoted exclusively to the topic. The *Counselor Education and Supervision Journal,* the flagship periodical of the Association for Counselor Education and Supervision, began with its first issue in 1961. Counselor Education and Supervision (CES) was originally dedicated to the transmittal of information, training, and supervision of counselors for the American Personnel and Guidance Association (APGA), the forerunner of the American Counseling Association (ACA) and all of its divisions. Again, primarily geared toward academics who train and supervise any of the many counselor types (mental health counselors, couple and family counselors, school counselors, etc.), the journal is a much overlooked source of supervision thought and training, as well as a source for other guilds in the field of clinical supervision. A second journal, which began in 1983, is *The Clinical Supervisor,* dedicated to providing a cross-pollination of ideas and research of the supervision provided by all clinical guilds, including social work, psychology, counseling, couple and family therapy, and substance abuse counseling. It is just possible that these two journals are responsible for the dissemination of almost all of the current knowledge and direction that our field has up until now. Every book written since these journals' inception has relied on their fullness and richness of the breadth of our field to fill their pages. Anyone coming into our field should feel the pride of knowing that the shoulders we stand on are those of a diverse, dedicated, and interesting group of professionals who care to insure that clinical work has support and care beyond the managed care bosses.

In addition to the early literature, texts on clinical supervision informed those who wanted to learn and practice this craft. What follows is a look at the major books on clinical supervision in the aggregate. This is not an attempt to provide a microscopic look into these volumes but to place them in context historically in a large and ever growing field that is critical to those who learn, research, teach, and practice supervision. Every interested writer of clinical supervision since the "blossom" has explained their own view of what is meant by supervision, provides a framework for their particular manner of discussing the subject and then indicates that there have been several discrete changes or additions, if you will, to the supervision literature and methods throughout the early years, up

until now. Kadushin and Harkness' (1976, 2002) book on social work supervision begins with a definition, after a word about their particular history. Their definition breaks down its roots, indicating that it comes from the "Latin *super* (over) and *videre* (to watch, to see) . . . one who watches over the work of another with responsibility for its quality. Such a definition of supervision leads to the derisive phrase *snooper vision*" (pp. 18–19). I was pleasantly surprised to see the "pun" of one who snoops, as a part of the earlier view of supervision, and reflected on how I had earlier on changed the word to "co-vision," a word Bernard and Goodyear, trounced (2004, p. 12). Rather than taking the usual meaning of the term, Kadushin and Harkness (2002) defined it by looking at function, objectives, hierarchy, indirect process, and a means to an end, settling on the following definition: "A comprehensive definition of social work supervision attempts to combine all the elements noted in the five sections . . . an agency administrative-staff member to whose authority is delegated to direct, coordinate, enhance, and evaluate the on-the-job performance of the supervisees" (p. 23) . Using the traditional social work model of ecological systems (Siporin, 1975, 1980), they indicated the complexity and interconnectedness of all these functions and provided a definition that is very different from that of other mental health groups' range of vision. What is most punctuated, however, is that social work supervision is for those in the trenches, as opposed to being almost entirely directed at doctoral students. They then went on to address the social work agency and unit, the demographics of social work supervision, the nature of education and how it is different from supervision and therapy, as well as the relationship between the supervisor and the supervisee. These sections are rounded out with chapters on supportive supervision, including thoughts on burnout, stress that includes both the client and the organization as contributing factors, the problems that come with becoming a supervisor, and evaluation and innovations that include what we will cover as modes of supervision. Clearly, supervision for social workers is a comprehensive view of all the factors that are a part of the ecological process.

The current big three generalist books on supervision, written mostly for psychology and counseling doctoral students, are in the order of their first appearance: Allen Hess' *Psychotherapy Supervision: Theory, Research, and Practice* (1980, 2008), the duo of Janine Bernard and Rodney Goodyear's *Fundamentals of Clinical Supervision*—changing authorship position in the middle—(Bernard & Goodyear, 1992, 1998, 2004, 2006), and C. Edward Watkins' *Handbook of Psychotherapy Supervision* (1997). These volumes take a more unswerving look at clinical supervision than do the books on social work supervision. And although they are useful for those on a master's level, I wonder if any in-the-trenches supervisor ever looks for books on supervision. These three books are aimed at the training of doctoral-level supervisors and perhaps some master's-level students in programs that open their training to them.

Later, Hess enlisted the help of his wife Kathryn and daughter Tanya (Hess, Hess, & Hess, 2008) to update his original volume, which begins with a review of the supervision literature in Part 1 and then moves into the first four chapters in Part 2, which look at what it is like for supervisees to become professionals in the field. It then moves on to a personal perspective of being supervised, including supervising international students, to becoming a supervisor. From here, Part 3 discusses several psychotherapy models, or as they call them, orientations, such as psychoanalysis supervision and Narrative Therapy supervision. Then, for some reason, they move to Part 4, which includes a discussion of couple and family therapy supervision and hypnotherapy, which they consider special modalities. What is left out is the extensive literature on both the person centered and cognitive behavioral therapies. Part 5 is a discussion of developmental perspectives, and by this, they mean children, adolescents, and geriatric populations. Part 6 is a discussion of special populations, such as supervision of clinicians working with abuse survivors, those who are severely mentally ill, those in a correctional setting, and even those in the fast-rising motivational interviewing model, so prevalent in the substance abuse community. Rounding this work out are three short parts, namely (1) research and professional issues; (2) race, sex, and gender; and (3) the state of the field. Hess passed away recently at the age of 64, and for a man so young, he has left behind a hefty legacy of supervision ideas for budding and practicing supervisors. But because of the range of topics, his work is more appropriate for doctoral students who are learning more about the field of clinical supervision. The book has breadth but is short on depth, and it is more useful as a piece of literature from which researchers and supervisors may find a beginning on specific types of supervision.

Longtime supervision authors, Janine Bernard and Rodney Goodyear (2004), provide a 12-chapter book (not an edited work) focused clearly on the process and modes of clinical supervision. This is a teaching book; that is quite clear. Laid out in form for a good syllabus, with chapters enough for the usual university setting, the book moves from an introduction to the field of supervision, right straight to their academic point, that supervision is always about evaluation. Chapter 3 has excellent information about ethical and legal issues that most in-the-trenches supervisors should know well, along with information about graduate training programs. Next they provide an adequate view of the most modernist approaches to the field, followed up by three chapters on the supervisory relationship and its many parts and parcels. Here they have moved into the nuts and bolts of supervision practice, including parallel processes, triadic supervision, and clarity about what is going on in supervision. The next few chapters introduce the reader to organization of supervision; the modes of supervising, that is, group, live, and so forth; and supervising and teaching supervision. This is a fine book for doctoral students learning about the field, and in fact, it ends with a section they call the Supervisors' Tool Box (Bernard & Goodyear, 2004, p. xii). As someone who has made the transition from modernist to postmodernist, from objective reality to socially constructed reality, I understand but disagree with much of what they put forth. Their emphasis on hierarchy and evaluation from a single source who believes that he or she has special privileged knowledge that is *the* only truth leads to my finding fault with their premises a great deal of the time.

Finally, C. Edward Watkins' *Handbook of Psychotherapy Supervision* (1997), an edited book, covers all of the ground found in the previous two works, with an expanded section on supervision models. This 7-part, 31-chapter volume begins with a section on conceptual ideas and methods, defining supervision as they all have, as well as a chapter on evaluation and research. Part 2 has 12 chapters on what Watkins considers approaches (not models) to supervision, including all the big ones from psychodynamic to cognitive and rational-behavioral and developmental. Part 3 in Watkins' book is about training models for clinical supervision, while Part 4 lumps supervision of adolescents, children, and geriatric populations in with group and family therapy under specialized forms and modes. I would contend that the supervision of family therapy has its own special view of supervision thought, and it is really a modality, or as Watkins calls them, approaches. Bernard and Goodyear (2004) called this systemic supervision, while Hess et al. (2008) called it couples and family therapy and categorized it as a special modality. Next are sections on research and professional, legal, and ethical issues, and finally endnotes or thoughts. Each of these volumes is filled with the knowledge needed to know cognitively in order to provide solid clinical supervision from a modernist perspective.

Family Systems Supervision

One of the first books I purchased on supervision, other than Hess (1980), was Howard Liddle, Doug Breunlin, and Richard Schwartz's (1988a) edited work, the *Handbook of Family Therapy Training and Supervision.* After reading the existing literature on supervision, I see that this book parallels some of the more traditional books but with the language and rock stars of the systems thinkers. If there was ever any doubt that the more traditional views on supervision and clinical work and the systems models speak and think differently, this book brings that message home, for sure. Thinking structurally or strategically, or applying the concepts of cybernetics to videotaping in supervision, makes me salivate, while I understand fully that these concepts are completely foreign to many clinicians who live in a positivist, modernist worldview. Today, these concepts are taught as history of a field that has been all but marginalized by contemporary clinical work that clicks with managed care and big pharma, I fear. But a lot has happened since those early days when training was done in add-on, freestanding training facilities or adjacent to more traditional university settings without degree opportunities. Now, every guild's training has at least one class in couples and family therapy/counseling.

Preceding Liddle et al.'s (1988a) work by two years, Fred Piercy's (1986) edited work, *Family Therapy Education and Supervision,* has a full setting of chapters, with a different flavor of presentation. Nowhere in either of these two books are the usual discussions of what constitutes supervision. Instead, they focus on how systemic thinking, and the training and supervision of family systems clinical work, are different. Liddle et al. presented the following in a middle chapter (9), "Systemic Supervision: Conceptual Overlays and Pragmatic Guidelines" (p. 153), instead of the usual introduction to what supervision is in general. In Piercy's book, Robert Beavers' chapter is entitled "Family Therapy Supervision: An Introduction and Consumer's Guide." In it, he states the following: "Supervision in marriage and family therapy is both a legitimate offspring of individual psychotherapy supervision and a mutant, representing qualitative differences from the parent" (p. 15). He is saying that the supervision of marriage and family therapy is very different from the usual manner that supervision is perceived and practiced.

In Piercy and Sprinkle's (1986) conclusion to their chapter in Piercy's (1986) book, they state the following: "The key figures of family therapy were revolutionaries. They took strong, often unpopular, theoretical stands that ran counter to the Zeitgeist of their time and paved the way for the theoretical models taught today" (p. 12). That the American Association for Marriage and Family Therapy (AAMFT) had an approved supervisor status long before Professional Clinical Counseling or any of the other guilds speaks to the privileged knowledge it assumes AAMFT has as supervisors of family therapy. All candidates are expected to practice from a systemic orientation rather than the linear model of individual psychotherapy or counseling models, and unless one has had good training past a single class on family systems, it is hard to impart this special knowledge. AAMFT's requirements at first included the notion that special training in systems thinking was a prerequisite to supervise other family therapists properly. Today this notion is more lax as licensure has taken over and power struggles and turf wars have forced compromises as well as challenges to supervise, let alone practice systemically. Berger's (1988) chapter in Liddle et al. (1988a) speaks to this point prophetically when he stated that "the acceptance of family therapy theory as a way of thinking in psychology would require changes in psychologists' basic unit of conceptualization . . ." (p. 305). My experience has been similar, even for APA programs that are attached with a specialty program in child, adolescent, and family as a subspecialty. Supervision from a systemic perspective is very different from a traditional individual perspective. Appropriately enough, the AAMFT (2007) put forth its own book as a training tool for upcoming AAMFT-approved supervisors in training.

Some of the first recognitions of a cultural influence in clinical supervision appeared in these two books. Falicov's chapter, "Learning to Think Culturally," in Liddle et al.'s (1988a) book, is evidence that family therapists were out in front and aware of how culture influences systems and contextualizes treatment, thus supervision early in the game of supervision literature and practice.

I can say the same thing about the AAMFT book as I did about Bernard and Goodyear's volume (2004); it is complete, with chapters ready to go for a semester's worth of reading. The book includes a chapter on models (yes, family therapy, like individual therapy, has its own abundance of models from which to choose), a chapter on developing one's own personal philosophy of supervision (what, no right way?), and chapters on the tripartite of interconnected relationships in isomorphic proportion, such as supervisors, therapists, clients, within structures, assessments, modalities, ethics, and other issues. Does this sound familiar?

Much of the field of mental health—psychology, social work, professional counseling—has tried to make family therapy a separate subpart of its own training in the field and disregards the unique supervision frameworks that AAMFT and its approved supervisory designation mandates. The question that still baffles most others in the field at large is, can it be a treatment specialty like cognitive therapy, used by social workers, psychologists, and counselors, or is it really a very different way and philosophy about how to treat people? Is systemic thinking and the postmodern, social constructionist ideas that are a part of the systemic view a specific part of our larger field that is here to stay, or is it only relegated to working within those who use family systems thinking? Gerald Cory (2008) placed postmodern and family systems therapy on the same level as cognitive behavioral, gestalt, person centered, and all the rest. I mention this because next I address the supervision of substance abuse counseling, and rather than seeing each of these as specialties, thus specialties of supervision, one has to wonder whether it is a practice issue or a title protection issue. I think this becomes a topic for our field of clinical supervision. The questions become these: Who has the right to supervise what groups in the larger field? Does the training of specific treatment populations also require specific supervision models?

Substance Abuse
Counseling Supervision

Substance abuse (SA) and the counseling that treats it have always had their own unique and sometimes misunderstood ways of treating a problem that affects millions of people. The comorbidity/dual diagnosis with or because of other mental health problems makes SA a huge problem that has its own special treatments and myths. Substance abuse, in its many forms, also affects families with long-range concerns, some that last a life time. In addition, up until a decade ago, many SA counselors had little or no training, and then most of the training came from community colleges where the associate's degree was the terminal degree. I can't speak for all the training in the United States, but today in many states, the field has transitioned to insisting on master's degrees in some mental health field, and many physicians and psychologists are specializing in this field.

As with psychology, counseling, and other mental health fields, the field of substance abuse is also replete with multiple views on what causes SA and how to appropriately treat SA as a serious health concern. Having said that, it is interesting that there is only one book written on the supervision of counselors who practice in this area (Powell & Brodsky, 2004), while an examination of both Google Scholar and the PsycINFO database found a paltry few who even attempt articles on the subject (Anderson, 2000; Culbreth, 1999; Overholser & Ricciardi, 1992; Todd & Heath, 1992). Powell and Brodsky's (2004) book is laid out in similar fashion to the other leading works: There are three parts and an appendix with interesting forms and study information, with 17 chapters that establish a historical perspective, working definition, and traits of effective clinical supervision, evaluation, and feedback, contracting, ethics, and several models, while Chapter 3's section on leadership principles for supervision and organizational perspective is enlightening and exciting. "The principles and methods of clinical supervision espoused in this book are founded on fundamental concepts of organizational leadership: servant leadership, stakeholders, participatory management, and effective working environment" (p. 20).

Here is a real book on supervision, written for those in the trenches, not some ivory tower training for a hierarchical view of their world. They champion a leadership/supervision that sees supervisees as stakeholders in the process—stakeholders in relationship with their clients as well as the organization. Inspired by new views of what it means to be a leader, they also believe that being a supervisor does not automatically mean that they will be respected. How different this model of clinical supervision is from many of the standard, revered literature that has been informing us for years. They take the road of the new management and organizational philosophy that no longer adhere to a "linear, hierarchical, quasi-military structure, with top-down communication and little employee empowerment" (p. 24). Quoting the words of 6th-century father of Taoism, Lao-tzu, they put forth the notion that, "The superior leader gets things done with very little motion. He imparts instruction not through many words, but through a few deeds. He keeps informed about everything, but interferes hardly at all'" (Lao-tzu, cited in Powell & Brodsky, 2004, p. 22). This is a real book on clinical supervision for today, and it sounds exactly like what Mei Whei Chen and I put forth in 1999 (Edwards & Chen, 1999): Leave less footprints. When I began this viewing of the literature on clinical supervision I felt like Diogenes, and yet, in the most far-reaching place of supervision, in a place I would never guess might have what I desired, I have finally found two honest men.

HISTORICAL CHANGES IN MODELS AND MODES OF CLINICAL SUPERVISION

Neukrug (2003) defined the role of the supervisor as critical to a clinicians' professional responsibility, so much so that it is expected. He found it critical in a systemic way, so that the supervision can create change for the supervisee, as well as for the clients. Indeed, clinical supervision has become one of the most important factors not only in training, as well as accountability, but as a vehicle of change in the clinical process. After all, two heads are better than one.

Models of Supervision

The models of supervision, "the systematic manner in which supervision is applied" (Leddick, 1994, p. 1), came about in several different ways. As I have said elsewhere, "Most traditional supervision has paralleled conventional counseling, looking for what the supervisee was doing incorrectly or not doing enough of, mostly in the area of technique, and attempting to devise remedial solutions" (Edwards & Chen, 1999, p. 350). Supervisors use their favorite model of clinical work as an adjunct to their clinical supervision; the facilitative counseling taken from Rogers (1951) will model empathy, warmth, and genuineness in their supervision, while those adhering to cognitive behavioral therapy will stress supervision that parallels that model, and so forth.

Heath and Storm (1985) pointed out quite a while ago that most supervisors at some level use their own favorite model or models to inform their clinical supervision practice. As the field progressed, providing better research and more additions to clinical supervision thought, many ideas of how to supervise well became part and parcel of how some supervisors were trained at the university level, and this added to the collective fund of ideas that informs clinical supervision today. Like the field of clinical practice, clinical supervision increased its range of models. From psychodynamic, to person centered, cognitive behavioral, and the generalist systemic frames, that is, strategic, structural, narrative, and solution focused, supervisors use their own favorite clinical model as a frame for their supervision. As stressed elsewhere, these models of supervision—what Leddick (1994) called orientation-specific models

and Hess et al. (2008) and Watkins (1997) called psychotherapy orientations—are case-specific types of supervision suggestions, and depending on the guild from where the author(s) or editor(s) comes from, this might include supervision of supervisees using special modalities like couples and family therapy, hypnotherapy, and paraprofessionals, or special populations such as abuse survivors, substance abusers, different sexual disorders, and so forth (Hess, et al., 2008). Does this confuse you? Are you asking the same questions as I, such as why is there such chaos of models among the different authoritative books? One needs to look no further than the various guilds' insistence on turf and ownership of who does what. Most clinicians at some time or another, if they are practicing generalists in mental health, will come across any and all of these special populations, and hopefully, they will notice that there are many different ways to practice as well as supervise. It is also an indictment of our inability to learn from and accept one another that some find working with couples and families as modalities, while others see the same activity as a specialty. Several of these guilds have battled perception for a long time, longing to be seen as a separate profession (Fenell & Hovestadt, 1986), where a clinician can be called a Licensed Marriage and Family Therapist (LMFT), or a Licensed Clinical Professional Counselor (LCPC). These guild wars are an indication of our inability to learn from and accept one another. Turf wars and holdovers from our early days keep us from seeing our similarities and maintain our top-down views of each as discrete entities in a hierarchical pecking order from psychiatry, to psychology, to social worker, licensed clinical professional counselor, or licensed marriage and family therapist, and even on to addictions counselors. There has never been any concrete research which demonstrates that one group's practice outcome is better than the other, and I suspect that this is also true when it comes to supervisors. It is important, however, to note that the current models of supervision almost always maintains a hierarchical, evaluative, remedial position (Edwards & Chen, 1999), indicative of the medical model that is about "fixing" people. World-class social psychologist Elliot Aronson (2010), who has commented about his own field of psychology, said that his colleagues on the clinical side of the field are about "fixing" people, while he and his colleagues in social psychology are about change, saying, "Okay, you had a bad childhood, but let's change your environment, change your motivation, and give you new opportunities, and you can transcend your origins, your self-defeating attitudes, your prejudices" (p. xiv). This is very different than the usual views of mental health as portrayed by some guilds and the common nomenclature as presented by the American Psychiatric Association's (1994) *Diagnostic and Statistical Manual of Mental Health Disorders* (4th ed). This view is very similar to what is purported by strengths-based work, of sorting out and punctuating what people do well and by helping them stay on that course of development. Or like what Albert Bandura (1997), another great psychologist, called developing self-efficacy, whose methods are also a far cry from a medical model's remediation.

Additional to the orientation models are what Leddick (1994) called developmental and integrative models. These two models make up the rest of the usual models of clinical supervision that is both taught and used in training centers around the country. Leddick (1994) and Bernard and Goodyear (2008) have different meanings regarding a developmental model, when compared with Hess et al. (2008). Hess et al. defined development according to the client system being discussed during supervision, with clinicians treating three separate populations—child, adolescent, and geriatric. Leddick and Bernard and Goodyear defined development according to the skill level of the clinicians under supervision with respect to their stage as a clinician. Anyone interested in clinical supervision reading these various authoritative offerings would be confused and perplexed. For a better look, let us briefly move into the developmental perspective as defined by Leddick.

Looking at the developmental perspective of the clinician (and isomorphically the supervisor in

training), the main proponents of what I came to understand as a helpful developmental perspective were Bernard's (1979) discrimination model, and, beginning with Cal Stoltenberg (1981), a developmental model he called the counselor complexity model, which evolved into a unique and ever growing developmental approach coauthored with Ursula Delworth (Stoltenberg & Delworth, 1987) and recently Stoltenberg and McNeill (2009). Since I cover these two models as executive skills in Chapter 2, I do not dwell on the particulars of the model here, but I briefly talk about them and then discuss them in more depth, as well as what others might have written about them.

Despite the agreement in the field to think about the developmental stages of the supervisees with whom we work, and to adapt supervision accordingly, Kersey (1982) and Fisher and Embree (1980; as found in Marek, Sandifer, Beach, Coward, & Protinsky, 1994) suggested that supervisors generally do not take the developmental stages into account while they are supervising. This leads one to wonder if supervisors should even bother. However, by this time, thinking developmentally is part of the culture of informed clinical supervision. I can put forth my own personal experience. At least three or four times a year, during practicum and internship, students express their anxiety about not knowing where to go with their clients' discussions or what to do, or most often, they say that they just don't feel as if they have had enough training, thus they need more specific instruction (and when one speaks his or her anxious concerns, the other more timid ones will also chime in). A calming voice from what they perceive as a totally competent supervisor, stating that this is developmental and that this too will pass, quiets their fears. So, one of the issues of development is that of experience, rather than training or skill. I usually tell them a story from my favorite author, Malcolm Gladwell's (2008) book, *Outliers: The Story of Success,* where he demonstrates over and over again that success is based on a large quantity of experience. From the Beatles' luck at having a long-term gig in a German cave bar playing for eight hours at a time early in their career, to the success of hockey players in Canada based on their very early youth club experiences, to the high school shenanigans of Bill Gates with computers, Gladwell documented that a large fund of experience from which to draw seems to make a huge difference in one's success. There is a magic number of 10,000 hours that seems to have a large bearing on great success, but I do not tell them this often for fear of losing a whole lot of late-term clinical students to other careers. Although it is useful to know this about them and to normalize their situation, the original intent of Stoltenberg's developmental model, the counselor complexity model, was to identify not only skills that may be lacking but also to move them onto "a course of development that will culminate in the emergence of a counselor identity" (1981, p. 59). What was originally intended was to bring forth complete clinicians who have integrated skills and theory, as well as an awareness of themselves in relationship with others. If this is the case, and I am sure my astute colleagues will disagree with me on this point, why is there always so much focus on making sure that audiotape and videotape content is exactly like the microskills dictate? With over 400 models to work with, how in the world is a supervisor supposed to know what his or her supervisee should say or do? One of the beauties of this developmental model is its focus on more than just skill development, as it takes into consideration in each of its four stages the development of a clinician's identity. This focus on identity is portable to any of the several guilds or professions that rest in our field.

Interestingly, Stoltenberg changed his four-level complexity model (1981) to a simpler three-level model (Stoltenberg & Delworth, 1987), as he and Delworth put forth an integrated developmental model (IDM) "that relied more directly on developmental theory and provided more specific details regarding changes in supervisees over time and the types of supervision environments, including supervisor interventions, that were seen as most appropriate for each of the three levels of development" (Stoltenberg, 2005, p. 859). Again, this is a training model, useful to those who are

watching to see where a supervisee—a clinician in training—is situated in his or her development. It is specific to the training of counselors and psychologists, however, that all clinicians move along a developmental path as they learn more about their craft or a specific model. By integration, this model means to provide a clearer and more complete "set of identifiable skills and behaviors" that fit within an integration of them with a more complete set of developmental stages, as I understand IDM. I am, however, troubled by their use of so-called interventions meant to provide a perfect climate for change of what the supervisor sees as appropriate. This way of working is not only mechanistic, but it leaves out any discussion or collaboration within the work or understanding of the context of where the clinical work is being done. The clinician and other multiple factors should be included in any discussion, using the notion of development as a theory (not real) that can be redeveloped or jettisoned as needed.

Lee and Everett (2004) produced a primer book on an integrative family therapy supervisor model that, of course, is directed at those who think systemically, and yet it references some of the same concepts that individual, or perhaps, traditional clinical supervision includes (see Table 1.1).

Aside from the useful principles given in Table 1.1, this model and others have different meanings for the word integrative. The word integrative as used in this model allows that there are many different models of family therapy (as there also are with individual clinical work), but it reaches for a central core with which supervisors might attend to unique systemic concepts or theories with their supervisees. As an old-time family therapist and counselor, I resonate with several of the concepts that are placed within their framework of principles; they are central to a strengths-based model, so they bear mentioning here. But before that, it bears witnessing again that the two models—individual clinical work and family systems clinical work—are from two very different eras, thus they have different philosophies at root. I have never understood the "why" of this difference, as I am sure that many who have done any serious training in both models must also

Table 1.1   Basic Principles of Integrative Family Therapy Supervision

1. Supervision must be respectful.
2. Supervision, like therapy, must be a safe place.
3. A working alliance must be developed.
4. A supervisor does not offer therapy to the clinical family.
5. A supervisor does not offer therapy to the therapist in training.
6. Supervision operates within a clearly defined clinical training system that includes intergenerational subsystems and dynamics.
7. The dynamics of supervision include hierarchy and power.
8. Supervision develops through predictable stages.
9. Supervision interventions are driven by theory.
10. Supervision should be competency based.
11. The supervisor has simultaneous responsibilities to the therapist, the clinical family, the clinical setting/institution, and the self.
12. The supervisor, like the therapist, follows clear ethical principles of conduct and practice.
13. Supervision is unique within each training system.

Source: Adapted from Lee and Everett (2004, p. 4).

wonder. However, I do understand the how. We hold onto our theories, no matter that they are not real, as the only ways of thinking that have become imbued with not so subtle sociopolitical turf issues. As a personal aside, I remember being interviewed by two clinical psychologists in our department when I first applied for a job, some 20 years ago. They were very concerned that I might corrupt the students with my "radical" beliefs yet wanted someone that could teach the concepts they abhorred that proliferate the main family systems therapy texts. Strengths-based work, whether from systems concepts or the early works of psychology, all have a disdain for the traditional model that came from the medical field of deficit seeking and correcting. But I digress, so let us move back to the point I was making about Lee and Everett's (2004) book on integrative family therapy.

Lee and Everett (2004) utilized, as one would expect, the careful and skillfully crafted language of postmodern thinking, as they looked to "identify, and appreciated the unique qualities, resources, and constructions of reality of the many therapists and their clients . . ." so, first and foremost, "supervision must be respectful" and "supervision, like therapy, must be a safe place" (p. 4). This sort of care is found nowhere else as directly as it is here and in the family systems therapy literature on clinical supervision. The way in which this next principle attends to a major element and theory of family therapy, that "supervision operates within a clearly defined clinical training system that includes intergenerational subsystems and dynamics" (Lee & Everett, 2004, p. 7), references the systemic works of Murray Bowen (1966, 1971, 1974, 1976), Kerr and Bowen (1988), and Salvador Minuchin (1974, 1997), whose main theoretical thrusts are related to intergenerational perspectives and subsystems interactions. A point of order here is that Minuchin's idea of hierarchy can be divided into two complementary parts, the hard side and the soft side. Keim (1998) called these discipline and nurturance. The hard side of hierarch is that part that makes and maintains the rules, while the soft side provides for the nurture, care, and health of those who are being cared for. For hierarchy to be effective, both sides must be rules working for organizational systems to function well, and Lee and Everett recognized and imparted this piece of systems logic into their model of supervision. Their model is isomorphic to the systems models they use in their supervision. But then, I believe this model is important to all of clinical work, and it cannot be isolated to one specific model alone. Finally, congruent with the later, postmodern models of clinical work, such as narrative, solution focused, or languaging systems models, all adhere to a competency-based frame. "Supervision should be competency based," and as systemically oriented, looking for interrelationships between and with the various components that make up the whole of the system, it is demonstrated by the natural synergy that arrives when "the supervisor has simultaneous responsibilities to the therapist, the clinical family, the clinical setting/institution, and the self "(p. 4).

Integration can mean many things to many different folks. In the case of Lee and Everett (2004), they referenced integration of different systemic models, while Stoltenberg (2005) and his many colleagues meant to integrate the various developmental views with the supervisory conditions they suggested are needed to produce good clinicians in the end.

I have left out Bernard's (1979, 1997) ridiculously wonderful discrimination model that set the bar for all clinical counselor supervisors, discussed at length in Chapter 2 of this book as what I call an executive skill. Bernard suggests that there are three areas of focus that supervisors must pay attention to: "process skills, conceptualization skills, and personalization skills" (1997, p. 310), as well as three spheres of influence which a supervisor makes use of: training, consultation, and counseling. She then placed these on a very useable grid in order for supervisors to track the supervisory process. If you are not familiar with this work, you should read the originals or at least check out what I say about her work in Chapter 3.

Formats of Clinical Supervision

In addition to the various models, there are also different formats for providing clinical supervision to those who are in need of supervision, be they students in a clinical training site—usually a university or college, a newbie clinician just learning one of the skill sets from clinical models—or longtime skilled clinicians who feel the need to check out their own perceptions along with potential changes to their work. Each has his or her own uniqueness and also demands different sets of conditions and thoughts about how to be helpful. I want to say that again, because I think it is the most important part of providing supervision, that during the initial presupervision contracting, supervisors should check with their supervisee to ask how they might be helpful and what they might want to gain from their supervision. So, for supervision to be effective, and beyond that to provide excellent supervision, the work together must be perceived by the supervisee (the clinician) as helpful. Just like the use of clinical skills must meet the needs of the client's perception of being useful to be most effective (Lambert & Bergin, 1994), so, too, must clinical supervision be useful—helpful—to the person being supervised. Supervision usually means that persons who would like, or are in need of, input from a more advanced or skilled clinician for the purpose of case consultation, training in a model, or interpersonal change, are in some formal or informal social arrangement. In many cases, it is a remedial or deficit-based focus that a model takes, just like older, traditional clinical models. From individual one-on-one supervision, to group, triadic, live, videotaped, or audiotaped (now digital), interpersonal process recall, to reflecting teams, self-reports, and now online, texting, or other electronic means, each is discussed and commented upon. In addition, any of these models may also be used in a strengths-based model where the supervisee(s) will be seen as "at potential.

Formats or modes of clinical supervision include both the manner in which supervision feedback is provided to the supervisee, as well as the setting of the supervision. Feedback can include either positive exchanges or corrective exchanges, and both can be given in either a strengths-based manner or a top-down hierarchical manner. The method in which supervision feedback is provided includes such things as case presentations (Biggs, 1988), Interpersonal Process Recall (IPR; Kagan, Schauble, & Resnikoff, 1969), audiotaped supervision (Protinsky, 2003), videotaped supervision (Protinsky, 2003), cotherapy (Barnard & Miller, 1987; Hendrix, Fournier, & Briggs, 2001; Lantz, 1978; Roller & Nelson, 1991; Whitaker & Garfield, 1987), a bug in the ear (Boylston & Tuma, 1972), live supervision (Montalvo, 1973), a phone-in (Wright, 1986), a team break (Barthe, 1985), and reflecting teams (Andersen, 1992b; Stinchfield, Hill, & Kleist, 2007). Each of these methods of providing feedback or correction has its usefulness and drawbacks, and, as you will see, some may be dated as the times and the means have changed.

Case presentations are unequivocally the most used mode for presenting information about a clinician's case, either for help or to keep the clinician's supervisor up-to-date on his or her caseload, as well as getting suggestions and helpful consultation from the clinician's clinical supervisor. Biggs (1988) suggested that a case presentation format included looking at and identifying how to help a clinician make interferences from his or her observations to better use the clinical data presented, as well as talking about the process and expectations of the supervisory relationship. This could be considered the contracting phase, where goals and expectations of supervision are laid out for both parties to agree on. Finally, during the case presentation, goals for the client unit, including problems, personality, and factors that influence the problem, lead to an intervention strategy, according to Biggs. Bernard (1997) called this part of the supervision or consultation, and this can happen either during individual supervision, group supervision, or at a formal staffing of cases with

or without a consultant. Two issues always are present during supervision using a case presentation consultation format. First of all, memory fades—rapidly. So what might be talked about during a case presentation is always the clinician's own perceptions of a client system, and that is subjective. Depending on the relationship between the supervisor and the supervisee, the accuracy of the description can vary. People always want to put their best foot forward, and even within the best of clinical supervision sessions, the accuracy of the description of a past session or general progression of a specific client system will be filled with "writers' prerogative." Also, there is no guarantee that the suggestions and requests to use a different approach will be taken or appropriate when the situation comes about the next time.

Interpersonal Process Recall (IPR), first written about by Kagan et al. (1969), is usually attributed to Norman Kagan (1972); it is a supervision strategy that is used to help clinicians understand and act on their perceptions of cases that they might have difficulty accessing, for all of the reasons I outlined in the previous section. It is important to note that the use of IPR is a tool to use Socratically with the supervisee being the one who has the "highest authority about the experiences in the counseling session" (Cashwell, 1994, p. 1). The supervisor process, as Bernard and Goodyear (2004) see it, is not to "adopt a teaching roll and instruct the supervisee about what might have been done" (p. 220). Instead, questions that are designed to increase the supervisee's insight into his or her own blind spots, thus increasing competency, are used. A short "CliffsNotes" version of what all should or might be done using IPR is, as of this writing, readily available online (see Cashwell, 1994). The steps used in conducting IPR as well as a handful of recommended leads the supervisor might use are available.

Audiotaped supervision has been around for many years; in fact, Protinsky (2003) cited Gill, Newman, and Redlich (1954) as crediting Earl Zinn for having recorded psychotherapy sessions on wax Dictaphone cylinders. Protinsky went on to say that "it was generally agreed that Carl Rogers was most influential in the use of electronic recordings of the psychotherapy sessions" (2003, p. 298). Audiotaped supervision can be used with IPR or videotaped supervision. I have seen and heard about audiotaped supervision being utilized in several ways, including IPR. Early on in my career as a clinician, I used audiotapes as a means to discuss cases with my supervisors. I found that supervisors who used audiotapes as a means to help me with my case load usually asked me to bring a recording that demonstrated either a stellar moment in a session or a time when I was genuinely stuck and was looking for suggestions that were alternatives to my current way of engaging and working with a particular client. I found these times both uplifting and humbling. Depending on the clinical model of my supervisors, their interactions and "suggestions" might be helpful or shameful. I also know of supervisors and have had descriptions of supervision where the focus was on specific clinical responses and suggestions for alternative responses to client discussion. This sort of exchange may be appropriate for training in a specific model, but in my opinion, not for real-life cases where the situation changes in the week(s) before the next session. My guess on why this occurs later in clinical work is that supervisors are utilizing a training devise they learned while in their own clinical training, and without forethought, they continue to use the same format when they are raised to the status of clinical supervisor. We all tend to replicate the sort of clinical work and supervision we learned in our own training. This can occur especially with those who have had a very positive relationship with their trainer or first supervisor. We can place our trainers on pedestals, and it can be a long way to fall for all, when we see that their ideas are not always useful or the best.

Videotaped supervision goes as far back as 1968 as a vehicle to allow "teachers to apply clearly defined teaching skills to carefully prepared lessons in a planned series of five to ten-minute encounters with a small group of real students, often with an opportunity to observe the results on videotape" (Allen, 1967, p. 5). What the Stanford group found unique was its ability to provide immediate feedback by supervisors and colleagues, as well as the ability to demonstrate skill progress in a measured way. Feedback had come of age with the knowledge and expectation that more immediate feedback provides better learning opportunities and a chance for course corrections and practice. No longer were case consultations, even with IPR, considered to be the gold standard for supervision and training.

With the opportunity for peer colleagues in-training, in addition to clinical supervisors to interact and provide feedback, a new wave of influence was held to a higher standard. First of all, one needs to acknowledge that there is a distinct difference between training and supervision. I make this point repeatedly throughout this book: Our interns and clinicians, regardless of the program from which they come or the field of endeavor they call home, are some of the finest and best clinicians ever. However, training is the acquisition of skills and knowledge in preparation for real clinical work, while supervision is something else again; yet all too often, the literature for clinical supervision is set to accommodate both. Second, as Todd and Storm articulated (2002), videotape allows supervision groups to participate in the process and add their own perspectives; videotaped supervision allows for multiple perspectives, rather than a singular "correct" answer. In addition, this multiple perspective allows for a flattening of the hierarchy usually inherent with supervision. This flattening, when encouraged and allowed to grow, brings forth more accurate descriptions with regard to cultural and gender perspectives when supervisees (sometimes even seen as part of a team rather than students of the supervisee) are allowed to bring forth their own perspectives and views, creating a rich and thick description of the clinical work, with multiple perspectives from which to choose.

I remember learning to supervise this way while doing my supervision of supervision during my doctoral work in the late 1980s. I had previously trained as a postmaster's student in one of the typical "family therapy free-standing" training programs that had sprung up around the country, and I was used to having one of my trainers step out from his or her perch behind the one-way mirror to knock on the consultation room and ask if he or she might join the session with my clients and myself. The use of the phone-in seemed more elegant to me than the suddenness of a knock and the intrusion of an "expert" joining us, but in retrospect, the clients knew that I was in training and expected some form of course correction from an outside source. They had been informed of the training protocol and even seemed to welcome this intrusion, as much as all of us in training dreaded the knock. The point of it all, however, seems to be consistent with learning theory, in that the shorter the time between when someone makes a mistake or misses an opportunity to move in a more productive manner and the correction, the better the connection. This is the core of Lewinian Action Research and laboratory training (Kolb, 1984). Interestingly, there is also research to suggest that live supervision is beneficial to the trainee or supervisee, but the clients do not seem to notice any more progress during their sessions than those who do not have live supervision (Silverthorn, Bartie-Haring, Meyer, & Toviessi, 2009). Since the early 1970s, there has been a plethora of research done on live supervision from investigating many of the aspects of its use and the many additional modalities used to provide feedback to the supervisor.

According to Champe and Kleist (2003), all of the guilds in the mental health field utilize live supervision for training, and many agencies are using it, with its different modalities, for treatment or serious internship training. We look at these modalities from an historical perspective, rather than a usage, as it demonstrates how technology has been instrumental in the provision of training and supervision.

Cotherapy is a wonderful experience for a trainee or new clinician to watch and learn at the side of a more senior clinician (Barnard & Miller, 1987; Hendrix, Fournier, & Briggs, 2001; Lantz, 1978; Roller & Nelson, 1991; Whitaker & Garfield, 1987). It is usually implemented in the training and supervision of family therapy. Maclennan (1965), and much later Dugo and Beck (1997), also used cotherapy for the training of group work. Drawing on a "two heads are better than one" philosophy, cotherapy allows the new clinician to participate in actual sessions with a more skilled clinician and to feel the joys and shakes while feeling more secure than when all alone. Depending on the senior clinician's skills, personality, clinical model of choice, training or supervision intent, and relationship with the cotherapist, the experience has the potential to be really great or otherwise. I first used cotherapy at the state mental health clinic I worked at outside of Chicago, where we utilized it during our family and group clinical sessions. I was in group therapy training during my master's program, and at the Family Institute of Chicago's two-year, free standing marriage and family therapy training program, by a cotherapy team during both years of clinical training. When cotherapists are working well together, it is wonderful. One person can be working on content, while the other can work on process. When one becomes stymied, the other may have seen the session from a different perspective and be able to open up new, constructive dialog. It allows one to take a break and just watch what is happening during the clinical experience, while the other clinician may be fully engaged in the process, modeling good communication and discussing in front of the clients how both therapists are seeing what is going on. Again, the process is always to open up the session experience to new and multiple ways of understanding. I always liked working in a cotherapy team as long as we were collegial and open to the experience and feedback. Again, this is seen primarily as a training and supervising device, and at some point, even though it is believed to be more useful for the training of clinicians, it is more costly and complicated. In the early 1980s, it fell from grace as anything other than a training devise, due to economic constraints in most clinics and agencies.

Bug in the ear (Boylston & Tuma, 1972; Crawford, 1994; Gallant & Thyer, 1989; Klitzke

& Lombardo, 1991; Mauzey, 1998; Smith, Mead, & Kinsella, 1998; Trepal, Granello, & Smith, 2008) is a remote system where the trainee or supervisee wears a receiving devise much like a hearing aid, while providing clinical services. The supervisor or trainer sits behind the one-way mirror and provides feedback (sometimes called course corrections) to the trainee by speaking into a microphone that is connected to the bug in the trainee's ear. Feedback is directed to either provide additional input or correct a mistake in clinical procedure. I also learned how to supervise using this type of feedback modality during my doctoral program. It is just my perspective, but I found the use of a bug in the ear cumbersome and rather detrimental to the clinical process. I mean, after students have had several classes in techniques, how much damage can they do? And my experience is that students or most trainees in a new clinical method really focus on what they are doing wrong anyway, and they usually need feedback that gives them courage to continue and focus on what they have done well. They already know about any glowing mistakes. But again, this is a training method, more so than a supervisory tool.

Live supervision seems to have begun with the family therapists (Montalvo, 1973), and according to Hardy (1993), it was one of the salient components of the discipline that sets it apart from other disciplines. Selvini and Selvini Palazzoli (1991) credited Nat Ackerman and his staff at the Jewish Family Services for first watching "each other's therapeutic work using the one-way mirror" (p. 31). They went on to say that during the 1950s and 1960s, "much therapy theory building was characterized by the use of observation and team work, including Bateson's (1972) seminal research project, undertaken in collaboration with Haley, Weakland and later, Jackson, and The Multiple Impact Therapy group (MIT)" (p. 31). Live supervision is a training and supervision medium where the clinician is guided in the process through several discreet feedback modalities I discuss later. Montalvo's (1973) article is the earliest recorded literature I could find in any searchable database, and he described

it as having a supervisor behind a one-way mirror, occasionally making suggestions to the clinician via phone calls. But Montalvo was followed by a flood of other contributors to the field, such as Birchler (1975), Gershenson and Cohen, (1978), Smith and Kingston (1980), Berger and Dammann (1982), Liddle and Schwartz (1983), and Wright (1986), followed by those in psychology, such as Kivlighan (1991) and Heppner and Kivlighan (1994), and, in counselor education, Bubenzer (1991) and Champe and Kleist (2003).

Phone-ins during clinical supervision were one of the many novel and forward thinking ideas from the field of family therapy. Wright (1986) stated that the benefit of the phone-in component of live supervision is "that trainees are able to receive immediate feedback on the development of their skills" (p. 187). Again, during my doctoral studies in the mid-1980s, I was trained to use phone-ins as a method of providing supervisory input. It was, to me, a step above the bug in the ear or the knock on the door, but it could still be awkward and clumsy, as the supervisor had to make the choice of providing immediate feedback, thus stopping forward momentum of the clinical work, or waiting until there was a natural break in the flow of dialog, and then, perhaps missing the opportunity to help change the clinical course. I never did any research on this, and I have yet to find any, but I often wondered if I were to just let things be, might the session turn out just as well?

Team breaks are also a part of the varied history of family therapy that somehow filtered over to more traditional individual clinical work as well as group therapy. The Milan team, a psychiatry group practice from Milan, Italy (Selvini Palazzoli, Boscolo, Cecchin, & Prata, 1978), devised a model of clinical work that utilized a team behind a one-way mirror and a cotherapy team providing the direct work with the family group. The Milan model went through several evolutions and revisions, as the original team split and group members refined their way of treating seriously disturbed people from a family systems model. Originally working with the systemic ideas of Gregory Bateson, they attempted to see family life with the communications and game theory that had come from that work. Their model included five interlocking stages, presession, session, intersession, intervention, and postsession discussion (Boscolo, Cecchin, Hoffman, & Penn, 1987), and thus began the team concept. During the intersession, the whole team would take a midsession break and meet together to discuss what they saw and devise a strategic intervention that would be given to the family in the consultation room. It is most interesting to me that their version of a team break was of a clinical nature and led to many other versions of the use of team breaks with other clinicians. Sometimes the break is used as a training vehicle to help course corrections in the clinical exchanges. One advantage most teams pointed to is that the intervention strategy was always the team's message, rather coming directly from the clinicians, thus the clinicians working directly with the family, individuals, or groups could have a great deal of maneuverability, should the client(s) disagree. As part of a strategic intervention, the clinician could "blame" the team for not fully understanding or sometimes suggest that perhaps team members might have a better perspective because they are not so close to what is happening in the room. Strategically, this can give the team an opportunity to ask the family to refine their own view of themselves. My colleague Mei Chen uses the team as a way of providing input to groups in both a supervisory method as well as a training model (Mei Chen, personal communication, 2001). It has also been researched for use with group supervision of school counseling interns (Kellum, 2010), for clinicians treating comorbid alcohol and mental health problems (Copello & Tobin, 2007), as a means to help social workers who live in politically tumultuous times (Shamai, 1998), and back again to Europe, mostly Germany (Barthe 1985; Fatzer, 1986; Meidinger, 1991; Schott, 2007; Spiess & Stahli, 1990), as well as France (Kuenzli-Monard, & Kuenzli, 1999; Meynckens-Fourez, 1993).

Selvini and Selvini Palazzoli (1991), however, lamented the loss of the team in both training institutions as well as in private practice. They posited that even though some have discussed the disadvantages of teams in terms of financial issues, there are more factors weighing in favor of the use of teams, such as how clearly and quickly teams have "striking results" because everything is clearer (p. 34). Emotional intensity is easier to deal with, because "a situation which is potentially so charged, with tensions can confuse an isolated therapist who will more or less consciously tend to defend against the intensity" (p. 35). Also, the use of a team tends to subjectify what team members are observing and the multiplicity of meaning—the polyvocal meanings of what is being seen becomes apparent, leading to more potential for outcomes rather than stymied situations. This honoring of multiple voices and meanings leads to a lessoning of the hierarchical nature of our more traditional supervisory situations.

Reflecting teams have been a unique addition to training and supervision from the postmodern, social constructionist perspective. Most often affiliated with family therapy (Edwards & Chen, 1999; Hardy, 1993), they have also been used in group therapy training (Chen & Noosbond, 1997a; Chen & Noosbond, 1997b; Chen & Noosbond, 1999; Chen, Noosbond, & Bruce, 1998), as well as with individual skills training (Chen, Froehle, & Morran, 1997; Chen & Noosbond, 1997b).

I was introduced to this modality during my doctoral program while I was working toward my Approved Supervisor Designation for the AAMFT. For about half of the year, I worked with master's students using the typical phone in modality, then my supervisors of supervision Tony Heath and Brent Atkinson were introduced to the reflecting team, and they introduced it to their students. Credit for the reflecting team usually goes to Norwegian psychiatrist Tom Andersen, whom I met through my associations with Heath and Atkins, but Finnish psychiatrist Ben Furman and his associate Tapani Ahola were out to dinner with a group of us after they had given a lecture/workshop, and they had a much different perspective on the reflecting team beginnings. As they told it, during the early days when the model of team breaks a la the Milan team moved from prescriptive messages to team reflections, Andersen and his group had more financing for their two-way mirrors, so that the lights might go down in the treatment room at the same time that the lights would go up in the adjoining team consultation room. "Those Norwegians had more money than us poor Fins," said Furman. "We were so poor we used an old lady's nylon stocking we put over our heads, instead of a one or two way mirror!" (Furman, personal communication, 1989). The intention was not lost on the rest of us sitting around the table—Andersen got the credit, instead of Furman and Ahola. We will never know whether this is a true story, but it is a funny story demonstrating the interest, competition, and revolutionary spirit that existed in those earlier days.

The reflecting team, comprised of a small group of colleagues, watches the clinician and client(s) from behind the one-way mirror, and then, after a little more than halfway through, group members switch by either having the lights go down in the clinical room and up in the team room, or they actually switch places. Then the members of the reflecting team talk about what they have seen, using their own reflections or thoughts. Andersen (1992b) started with the premise that reflecting team language "tended to move professional language towards daily language" (p. 58). Relying on Bateson's (1972) concept of a difference that can make a difference, Andersen wanted language and ideas to be different from what the clients have already experienced, in order to make that difference, but not too different, so that the clients do not reject it. We talked previously about how the narrative function of the brain has top-down functioning that, in Siegel's (2007) thinking, enslaves our meaning to the present set of values or "views." This Batesonian manner of talking is a means to get around those settings by adding novelty that will make the difference. It is close enough to not create dissonance, yet different enough to make change—a difference that makes a difference. Andersen also said that clinicians using the reflecting team should always be flexible enough

to allow the clients to "turn away from that with which they feel uncomfortable," and when talking in the reflecting team, "restrain themselves from giving negative connotations" (p. 60). When first observing the team at work, most clinicians and clients are surprised at the lack of "problem talk." Many clients, upon returning to discuss what the team has said, comment that they were pleasantly surprised to find that the team didn't flood them with talk about what is wrong with them but instead had much to say about how well they have been coping or trying. Life and our dilemmas and attempts to right them can be punctuated—viewed if you will—with either positive or negative valences, given context. However, we are, indeed, a society that is facing what we think is wrong, rather than perceiving what is right or going well.

The opening of the reflecting team clinical meeting situates how the clients would like to use the session and then explores the history of the dilemma with all its socially constructed parts. The clinician and clients talk for about half the session, then switch rooms with the team members. The team members then talk among themselves, while the clients and clinician watch and listen. They then switch rooms again, and the clinician asks the clients what they heard from the team while the members were talking, what they were thinking about during the discussion, and whether they wished to discuss anything or found something interesting. After this reflection on a reflection, the session ends, and the team members and clinician may talk some more, privately. The expectation is that this will result in providing many positives for what the clinician has done during the session. In making sense of the use of reflecting teams in triadic supervision, Stinchfield et al. (2007), in reflecting the current directions of Andersen, wrote that, "it is the process, and not the team, that holds therapeutic power and influence" (p. 175). Social construction occurs when novel information that is interjected in conversation provides a difference that is not offered as truth but as a person's own reflections about what he or she is observing in a way that does not dictate truth, so much as perhaps an alternative view. The view is close and congruent enough that an alternative reality is visible, and perhaps internalized, thus creating change. As of this writing, there has been only one empirical study of reflecting team use for supervision (Moran, Brownlee, Gallant, Meyers, Farmer, & Taylor, 1995), and the need for more research is obvious due to the many that use and rely on it.

Supervision Configurations

Supervision also has several configurations, from the typical one-on-one, to triadic, group supervision, and peer supervision. The purpose of any supervision configuration is the same, to provide input and feedback to clinicians who are in need or desirous of another perspective on how and what they are doing with their clients. Supervision can be for those in training in a clinical skills class, training of a new or procedural change or during practicum and internship, as well as an ongoing experience at a clinic or practicum situation regarding specific cases or updates of a case load. Most commonly, the supervisor and supervisee(s) discuss procedures, expectations, beliefs, and experiences of their supervision, numbers of meetings, goals, times, and dates. Depending on the model used, contractual agreements taking into account these factors will dictate process and procedure of the supervisory relationship.

An important part of the contract is the use of informed consent, just like in a clinical situation. In several of the formal workshop trainings I have provided, some of the supervisors that are already practicing report that they are still using person-of-the-therapist supervision. Person-of-the-therapist supervision is similar to the sort of supervision psychoanalytic supervision uses, where the supervisee is required to talk about his or her interface/countertransference issues in depth. Supervision becomes more like therapy than it does during clinical supervision. These supervisors should obtain informed consent before they stumble around into their supervisee's psyche. Supervision is not clinical work,

although it comes close at times. If the supervisor and supervisee enter into this sort of supervision, informed consent should be obtained first.

Individual supervision is the typical one-on-one supervision that most think of when addressing what supervision is. This is the version of supervision where Bernard's domains were most helpful to me during my formative years as a supervisor. And I must say that in the early days, her tripartite model—easy to remember and simple to use—included teaching, consultations, and counseling. Much of the early supervision I received, especially from those who had definite psychodynamic leanings, involved a great deal of introspective work. Looking at my own motives in why I did something with one of my clients was seen as relatively important to the movement of my clients in a clinical sense—know thyself, and you can help your clients move to the same spot. Parallelism was important to the work. Even in the early days, the family systems thinking of Murray Bowen (1966, 1974, 1976) suggested that his theory was not one to be learned as a technique, but it had to be practiced on oneself, thus clinicians could not take their clients further than they had gone themselves.

Triadic supervision came about, according to Stinchfield et al. (2007), from the 2001 Council for Accreditation of Counseling and Related Educational Programs (CACREP) standards that allow for triadic supervision for students, as well as for individuals. These authors alluded to the significant increase in programs (52% for CACREP programs from 1999 to 2004), as well as in students, as one of the reasons for allowing triadic supervision. I do, however, remember having triadic supervision as far back as 1971, as a means to deal with the time commitment a program in the Illinois Department of Mental Health had with respect to availability of a consulting supervisor. We thought nothing of it in those days; however, we were well aware that our supervision was to be confidential due to the nature of person-of-the-therapist supervision in our psychoanalytically oriented program. My personal experience lately with triadic supervision has also been overwhelmingly positive, as each member is also encouraged to comment, give opinions, suggestions, and encouragements. The students really like to hear from and give support to each other, as well as feel like others value their contributions to the corporate clinical growth. Stinchfield et al. have a unique version of triadic supervision that includes the use of a reflective process adapted from Andersen (1987) that has excellent potential for use in strengths-based supervision, especially as it is one of the frameworks of strengths-based work.

In this model of triadic supervision, Stinchfield, Hill, and Kleist (2007) pointed out that Andersen has discussed, as one of his ideas about the reflecting practice, that there are both inner and outer dialogues going on all the time, and it is this that makes the practice during supervision so powerful. But first, let us take it step by step to help understand the practice.

First, the authors suggest that the reflecting part of supervision, using the Reflecting Model of Triadic Supervision (RMTS; Stinchfield et al., 2007), should be offered to students, rather than as using it as something that is a usual part of common everyday practice. The invitation and pre-discussion of what RMTS is reflects collegial respect, or as they maintain, presents the opportunity to participate in either RMTS or individual supervision in order to "maintain a sense of safety" (Stinchfield et al., 2007, p. 181). Most likely, if they do choose to participate in RMTS, trainees will pick people whom they know well and trust. It is the authors' belief that offering choice also cultivates a trusting relationship with the supervisor, thus potentiating their involvement and comfort in the reflecting model. Next, for those who choose to participate in this form of triadic supervision instead of one on one supervision, the two supervisees meet with their supervisor, and every other week one of them present a case situation—in the authors' setting, the use of videotaped clinical work is used. The supervisor describes the process of RMTS, including an informed consent, and as a usual part of goaling or contracting, the supervisees further agree to this model by either verbal assent or through formal supervisory

contractual process. Then the presenting supervisee proceeds with the formal presentation while the official supervisor and the reflecting supervisee listen. The supervisee presenting the case specifies what they want to show, as well as, perhaps, what they might want the two reflectors to watch for, and what he or she might want to gain from this experience. Then they proceed, and the supervisor and reflecting supervisee listen, and the presenting supervisee and the supervisor may discuss the counseling session. After some time, they shift to the reflecting piece, and the supervisor and reflecting supervisee engage in a reflection of the supervision piece. It is interesting to note that Stinchfield et al. (2007) suggested a 1½-hour time frame and that they also meet with their supervisees every week. At this point of the reflection, the presenting supervisee is not required to speak or comment; only to listen. After the reflection piece of "approximately 10 minutes" the supervisor turns to process the reflection part of RMTS (p. 177). I am intrigued by their use of the "process," as it seems more modernist than postmodern in its usage. In clinical work or supervision, my usual words to those listening to the reflection are, "So when you heard the team's reflections, what were your own thoughts, ideas, or feelings? What stood out for you as you listened that you might want to comment on?"

Now, let me get back to the comment I made at the beginning of this reflection of triadic supervision reflecting teams. Andersen (1992b) clearly has set the standard for what goes on during conversations, especially during supervision, with his discussion of inner and outer dialogues or conversations, as he prefers. He makes clear that when people converse, "they are engaged in an "outer" dialog. When they are listening, they are talking to themselves in an "inner" dialogue. Each of the participants is engaged on the same issue from those two different perspectives; talking and listening, the other and inner dialogue respectively" (p. 88). Reflecting on this, and mulling over what Siegel (2007) has taught us about the brain (see Chapter 4 in this book), our "enslavement" is either taking the conversation in, or filtering it out, depending on the way the language and conversation is constructed and presented, as well as how the receiver's enslaved view is accepting it. To use Narrative Therapy terms, as clinicians and supervisors we can either work to open space for conversation, or close that space. The structure of the RMTS and reflective work of any kind sets the stage for a release of enslavement and opens us up to understand each other and appreciate what others have said, perhaps not to agree. To deeply understand another point of view, thus to open space for other possibilities, one needs to experience being heard or received. "Pain is created by not being received" (Loegstrup, cited in Andersen, 2001, p. 11). The space for reflection is opened, according to Andersen, because the obligatory rush to answer, that is culturally constructed, especially in some countries and occupations, is changed to allow for longer periods of reflection. Our profession places a high value on responding to a client/supervisee (our inner conversation), in order to be helpful. When this rush to answer is replaced with a rush to pause and listen, inner reflections can be opened for the difference that makes a difference that we discussed earlier (Bateson, 1972). For information to be taken in, and an impact made, means that the reflection piece—the internal conversation—has to have taken place in a way that makes sense to the receiver. The receiver does not have to agree with it in total, or in part, but he or she needs time to reflect and see if it fits and also to have an opportunity to voice his or her own perspective and have that received. The Taos Institute folks argue that meaning is constructed in relationships, and it is by this reflective, recursive manner that our internal conversations are stored, from "our history of relationships—from our early childhoods to our most recent conversations . . . that we determine what is real and valuable for us" (Anderson et al., 2008). It is here that the most important piece

of how to supervise becomes apparent, not only for triadic reflective supervision but for all of supervision. The time to process, reflect, make sense of, and be understood, as well as to acknowledge that supervisors understand too why they have a difference from ours, creates the safe space where new meaning can be constructed. What Andersen said is that "one does not even need a team to alternate talking and listening roles" (1992a, p. 88). People can do that themselves under the right conditions of serious open reflection.

Group supervision or group soup is just what it says, a supervisor or facilitator and a bunch of people that gather to talk about and get ideas of what to do with their clients. I remember in the early days, we used a group soup format to have case staffings, usually with a psychiatrist or clinical psychologist to listen, evoke thoughts from the group, and then pronounce a plan of action with the client. In agency or residential settings, it might also include members of a therapeutic team, such as clinicians of many stripes, such as social workers, activity therapists, dance therapists, aides and or child care workers, psychiatrists, and agency directors or supervisors. From this model, group soup naturally ends up as a training venue to teach models or supervise interns both on site and at the university from which the degree will be granted.

Peer group supervision is just what it says: A group of clinicians gather together and provide support and suggestions with difficult cases. The absence of a designated or assigned supervisor with responsibility and ties to an agency or organization of some kind changes the dynamics of power and hierarchy most supervision configurations have. There is a scarcity of literature on the subject (Kassan, 2010), demonstrating the lack of informal—or should I say unofficial—forms of supervision that occur. Kassan (2010) made the point that peer supervision can become a great source of comfort and help to those in independent practice. Worrall and Fruzzetti (2009) presented an Internet-based training system "designed to help increase the skill with which peer supervisors discriminate more effective from less effective interventions, allowing them to deliver more effective feedback to their peers or supervisees" (p. 476). Whether it is for training and supervision in Dialectical Behavior Therapy, or simply based on the unique availability of an Internet method, should demonstrate that there are many ways of delivering supervision and that there are many theoretical models for clinicians to use that need supervision from those more fully trained.

Peer group supervision has been written about for the development of school counselors (Wilkerson, 2006), as an adjunct to individual supervision (Akhurst & Kelly, 2006), as a vehicle to collaborate between health workers and mental health workers in the field of infant mental health (Thomasgard, Warfield, & Williams, 2004), with music therapists (Bird, Merrill, Mohan, Summers, & Woodward, 1999), in social work (Hardcastle, 1991), and in counselor education (Benshoff, 1993), showing that it has versatility and usefulness. Although the research on peer supervision follows the usual course of the next new big thing in this field (see a list of research from 1987 to 1997, in Christensen & Kline, 2001), the topic of peer supervision seemed to peter out in the literature after the Christensen and Kline (2001) article was published. Their premise echoes what most group supervision models expect, that "the support for peer group supervision is based on the belief that it offers opportunities for vicarious learning in a supportive group environment." It is argued that once established, this environment contributes to decreased supervisee anxiety, increased self-efficacy and confidence, and enhanced learning opportunities. Christensen and Kline also postulated that because of the dual factors of being a group, and being a peer-led supervision modality, the issue of hierarchy and dependency that is found in most problem-focused individual supervision, is diminished. In unpacking Christensen and Kline's research subjects' qualitative responses, it seems that the same sort of expected outcomes for any group process is evident, meaning that their peer group supervision is no more or less effective than any other

group. Their model also lacks true peer group supervision, as the university supervisors facilitate the group process:

> Supervisors supplied initial structure, but as supervisees became more effective in their roles, supervisors served as group process facilitators. From the perspectives of the supervisees, supervisors were most effective when they facilitated feedback, focused on interpersonal dynamics, and intervened to resolve process issues. (Christensen & Kline, 2001, p. 96)

However you slice it, new clinicians value any feedback they can get, including that from peers, who the new clinicians experience as "being highly valuable and important" (Christensen & Kline, 2001, p. 97). One can hope that they feel the same way about their clinical supervisors also.

Peer supervision is an outside-of-formal training and supervision model that allows a clinician to get feedback from his or her peers regarding cases that might be in need of alternative points of view, but they should be differentiated from a "stuck-case clinic" (Quinn, Atkinson, & Hood, 1985), which is a fairly rigorous and formal group supervision model for couple and family therapy.

Training contexts are the last metagroup of clinical supervision I want to address. It must be fairly evident to you at this point that the separate field of supervision has become a force of reckoning in the various fields of mental health clinicians and thus in the literature. Supervision is a method of training and maintaining integrity for the client and the clinician, as well as the organization. Depending on the clinical treatment modality being used for family therapy, individual counseling or therapy, or group counseling/therapy—each treatment modality may have its own worldview, thus its own model of training and supervision. To some extent, they have maintained their own views about clinical practice as well as clinical supervision. In my experience, this also happens between the various guild groups, such as psychology, social work, couple and family, and professional counseling. That we rarely read each other's literature is a sad commentary on scholarship, but that some refrain from using excellent models of clinical supervision or clinical work limits our ability to be helpful to those we seek to serve. I believe that this is exactly what Jane Speedy (2000) meant when offered her critique of most literature regarding clinical supervision when she said, "It is not a humble or exploratory literature" (p. 428).

Strengths-Based Supervision

The strength of *Strengths-Based Supervision in Clinical Practice* is that it is different and more current than any of the books on supervision I have read and referenced. It is the paradigm shift that needs to happen in the field of clinical supervision to fit with the strengths-based clinical work that is current today. Based on Information Age/Connectivity Age and strengths-based concepts, strengths-based supervision moves away from the "more of the same" mentality that has dominated the supervision field for so long. In reframing the focus of supervision from doing something *to* supervisees, to collaborating *with* stakeholders, the assumptions of supervision change significantly. Assuming that typical supervision competencies *do* provide needed executive skills, strengths-based supervision provides nine strong basic skills that are typical for any good supervision work and replaces the usual medically modeled deficit and problem remediation focus with the primary four contemporary strengths concepts—Narrative, Solution Focus, and Resiliency means, as well as Positive Psychology—for the operating principles that move the supervision process past mere effectiveness, onward toward excellence. In addition, supervision excellence is assured by using research from social psychology, management, and leadership, all tested and proven concepts that work and should have been a part of clinical supervision from the beginning.

All of these concepts are unpacked in Chapter 4, which looks at how postmodern and social constructionist models inform strengths-based supervision, and in Chapter 5, how Positive Psychology and resilience research adds weight to strengths-based supervision.

2

EXECUTIVE SKILLS OF STRENGTHS-BASED SUPERVISION

The meeting of two personalities is like the contact of two chemical substances: if there is any reaction, both are transformed.

—Carl Jung (1933, p. 49)

Travel is fatal to prejudice, bigotry, and narrow-mindedness.

—Mark Twain (1869, p. 491)

Most clinical supervision is done by competent and well-heeled supervisors in the trenches who are not attached to academia in any way. This is somewhat contentious to academics, yet the bulk of supervision literature and training is geared toward doctoral students and academics in ivory towers and laboratories. There are far more supervisors without doctoral training (West Russo, 2010), and they deserve our respect, admiration and thanks, rather than the failure of inclusion that occurs in literature intended for doctoral students. There is, it seems, a pejorative favor of doctoral training of supervisors over "in the field" supervisors in the literature's availability and focus, while in reality there are more of those in the field, and they are doing good solid work. I have nothing but admiration for these folks who provide the bulk of clinical supervision in our world. Thus, the executive skills I present here are aimed at

providing a flavor of the literature on supervision, while at the same time adding up-to-date material past what was originally written. I do so to provide a more current, albeit personal, version in order to round out what many site supervisors never got because they chose to provide quality work in our collective field.

Strengths-based work, yes I will get to it eventually, cannot exist alone, and neither can any form of supervision or clinical work. It is executive skills that provide the groundwork for whatever we do. They are the nuts and bolts of clinical supervision, while resiliency and strengths are the frame through which we must see our supervisees. Several universal concepts from clinical work form the basis of executive skills that help clinical supervisors stay on track regardless of the model they use. This is also a partial review of many of the foundational thoughts of supervision that can inform those of us who supervise or desire to do so that we just covered. While some experts have suggested that clinicians should work from a strategic frame, while maintaining a structural position (Kottler & Shepard, 2008), I advocate for thinking strengths-based, while adhering to principles that assure quality and ethical work, both clinically and as a supervisor. Each of the executive skills described here is punctuated with actual case material.

Regardless of the model or mode used, clinicians or supervisors, to do their job, must understand and utilize the 10 executive skills: (1) cross-cultural or multicultural competencies, (2) the domains of a supervisor, (3) ethics, (4) developmental stages of a clinician, (5) isomorphs and parallel processes, (6) boundary issues, (7) interpersonal relationship skills, (8) conflict resolution, (9) enhancement of self-efficacy and personal agency, and finally, (10) session management. Each of these areas that I include as a specific executive skill has been researched and written about in great detail, so I will only provide an overview. But I sincerely believe that to be a competent supervisor—even a strengths-based one—these areas need to be understood and continue to be a part of a lifelong learning update that we maintain. Even in the last few years, from when I began the formulation of this book, new and exciting changes have happened in each of these areas.

Over the years, as I provided workshops for new supervisors and those who had no formal training, it was clear to me that the literature compartmentalized a series of skills that were needed to provide adequate supervision. However, although they may all have been situated in edited texts, no one has actually placed them together, and like the executive skills necessary to provide quality clinical work (office rules of conduct, how to start and stop sessions on time, what to do if someone talks too much or too little, etc.), they are the bedrock of quality clinical work and supervision but are rarely taught or written about. An examination of the literature shows that little work has been focused on these "high-level" skills—skills that help clinicians and supervisors pay attention to a

group of guiding principles that help to organize specific events and issues in sessions that lead to smooth and beneficial collaborative work. Executive skills are metaskills, rarely taught in a university setting and from the lack of literature, rarely spoken of or researched, yet seasoned clinicians and supervisors know how to incorporate these in order to run a session smoothly. Especially today, managing the session from entry to exit, from upset to joy, it is useful to know how things work in one's office during a session. It is important to have a skill set that goes above and beyond one's model or orientation in clinical supervision. Ironically, the only place I found references to executive skills in counseling was in Chen and Rybak's book, *Group Leadership Skills* (2003), and in an article on family therapy training by Tomm and Wright (2004). In this chapter, I review what I consider to be the executive skills of a clinical supervisor. Each of the executive skills is punctuated with actual case dialogue. Let us unpack the supervisory executive skills one at a time and understand the synergy they create for competent clinical supervision.

While evidence-based practice may be the current gold standard, statistically proven protocols don't always work. When they fail, clinicians and supervisors often place blame for the errors and failures on the client, saying the client wasn't ready or psychologically minded (Hubble, Duncan, & Miller, 1999). Time-bound models do not account for novel or random events that occur in our stakeholders' lives, so even the best constructed model will not account for a mother's loss of food stamps, a child's sudden desire to begin using drugs, or other systemic barriers to smooth sailing treatment. Like a well-trained clinician who has a developed maturity and personal agency and can move with the flow and be flexible when needed, great supervisors are ready to attend to the sudden stops and starts, all the while looking for the supervisee's strengths and resilience, pointing them out at an appropriate time. Most supervisors have had times when a supervisee experiences a death of a loved one, a romance gone sour, family problems, or a tragedy. These experiences require supervisors to be on their toes and ready to help their supervisee bring forth his or her natural resilient resources. The supervisor's ability to be flexible is imperative, and our executive skills, if understood, can kick into gear and help smooth out these transitory life events. I have had at least two women give birth and need to be in internship class soon after. Both needed to express their breast milk for their baby at home, during class, so I left them alone in my office, showed them where the refrigerator was, and started class with the expectation they would join us later. In addition, we videotaped the sessions they missed and sent the tape to them so they would still feel a part of the class.

PERSONAL CARE FOR PERSONAL AGENCY

Jennifer was in her last semester of internship at a program designed to work with women who have experienced sexual abuse at some point in their lives. She had talked several times in supervision about one of her clients, a woman who also had an advanced degree in counseling and who had at times been suicidal. Jen had, according to the agency plan, written a suicide protection contract, but the women had laughed and said, "This is really more for you than it is for me, isn't it?" The woman had no plan at the time, but she had also talked about knowing that at some point in time she would follow through with ending her life.

Then one day, Jen came in looking really stressed and said she had received another client who had been suicidal once before and that this client was always in crisis mode. The wear and tear on this intern was showing, and I asked if she was talking care of herself well enough to have the energy to be present for her clients. Her personal agency was at risk. I asked what were some of the things she used to do that gave her joy and filled her life with energy. The mood in the room changed from hopeless to more hope filled as she discussed how she enjoyed singing in a choir, had not spent any time during her graduate studies doing this, and was waiting until she graduated. Signature strengths when applied can balance the work stressors we all have, and as Jen and I discussed this, we both agreed that the sooner she started this course of action, the more likely it would be that she would continue it as a regular part of her life. The offshoot might possibly be better energy and focus on her clients. I then asked her to describe a time in her sessions when she felt the work she was providing with one of these clients was really profound and solid forward progression. She was able to describe several of these times—she was in the moment—flow—and the clinical work was, in her opinion, the best of the best for client and clinician. As we take care of our supervisees, they will do the same for their clients.

CROSS-CULTURAL AND MULTICULTURAL COMPETENCIES

As I was thinking more about the issue of culture and how it plays into supervision, I chanced to have lunch with my two colleagues and friends, Drs. Anita Thomas and Sara Schwarzbaum, authors of two fine texts about multiculturalism (Thomas & Schwarzbaum, 2005; Schwarzbaum & Thomas, 2008). So I asked them what they thought would be important to get across to supervisors regarding multiculturalism. Thomas quickly said, "Talk about it" (A. J. Thomas, personal communication, March 31, 2010). Schwarzbaum agreed. This is good sound advice, but of course, there is more.

Multicultural and cross-cultural thought, including, for instance, the feminist perspective (Nelson, 2006), gender and sexual orientation (Singh & Chun, 2010), cultural (Constantine, 1997; D'Andrea & Daniels, 1997; Dressel, Consoli, Kim, & Atkinson, 2007; Gonzalez, 1997; Inman, 2006; Lassiter, Napolitano, Culbreth, & Ng, 2008; Martinez & Holloway, 1997; Stone, 1997), racial (Butler-Byrd, 2010), and spirituality and religion issues (Puig & Fukuyama, 2008), have become central to the field as we train future generations of clinicians as well as supervisors to work sensitively with all people. Most of the work of cultural sensitivity includes a healthy look at our own epistemological view of who we are and how we learned how to think about and get along with those who are not the same as us. We tend to believe that the way we have been taught to think and believe (social constructions) is not only the right way but that those who are different from us are wrong. Even those with multicultural sensitivity can still carry around messages embedded from years of walking around in a country and culture that continue to institutionalize racist policies and practices. For example, in 2009 a justice of the peace, of all people, refused to marry a couple because they were of different races, while prominent public figures of color continue to be mistaken for each other and parts of our nation are enacting strict and potentially dangerous legislation that effects cultures that might be racially profiled. These actions are the most obvious of concerns, as ever more critical human rights are overlooked as we debate the rights of all people to share in the common good, equally. Those of us who supervise and practice must always be aware of our own worldviews.

Cross-Culturalism and Multiculturalism

There is a distinction between what is meant by cross-culturalism and multiculturalism. Cross-culturalism has to do with the similarities and differences among discrete cultural groups beyond the constraints of a nation, state, or other structure, while multiculturalism has to do with differences among groups within a larger group such as a nation, or even within the boundaries of a single cultural group. Cross-culturalism would be interested in how blacks who have ancestral roots in Africa are different from Asians or differences of psychologists in the United States from those in Sweden, while multiculturalism might focus on differences and similarities of white Eurocentric males in the United States or compare the Hells Angels from Los Angeles to the Aryan Brotherhood Wonderland Gang from some of our southern states.

For our purposes of supervision in clinical settings, however, as early as 1997 Constantine (1997), as well as D'Andrea and Daniels (1997), suggested that the term multicultural is far more appropriate, because these days the nature of clinical work, thus clinical supervision, is reflective of "multiple cultural factors" (D'Andrea & Daniels, 1997, p. 293). Fong and Lease (1997) made the point that "all supervisors, regardless of racial/ethnic background, need to seek professional development in the knowledge and skills of cross-cultural supervision" (p. 396). Today, we know that to be true, however, as multicultural supervision. Many years later, the field has increased our understanding of multicultural supervision by many folds, making it a rich and growing endeavor that continues to need more professional development training.

Smith (2006) suggested "a core component of the strength-based theory is that culture has a major impact on how people view and evaluate human strengths. All strengths are culturally based" (p. 17). She believed that any time clinicians are involved with counseling where culture is a factor (and almost all are), they should be focusing on cultural strengths rather than on their potential to be victimized due to discrimination, and she noted that strengths-based work has roots in researchers who began to question the relevance of some assumptions of the field, due to their cross-cultural implications.

Furthermore, the implications of a philosophy that adheres to a postmodern and socially constructed practice have similarities and congruence with those of multiculturalism (D'Andrea, 2000). It moves us away from a universalist perspective to a multiverse, providing opportunities and ways of truth farther past fundamentalism. The standardization of traditional clinical theory and models can be called into question and required to make way for multiple perspectives, due to our understanding of top-down socially constructed beliefs, and this moves us away from holding to any single truth. We are forced to admit and see that our way is only best for us, not for all, and that we may also adopt and rewrite our views over time. So, what does this all mean in regard to multiculturalism embedded in strengths-based supervision? I will give you, the reader, a broad stroke view of the field.

Multiculturalism and Supervision

Earlier in the study of multiculturalism and supervision, Stone (1997) noted a growing problem in a growing field—the literature is slim. Those who are studying this niche of the field disagree on what the focus should be; defining multiculturalism from either an inclusive or exclusive approach uses ambiguous terms such as race, nationality, ethnicity, gender, and so forth, in addition to who should be included in what is called culture. Pointing to a study of biological aspects of ethnicity, the position is made that the boundaries of culture are blurred as there are no discrete boundaries genetically between races (Chapman, 1993, as cited in Stone, 1997). Making an observation that I think is an early precursor to strengths-based thinking, Stone said the following: "One general, unfortunate consequence has been the view of culture as an obstacle to overcome in counseling practice rather than an opportunity to enhance practice" (p. 268). Culture as a strength is centered and put forward, with the caveat and understated notion that multicultural training is cited in the literature for the purposes of training competent clinicians, while we noted earlier that the focus should also be on the training of supervisors.

Throughout the literature, the issue of power and privilege resonate for the supervisor with respect to issues of gender (Nelson et al., 2006), sexual orientation (Singh & Chun, 2010), and cultural (Constantine, 1997; D'Andrea & Daniels, 1997; Dressel et al., 2007; Gonzalez, 1997; Inman, 2006; Lassiter, 2008; Martinez & Holloway, 1997; Stone, 1997); and supervisor competencies (Dressel et al., 2007; Inman, 2006; Lassiter et al., 2008; Ober, Granello, & Henfield, 2009). The issue of power is a standard part of supervision, one I have tried to deconstruct throughout the section on strengths-based models. Some of the issues of power and privilege that come along with the title of supervision are more likely to be jettisoned, depending on where the supervision is done. The natural consequences of a hierarchical grade-giving occupation as professor *and* clinical supervisor make the problem just that much harder to deal with, yet as we see throughout this book, supervisees want to be treated as competent and collegial members of a team (Heath & Storm, 1983; Heath and Tharp, as cited by Thomas, 1996). Awareness, self-reflection, and open discussion work to maintain open communication and level the hierarchical playing field. Indeed, the importance of self-examination is considered one of the themes that came out of the work of a two-day meeting/discussion of the Supervision and Training Work Group at the 1998 Advancing Together: Centralizing Feminism and Multiculturalism in Counseling Psychology Conference (Nelson et al., 2006). Nelson et al. (2006) also pointed to the ability to contain ambiguity and anxiety as it relates to multiculturalism within supervision, a notion I have experienced quite often while writing this section for this book. "The capacity to make such admissions is related to a supervisor's ability to acknowledge her or his own limitations in supervision with trainees. Admission of what one does not know is related to the capacity to remain open" (Nelson et al., 2006, p. 116). Regardless of my experience working with urban populations and counseling in multicultural settings for the better part of my 43 years, I have not had sufficient training in a broad understanding of what it means to supervise multiculturally. Sometimes I have felt like a fraud writing a section in which I have experienced but not had formal training. Multicultural competency training was not a required part of my education when I was in graduate school, and I am the product of a family that didn't think twice about its white power; my beloved father liked only his own kind during an era much different than the one I live in today. We are socially constructed, but that can change through training and self-examination and being open to our own limitations. Thus began a career where my work comprised almost 70% nonwhite clients.

During the writing of this section, I had a supervisory session with a Latino gay man who was stymied in his work with a gay man of South Asian descent. The client presented as depressed and expressed that there is nothing about where he came from to be proud of or like, and that there was no one in this city to whom he relates. Irony: a straight, white 64-year-old male supervisor helping a Latino gay supervisee who is struggling with a situation neither I, nor my supervisee, know very little about. My only hope is that I have recently read several articles for this section, especially Singh and Chun's (2010) *From the Margins to the Center: Moving Towards a Resilience-Based Model of Supervision for Queer People of Color Supervisors* and Field and Chavez-Korell's (2010) *No Hay Rosas Sin Espinas: Conceptualizing Latina-Latina Supervision From a Multicultural Developmental Supervisory Model;* and I have reread Smith's (2006) seminal article on strength-based work. Smith's mantra, again, is that strengths emanate from our culture—work with the cultural strengths and you are working strengths-based, while Singh and Chun advocate for a resiliency model. I feel at home again. My dual cultures of English, which can sometimes be perceived as arrogant and standoffish, are tempered by the knowledge of what my Scottish ancestors had to do to gain their rights for freedom. This is a useful clash, I might rather suspect, but I acknowledge my own limitations. My Celtic epistemology tells me that the universe will provide, while my Scottish Presbyterian epistemology tells me that the Lord will provide if I have been predestined. She (God) did, so we dig for strengths and resiliencies of his client's culture, but we are both unsure of what they are. I start to suggest that he have the young man watch the story of Harvey Milk—what

a mistake; he is white. And I am really glad that there are no roses without thorns—*no hay rosas sin espinas.* So my supervisee goes off to find out about that part of the multicultural situation—his South Asian gay man, coming from a culture where there is no word for gay or homosexual in his language, and he is living in a very multicultural urban city. I am not in Kansas anymore, that's for sure. There is a lot to know when one becomes a multicultural supervisor.

Let us take a look at some suggested skills we need to have and what to do to get there. But before you do that, you should look at the multicultural competencies of the Association for Multicultural Counseling and Development (AMCD), a division of the ACA (Figure 2.1). In addition, both the American Psychological Association (APA; 2002) and the National Association for Social Workers (NASW; 2005) have articulated practice and training stances on multiculturalism.

Dressel et al. (2007), in an attempt to find what successful and unsuccessful multicultural supervisory behaviors might be, conducted a three-round Delphi study with 21 supervisors referred by university training directors, who met the criteria for the study—many years as a supervisor with multicultural experience (number unspecified) and evidence of scholarship in multicultural supervision. The final number of supervisor panel members who stayed with the project to the end was 13. The final results indicated that of the 27 behaviors the respondent group put together for successful multicultural supervision, the most favorably rated behavior was "creating a safe environment for discussion of multicultural issues" (p. 58). The next highest ranked behaviors were those that had to do with supervisors developing their own self-awareness with respect to culture and ethnic identity and communicating respect for their supervisees' ethnicity, ideas about cultural influences in a clinical situation, and openness, empathy, genuineness, and ability to be nonjudgmental (Dressel et al., 2007). Of the 33 behavioral statements the panel decided on, the highest rated behavior to indicate unsuccessful multicultural supervision was a lack of awareness

Figure 2.1 Association for Multicultural Counseling & Development (AMCD) Counseling Competencies

I. Counselor Awareness of Own Cultural Values and Biases

A. Attitudes and Beliefs

1. Culturally skilled counselors believe that cultural self-awareness and sensitivity to one's own cultural heritage is essential.

2. Culturally skilled counselors are aware of how their own cultural background and experiences have influenced attitudes, values, and biases about psychological processes.

3. Culturally skilled counselors are able to recognize the limits of their multicultural competency and expertise.

4. Culturally skilled counselors recognize their sources of discomfort with differences that exist between themselves and clients in terms of race, ethnicity, and culture.

B. Knowledge

1. Culturally skilled counselors have specific knowledge about their own racial and cultural heritage and how it personally and professionally affects their definitions and biases of normality/abnormality and the process of counseling.

2. Culturally skilled counselors possess knowledge and understanding about how oppression, racism, discrimination, and stereotyping affect them personally and in their work. This allows individuals to acknowledge their own racist attitudes, beliefs, and feelings. Although this standard applies to all groups, for white counselors it may mean that they understand how they may have directly or indirectly benefited from individual, institutional, and cultural racism as outlined in white identity development models.

3. Culturally skilled counselors possess knowledge about their social impact upon others. They are knowledgeable about communication style differences, how their style may clash with or foster the counseling process with persons of color or others different from themselves based on the A, B, and C, Dimensions, and how to anticipate the impact it may have on others.

C. Skills

1. Culturally skilled counselors seek out educational, consultative, and training experiences to improve their understanding and effectiveness in working with culturally different populations. Being able to recognize the limits of their competencies, they (a) seek consultation, (b) seek further training or education, (c) refer out to more qualified individuals or resources, or (d) engage in a combination of these.

2. Culturally skilled counselors are constantly seeking to understand themselves as racial and cultural beings and are actively seeking a nonracist identity.

(Continued)

Figure 2.1 (Continued)

II. Counselor Awareness of Client's Worldview

A. Attitudes and Beliefs

1. Culturally skilled counselors are aware of their negative and positive emotional reactions toward other racial and ethnic groups that may prove detrimental to the counseling relationship. They are willing to contrast their own beliefs and attitudes with those of their culturally different clients in a nonjudgmental fashion.

2. Culturally skilled counselors are aware of their stereotypes and preconceived notions that they may hold toward other racial and ethnic minority groups.

B. Knowledge

1. Culturally skilled counselors possess specific knowledge and information about the particular group with which they are working. They are aware of the life experiences, cultural heritage, and historical background of their culturally different clients. This particular competency is strongly linked to the "minority identity development models" available in the literature.

2. Culturally skilled counselors understand how race, culture, ethnicity, and so forth may affect personality formation, vocational choices, manifestation of psychological disorders, help seeking behavior, and the appropriateness or inappropriateness of counseling approaches.

3. Culturally skilled counselors understand and have knowledge about sociopolitical influences that impinge upon the life of racial and ethnic minorities. Immigration issues, poverty, racism, stereotyping, and powerlessness may impact self-esteem and self-concept in the counseling process.

C. Skills

1. Culturally skilled counselors should familiarize themselves with relevant research and the latest findings regarding mental health and mental disorders that affect various ethnic and racial groups. They should actively seek out educational experiences that enrich their knowledge, understanding, and cross-cultural skills for more effective counseling behavior.

2. Culturally skilled counselors become actively involved with minority individuals outside the counseling setting (e.g., community events, social and political functions, celebrations, friendships, neighborhood groups, and so forth) so that their perspective of minorities is more than an academic or helping exercise.

III. Culturally Appropriate Intervention Strategies

A. Beliefs and Attitudes

1. Culturally skilled counselors respect clients' religious and/ or spiritual beliefs and values, including attributions and taboos, because they affect worldview, psychosocial functioning, and expressions of distress.

2. Culturally skilled counselors respect indigenous helping practices and helping networks among communities of color.

3. Culturally skilled counselors value bilingualism and do not view another language as an impediment to counseling (monolingualism may be the culprit).

B. Knowledge

1. Culturally skilled counselors have a clear and explicit knowledge and understanding of the generic characteristics of counseling and therapy (culture bound, class bound, and monolingual) and how they may clash with the cultural values of various cultural groups.

2. Culturally skilled counselors are aware of institutional barriers that prevent minorities from using mental health services.

3. Culturally skilled counselors have knowledge of the potential bias in assessment instruments and use procedures and interpret findings while keeping in mind the cultural and linguistic characteristics of the clients.

4. Culturally skilled counselors have knowledge of family structures, hierarchies, values, and beliefs from various cultural perspectives. They are knowledgeable about the community where a particular cultural group may reside and the resources in the community.

5. Culturally skilled counselors should be aware of relevant discriminatory practices at the social and community level that may be affecting the psychological welfare of the population being served.

C. Skills

1. Culturally skilled counselors are able to engage in a variety of verbal and nonverbal helping responses. They are able to send and receive both verbal and nonverbal messages accurately and appropriately. They are not tied down to only one method or approach to helping but recognize that helping styles and approaches may be culture bound. When they sense that their helping style is limited and potentially inappropriate, they can anticipate and modify it.

2. Culturally skilled counselors are able to exercise institutional intervention skills on behalf of their clients. They can help clients determine whether a "problem" stems from racism or bias in others (the concept of healthy paranoia) so that clients do not inappropriately personalize problems.

3. Culturally skilled counselors are not averse to seeking consultation with traditional healers or religious and spiritual leaders and practitioners in the treatment of culturally different clients when appropriate.

4. Culturally skilled counselors take responsibility for interacting in the language requested by the client and, if not feasible, make appropriate referrals. A serious problem arises when the linguistic skills of the counselor do not match the language of the client. This being the case, counselors should (a) seek a translator with cultural knowledge and appropriate professional background or (b) refer to a knowledgeable and competent bilingual counselor.

(Continued)

Figure 2.1 (Continued)

5. Culturally skilled counselors have training and expertise in the use of traditional assessment and testing instruments. They not only understand the technical aspects of the instruments but are also aware of the cultural limitations. This allows them to use test instruments for the welfare of culturally different clients.

6. Culturally skilled counselors should attend to as well as work to eliminate biases, prejudices, and discriminatory contexts in conducting evaluations and providing interventions, and they should develop sensitivity to issues of oppression, sexism, heterosexism, elitism, and racism.

7. Culturally skilled counselors take responsibility for educating their clients to the processes of psychological intervention, such as goals, expectations, legal rights, and the counselor's orientation.

Source: Adapted from Arredondo, P., Toporek, M. S., Brown, S., Jones, J., Locke, D. C., Sanchez, J., & Stadler, H. (1996). Operationalization of the multicultural counseling competencies. Alexandria, VA: AMCD.

by a supervisor of his or her own culture or bias. This was followed up in rank order by failing to bring cultural issues into supervisory discussion, being defensive about multicultural issues, and more general behaviors such as not establishing a working alliance or recognizing the hierarchical power differential. What is interesting to me is that many of the statements this panel has set forward are general skills one would expect of any supervisor, and they have limited content connected to multiculturalism specifically. For instance, the highest ranked statement for successful multicultural supervision is to create a safe environment for the discussion of multicultural issues. And although I am at first incredulous that any supervisor would shut down discussion of this sort, I know and have an example of such behavior in a later section discussing boundary issues, where I provide a case example called "Muriel and her Beliefs."

In an interesting study by Inman (2006), it was hypothesized that supervisors who were perceived by their supervisees to have multicultural competencies and by their working alliance or both would have an effect on supervisees' multicultural case conceptualizations. Results of this found that supervisors' multicultural competencies were positively correlated with working alliance and

supervision satisfaction, but they had a negative relationship with supervisees' etiological conceptual abilities regarding multicultural factors. Again, supervisors' knowledge of multiculturalism as perceived by supervisees has a positive effect on working relationships with their supervisees.

Two protocols for the development of multicultural competencies in supervision are worth mentioning. Lassiter et al. (2008) presented a structured peer group supervision (SPGS) model where a supervisee tapes (audio or video) and selects a 10-minute segment to share and has a series of questions, concerns, and areas to focus on, while the peers choose roles they will address, such as nonverbal behavior of either client or supervisee, reactions and possible perceptions of the client, how significant others to the client might react if they were present, multicultural concerns of the case, and so forth. These people then voice their perspectives after the presentation, with the expectation that this will increase hidden concerns or factors of which the supervisee might be unaware.

Ober et al. (2009) proposed a synergistic model (SMMS) combining Bloom's Taxonomy model (Bloom et al., cited in Ober et al., 2009), which promotes cognitive development, with the Heuristic Model of Non-Oppressive Interpersonal

Development (HMNID; Bloom et al., cited in Ober et al., 2009), with process learning and multicultural counseling competencies (Sue et al., cited in Ober et al., 2009). This is a very curricular model, intended for classroom learning, and it is not, in my opinion, practical for applications in group supervision, where the focus is on case conceptualization and strengthening supervisees' skill and personal agency.

During my research for this section, I was enthralled with the manner in which a group of women (Nelson et al., 2006) went about their discussion of multiculturalism. I was also shocked and dismayed at how lengthy, and to my mind, cumbersome and academically oriented, the two models seemed. I have tried to write this book for both those in academics as well as those in agency sites, and I wanted to provide a simple yet easy way to go about training that would benefit their interest and knowledge of multicultural supervision, so I invented and later tested my model with my group supervision class. The procedure used a person-centered group format for the discussion on multiculturalism, facilitated by an outside person. The interns are asked to read five readings, which are referenced in this section, prior to this experience: Nelson et al. (2006), Field and Chavez-Korell (2010), Singh and Chun (2010), Butler-Byrd (2010), and the list of multicultural competencies of the AMCD. After reading these, the supervisor (me) and supervisees (my group supervision class) met for $2\frac{1}{2}$ hours of open discussion facilitated by a skilled group leader. I wish I had done this earlier in the year, because the discussion and openness were wonderful. I would like to include a reflecting team to further facilitate discussion.

Further Discussion on Multicultural Supervision

What strikes me first from all of the literature is that a supervisor's openness to discuss multicultural issues, rather than a supervisee's perception that his or her supervisor is open to these discussions, is most important. Second, what stands out is that the process of imparting

multicultural expectations as part of our supervisor's responsibility begins with us and our own work on our own cultural context and processes and our own openness to explore this during supervision. For me, as a white male supervising in a university that prides itself as the most culturally diverse university in the Midwest, that means I need to attend to my own top-down beliefs about my power and privilege and the fact that as supervisors we have assigned to us, by our supervisees' perceptions, a power and privileged rank that we may not choose but have to accept. Knowing this makes it all the more difficult to deconstruct those perceptions of my supervisees in order to be more in tune as a supervisor who cares about working with and for a multicultural stance. Is being open to discussions and aware of my position in these supervisory relationships enough? Does it matter that I understand and have pride in my own cultural pedigree? It seems important that I am not only willing to immerse myself in understanding other cultures and contribute to an equal footing of all cultures but also that I see them as important to the substance of our growth and resiliency as clinicians who work in a multicultural world. Understanding and promoting multicultural competencies are not only for clinicians but for supervisors as well. If we believe we know it all, we have lost the ability to take risks, be open to the complexity of our supervisory relationships, and "tolerate ambiguity and anxiety related to a lack of certainty" (Nelson et al., 2006, p. 113). In my experience, this is aimed at us all, regardless of our culture, race, gender, or station in life.

Focus Areas and Domains of a Supervisor

Janine Bernard (1979, 1997) was the first to actually pinpoint what areas should be attended to when a supervisor begins to work with a clinician. She put forth the idea that there are three areas of focus that supervisors must pay attention to: "process skills, conceptualization skills, and personalization skills" (1997, p. 310), as well as three spheres of influence which a supervisor makes use of: training, consultation, and counseling. She placed these in a grid so a supervisor can track and situate the supervisory process. Someone having a problem with, say, conceptualization of a counseling situation, can be supervised either by training, consultation or counseling, and so on. Bernard's work was an effort to provide an easy to understand map that supervisors could conceptualize and use quickly, in order to make interventions. I used this model for quite a long time with success, but lately, I have found its underlying philosophy to be contrary to my views, as it is deficit-based and hierarchically oriented, rather than strengths-based conceptually. I spend more time on this in Chapter 4. But for now, let us look at its parts and what they provide for clinical supervision as an executive skill.

Process Skills

Bernard changed her original version from what she called process skills (1979) to intervention skills (1997), because she believed that the concept of process is not as elegant as the term intervention. What she is talking about, from her reference point I believe, is the observable activities and technical interactions a clinician does while engaged in clinical work. Such things might be when to confront, when to reflect, when to reframe, when to use circular questioning, when to listen, and so forth. This way of working is from a modernist perspective and has a flavor of what Nichols and Schwartz (2001) stated postmodern clinicians avoid, because "too often clients aren't heard because therapists are doing therapy *to* them rather than *with* them" (p. 205). I have the same dilemma with the term intervention, as it has too many connotations, from planned and orchestrated strategies applied with substance abusing individuals, to the all too frequently used term associated with the military. I think Bernard's intentions are good, and I would hope that she might agree with my concerns, after

further thought. A better way of thinking about it, I believe, has to do with how clinicians make meaning of and structure their contacts with clients or supervisees during presession, intrasession, and postsession. For instance, I might want to ask myself, what do I want to punctuate, what do I want to listen for, ask questions about, and where in the session do I want to see if I can help coconstruct different means or find opportunities to add or expand different meanings in the session? I would also want to think about when I abandon sharing my ideas in favor of my clients. I also might want to ask myself where can I use Positive Psychology ideas or consider how to help the client use narrative reediting, and so forth. So, I agree that supervision as well as clinical work is not just a process of reflecting or being in the here and now but a self-reflective engaged process of human interactions that can change and evolve over the course of a session and the length of clinical involvement.

Conceptualization Skills

Bernard considers this a more subtle part of clinical skills because it has to do with how the clinician (and supervisor) makes meaning of what is going on during a session. She also hooks this up with how to decide what responses to make during the session, so it is in her mind a two-part process. If I am attempting to make assessments of my client's discourse, of course I am attempting to make meaning of what is meant and where to go with the discourse—in other words, I am in charge of the session and its direction. My druthers again would be to ask the supervisees to be in charge of telling me how *they* are making meaning of what we are doing together and to have *them* evaluate whether what we are doing together is useful (Miller et al., 2007). My conceptual skill, rather than being on evaluation and intervention, will be on asking and refining what we do in the session that can be of more use to the client. My conceptualization skills would be self-reflective as well as interactive, to help define how the session can change to be more useful. I have heard many discussions that question if supervisees or clients are truthful or fully committed to their own treatment, and in fact I have even experienced those sensations myself. My experience has been that when I believe my client to want something positive out of his or her time with me, it generally happens, and we find a way. Again, the Pygmalion effect as a socially constructed idea is central to this concept. Cooperrider (2000) stated the following:

> One of the remarkable things about Pygmalion is that it shows us how essentially modifiable the human self is in relation to the mental projects of others. Indeed, not only do performance levels change, but so do more deeply rooted "stable" self conceptions. (p. 36)

If I believe in my client's ability and see that person as capable and honest, it has been my experience that it seems to work out. An old tale about hypnotherapist and founder of the strategic model Milton Erickson confirms for me that recursive interactions of how I perceive and act toward others will have an effect on how others may act in return. The tale, one I cannot identify or provide citation for, that has been told to me years ago, goes like this: When asked by someone what he (Erickson) does when he finds a client to be so reprehensible as to make it impossible to work with, he responded as follows: "I form a mental picture of the person and envision him or her as having some genuine desirable traits, and then I act toward him or her as if they are true." The power of our projections is amazing, as well as verifiable. If I had to decide on one conceptual skill I would want my supervisees to have, it would be an ability to see their clients in a positive light, and somehow that sounds to me like unconditional positive regard.

Personalization Skills

These "skills" are what some believe to be the most important to clinical work, as well as supervision (Luborsky, McLellan, Woody, O'Brien, & Auerbach, 1985). Bernard said that they are the makeup of who we are: personality, culture, sensitivity, humor, to name a few. How we use ourselves during sessions, make up our personalization skills, and how we make the sessions and work our own, I guess would be another way of looking at it. These skills are also what make up a good deal of feminist clinical ideas (Goodrich, Rampage, Ellman, & Halstead, 1988), so that the person-of-the-clinician (personalization skills) bridges from the technical (techniques and hierarchical stance) to the personal and collaborative. But they can also work to a clinician's detriment when they undermine a working relationship because of transferential or interface issues—personal blind spots caused by top-down personal narratives. Because this component is one of the most critical, when it becomes a focus of supervision, it can be very tricky. Supervisors must continually monitor themselves, reflecting on their known and potential unknown places of vulnerability. The three areas we discussed earlier, what Bernard called skills, fit with the three domains of activities or roles that follow.

Training

Training supervisees is something we all do a time or two or more. Depending on their sophistication, education, and experience, supervisors will find themselves in a spot discussing new techniques or reviewing older but perhaps more appropriate models that might work better with a certain client. This means that the flexibility of a supervisor, with respect to models, should be fairly wide. In these days of evidence-based treatments, or Solution-Focused brief Therapy, there is a tendency to be locked into one method—a one-size-fits-all mentality, that not only violates ethical responsibility but may purposefully avoid techniques that could be used for clients with specific complaints. We discuss more of this in the ethics section.

I have made a conscious effort to make clear that I believe our supervisees are the most well-trained and well-informed clinicians ever due to the explosion of media and technology. In addition, the efforts in the last few years to increase the competitive edge through training followed by continuing education requirements for licensure have made our clinicians more competitive and better trained than ever before. It is well known that since the mid-1980s there has been over a 275% increase of persons who have trained to be mental health clinicians (Hubble et al., 1999). Those of us who train and teach in universities have felt the impact for our students both for internship placements as well as jobs postgraduation. Those of us who supervise or administer agencies know all too well the competiveness for jobs and the lack of financial resources to provide clinical services for the clients we serve. It's a highly competitive market, fueling a highly trained clinical surplus. But the point still remains that supervisees are extremely well trained.

Despite this increase of clinical "right stuff," universities have had to cut back on extra elective classes, as course work becomes centralized around guild requirements and students' funds for elective classes past the minimum requirements are usually not available. Add to that the financial crunch put upon agencies where dollars for continued training was routine and now the place where advanced elective training may be collected is during supervision. A supervisor may have a set of skills that is different than what the cadre of Licensed Clinical Professional Counselors, Licensed Clinical Social Workers, clinical psychologists, and so forth, might be provided by a supervisor who has advanced training, or at an agency where a specific model is used, and new clinicians are taken on with the expectation that they will learn those models' skills along the way (B. Atkinson, personal communication, March, 2010; J. Walter, personal communication, October, 2008).

In my internship classes with community and family counselors who are headed out the door soon to begin their clinical life's work, I try to teach them some other strengths-based skills, past the foundational microskills course that is core to our program, during group supervision. Also, it has been my experience that many programs typically require only one class in family systems, so when the newly trained clinicians hit the market, they might get the additional training during their clinical supervision at their internship site where family therapy is part of the usual treatment routine.

All of this leads me to agree with Bernard, that training can be critical to supervision practices and that supervisors need to know more than a few models and knowledge of the different styles of learning. In my experience, many of our supervisees already have preferred conceptual orientations and approaches to learning. Ed Neukrug (2011) has developed an assessment tool supervisees can take online that will help them and (if they care to share) their supervisor find their preferred clinical conceptual orientation (see http://www.odu.edu/~eneukrug/therapists/booksurvey.html). I have used this with my supervisees to help them assess where they are in their development and what they like most from the breadth of the 12 theoretical approaches, as well as the four conceptual beliefs Neukrug has situated in the field of counseling and psychotherapy. After having my group supervision class take the test, I have them discuss what it is about those approaches that they like and don't like. This not only gives us a clue about what they feel comfortable with, but it also provides multiple models that allow for additions and increased readiness to learn different models that they might find useful in the future.

Consultation

Consultation practice has made interesting strides in the past 20-some years since Bernard first wrote her discrimination model of supervision. What has remained constant in the focus and application of consultation skills is that it is a voluntary relationship where a person or persons (the consultant) are in dialogue with a second person or persons (the consultees), regarding a third person or situation, for the purpose of potential change. Consultants are supposed to provide an assessment of needs and then give suggestions and advice, providing alternatives and objectives that the second person may or may not follow through on. The responsibility for follow-through is always left to the consultee to decide, and over the years consultants have devised a set of operational principles that can influence the follow-through. Block (2000) suggested much of the following: (a) effective decision making should require free and open choice—the consultee (supervisee) always has a choice whether to follow the suggestions of the consultant, (b) implementation requires internal commitment—the consultee and his or her organization needs to be committed to the process of change and believe the process is appropriate, (c) the first goal of consultation is to establish a collaborative relationship and solve problems together *so they stay solved,* (d) change works best when consultees feel the need and understand that the goals and solutions are mostly their ideas, (e) to begin the process means the examination of all data and choice making of commitment, methods, and intended outcome, and (f) collaboration works best, over that of an "expert" role. This is nothing new to most clinicians, as we have recognized for a long time that collaboration—helping clients feel that they own a large part of their changes and helping them experience the solutions as their own—contributes to a successful outcome (Lambert & Bergin, 1994). The last point is the most interesting. Collaboration over "expert" roll fits very well with a strengths-based perspective, such as reflecting teams, narrative, and so forth.

Counseling

This final domain or task Bernard points to is vexing to me. As she intends, counseling is to create a place where supervisors provide an opportunity to reflect on what has happened in their clinical work and to explore the meaning. "Therefore, the supervisor as counselor is more likely to instigate moments for the trainee when things 'come together,' when thoughts, behaviors, and personal realities merge to enhance professional development" (Bernard, 1997, p. 312).

This view has an historical basis, and anyone familiar with the way psychoanalysts were trained will be more than accustomed with how this one works. Psychoanalytic training includes going through the process yourself, as part of your clinical work. I remember working with my supervisors, talking about my own family (of origin or nuclear) and how that part of my life was affecting my clinical work. Today, however, ethics dictates that counseling your supervisee might be construed as a dual relationship. I have trained numerous supervisors who blink with distress when I suggest that supervision in this manner could be considered unethical, especially if they have not provided informed consent about their way of supervising and had it agreed upon by their supervisee. If the relationship is voluntary, the client has the right to agree or disagree. If supervisors are working in an agency, they must provide a less "clinical" form of supervision if their supervisee rejects counseling as a part of supervision.

Now there are many times in one's supervisory life when it is as plain as the nose on the face (given our own top-down constructions) that counseling, either long term or short, would be helpful to the process for a supervisee. Our field has a fair number of impaired clinicians, including those with all the common problems our clients might have, as well as a significant number of clinicians who cross the boundary sexually with their clients. Bringing these issues up to supervisees and providing suggestions for ways they can work things out or even perhaps (and I say this with great trepidation, knowing that there are those out there who love psychic voyeurism) using part of a supervision session to explore how supervisees interface issues might be negatively affecting clinical work. But supervisors need to have a mandate from their supervisees to do so. Supervisors need to explain themselves clearly and make it known that this is a choice the supervisee has. Just as in our own clinical work, it is necessary to provide informed consent, with stipulations that there will be no repercussions if the supervisee says no and suggestions for providing alternative means to work things out. Even then, supervisees have the right to self-determination, and unless their interface issues are harming clients and it can be documented, they have the right to reject their supervisor's suggestions, without reprisal for following their own path.

The Bernard model leaves us with a short and sweet way of understanding what can and does happen during supervision. Supervisors will consult regarding cases that their supervisees' are seeing, they will teach new or deeper understanding of clinical skills, and they will find themselves in instances where interface issues (countertransferences) occur, and they may have to do something about that in order for the supervisor to move forward. This last piece can provide difficulties, if we think that the traditional concept of counseling always applies. And maybe there are not any difficulties, if we think of evaluation and counseling from a strengths-based perspective.

KAREN: AN EXAMPLE

Karen was open about her reasons for interning at a domestic violence shelter. She had been beaten many times by her husband before she finally got the courage up to leave him, their children in tow. So, when she began her internship, she ended up talking fairly regularly about the bastards that beat up their wives, and after some time, she began tirades about how gutless were the women who had gone through the program, only to reappear again and again. I spoke with Karen about her anger and asked if she thought maybe seeing one of our free-for-students counselors at the university counseling center would help. She responded fairly angrily that she was fine, but she said she would not speak so blatantly in group supervision in the future. However, her attitude didn't change, only her use of pejorative words, and one day soon after our supervisory "talk," several of her colleagues in group supervision began to take her down for her attitude toward both her clients and their men. She fought back, angrily, and left the class in tears; I followed her out and down the hall, to comfort and talk, leaving the rest of the group members to continue their talk and their regret. Karen didn't want to talk much, especially when I suggested again that she seek help from someone at the center or seriously think about where she is interning and if it is best for her.

Karen slowed down in class with her attitude, didn't participate as much, and told me once she felt as if she didn't belong anywhere. No matter what I suggested, it just didn't seem to help. One day, however, she came to my office smiling and said that she would finish her internship, that she and her site supervisor had also talked, and she had decided that instead of being a domestic violence counselor, she was going to become the agency's marketing and development director, as she had these skills from her past work experience in business. I was relieved, she was overjoyed, and her relationships with her peers began to get a whole lot better. She graduated on time and felt as if she had learned a great deal from her experiences and from the internship. Her distance from the direct services over time gave her perspective, and the last time I saw her, she was doing well.

I do not know why people gravitate to a place where the clinical work is so close to them that interface issues get in the way. Well, that's not true, and as soon as I started to write that last sentence, I knew it was silly. Recovering addicts go into substance abuse counseling treatment, many African American counselors I have supervised want to work with people from their communities, gay and lesbian counselors seek out centers for people with HIV, and I ended up seeing lots of divorcing clients as I went through my own separation and divorce. Unconsciously, or consciously, we work out our own issues and give back to others who are experiencing the same sort of pain we have overcome or in some cases are still going through. Or maybe the universe in its infinite wisdom calls us to this profession as wounded healers. Whatever, rather than being one-up and all knowing, I am glad that I spent time with Karen but let her work it out herself. I'm also pleased that her site supervisor was willing to find her a space that fit where she was at the time, rather than making it a huge pathologizing event. The takeaway for me was that supervisors should never be supervisees' counselors, but they can be an open ear, make suggestions, provide support, and describe their own time when they had to seek counseling for their own interface issues.

ETHICS

One of my favorite colleagues used to start off all her classes on ethics by saying, "Don't sleep with your clients." That was her mantra and a well-intended and needed one at that. The statistics on clinicians of every ilk who still break the sacred and ethical bond is startling. Aside from the fact that every guild from clinical counseling on down to psychiatry has ethical guidelines about dual relationships, and specifically about sexual relationships, it still needs to be said. They are defined as inappropriate; we all know that it is a hierarchical problem, and yet clinicians are human too.

It should be enough that I stress that ethics for supervisors are the same as those for clinicians. It is not by accident that the lawyers in the most famous of all ethical cases for clinicians, the Tarasoff case, sued the supervisor as well as the consulting psychiatrist for not insuring that a clinician followed the duty to warn another person of possible danger, when the clinician had information that might have prevented harm. Supervisors must live with these ethical and legal requirements also, even when they cross another ethical guideline of confidentiality.

As I have noted elsewhere in this book, supervisors have a responsibility to provide informed consent to their supervisees, especially when they are using forms of supervision that might cross other boundaries such as person-of-the-therapist supervision where the supervisor assumes the role of clinician during supervision to help supervisees move past stuck places, or as in early psychodynamic supervision, where it was expected that clinicians learn their craft by being analyzed (Aponte, 1991; Watson, 2005). Early in my career, this was the typical mode of supervision as I was trained by people for the Chicago Institute for Psychoanalysis, but I was never given informed consent back then; my supervisor just plodded on through as a natural course of our supervision. These days, it is a boundary issue and an ethical problem of dual relationship, as well as an issue of informed consent. In my training of clinical supervisors, I have been perplexed that this still goes on as part of business as usual supervision. I have had several supervisors in training who have been taken off guard by the knowledge that they had been crossing the ethical boundary of informed consent as they openly did what I consider to be psychic voyeurism, unnecessarily and unethically. As Hess (2008a) stated, "Sadly, chapters on ethics are necessary because one or both parties does not see the other's interests, values, or being" (p. 522).

An issue of confidentiality and boundary issues under threat in many states (D. Stasis, executive director, Illinois School Counselors Association, personal communication, February 20, 2010) centers around the issue of school counselors who are expected to "give up" any information that their administrators want to know about students who are in their care. This issue affects not only school counselors but school social workers and school psychologists as well. Legislation has been passed but not without a fight from school administrator associations who feel that all information should be held as non-privileged with regard to their need to know. Again, unless it is a situation of duty to warn of imminent harm, confidentiality is believed by most clinicians to be confidential under the codes and laws of mental health practices.

Finally, every guild has an ethical component that speaks to practicing outside of your boundaries. For instance, the AAMFT'S code of ethics stated the following:

> While developing new skills in specialty areas, marriage and family therapists take steps to ensure the competence of their work and to protect clients from possible harm. Marriage and family therapists practice in specialty areas new to them only after appropriate education, training, or supervised experience. (AAMFT Code of Ethics, 2001)

Similarly, the ACA's code of ethics, in addressing boundaries of competency, stated the following: "Prior to offering clinical supervision services, counselors are trained in supervision methods and techniques. Counselors who offer clinical supervision services regularly pursue continuing education activities including both counseling and supervision topics and skills" (see C.2.a., C.2.f., ACA Code of Ethics, 2005, p. 9). All of the guilds, including the APA and the NASW, have codes of conduct related to competency, and this always includes the training and education of supervisory practices. What this means for clinical supervisors is that our guilds mandate competency in clinical supervision, through appropriate training, and in some cases supervision of supervision,

before one can practice the art and skill of clinical supervision. As a part of that training and responsibility, supervisors are bound to their own codes of ethics for all members. Abide by your guild's ethics and the law of the land where you practice, and as a supervisor you will be an ethical supervisor.

DEVELOPMENTAL STAGES OF COUNSELORS

As Stoltenberg and Delworth (1987) taught us years ago, clinicians go through developmental stages. This developmental process is organic, rather than static. One is never stuck in one stage but may be working at issues in several of our arbitrary descriptions of development. In fact, the transformation of one's experiences are expected or hoped to be changed into meaningful information. Thus, the emerging clinician is seen as moving toward a goal or end state through the incorporation of new more meaningful information (Stoltenberg & Delworth, 1987). Growth is organic, ever changing. I would add that these stages are isomorphic to the process supervisors go through also. In addition, as I have said elsewhere, most supervisory research and literature are intended for academics, but they are also a useful way of understanding any supervisory relationship or context—be that of new supervisees and/or supervisors beginning new relationships or learning new skill levels. I will try to synthesize Stoltenberg and Delworth's work here with an attempt to stay within the spirit of that work. As they pointed out, there have been discussions prior to their early work (Blocher, 1983; Hogan, 1964; Hunt, 1971; Littrell, Lee-Borden, & Lorenz, 1979; Ralph, 1980; Stoltenberg, 1981; Yogev, 1982), and several since their work began (Rønnestad & Skovholt, 1993, 2003; Skovholt & Rønnestad, 1992, 1995), but Stoltenberg and Delworth's ideas remain an important way of viewing the clinician's progress and development (Stoltenberg & Delworth, 1987). To reiterate, their stages follow.

Level 1: The Beginning of the Journey

During this beginning stage, clinicians are usually very dependent on their supervisors, and they may imitate them a great deal. They can lack self-awareness, think about their cases and clinical work categorically, and show the world, unbeknownst to themselves, that they have limited experience (Stoltenberg & Delworth, 1987). Graduate student supervisees can quote little know facts about Carl Rogers, Aaron Beck, or Steve deShazar, depending on the guild with which they are associated, while supervisees in agencies can tell interesting stories about their supervisors and how cleverly they were able to help them. They are using role models as a way to learn socially about their field and practice.

Supervisees at this stage have high motivation to do well, and their anxiety can be channeled into hard work—almost overdoing their clinical responsibilities. They are also focused on skill acquisition, building up a grand library of half-read books on every form of counseling known to man. They are highly dependent on supervision, so supervisors can use this to their advantage by providing a supervision environment that provides well-defined structure, thus keeping the new clinicians' anxiety low. By providing positive feedback regarding counselors' abilities and focusing on specifics rather than on the supervisee, you can ease them into a good working alliance and begin to build their confidence. It is also at this stage that criticism of their work is taken very personally and can hinder the relationship. As in any relationship that will be of great importance to both parties, care must be taken to move slowly, and the use of positive connotations and relationship building is essential to future contacts (Stoltenberg & Delworth, 1987). Kind words about their ongoing fund of techniques or how well they did with difficult cases will go a long way to an ongoing bank account of a positive working relationship. I remember a supervisor who told me, "You helped me to believe in myself, even when the cases were very difficult, and when I was not doing my best—you still believed in me, and that helped me to keep on going. You saw my strengths when no one else including me could see them."

Level 2: Trials and Tribulations

The second stage can be challenging, both for the supervisor as well as the supervisee. Much akin to an adolescent stage, Level 2 supervisees show a fluctuating motivation, great striving for independence, and more self-assertive, less imitative behavior and the typical dependency/autonomy conflict that goes with most middle growth stages. Stoltenberg and Delworth (1987) conceptualized this stage as one of confusion, and rightfully so.

As can be true with adolescences, during this stage a supervisee's various skills, strengths, and weaknesses are becoming more evident. But also, now that supervisees know that this is a job they can do—they are over the frightfulness of sitting with someone who has problems and conversing—they begin to have an awareness that this is not a job for the faint of heart, that there is more to this profession than using good counseling skills and technique, and that not all cases respond as hoped for, even with good skill level usage. Many of the supervisees with whom I have worked had the largest collection of technique books on the widest variety of models known to mankind, all with the first two chapters dog-eared, highlighted, and underlined, as they searched for the silver bullet that would fix all their clients. They often tend to mix methods, such as solution focused therapy and cognitive behavioral work. Or they think that all family therapists use genograms or ask for narrative stories.

They begin to see how certain professional ethics like boundaries relates to the work and that some of their case load may have severe and traumatic, even toxic horrific situations that illuminate the limitations of counseling process with certain clients. These factors can lead one to "take home" the situations, as they work out how best to deal with situations they have not known before. At the same time, supervisors are also inclined to increase their supervisees' autonomy, while noting that they may not actively seek opinions or the advice of their supervisor, if not altogether resist discussion of cases. This is a wrongheaded, albeit natural protection devise that occurs so that they do not look foolish or incompetent to the supervisees who they have been trying to imitate.

Strategies that most often work during this time are to provide a highly autonomous supervisory situation, with little structure. As with clients who present with similar profiles, allowing them to go it alone not only gives them the autonomy they wish for but also the flexibility to work out problems for themselves. Other strategies include providing supervisees with a good blend of client types, so that they see a broad variety of clients where difficulty is not generalized to the entire field but can be seen as case specific. Providing a supportive environment that is consultative, where generalizations can focus on theory and its application can be useful. I always ask supervisees to provide me with several alternative views of clients as a way of broadening their repertoire of theory and technique. I am displeased with the notion that one model of counseling should fit well for everyone. And though I am not fond of eclecticism, I do think that understanding more than one way of working with people increases the chances for success.

Another means to being helpful with supervisees is to use your relationship. Many new supervisees are fearful of developing a strong relationship clinically, thinking that they might lose their "objectivity." My experience is the opposite. Those supervisees who have positive, caring relationships with me have almost always been willing to listen to my suggestions, as well as be up front about why my ideas will not work with certain cases or situations. In fact, most supervisors at one time or another will be their own worst critic. This is the sort of give and take you develop with both adolescents as well as supervisees during this stage.

I remember with fondness one of my last doctoral supervisors of my own supervision, focusing and building on our relationship, with little care toward "professional boundaries." Instead he was always interested and mentoring me as if we already had a collegial relationship. While it presented some of its own issues, it also served to increase my feelings of competency and professionalism, as we worked together in several other venues including publishing, attending, and presenting at conferences. Interns especially like to hear the stories of my own trials and failures, as it seems to make me more human to them. Collegial mentoring supervisory relationships have to be real, I believe. One of my classes with advanced doctoral group counselors took me on and all but tore me apart because of a serious mistake I had made. In the efforts to repair the situation, one of them said, "I just don't understand; most of the students here think the world of you—put you up on a pedestal as someone to really learn from, and here you did such a stupid thing" (it wasn't that stupid). My reply was that I didn't like being put on a pedestal, because the fall is always hard. But being real with supervisees is what they like the most from us—the reason that they look up to us, and yet that very act that can make us a great model can also be the one thing that works to keep us out of reach. This closeness of relationship carried over to the relationships I had with my clients and my own supervisees, and they too experienced a change in their relationships with the clients they were seeing. It is isomorphic. This movement away for a purely clinical view of clients (supervisees) to a more human attention of focus on relationship, both with client and during supervision, was a wonderful change from earlier days when we were always analyzing interactions from a purely clinical perspective. This posture or position helps supervisees begin the process of differentiation from their supervisor, and supervisees will find that they are ready and can be less inclined to take the supervisor's word as final, without first critically evaluating supervisors' suggestions as applied to clients. Their own trials and tribulations need to be critically evaluated by their own hand and supported within a collegial relationship, rather than at the foot of some almighty all-knowing supervisor. Again, the metaphor of adolescence is appropriate, as good enough parents allow their offspring to try out new ideas, support autonomy, while at the same time providing a background of operating principles of adult behavior.

Supervisees generally know what they should be doing, even when difficult cases present themselves. The skilled supervisor supports their supervisees' decisions, while at the same time holding up professional competency as a model for them to judge their own work. Supervisors should work with the idea of attraction, rather than submission. As Heath and Storm (1983) have said elsewhere, supervisees will work better if they believe that their supervisor has something to offer them that is helpful, rather than criticism.

In a later chapter I provide a case example of a supervision session I had with one of my supervisees. She began her session by telling me what a hard, horrible day she had been through and ended with a story of a mother and teenage daughter that used horrible obscenities toward each other. But there will surely be worse human tragedies that our supervisees will be a witness to: sexual abuse of children, rape and physical abuse, potentially dangerous clients, and substance abuse of every kind. If our firefighters and police officers see the horrible, seamy physical events of life, then surely clinicians in our field see the same as remnants of the same in relational, interpersonal, and psychological troubles. To work with our supervisees as if this were merely a clinical event and miss seeing the trauma or providing empathy and support, supervisors miss the point, in my estimation.

I have made the analogy that this second stage is like that of an adolescent, where basic skills are evident, but their knowledge of their own abilities has not been refined. Like a new teenage driver, they can drive most competently but have not refined the skills and maturity that need to go with it to become sophisticated and mature behind the wheel. This takes several years, perhaps a dent or two in their parents' car, as well as a speeding ticket or two, perhaps. Sometimes overconfident, sometimes underconfident, but also unwilling to share these feelings or thoughts for fear they will look foolish, or worse yet, not ready to take their place in the adult world, this stage takes life lessons that have to happen on their own. Parents, or in our case clinical supervisors, cannot hold their hands forever but should stand ready and open to discuss and even bring up issues to discuss in a way that also depersonalizes the situation, so that the new clinician is not humiliated. Pointing out their strengths is always a good place to start these discussions.

Level 3: Challenge and Growth

The third stage of development is one where their personal sense of counselor identity and self-confidence begins to shine. Whatever the clinician's guild may be, they begin to feel membership. Because their motivation to continue learning and doing this work is more stable, they feel more comfortable in talking about both their struggles as well as their strengths. Their autonomy is not threatened by their supervisor, and they seek the supervisor out to discuss cases as consultation and their own self- and other awareness is heightened. Having moved through the first two levels successfully and now unencumbered from the fear of not measuring up that they encountered in the first level, and confronted with the realities of how difficult and responsible this job can be as in the second level, a second-order shift has occurred. They have moved up from going through the motions and can now fully participate in clinical work with all its trials and tribulations, knowing that they are well prepared and supported (Stoltenberg & Delworth, 1987).

At this point, supervisees are able to be with their clients, and most are not drawn into the various traps that may be a part of the work. Aware of transferences and countertransferences, and hopefully, having begun to deal with some of their own interface issues, they are able to pull back from the relationships and evaluate what has to be done for good clinical work to occur, as well as understand where they stand relationally with their clients. They do not have their ego invested in their clients' process, most often, and can tell pithy stories about their own mistakes, laughing about how such and such client evaded them or how they missed important pieces of their clients' lives. One of our biggest problems is how serious we can take ourselves and our work, while at other times feeling like a fraud. One of my doctoral mentors once told me that all of the good clinicians will feel like imposters at many times during their lives. Our pitiful hour or two a week, as important as it is, has a hard time competing with the rest of their lives or the cacophony of competing suggestions, world-views, and family of origin operating principles. And at this level, they hopefully recognize that their clients' growth, change, or wellness really depends on the clients and that although as a clinician they may be a help giver, the journey is not theirs to travel but can sometimes be a support system, sometimes a guide, and sometimes a mirror to their clients as they do the walking. But the journey always rests with their clients: their choices, their moves, their life.

Generally aware of their own strengths and weaknesses, Level 3 clinicians can think of individual differences of their clients. It is during this third stage, with good supervision and mentoring, a new or new to a model changed clinician begins to understand the ethics involved and to assimilate the professional perspective of such a change. Energy has been freed up from the first two levels, and these higher level aspects of clinical work, albeit most important, become integrated.

Again, Delworth and Stoltenberg (1987) have provided the beginnings of what is helpful in the supervisory environment during Level 3. Remembering that they have named this final level one of challenges and growth, it seems natural that supervision should both acknowledge the supervisees' strengths as well as those areas where they may still have some dependency on their supervisor for more support and/or consultation around specific areas that affect their clinical life. Most often, as with previous stages, case accountability needs to be provided, but within the context of support and growth, rather than as a check and balance that may be present during the previous levels.

Supervisees may be beyond formal, regular supervision, but they may seek help with specific cases. There is a need for supervision to advance past a single theoretical framework, broadening the supervisee's repertoire. Focus should be on integration of all aspects of the counselor (Delworth & Stoltenberg, 1987).

Equipped with the understanding of the developmental process of counselors, both newly trained, as well as those retrained in a new framework or model, clinical supervisors need a tool to increase clinicians' competencies. It is at this level that basic executive skill comes into play. Clinicians need to believe in their skill levels as well as their ability to work toward proficiency and competence.

ISOMORPHS AND PARALLEL PROCESSES IN SUPERVISION

The word comes from Iso—meaning same, and morph—meaning structure. Any two systems that are connected are said to have isomorphic properties when there is similarity between the two. Isomorphy refers to the part of two or more structures that have a correspondence. As there is an interconnection between all systems that are interrelated, this correspondence has the potential of influence (see Figure 2.2). I assume that all systems in relationship will have this correspondence and thus will be open to the potentiality of influence, when recognized. Conceiving of a client system, be it individual, family, or group, the interconnectedness of those systems with their own systems are also affected by the connection to a counselor, as there is an interconnection between the supervisor and the counselor they have been asked to help. A change in one part of the system will create a change in the corresponding parts. This is basic systems principles at work. A stuck client system—group, family, or client—can create (not cause, but contribute to the creation of) a stuckness between the client and counselor, which will then affect or potentiate a stuckness within the corresponding counselor or supervisor system. They are nested systems, with a correspondence.

Figure 2.2   Isomorphic Structure

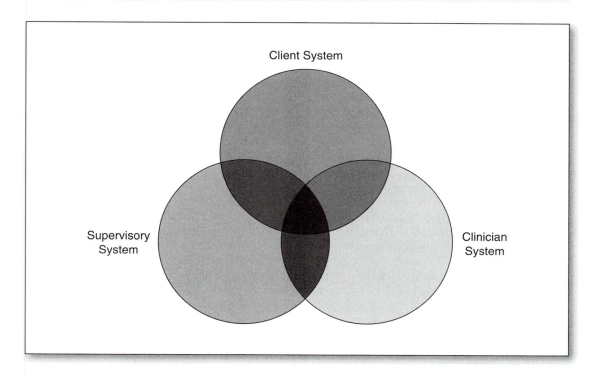

The more commonly understood concept of parallel process is often cited in the literature (McNeil & Worthen, 1989; Williams, 1997). Originally referring to a part of transference and countertransference of psychoanalytic treatment, early analytic supervisors noted that what was happening in supervision between supervisor and supervisee was also happening in the transferential relationship between the therapist and client (Morrissey & Tribe, 2001; Sumerel & ERIC Clearinghouse on Counseling and Student Services, 1994). Parallel process represents something that can be worked through or an issue that needs addressing, while an isomorph epitomizes patterns of interrelated systems that remain similar in form, despite a context change. The roots of these two phenomena are similar to the two models from which they come. Parallel process concepts in clinical work were first recognized in conjunction with psychoanalytic models (Heuer, 2009; Rodriguez, Cabaniss, Arbuckle, & Oquendo, 2008; Sumerel 1994), while isomorphs are most often associated with the training and supervision of family therapists (Liddle, Breunlin, & Schwartz, 1988b; Liddle & Saba, 1983; Liddle & Saba, 1985). As Sumerel (1994) suggested, "The concept of parallel process has its origin in the psychoanalytic concepts of transference and counter transference. The transference occurs when the counselor recreates the presenting problem and emotions of the therapeutic relationship within the supervisory relationship" (pp. 1–2). Morrissey and Tribe (2001) described parallel process to be "the unconscious replication of the therapeutic relationship in the supervisory situation" (p. 103). Much of the literature regarding parallel process suggests that the cause is related to the anxiety of the supervisee, regarding the supervisee's work with a client who is similar through projection identification, as the client projects his or her own feelings onto the clinician and the clinician projects them onto the supervisee. But there are multiple views of what parallel process is and the causative nature of this action or event (Morrissey & Tribe, 2001). In any case, the concept of parallel process runs parallel to the models from which it comes, being seen as intrapsychic, linear, reductionistic, and from a problem-focused model.

Liddle and Saba (1983) introduced the concept of isomorphs in the training and supervision of family therapy, staying true to a systemic frame work, rather than a more linear model that might be associated with analytic or other models of counseling and therapy. Believing that isomorphs are a valuable tool for trainees of family therapy, White and Russell (1997) suggested that the concept crosses all forms of clinical work despite their theoretical model. Noting that contexts being replicated at multiple systems overlays, regardless of their dissimilarity, are not conceived of as linear or work in only one direction because the rules of the larger system seem to constrain and provide principles for how they should behave. Isomorphs are common culture to mathematicians and physicists and also stem from general systems theory, providing a fuller, more complete view of what happens between a client system, up through a client/clinician system, and through, perhaps, to a client/clinician/ supervisor system where it may, "not existing with a reductionistic certainty, but as showing tendencies to exist. Such an analogy allows context replication and mirroring of sequences to be thought of in other than the familiar domino-effect, cause-and-effect ways" (Liddle & Saba, 1983, p. 10). Oh, these systems folk! You gotta love 'em.

White and Russell (1997) made the point that the concept of isomorphs is a standard part of understanding supervision within the field of marriage and family therapy, and yet, there is a lack of clarity with regard to its usage and meaning. They noted that there are four different phenomena identified and discussed in the literature: (a) identification of repetitive or similar patterns, (b) translations of therapeutic models and principles into supervision, (c) acknowledgment that the structure and process of therapy and supervision are identical, and (d) isomorphism as an interventive stance. In their treatment of isomorphs, Bernard and Goodyear (2004) suggested that "the supervisor who is aware of this process will watch for dynamics in supervision that reflect the initial assessment that the supervisor has made about what is transpiring in therapy" (p. 141).

Isomorphs in Practice—An Example

Mary had a 13-year-old son, Tony, the identified client who was referred to our therapeutic day school for severe acting out behavior, running away from home whenever mom confronted him, and on at least one occasion, pulling a jack knife out to threaten her. Mary would then try to console him and end up giving in to his demands. When she tried to step up to the plate with some parental authority, he would become more abusive and confront her with her inadequacies as a parent and woman.

Mary had divorced her husband Bill 3 years previously, because of Bill's verbal and occasional physical abuse to her, and although there was still contact between the boy and his dad, Mary was adamant that she did not want him in family sessions. However, whenever Tony became abusive toward Mary, her first response was almost always to call Bill for help.

As was typical of our program, both son and mother were required to have counseling sessions—both together, as well as separately. The resulting feelings of defeat, anger, and resentment toward her ex-husband Bill and her powerlessness with son Tony were almost always the subject of discussion during Mary's "parent consultation" session with her therapist Joan. Joan's attempts to get Mary to both back off from calling in Bill's help, as well as to "reward" Tony's misbehavior with more placating and lack of consequences, was repeatedly met without interest, and Mary stated that she didn't know what else to do.

Corresponding with the these issues, Joan's supervision with me became almost identical, process-wise, to what was happening in other parts of the system. She repeatedly expressed exasperation and a sense of defeat in her sessions with Mary, as well as when they had family therapy. In her individual sessions with Tony, he was polite, and almost too sweet, while in their family sessions, he would rule the roost. The more that this happened, the more Joan hung around my office asking for help. Parallel process describes the experience to some extent, but understanding it as an isomorph gives one the knowledge that the dilemma can be changed. As soon as I recognized the pattern, I stopped being so willing to give up suggestions and began asking Joan to brainstorm ways she herself could get out of her own pickle. This led to a different sort of work between Mary and Joan, which was similar to the work between Joan and I; it enabled Mary to begin acting differently in her relationship with Tony. Once again, Tony predictably acted out and pulled a knife on his mom. This time, rather than backing down to the seriousness, Mary called the police. This is a responsible and appropriate act to the potential violence, and it underlines the seriousness of Tony's actions. Counseling could now once again be back on track, and it dealt with Mary's feelings, as well as her responses to setting better limits and consequences that matched Tony's actions. Mary could be commended for her parenting response to a very serious situation. In addition, Joan could be commended for her work with this system.

By knowing about and being aware of isomorphic properties in relationships, supervisors may discern when this aspect is jeopardizing progress and how to move away from the pull that is common to all parts of the system involved. For our purposes, with regard to strengths-based supervision, I am strangely interested in how both parallel and isomorphic processes can be viewed through a similar lens, darkly. Friedlander, Siegel, and Brenock (1989) said similar things about parallel process when they noted that a new supervisee, who is having a difficult time with a client that seems helpless, may also act in a similar fashion by becoming "helplessly dependent on the supervisor's advice.

If the supervisor resists responding to the trainee's self-effacement and instead helps the trainee to take more control, the trainee may adopt a similar strategy in the next session with the client" (p. 149). It sounds the same, doesn't it? Well, perhaps someone more knowledgeable about both concepts could straighten me out, but here is my take with respect to strengths-based supervision. Like the concepts of resiliency, the issue seems to be one of attitude. Family systems folk went a long way out to provide a concept that did not replicate parallel process, a concept from the grandmother of all problem-focused thought. Liddle and all his colleagues were set on using an idea that did not pathologize their supervisees, by recognizing that there were similarities among clients, supervisees, and supervisors when they were in cahoots with each other. They were normal events that supervisors could use to produce learning for their supervisees in a manner that might help make the learning become their own, rather than something they learned at the feet of their master practitioners.

BOUNDARY ISSUES IN CLINICAL SUPERVISION

The worrisome issue of boundaries is a holdover from clinical work; however, research has demonstrated that at the graduate level of training, severe boundaries are not as helpful as a professional collegial relationship. There are different parameters and factors at work when training and supervising that necessitate a second, perhaps less stringent look at boundaries between supervisee and supervisor, than would be held to between a clinician and a client. Aside from some of the more serious boundaries, such as those that are sexual, there are differences between clinical and professional boundaries. This section explores some of these.

As Herlihy and Corey (1997) pointed out, there is a diversity of opinions on the topic of dual or multiple relationships in counseling supervision, leading one to believe that there are many ways and reasons that boundaries may be bridged and very few that present a hard and firm boundary that should never be crossed. Sexuality and issues of unequal power differentials between supervisor and supervisee are some of the issues that have strong agreement as to their problem potential, as well as being unethical. Ironically, the issue of conflict within the supervisory relationship points to three issues beyond inappropriate sexual contact or harassment. Nelson and Friedlander (2001) studied conflictual supervisory relationships from the supervisee's point of view and found that the issue of availability was bidirectional, in that supervisors who were seen as distant and remote, as well as those who seemed overly friendly or too familiar, were found to be of concern (Nelson & Friedlander, 2001). Nelson and Friedlander as well

as Moskowitz and Rupert (1983) found that conflicts can also be problematic around the issue of the type of counseling model being used, although Nelson and Friedlander pointed out that these issues are lower on the concern scales and can usually be worked out. The conflicts that can arise from a more senior clinician being supervised by a rather new and less clinically experienced supervisor, however, can be more problematic than a supervisor who requires a specific model being required. These issues of conflict are also breaches of boundaries, because they entail relationship issues that can be very personal.

According to Gutheil and Gabbard (1993), boundary issues can be viewed as being harmful or not harmful. Areas such as time, money, gifts, services, self-disclosure, and physical contact, when shared in a counseling or supervision relationship, may be considered items where breech of boundary exist but may not be seen as overly harmful. Sexual misconduct and other areas where power differentials are evident are in a harmful category. The issue of boundaries can be a difficult and important concept within the supervision relationship. Problems with boundaries usually come from novice, unsure or unclear supervisors, and sometimes with impaired clinicians. A review of the literature found that the majority of writing and research in the area of boundaries for our profession focused on the area of inappropriate dual relationships, mostly regarding sexual misconduct or abuse (Clipson, 2005; Evans & Hearn, 1997; Glosoff, Corey, & Herlihy, 1996; Lamb, Catanzaro, & Moorman, 2004; Lamb, Catanzaro, & Moorman, 2008; Moleski & Kiselica, 2005; Pearson, & Piazza, 1997; Rinella, & Gerstein, 1994; Robinson, 2006; Shavit, 2005a; Shavit, 2005b). These are the sort of boundary issues that when crossed, give a bad name to all professions. We have ethical standards as well as legal and professional consequences for those who stray. But sometimes, especially in the venue of supervision, they are based on a prejudicial view of the one in the supervisor seat. The literature on conflict in supervisory relationships references two specific issues reflected in boundary problems, other than sexual, as detrimental to the process of supervision. One is how close or distant the supervisor seems to be as perceived by the supervisee, and the other is forcing a model on to a supervisee that is counter to what he or she has already learned and is comfortable with (Moskowitz & Rupert, 1983; Nelson & Friedlander, 2001) without a prior contract and updated discussions). Two case vignettes will demonstrate how this can get out of hand.

MARIE AND STRENGTHS-FORCED SUPERVISION: AN EXAMPLE

Marie and Jake were interns at the same internship site, with the same clinical supervisor. The clinical supervisor of the site was a well-known strengths-based clinician, and both students were eager to intern with this site and their supervisor, Kate. Both the site and the supervisor had a good reputation in the state and locally, and both interns were given ample opportunity to learn and practice strengths-based clinical work from this master practitioner/supervisor. Somewhere in the middle of the clinical experience Jake became unhappy with his supervision. He would present cases to Kate and then almost slyly say, "So Kate, you keep telling me that I should only work on the presenting problem and work from a strengths-based position, but the records have indicated that this client has had a severe substance abuse problem in the past. I think we should be talking about relapse prevention strategies. What do you think?"

When Jake would talk with me about his site supervision, I could tell that he was having trouble. My usual default modus operandi is to listen carefully to see if there is a serious risk and then default to their site supervisor's thinking, unless it was way off base. Sites "own" their clients, their methodology, and their risks. Universities do not have privileged positions with agency sites, above and beyond any contractual agreement. I began to believe this after being a site supervisor for many years, when a brand new PsyD university supervisor with limited family counseling experience attempted to change the methodology our agency was using, expecting the students to work outside of our agency's established family protocol. Even experienced and savvy university supervisors can never have all of the information in front of them to make snap clinical judgments when they are only armchair supervising.

I encouraged Jake to explore his own motivations and worldviews that informed this case, and I commented on how hard it is to learn a new model that can seem to be at cross-purposes with an old model we know well. He agreed, and for a short time, his case presentations with me were again on track, but not for long. The same challenging situation came back several times, and he commented that the strengths-based model was too restrictive and did not take into account many of the elements of counseling he had learned in his counseling skills class—a modified person-centered model. "Besides," he said, "she is really pushy about learning all of the skill sets and won't let me see clients without her being present. All my fellow interns and classmates are seeing clients alone by now, including Marie. She seems to be Kate's pet pupil."

A discussion on the phone with the site supervisor indicated that this was only partially true, that Marie was seeing a woman alone that they had seen together for a time. Also, Kate said that Marie had, in her opinion, learned some of the basic tenets of strengths-based

(Continued)

(Continued)

clinical work well enough that she thought the case would be better off with only one clinician in the room, with videotaped supervision. She was well aware of the dynamics of her two interns and her own relationships with them, and she really believed that Jake was coming along fine, albeit a bit slower than Marie. She agreed that it may seem unfair to Jake, that Marie had "her own case" to work with, but that Jake was slated to get a case of his own soon.

At our university, clinical experience is a year long, over three semesters, and many normal life events occur during that time, including, on rare occasions, switching clinical sites. So, I told Jake that if he was really unhappy and wanted to switch sites, we could look into it. He decided that maybe he would stay and learn something after all. He also stated that he wanted to go back to working with the substance abuse community when he finished and I wondered if some of what he would continue to learn might rub off and will be useful in his future clinical work.

In retrospect, I think that the turning point was when I offered up my support to Jake in the form of an option to find another site. Rather than feeling as if the strengths-based model was forced on him, it once again became his choice.

MURIEL AND HER BELIEFS—AN EXAMPLE

Muriel was a nonpracticing, cultural Jew, and her internship supervisor Mike was an evangelical Christian. One day one of Muriel's clients was talking about an argument she had had with a colleague regarding her religious beliefs, especially creation versus evolution . . . being more on the evolutionist side. Muriel listened and validated her client's right to believe what she wanted, while Mike watched from behind a one-way mirror. When Muriel went for her consultation break to discuss the case, Mike was clearly upset and pursued Muriel with questions regarding her own views of creation versus evolution. Muriel was very clear with Mike, to her credit, that this was out of bounds for their supervision discussion, but Mike persisted, wanting to know specifically what she believed. Muriel finished the case, somewhat upset, and later, she made her point with Mike that this was uncomfortable territory for her because of their differences in religion. The next day, he persisted again, and again she made it clear that she did not want to discuss this issue, but she remained worried that this interchange could change the dynamics of their clinical relationship. Muriel went to the site's clinical director and was later changed to a different site supervisor.

I was very proud of Muriel for sticking to her guns, using her voice, and risking a problem by going over Mike's head. The issue of Muriel's beliefs is not an issue to be challenged, but perhaps Mike's views and insistences should be a subject of his own supervision with his immediate supervisor. To this agency's credit, Mike's supervisor did spend some time with him regarding this issue, and he later apologized for his inappropriate boundary breach.

The point to these stories, of course, is that some boundary issues should be clear and out of bounds for supervision. There are simply issues and places that supervisors should not go with their supervisees; for instance, differences in religious beliefs are clearly inappropriate for discussion, especially when pursued in such a hostile manner. If the issue was one of clinical concern, then the issue is in bounds for discussion, but in Muriel's case, the supervisor had no right to pursue her because of his own issues. And even if there was a shade of difference, the fact that Muriel said she was uncomfortable in discussing the issue should have been enough. The other case could be perceived as crossing over into a conflictual place if a supervisor had not made it clear and provided informed consent in regard to training and supervision with a specific model. If a supervisee begins to feel pushed into a direction he or she clearly does not understand or agree with clinically, the supervisor has a responsibility to discuss the meta-issue and stop pushing the model until that issue is cleared up and a forward direction agreed upon between supervisor and supervisee. Clear expectations, using and encouraging "voice," and good feedback will establish an open collegial boundary with good expectations of both participants and "soft influence," thus avoiding pitfalls.

Interestingly, some areas of boundary crossing can be viewed as useful to both parties. For instance, a qualitative investigation of patterns of interaction in clinical supervision found that the process of supervision appears to have much to do with the nature of the relationship, and that openness between supervisor and supervisee can be relationship-focused *and* multihierarchical (Keller, Protinsky, Lichtman, & Allen, 1996). During this research, Keller et al. (1996) discovered that discussing supervision processes (transparency and metacommunications) between supervisee and supervisor increased the level of trust and collegiality between students and supervisors. It was found that supervision can be enhanced by increasing vulnerability on both sides of the relationship and collegiality, without harm to boundaries. It may be that seasoned

ethical supervisors do not worry much about the boundary issues and focus on relationship building in the process. Ethical supervisors may not have to worry about rigid boundaries and thus can spend time forming long-lasting, interesting, and ethical collegial relationships. I, for one, found myself in the lucky situation of having three very competent and well-known supervisors in different situations during my doctoral program. These very generous educators gave their time and talents to help me develop supervisory skills, as well as writing and publishing skills, that I would never have gotten if they had not reached out and developed personal relationships with me.

In agencies, the issue of hierarchy and boundaries are very different than they are in the university setting. Setting us straighter on the appropriateness of boundary issues between our supervisees and ourselves, White and Russell (1997) suggested an alternative, more realistic collegial position, as they pointed out that the more rigid boundaries of therapy are not the same as those supervisors might have with supervisees. Using their training with burgeoning marriage and family therapy students, they made the point that our socialization (social constructs) have taught us to believe that personal and more intimate relationships with clients are regarded as off bounds. While this may be true for our clients, it might often not be true with our supervisees, as this relationship involves creating future colleagues (Ryder & Hepworth, as cited by White & Russell, 1997). "We expect to meet them at future conferences, publish with them, refer clients to them, and so forth" (White & Russell, 1997, p. 330). I believe this to be true, and maybe even more so in agency supervision; at least this has been my experience both personally, as well as with colleagues from agencies where they publish together and also spend time together outside of work, publish and even go to festive conferences away and outside of work. So, supervision relationships do and can cross boundaries, but what seems to keep them from crossing that chasm to the dark side? Lamb et al. (2004) studied the issue of multiple relationships with psychologists and found that their values of ethics and morals were most often indicated as what helps them from moving outside the boundaries; however, this does not always hold true with supervisees.

I have experienced firsthand in several settings how boundaries can blur and be both beneficial as well as problematic. It is important to remember that boundaries are not real, concrete "things," but they exist in our minds, formulated and socially constructed by what we have learned from those who teach us, as well as past and current situations. Each circumstance is different and constructed as people come together and utilize their own construct of where they want to go with each relationship. The caution is to be aware that hierarchy can be powerful and abused on both sides. If it feels wrong, check it out with others, and talk about it openly. If you cannot do that, or feel uncomfortable doing so, ask someone else about it, and get good council. The power differential can be a true double bind, where there are mixed messages and one of the parties is uncomfortable with talking about it for fear of reprisal. If that is the case, get out of the relationship and go to someone at a higher level that you trust to talk it out. I do not want to give the impression that all dual relationships are bad. Due to the culture or the whereabouts of the supervision site, the context will change.

When I was a brand new professor, I went to lunch with a site supervisor and our shared student, toward the end of her internship experience to celebrate the end of her term. I intended to pay my own way, but I was stopped by the site supervisor when I went for my wallet and told that our student would be offended if I did not accept her gracious gift. She was Vietnamese and was very proud to "pay back" her two supervisors with a lunch for the time and interest we had given her. So, I got a great Vietnamese lunch and learned about wonderful French coffee that I still love to this day.

The newest issue to come up regarding boundaries is about the ubiquitous social networking sites on the Internet. The CEST-Net, an electronic mailing list for counselor educators, has had a very active debate in regard to the potential for problems with being "friends" with students or supervisees on these sites. Immature and risky young people can say and post things that perhaps should not be seen anywhere, but they are fearless and sometimes do not understand the risks. Posted information is seen by some as a dual relationship, especially if that information is being shared with supervisees or supervisors.

During this debate, someone mentioned that they hated Facebook and would like to have it disbanded, but she had never been on the site to see for herself. Media changes so quickly. According to a YouTube video from "Did you Know," there are 200 million registered MySpace users and 31 billion searches on Google every month (see http://www.youtube.com/watch#!v=PHmwZ96_Gos&feature=related), and the video concludes that we live in exponential times, ever expanding our knowledge and the electronic social media we use. Supervisors and educators cannot hide from this, but we can be careful and set out our own parameters, as it has not been set for us as of yet. During this electronic mailing list debate, a woman spoke against all of the cautious writers to say the following:

I have seen the "establishment" rebel against computers, video tape, white board instead of chalk, computer based training, going from disks to USB drives, etc.

Well, it is media, plainly. That is all. The telephone probably started similar discussions.

By the way, if you are relying on a "chain of command" type respect from students, then you probably do not have it now—fear is a bad motivator. Respect is from being professional in your dealings and knowing what you are talking about. If you are honest, you do not have to have two personas.

I had 250 people that used to work for me. Most called me by my first name or nickname, only strangers used my rank. They also generated more output than any other similar organization in the USAF. I never doubted their respect. They did what needed to be done because I asked them to, even when going to war. Their efforts went well beyond what I expected. These sterile "I am the leader" theories that gave birth to some of these "boundary" discussions are what they seem to be—authoritarian and antiquated. One earns respect. (Fisk, 2009)

There is something about what Lt. Col. Fisk said that rings simple truth for me beyond our attempts to regulate behavior of clinicians and supervisors. If we act professionally and yet are human within the context of our professional regulations, we can extend the professional relationships to become clear and further refined beyond their constraints. I am reminded that Thomas found several of Heath and Tharp's (1991) points of the supervisory process to be what clinicians want most: a relationship based on mutual respect and a supervision process that becomes a human experience (Heath & Tharp, cited in Thomas, 1996). I do not think it is over-kill to point out that White and Russell (1997) suggested a realistic collegial position, where there are less than usual ridged boundaries found in therapy, because we might bloody well be meeting former students at conferences and even publishing with them (White & Russell, 1997). Finally, again I present the words of someone who has been at the top of a hierarchical relationship and who seems to know better: "These sterile 'I am the leader' theories that gave birth to some of these 'boundary' discussions are what they seem to be—authoritarian and antiquated. One earns respect" (Fisk, 2009).

INTERPERSONAL RELATIONSHIP SKILLS

Important to what supervisors and clinicians do is how we relate to one another. If not for our interpersonal relationship skills in forming and maintaining relationships, we would have nothing. Sometimes called people skills, they include such things as using active listening and reflections and watching how you say things to people—for example, being too gruff, too soft, and so forth—they are the basis of how we relate to one another in everyday life as well as our professional life. Interpersonal skills can also include such things as how you carry yourself and interact with people. Do you appear confident and yet empathic and caring? Are your words congruent with your facial gestures and body posture? Those who studied communications theory and used it as a model of clinical work (Watzlawick, Beavin, & Jackson, 1969) suggested that all behavior is communication. For example, if my daughter Zoe were to come in our house after school, throw her books on the table, and run up to her room shutting the door quickly without saying hello, I am being told something. How I begin to decode that message will depend on our previous socially constructed meaning making of such or similar behavior. Also, communication is broken down into patterns of what is called report and command or digital and analog processes. Researchers postulated that all communication has both a report (general content) and a command (do something about what I am saying). Nichols, in explaining these phenomena, described it thus: "The report (or content) of a message conveys information, whereas the command is a statement about the relationship. For example, the statement, 'Mommy, Sandy hit me' conveys information but also implies a command—Do something about it" (Nichols, 2009, p. 111).

An interesting study by Klein (2009) looked at, among other qualities, what has typically been called the Big Five (see Digman, 1990) of broad domains of personality, in regard to finding the existence of antecedents for higher levels of learning and using interpersonal skills. The results of these analyses provided evidence for the existence of meaningful antecedents of interpersonal skills. The Big Five has been one of the most empirically researched and comprehensive models in human sciences and also one of the most debated. The five factors are Openness, Conscientiousness, Extraversion, Agreeableness, and Neuroticism, not necessarily in that order. These factors can be rated on a continuum, from those who show high to low, and perhaps the antithesis of the named trait. For instance, one can measure high on the agreeableness trait or at the opposite end that would be high as disagreeableness. Each of these factors also has constituent traits that cluster around the other factors. Briefly, I describe the factors and their traits:

- Openness as a factor includes an appreciation for the arts, adventure, imagination, curiosity, and experience—largely, this factor usually is considered to differentiate between people who are down to earth and those who might be more imaginative.
- Conscientiousness as a factor includes self-disciplined individuals versus those who tend to be more spontaneous.
- Extraversion as a factor includes people who are engaged in life, have lots of positive energy, and enjoy being with people, while introverts can lack social involvement, even though they also may be active and energetic.
- Agreeableness as a trait includes those who are compassionate and caring, tending to be more optimistic and cooperative, rather than suspicious and oppositional.
- Neuroticism as a factor tends to include people who have more negative emotions than positive, potentially being more angry, anxious, or depressed, while at the other end of the continuum includes people who are more relaxed, are most often calm, and do not get rattled as much.

Of interest to those in the training and development field are the findings that two of the personality dimensions, Openness and Extraversion, are related to performance outcome in training programs (Barrick & Mount, 1991). Jang, Livesley, and Vemon (1996) concluded their work noting that the factors of the Big Five have about equal portions of being hereditary and learned, meaning that having good interpersonal skills can be either learned or improved through training; but also we know that they have a big impact on outcomes and openness to change. Interpersonal skills are an indication of how supervisors can influence outcomes because of the way they interact with their supervisees in relationships that are open, engaging, and optimistic. Supervisors who show genuine concern and are open to different experiences rather than being one dimensional seem to engage relationships more than those who are closed off and have negative views and attitudes toward novelty with their supervisees.

Relationships can be fragile, and yet they are extremely important. We are creatures that are made to relate with one another, and we need to be in relationships to survive. Relationships are the building blocks of our interconnection and human behavior, depending on our interrelationships to work, play, cohabitate, cocreate, and nurture our young. Relationships are built on trust and mutual respect. Good relationships are the meat and potatoes of good working clinical relationships. Guidelines for good relationships include being respectful of each other. Name calling and sarcasm, or providing hurtful and harmful feedback, can damage relationships. Showing respect for others as human beings can increase the currency with which relationships depend. When discussing a problem, keep the problem the problem, and do not blame or use language that can be construed as adding fuel to a complicated situation. Do not personalize the discussion, but stay focused on the issues, and use basic "I" statements when in disagreement.

During any conversation there is a tendency to drift from the subject being discussed, to other subjects that one might be reminded of from the conversation. Goal-oriented conversations should, however, have a point. Staying on subject is a great way of making sure conversations progress, and it is the supervisor's task to do so in a careful and courteous way.

Make it a habit to use reflective, active listening, so you can really understand each other. We all have a basic need to be understood and feel that what we say is important, and our opinions are valued. This means that you should try to see others' points of view, and let them know you understand, even if you don't agree. And above all, accept each other with positive regard; basic attending skills make excellent relationship skills.

When we take interpersonal skills into the consulting room, other dimensions and behaviors can also be helpful. If someone is rambling on, it may be appropriate to say quietly and respectfully,

"Can I jump in here please?" But then, after saying what is on your mind, remember to again get back to the person you are discussing with, regarding where you left off. Even restating what you heard the person saying before you interrupted will show that person respect as well as interest. Many of these skills are also useful in conflict resolution, as we shall see.

Conflict Resolution: A Beginning

Not an afterthought, conflict resolution skills are an extremely important part of supervision not usually taught as typical supervision skills. Several authors have researched and discussed the need for conflict resolution skills by supervisors, and have demonstrated that conflicts in supervision sessions are that it is one of the most detrimental factors for new clinicians in how they behave and solidify clinical learning (Korinek & Kimball, 2003; Moskowitz & Rupert, 1983; Nelson & Friedlander, 2001). Issues are discussed, typical critical points in clinical supervision are raised, and suggestions for resolving them are presented.

The research and discussion of conflict and conflict resolution skills in clinical supervision is scarce but entirely needed (Jackson, Junior, & Mahoney, 2007). During a review of the clinical supervision literature, I found that there are very few that mention conflict resolution skills, and yet those who have done supervision for any length of time know that there is a need (Moskowitz & Rupert, 1983). Those who have studied and researched conflict within the supervision process have imparted us with an incredible amount of useful data; all that points to the need for better training in conflict resolution. Over and again issues of conflict during supervision seem to cluster around central issues. The anxiety of the supervisee seems to be central to conflictual situations during supervision. The hierarchal relationship positions the relationship in such a way that the supervisee is subordinate to the supervisor. The very nature of the hierarchy places the supervisee at a lower power level, which leads to either obedience or insubordination whenever a conflict or disagreement occurs. Conflict resolution assumes a few basic ideas—simple to understand, easy to practice, harder to use in the heated moment unless you have trained and worked at using them. According to conflict resolution theory, conflicts arise when someone becomes uncomfortable with how a current relationship or situation is working. For conflict resolution to become effective, one of the participants needs to at least acknowledge that there is a problem or conflict and speak up with the hope of resolving the current conditions. Next, all parties involved need to be receptive to the idea of resolution. Conflict arises when there are differences in the way two or more people see the situation and/or because they have different value systems or objectives. Polarization of positions creates a tension building up to the point where someone finally says something, and it is acknowledged by all parties. At this point, especially within situations where a perceived hierarchy occurs, the parties will either begin to work toward a solution or insist that the problem is not real, or worse yet, assume that the person who brings up the conflict is the cause.

Dealing with conflict in a supervision relationship, or in any relationship, has two methods or negative outcome reductions. The first is prevention; the second is intervention. As with most mental health concerns, it is less costly emotionally to provide prevention strategies, thus avoiding the problem, than it is to head into intervention strategies after the fact. We look at interventions first, because they also provide us with a series of behaviors that can be useful preventatively.

As we apply conflict resolution to clinical supervision, we must be reminded that (a) the quality of the relationship is seen as essential to positive outcomes in supervision, and (b) the hallmark of successful supervision is the resolution of conflict that occurs naturally because of the power imbalance between supervisor and supervisee (Holloway, 1995; Worthen & McNeil, 1996)—it is a natural component of supervision and almost any hierarchical relationship. While people battle over opposing positions and solutions—"Do it my way!" "No, that's no good! Do it my way!"—the conflict *is* a power struggle. What is needed is to change the agenda in the conversation?. One must adopt a win–win attitude that says, "I want to win and I want you to win too." The challenge then is how to have this happen.

A Synthesis of Basic Strategies

Let us look at some generic thoughts about conflict resolution strategies and apply them to the supervisory relationship. To begin with, the challenge of adopting a win–win approach decidedly suggests that to be effective, one must change his or her view of a supervisee from an opponent to that of a partner in the conflictual relationship. Both supervisor and supervisee want something out of this relationship. This is consistent to my premise that those with whom we work are truly costakeholders in the process. If a supervisor can remove his or her ego from this process and focus on resolving the conflict rather than being right, a shift in attitude for both will take place that can alter the dialogue that will follow; in fact, dialogue really becomes possible. But, as creatures of habit, we most often find that our default behavior is to defend ourselves when we feel attacked. So, it takes forethought and practice, but in the end, it is well worth it.

Next, research suggests that talking about each other's needs can significantly change the direction of outcome to a win–win position. Attempting to find what is fair for both parties and working slowly to reach that point in discussion is key. As in Bowenian systems therapy (Bowen, 1978), the secret to most productive change is to remain engaged while maintaining a nonreactive attitude to statements that may enflame. Remembering that all situations can be seen as either problems or as opportunities reframes the supervisor's intentions and provides a context for the win–win situation all parties hope for, while looking for a creative response

to the conflict can be a turning point in changing problems into possibilities.

The use of empathy for the supervisee's position can lessen the potential emotional reactivity that will lead to conflict, so good interpersonal skills, active listening, and a building of rapport and openness on both sides can go a long way to defusing conflict and producing solutions. Rather than focusing on personalities and traits that may be irritating, focusing on data—information on both parts in order to get a clear nonemotional picture of what the problem is on both sides—will help. For instance, a supervisor might say the following: "One of the components of supervision is that we have goals that we both agree with. What are you wanting from our time together?" This might be followed up with this: "I understand that you have had lots of experience in CBT, and now you are at an agency where we use Solution-Focused Therapy. I would like to see you succeed in learning the model in addition to your skills in CBT. I believe it might be useful to you in the long run, not that you will have to be chained to it forever. Does that sound reasonable to you? What do you think we might do together to help you in that direction, because I want you to be successful here in your time with us."

In the scenario I just provided, I was appropriately assertive in speaking about what my goals for this supervisor are in regard to some expectations, and I used "I" statements. The essence of being appropriately assertive is being able to state your case without arousing the defenses of the other person, giving credit for the other person's skills, saying how it is for you rather than what he or she should or should not do. Your "I" statement is not about being polite; it is not necessarily soft, but it also is not rude. It is about being up front without being reactive. Managing how you are feeling while you begin the process of de-escalating the conflict is very important.

Once the process is moving past the initial conflictual emotions, look for options. Make it explicit that you both have outcomes you desire, and make those outcomes explicit. You might want to suggest that both parties take some time to take a break and write a list of desirable outcomes—of potentials—so that you can both look at your lists and see where there are commonalities. Looking for common ground makes for a universal position and says we both have some things we want from meeting together that can be agreed upon.

Coleman and Deutsch (2006) suggested two rather out of the box creative components of conflict resolution. One is that after making some decisions regarding outcome, each party takes a break and is so quick to complete a contractual agreement. What is the rationale behind this thinking? They suggested the following: "Research has shown that humans tend to be poor decision makers because they often choose the first acceptable solution to a problem that emerges, even if it is far from being the best that could be developed" (p. 407). They believed that creative tension and not giving in to the first solution can make for longer lasting satisfaction for both parties, because of the engagement and creativity that comes from exploring all the possibilities. Why settle for the first outcome when others that are better might come along (Coleman & Deutsch, 2006)? In addition, they also suggested moving the venue of discussion from one location to another to get perspective and to try to see some humor without being disrespectful, to help both parties move past the seriousness of the situation as "disputants often approach their problems grimly" (p. 408).

During the problem-solving stage of conflict resolution it is useful to break out outcomes and solutions into smaller parts that are easily accomplished. It is also useful to make problems into solvable behaviors that can be tried out first before committing to complete change. Finally, find a location that is common ground, rather than meeting in an office of one of the parties (The Carroll-Keller Group, n.d.). There is too much psychological baggage imbued with an office where the conflict may have begun or where the power of the hierarchical relationship looms overhead.

By taking a broader perspective you may be confronted with the enormity of the difficulties.

Identify what you can do to affect a particular problem, even if it is only a small step in the right direction. One step forward changes the dynamics and new possibilities can open up.

Preventing Conflict

Several ideas I have used successfully come to mind that have prevented potential conflicts in supervision. The first is a concept that is close to what Russian psychologist and educational specialist Lev Vygotsky (1987) suggested, called *scaffolding*. Scaffolding is a teaching pedagogy that includes helping to prop up new learning by providing support, so that the student will succeed rather than fail. There have been many times when I have had students with experience in other similar fields, such as music therapy, or substance abuse counseling, where they have some great skills that could be expanded some. Usually they have a concreteness in their view of the professional relationship and are more like what we discussed in the first stage of development (Stoltenberg & Delworth, 1987) where they hold on to concepts as if they are absolutely true, wanting to show their supervisor that they know something. Later in this book I will tell the story of a student who was a music therapist who had left a doctoral program because one of her professors had told her she needed to abandon all of her previous experience and ideas if she was to succeed. I embraced her previous experience instead and encouraged her to learn even more and complementary techniques so she could be an even better music therapist, as well as a licensed counselor. I utilized her skills to encourage new learning. I know I routed potential conflict right out the door that day.

Next, I have discovered that by naming potential problems now and by dialoguing about them, we collaboratively create potential possibilities and solutions ahead of time. I find it far better to head off problems that I see coming than to deal with them later. Conflicts and differences need not be a problem, if supervisors anticipate, use forethought and creativity to change them into opportunities.

MARY JANE AND CONFLICT—AN EXAMPLE

Mary Jane was the director of clinical experience at a large mental health agency, and she was having difficulty with her boss Paul, as many people have had before her. Paul, a rather newly hired CEO, had been experienced by staff as someone who was dictatorial, ran a top-down hierarchical organization, and "bullied" people into submitting when he wanted his way. Mary Jane was just like her boss; she didn't give an inch but she was also on the board of directors, and so she had some leverage. Paul demanded a face-to-face meeting in his office to settle their conflict, and she had put him off saying she wanted to think about their situation and her options. She asked me to consult to see if there might be a way of leveling the playing field. We talked about options, and she wanted to go after him, invoking the support of friends on the board of directors, to give Paul his walking papers. I suggested that they were not about to run him out of town, but she might gain some leverage by doing three simple acts. First, she needed to stop being so reactive to what Paul did, and think logically. Next she needed to prepare for any meeting, and bring along an advocate so that Paul's usual bullying would either be corroborated by another or would not happen. And finally, she needed to have the meeting on neutral grounds, rather than in Paul's office. As a good consultant, I talked with her about this, attempted to get a commitment from her to follow through on my suggestions, and let her go to work on this plan. She was able to complete two of the three, but Paul was adamant about meeting in his office. The meeting terms were negotiated and she met with a list of complaints, which included conditions for other workers; she also requested that he stop his bullying behavior or she would bring it to the board of directors. All conditions were documented, because her advocate was present, and Mary Jane felt satisfied. Although she did not get everything she asked for, the meeting was productive, and the organization began to run better.

Promoting Counselor Self-Efficacy and Personal Agency: A Core Executive Skill

An individual's beliefs about their ability to carry out behaviors, and their beliefs about the connections between their efforts and the results of those behaviors to affect motivation, behaviors, and the persistence of effort, are called self-efficacy (Bandura, 1977b). Self-efficacy is the belief in one's capability to organize and execute the sources of action required to manage perspective situations (e.g., "I know I can do it"; Bandura, 1986). Personal agency is the ability to originate and direct actions for a specific purpose (e.g., "I have the skills and knowledge to set a goal, begin working toward that goal, and complete a task"). Personal agency is directly linked to the person's belief in his or her ability (self-efficacy). Personal agency is characterized by a number of core features, including intentionality, forethought, self regulation, and self-reflectiveness about one's capabilities, quality of functioning, and the meaning and purpose of one's life pursuits.

Counseling self-efficacy (CSE) and the personal agency that goes with it are key to both basic and strengths-based clinical supervision principles (Daniels & Larson, 2001). But where does it come from? How do counselors obtain or learn to have agency? They gain agency every time they have a mastery experience in the field. Watching new counselors realize that they can make it through a session with a new client and noticing that they don't stall, or that they ask the right questions and noticing that their client smiles when they are leaving—that is a mastery experience. Each time puts more experience in their bank. Clinicians gain agency when they watch their supervisor actually do a live clinical session and know that they can replicate a technique or skill they watched, again adding to their bank. As supervisors encourage their supervisees, they are persuaded to try new things or take stock in how far they have come.

To have personal agency is to intentionally make things happen through one's actions. The core features of agency enable people to play a role in their own self-development, adaptation, and self-renewal with changing times. Personal agency comes from several sources: mastery experiences, vicarious experiences, verbal persuasion, and personal psychological states. As supervisees try out their new learning, they receive internal (and perhaps external) feedback of their successes, adding to their fund of agency regarding a specific task (mastery experiences). Vicarious experiences as well as verbal persuasions from their supervisor can increase their agency; as they are asked questions regarding their own views of their behavior—meaning-making questions—supervisees begin to internalize their successes. According to their own internal psychological state, supervisees will include these skills as their own, value them, and evaluate them. Some supervisees have a greater capacity to look at their own skill levels and learn with optimism, while others do not learn self-efficacy and may need more time to begin changing their internal views. It is useful to see these psychological traits as learned, rather than as personality traits. Optimism has been shown to be a learned phenomenon (Seligman, 1996).

In my experience, CSE is cocreated by, and includes the use, of strength-based clinical values, supervisory forethought, and finding and using one's own voice (Covey, 2004). Others have also included intentionality (a representation of a future course of action to be performed), forethought (setting goals, creating a course of action likely to produce desired outcomes, while avoiding detrimental ones), self-reactivity (in order to self-motivate, and give shape to the course of action), and self-reflectiveness (Larson, & Daniels, 1998). This becomes perceived self-efficacy, and it can influence whether people think pessimistically or optimistically—and are self-enhancing or self-hindering. None of the components of agency are more central than the belief in one's capability to exercise a measure of control over his or her own functioning and environmental events. To be efficacious, counselors must orchestrate and continuously improvise multiple subskills to manage ever-changing circumstances in the session. It is one's *perceived* self-efficacy and personal agency that allows one to make judgments of how well one can execute the actions and make corrections to shape the future. The use of agency questioning has been used in both Solution-Focused Therapy as well as Narrative Therapy. Questions that ask people for their input into their own positive processes help them to interpret and restory their events in a way that illuminates their own successes in some endeavor, in this case success in a clinical session. Questions such as "How do you think you were able to do that?" or "Given your struggles to achieve a more successful outcome with that client, in what part of the discussion (with the client) did you find you were playing a more useful role with your client, and how were you able to do that?" play an important role in helping clinicians see their growth and successes during a part of their own development, when they might be prone to look in the other direction.

Several behavioral components are important to following through with one's personal agency: people must have forethought; their behavior must have directionality and intentionality; they must be able to self-regulate their actions, rather than be cast to random thoughts and feelings; and finally, they must be self-reflective, using evaluative feedback, correcting their efforts back toward their goals should they error. What determines forethought's direction, however, are the personal standards and values of the agent. This is a circular process and an evolving process. According to Bandura (2001), people check on their actions through what he called performance comparisons with one's own goals and standards, all of which are imbedded in our personal value system or what he believed to be our "moral agency." Self-efficacy is far easier to explain than it is to teach rationally. One can, I believe, facilitate the building of someone else's self-efficacy through modeling, giving praise, and positively punctuating when someone is on track by our discussions, but for the actual learning, the self-feedback must come from and be internalized by the person living the experience of growing self-efficacy.

This personal feedback process, which others call second-order cybernetics (Bateson, 1979), or the newer term top-down metacognition (Siegel, 2007), is the internal guidance system that keeps us on track but that is always inputting new, novel information, thus learning. The interesting part of this concept, now proven through brain research, is that it filters out "negative" information (information that doesn't fit with what one already "knows" to be true or believe) and only attaches meaning and interest in change (learning) when presented in a way that allows for adaptation. In other words, we attempt to maintain what we already believe to be true, while canceling out what we believe to be false, even when presented with evidence to the contrary. Learning is homeodynamic.

Thoughts on Self-Efficacy and Personal Agency

In my opinion, one of the most important components of supervision is the continued imparting of our belief in our supervisees and the development of their own agency. It is my opinion that supervision—as in clinical work—should be agentic in all we do. I believe it is the crux of strengths-based work. Agency helps us to have voice, morality, and a sense of self as a basic creator of our personal and professional lives and our ability to produce quality work; at the same time we learn from our mistakes without being overly upset by them. Agency is recognizing that we can create our own way, not as something perfect, but with excellence—with elegance. As Michael J. Fox has said, "I am careful not to confuse excellence with perfection. Excellence, I can reach for; perfection is God's business" (Fox, n.d.). Personal agency also means knowing how to pick one's self up and move on, learning from our efforts, so we might adapt and be resilient. This is the most critical piece of supervision we can provide—to our supervisees, our clients, ourselves, and to others.

Session Management

Many of the clinical mechanics are the same for both clinicians and supervisors. When and how do you start a session? Do you contract for goal-oriented outcomes or do you just open the session up to listen and talk? How do you terminate supervisory contact? Do you do it when they retire or graduate or never? What happens when your supervisee is cranky or angry? How do you de-escalate the process, and how do you bring the session and the relationship back to a working productive venue? Session management includes those behaviors and processes that we all do and mostly do well. My take on it is that we as supervisors should consider what we do from the beginning of a contact—opening moves with first-time supervisees—to the ending. I also think we should not only model these for our supervisees, we should ask them to consider how they want to run their sessions with their own clients and help them develop their own operating principles for session management. After all, it is not our session, but they may pick up the fact that we trust them but want them to consider how to have a session that has forethought and alternatives for potential problematic situations. I want my supervisees to have back doors of escape (sometimes literally) and a thought-out plan for session management that will provide comfort and structure for both them as well as their clients. I cannot tell them how to do it, but I can have a discussion about how I have done specific things that work for me. So, I end this chapter here and suggest that you outline potential sessions' management from beginning to end, right now.

THE RELATIONSHIP BETWEEN SUPERVISOR AND SUPERVISEE— PERSONAL AND PROFESSIONAL

Reflections

The novice as well as a seasoned supervisor needs to hone his or her executive skills, which I laid out earlier. Without them, supervisors will float in the flotsam of the events, conflicts, and processes that occur while helping supervisees work in their area of expertise. In clinical work, this means that developing executive skills are as necessary for clinicians as they are for supervisors—the processes are isomorphic.

It is the executive skills that transcend the models, clinical beliefs, and dilemmas that clients come with. Seeing one's supervisee—covisee or stakeholder—as the main person the supervisor is responsible for places the supervisor in a position to be most helpful to the supervisee's growth and development, rather than as a super astute manager of someone else's cases. These executive skills allow the clinical supervisor to move ahead with what Covey (2004) believes is a change from effectiveness to excellence.

PART II

A Time for a Change to a New Model

I don't know about you, but I was not aware of a solid model to use when I became a clinical supervisor, other than that at the time I knew more about clinical work than any of my charges. But those were the easy days. There were only a few solid models of clinical work; most of us practiced from a psychodynamic point of view and later a generic family systems model we were all learning together from the host of "experts" we hired as consultants. There was something interesting and beautifully simple about the 1960s and early 1970s. We were all in it together for altruistic reasons. I remember supervising a new psychiatric intern in children's group play therapy, and she was grateful for any help she might get. Nowadays there are well over 400 models of counseling and psychotherapy; some have been tested in the labs of universities using protocols for outcomes (efficacy), and some have the even more unique ability to be tried out in the field (effectiveness). But none of them can really be tried out under all of the interesting and unique conditions that most of our real-life clients present under their own typical conditions. If we seriously consider our clients' "problems" to be a multicausal, recursive system—a bio-psycho-social-spiritual-clinical interface—we must also include the relationship between client and clinician, and the clinician and the supervisor, too. It's a soup! And our field is lagging behind current models of leadership and management as well as clinical models, stuck in a metaphor that is more adequate for physical problems. Any supervisor who has even given a second thought to what I am saying has to admit that at best we often provide direction that may not be used, rather than encouraging interesting, rich, and novel collaborative client and clinician thought and solutions. And we know full well or at least we should, that most clinical dilemmas get better significantly when our clients feel a part of the planning.

3

A TIME FOR CHANGE

It is the nature of man to rise to greatness if greatness is expected of him.

—John Steinbeck,
American novelist (1902–1968)

For years, clinical supervision has been the most effective method of helping new clinicians to adapt, practice, and gain strength with their clinical skills. Clinical training was mostly done through lecture and discussion, followed by clinical practice under the watchful eye of senior, more experienced clinicians. Beginning with the basic training model of psychoanalysts who would undergo their own psychoanalysis as a means of apprenticeship, the field of clinical supervision practice has adapted to a medical model. Later, again, adapted from our siblings in medicine, we used the surgeon's "watch one, do one, teach one" method of training, practice, assessment and evaluation, and remediation. Bug in the ear, consultation breaks, and such were surefire methods to both supervise eager to learn new clinicians while training interns watching behind the mirror, as the trainee worked with clients, awaiting a call for course corrections. And we have done well for many years using models that fit our theories of change. The complementary field of clinical and agency supervision usually parallels the in-vogue models of clinical work. The literature of supervision blossomed and now the average clinical supervisor has at hand a large theory base that will inform the novice how to handle most situations, along with a fund of methods that will provide security and competence. Early edited works on supervision provided us with methods of supervision to fit the clinical model being used (Liddle, Breunlin, & Schwartz, 1988; Watkins, 1997). In a later chapter, I plow through the more prominent models and offer a second opinion.

Because our clinical models have been changing during the last two decades, strengths-based work has become more and more the "soup du jour," as "increasingly, psychology is moving toward a strength perspective in both philosophy and counseling practice" (Smith, 2006, p. 13). There have been significant pushes to move the strengths-based model forward (Smith, 2006) and more than enough iterations of strengths-based models to make a very sizable dent in tradition. As the field moves into a stronger strengths-based clinical model, it is important that supervision more than parallels the clinical field; it is time it leads.

Yet, the field of mental health has had an on-again off-again relationship with strengths-based models of treatment, interspersed with major pushes to move us back to the medically modeled view by those deep-pocketed groups who are reluctant to move toward a model that might spell a relinquished power and financial base for them.

> In the last fifteen years, HMO's, insurers, pharmaceutical companies, hospital corporations, physicians, and other segments of the industry contributed $479 million to political campaigns—more than the energy industry ($315 million), commercial banks ($133 million), and big tobacco ($52 million). More telling is how much the health care industry spends on lobbying. It invests more than any other industry except one, according to the nonpartisan Center for Responsive Politics. From 1997 to 2000, the most recent year for which complete data is available, the industry spent $734 million lobbying Congress and the executive branch. (Barlett & Steele, 2004, p. 97)

Despite the many changes and positive advances in traditional supervision, a 2001 study of some 20,000 exit interviews found that the number one reason people leave jobs is due to poor supervisory behavior (Enbysk, 2006). Although the survey was taken in the business sector, there is reason to believe that this information is similar in the mental health field. One of the early reviewers of this book objected that I use a business informed piece of research to make this point, but I see no reason to believe that this worrisome piece of news is any different within our field. In fact, I think that to make the assumption that it is not indicative of our field is to hide an overconfident head in the sand. The last two times I presented workshops on strengths-based supervision I mentioned this criticism and was flooded with anecdotal information that the same conditions are happening in the mental health field. As a university supervisor and former departmental clinical coordinator, I know that a portion of my efforts were directed at smoothing out conflicts between site supervisors who believe clinical work should progress their way, while the previous training of the intern was clearly in another camp. The level of unresolved conflicts between clinicians and supervisors is higher than one might expect in a field such as ours. Researchers have documented that conflicts occur all too frequently (Korinek &

Kimball, 2003; Moskowitz & Rupert, 1983; Nelson & Friedlander, 2001). This information should alarm administrators and seasoned supervisors alike, and novice clinicians and new supervisors should sit up and take notice. The continued model building along the traditional supervision format has not provided a major paradigm shift, until now with the advent of strengths-based models available for supervision too. And, to boot, some research supports the notion that not even doctoral students are adequately trained in the fine art and science of clinical supervision (Scott et al., 2000).

If these words rub you the wrong way now, I understand. Expecting a complete change in one's epistemological view is not a reasonable request or expectation on my part. I know what it is like to move from a time-honored, problem-focused worldview to one that seemed Pollyannaish and certainly not what I learned to be correct during the first 25 years of my professional life. But bear with me, and look at my facts in the next few chapters before putting this book down.

Several reasons for change come to mind from fields other than the clinical that indicate to me it is time for a change if we wish to move from simply effective clinical supervision to one where empowerment and greatness is the norm. I discuss them in the remainder of this chapter, but briefly they are *management, leadership, and organizational reasons for change,* the fact that our field is *awash in contradictions,* that our use of *best practices and who decides* is problematic, understanding the importance of *what really makes a difference* in clinical work, as well as what is *beyond clinical skills,* and finally, *a glimpse at strengths-based clinical supervision.* I begin to unpack these reasons here and return to them in several later chapters to further our understanding.

Management literature has pointed out that we live in the Information Age as highly trained and educated professionals. Many in our field, as well as those who fund us, hold on to an out-of-date paradigm of supervision and management that still holds onto an "Industrial-Age Worker" paradigm, when we have moved onto a "Know-ledge Worker" paradigm and now into an "Information Worker Age" (Drucker, 1968). Note that Drucker (1968) made this point way back in the 1960s. Despite the extremely well-trained clinicians our universities provide, we still main-tain a top-down hierarchical structure. Our stu-dents are better trained, have at their fingertips far more information and opportunities than most of their trainers did even 10 years ago, and by and large, we cull them out well, admitting the bright-est and the most educated. Highly trained people can work on their own for other reasons than the time worn carrot and stick (Florida & Goodnight, 2005). Yet, psychiatrists, many who have never had a course in psychotherapy or counseling (Breggin, 1991), supervise psychologists, who supervise licensed masters-level clinicians, and on down the historical pecking order without one single shred of evidence that their guild or educa-tion makes them better clinicians or supervisors. Supervision skills and practice in the counseling field are based on a premise that someone else needs to make certain that workers below them (clinicians who are doing the work) have some-one above them who is responsible for evaluating and correcting them, keeping them on track with the currently held "best practice" model or at least their version of it. We have a long history of hierarchical relationships in the field of mental health, at a time when hierarchy is disappearing in many enlightened fields (Friedman, 2005). In addition, our models of supervision have evolved from our models of clinical practice, filled with the medically modeled view that looks to what is wrong (problem focused) and attends to teaching or correcting the supervisee (remedial). Anyone who has practiced for a while knows that there are social workers who know more about therapy than psychiatrists and seasoned clinical counsel-ors who could teach us all a thing or two. It isn't about one field knowing more or even about seasoned professionals setting novice clinicians straight. Today's version of supervision practice is all too often nothing more than something that is tied to financial bottom lines, legal liability, and fear of law suits.

TOO MANY CONTRADICTIONS

Research has shown us that the field is full of inconsistencies and myths about what we can do. Paraprofessionals can be at least as helpful as those who are clinically trained in many clinical situations, and in fact, there is evidence that training might just be the "clinical" death null to those who have natural abilities but who seek training (Baker & Niemeyer, 1999; Berman & Norton, 1985). Add to that the fact that there are close to 400 and still counting models of counseling and psychotherapy, all more or less equal in outcome, and the field gets muddier and muddier (Smith, Glass, & Miller, 1986; Stiles, Shapiro, & Elliot, 1986). The use of Evidence Validated Therapies (EVTs) has not really furthered our field, as only easily re-searched models become the gold standard because of the ease of converting protocols into statistically significant products (Asy & Lambert, 2001). Other, less convertible models go by the wayside or are practiced almost cult-like by dedicated bands of clinicians who don't seem to worry about getting financed by managed care or who choose to fake documentation (Edwards, Chen, White, & Bradley, 2003). Seligman (2005) stated the following:

> The search for empirically validated therapies (EVT'S) has in its present form handcuffed us by focusing only on validating the specific techniques that repair damage and that map uniquely into DSM-IV categories. The parallel emphasis in man-aged care organizations on delivering only brief treatments directed solely at healing damage may rob patients of the very best weapons in the arsenal of therapy—making our patients stronger human beings. (p. 7)

The idea that one model fits all, even if it has been subjected to statistical analysis and shows promise, denies that people are different and may not all respond the same, and as the sign over Einstein's desk said, "Not everything that can be counted counts, and not everything that counts can be counted."

An interesting example of how quickly change occurs in our field is the case of Francine Shapiro's now famous Eye Movement Desensitization and Reprocessing (EMDR) for the treatment of trauma (Shapiro, 2001). While writing about EMDR for another book (Edwards & Heath, 2007), my coauthor told me, and in fact showed me, documentation from managed care pooled research that claimed there was no significant level of success using EMDR for the treatment of trauma. When I went to the EMDR website, lo and behold, it was documented that the American Psychiatric Association, the Department of Veterans Affairs, and the Department of Defense strongly recommend EMDR and gave it the highest level of recommendation for the treatment of trauma (see http://www .emdr.com). We were both surprised.

Change is inevitable! Science marches on! Models that were once seen as unquestionably true are later replaced by new "truths." Thomas Kuhn's (1970) *The Structure of Scientific Revolutions* demonstrated that paradigm shifts occur all the time in any field. These shifts convert what was once considered "normal science" to ideas that are outdated, while a "new science," beginning as an unaccepted new way forward, changes to "normal science" and then goes through the process again and again (Kuhn, 1970). Interestingly, Positive Psychology researcher and proponent Chris Peterson (2006) took issue with the use of the title "paradigm shifts," in this case, noting that Kuhn apparently suggested that psychology never had any overarching perspectives anyway and has always been up to creating new and novel ways of understanding what humans do and need. So maybe what we have going on is what country singer Vince Gill (2003) said, that we are all just looking for "the next big thing."

Our focus on "causation" is problematic and a contradiction as well. Again, beginning with the medical model, the idea of causation has been firmly planted in the heads of clinicians as well as the public as an understanding of "why" things happen. True dyed-in-the-wool systems thinking practitioners abandoned the idea of linear cause

and effect years ago, knowing that interactions and interrelationships are determined by recursive behaviors and multiple converging factors rather than a single causal factor (Edwards, Heath, & Todd, 1993; Furman & Ahola, 1988). Human systems are governed by these recursive multicausal events that influence our epistemology and behavior, rather than by singular linear causes. To understand this is to acknowledge then that any problem has multiple causes, all happening at the same time. Interestingly, Bertrand Russell (1953) asserted the following more than 45 years ago:

> The word "cause" is so inextricably bound up with misleading associations as to make its complete extrusion from the philosophical vocabulary desirable . . . the reason physics has ceased to look for causes is that, in fact, there are no such things. Law of causality . . . is a relic of a bygone age, surviving, like the monarchy, only because it is erroneously supposed to do no harm. (p. 387)

Or as I said years ago, "the discovery of 'causation' is abandoned as a relic of modernist linear thinking. Problems exist in a social context and are maintained by the manner in which all who are involved describe and view the dilemma" (Edwards, & Chen, 1999, p. 351).

But more than one supervisor has asked the question, "So why did you think that was best?" or "Why did you decide to do that?" All are looking for a single linear answer. The "how" question may be a far better one to ask, as in "How is it that you decided to choose that way of working with your clients' concerns?" This question asks for a full understanding of the process and resultant event. "Why" questions imply cause and blame, while "how" elicits a sense of curiosity and exploration of the multiplicity of thought and behavior. I think it is a more useful frame for supervision and leadership, to invite dialogue rather than other possibilities.

Finally, as Storm, Todd, Sprenkle, and Morgan (2001) echoed what Holloway and Neufeldt (1995) have put forth, it is hard to know if clinical supervision is actually effective. In the field of marriage and family therapy supervision, Storm and her colleagues noted that there is little evidence, either qualitative or quantitative, which shows that many of the field's beliefs about supervision and that it "rests mostly on faith" (Storm et al., 2001, p. 227). For clinical supervision for individual counseling, Holloway and Neufeldt (1995) stated emphatically that regardless of the research focused on what supervisees receive, it is impossible for them to "know what they need to know" (p. 211).

BEST PRACTICES: WHO DECIDES?

Because there are so many theoretical models, all of the researchers, clinicians, funding sources, and guilds are constantly trying to get it right. We have moved from the muddle of multiple untested methods that allowed clinicians to practice any old way they thought best, to an empirically tested only "paint by numbers" practice where statistics rule and guide guilds to a one model fits all practice. "Best-practices" models can still leave us in a muddle. Best practices stipulate parameters between which clinicians are required to practice and EVTs. Clinicians practice outside of these parameters and set themselves apart, risking liability, censure, and even loss of license. More problematic, best practices may lead many clinicians to falsify what they do during sessions (Braun & Cox, 2005).

Best practices hold us to standards that the leaders of our guilds and insurance companies insist are the best ways of practicing, and much like the *Diagnostic and Statistical Manual of Mental Disorders,* these theoretical truths are based on models that are made by a consensus and are socially constructed (Maddux, 2005). Best practices make no guarantees regarding a positive outcome occurring for every case. There is no assurance that a best practice model is more effective than other models; in fact, all models have been shown to be relative with respect to outcome (Luborsky, Singer, & Luborsky, 1975). Regardless, our reliance on these consensus-based truths (little t—meaning those that have

not been proven yet stand as what most believe accurate) do hold power to sway our clinical work in the direction lobbyists of special interest groups would like. And it can take the constructive critical thinking out of the client/clinician/supervisor relationship system when used exclusively for treatment conditions.

Actually, according to most business-oriented ideas, "best practices" continually evolve and should not bind to one inflexible or unchanging way of practicing. Really, best practices should commit us to a philosophy based on continuous learning, experimentation, and improvement, not a stagnant set of rules. Best practices continuously evolve as new ideas, learning, and improvement occur. Best practices do not have one template or form for everyone to follow. Best practices is a concept which holds that good process and planning is being followed in the execution of a plan and that dependencies and goals are being tracked, documented, evaluated, and refined. We as a field have been misusing the concept of best practices to suggest one best way of doing business.

The idea of "leading-edge practices" is more appropriate or at least more useful. The words "leading-edge practices" acknowledge that regardless of what some people would have us believe, there are no "single" best practices in our field. Best practices is a time bound concept and implies that we have found the "best" way to practice—static, with no reason to change in the future, and as we mentioned earlier, that has never been the case in our field. Best practices, as they are used today, are not meant to indicate that people should be inflexible or unchanging. It is meant to involve continuous improvement and change, thus a leading edge.

WHAT REALLY MAKES A DIFFERENCE?

If EVTs and best practices do not assure us of all-around success as counselors or supervisors, what should we do differently? It seems obvious that what could make fine skill-trained clinicians' more in line with what site supervisors want is not simply more case consultation, ethics, or iterations of what the current supervision literature suggests. Leading-edge, strengths-based clinical supervision is about instilling an attitude of seeing the supervisees as stakeholders in the process and helping them achieve their very best by being intentional and using strengths-based forethought.

Strengths-based clinical supervision develops personal agency and looks for what went right during supervision and clinically, with the client or supervisee. Stakeholders are encouraged to use their strengths-based work collaboratively and uniquely with their clients, practice ethically, and continue to elicit feedback from the clients they see as well as with outside supports. Supervisors and clinicians are isomorphically interconnected, with mutual recursive feedback systems operating, looking for, encouraging, and amplifying strengths and what is going well in the language system.

Support for this sort of thinking came from Miller et al. (2007) as they made the case that it isn't a top-down imposition of standardized practices that make for excellence in psychotherapy. In fact, they found that while the average clinician looks for how they have failed with their clients, the successful ones keep looking for and asking their clients what they are doing together that is helpful. They found that those who practice their craft well do so by finding their baseline of success, practicing, and seeking feedback that is then acted on. The feedback that is most important comes from their clients, and in fact, supervisors aren't even mentioned in their work. They concluded from their work that "supershrinks consistently seek client feedback about how the client feels about them, and their work together, they don't just say they do" (Miller et al., 2007, p. 34). Excellent clinicians seek feedback from their clients repeatedly—it becomes a routine part of their practice. Malcolm Gladwell's (2008) book, *Outliers,* gave us another look at this part of successful strategy. He cited research which shows statistically that success in *any* field is directly related to what he called the "10,000 hour rule." The closer people

get to that 10,000th hour of practicing their craft, the more superior are their outcomes. The Beatles playing all nighters in Germany before they ever cut a record, or Bill Gates who, at a young age, began his 10,000 hours of computer work, or the little kids in hockey leagues in Canada, who start their practices before they even enter kindergarten, are all grist for Gladwell's proposition that more is better when it comes to being really proficient.

Miller and his colleagues found that more successful clinicians divide their craft into three stages: thinking about future sessions with a client (presession), acting on what they have come up with (session), and reflecting on what they did and could improve on. As mentioned earlier, they found that top performers—those who consistently have more positive outcomes and maintain clients through the critical first few sessions—reflect on what they did during their session (performance) and identify actions and alternatives for reaching their and the clients' goals. However, they did not spend time hypothesizing about failed strategies (Miller et al., 2007).

Failures! Why do we always look for the negative rather than to strengths and possibilities? As I have said before, the supervision field we inhabit has almost always assumed a medically modeled view of the people we work with, including our supervisee, their problems, and how to fix them (Edwards & Chen, 1999).

Regardless of the successful forward steps in our field, much of the supervision is provided by persons who have not been trained or have a grand fund of experience; most have been promoted due to other factors of their employment. Rather than the doctoral-level-prepared basic supervision practitioners the literature is aimed at, most supervisors have been promoted up through the ranks with little idea that supervision has its own research base, techniques, and ideas. In addition to that, the university system can and does employ professors who come right out of their own doctoral programs, having little if any real-life experience past an all-too-brief clinical internship. They can lack depth of experience. As with clinical maturity, supervisory maturity requires many years of in-the-trenches work so that case conceptualization fits real life rather than theory; supervisors should have a large fund of clinical experience and empathy to provide their supervisees. This has significance for supervision and maintains the position for strengths-based work.

Jeffrey Zeig (1987), author of *The Evolution of Psychotherapy,* remembered a training/supervision session he had with Transactional Analyst and group therapy expert Mary Goulding:

> After finishing 20 minutes of work with the group, I turned to Mary for feedback. She said, "Jeff, these are the things that you did right." And she listed them. Then she told me, "Here are some options for things that you could do differently." She listed those. Then, she said, "All right, now you go back into the group and somebody else will be the therapist." I was shocked. Something was missing. I said, "Mary, what did I do wrong?" Mary looked at me quizzically and replied, "What do you want to know that for?" I said, "That's what my supervisors would normally have done. They tell me what I do wrong." Mary said, "It's not valuable information." When I reflected on her observation, I realized she was right! (p. 294)

Unconsciously or not, we use the medical model that looks for problems in our supervision to tell supervisees—our stakeholders in this process—what they have done wrong and how they can improve (remediate). And as Mary Goulding said, "It's not valuable information."

During the many workshops I have presented on supervisory skills, it has become clear to me that many seek training because they have been supervising for some time and feel unqualified—ungrounded. When I ask questions about their training, they are dumbfounded that there exists models and ideas that will help them be better supervisors. When asked about their own experiences with their own supervision, they are full of examples of unhelpful supervision they have had, yet they have limited examples of positive experiences. Those who have had good supervision experiences are repeatedly told by others in the class how lucky they are.

Supervisors are leaders and managers, and as such they should be prepared to work with their stakeholders in a way that helps them achieve their own goals and voice. The people we work with *are* stakeholders; they want be a part of the process, having their own ideas, and they want to advance not only their clinical skills but also their careers.

During a clinical skills workshop I was providing for a very large mental health and substance abuse treatment clinic, I was taken aback by one woman's urgent cry that all she needed from me was help in doing her interviews and paper work quicker. She was not interested in learning strengths-based treatment strategies. Later at the lunch meeting, the director of this organization gave out awards for employees who had the best records of productivity as measured by the number of clinical interviews and paperwork completed. I was dumbfounded but enlightened. Somewhere, somehow, this wonderful field that cared for those in need and provided them with understanding and empathy was choking if not dying. Yet, there were pockets of hope all over, demanding that our honorable field was deserving of much more. And yet, every crisis is an opportunity, and I finally understood what Einstein meant when he said that our theory determines what we see. A problem-focused lens as used by many clinicians and their supervisors will find a lot of problems, but so it is also true with a strengths-based lens. And the lens is always ours to choose.

Strengths-based clinical supervision, to be accepted, needs to be grounded in theory, but not in the usual modernist, deficit-based theories of our mental health fields. Theoretical signposts for strengths-based clinical supervision are based on the works of several influential and far-reaching people. From the clinical side, Albert Bandura's ideas of self-efficacy and personal agency as applied to counselor training, performance, and supervision, as well as the forethought that occurs as an element of personal agency, should be our foremost expected outcome. The constructivist and strengths-based work, such as collaborative language-based therapy (Goolishian, 1990),

Narrative Therapy (White & Epston, 1990), Solution-Focused Therapy (de Shazar, 1994), or a resiliency model (Walsh, 2006), plus Positive Psychology (Seligman, & Csikszentmihalyi, 2000) and strengths-based clinical supervision (Edwards & Chen, 1999), all add clinical strength and a framework for this model.

Current management and leadership work includes ideas regarding what motivates Information- and Knowledge-Age workers (Florida & Goodnight, 2005; Quinn, 2005), while there is a whole body of solid research to back up Tom Rath and Barry Conchie's *Strengths Based Leadership* and their StrengthsFinder 2.0 (Rath & Conchie, 2008). Organizational development research on appreciative inquiry provides strengths-based ways of reorganizing any kind of organization from a positive theory of change (Cooperrider, 2000). In addition, "value added" management and leadership ideas (Covey, 2004) about how to view our field differently have put a different spin on something that has really dragged behind in our perceptions of employees and trainees we continued to see from an Industrial Aged view (Drucker, 1968). Strengths-based clinical supervision is about good management, training, and well-run organizations. The current literature regarding how to manage well-educated and trained people is wide and vast and sets a new agenda for managing, educating, and training clinicians of any stripe.

EDUCATING ADULTS

I have mentioned, and will continue to do so throughout this book, that the majority of the literature and research on supervision have been by academics in their attempts to educate doctoral students. Let me put forth another thought about the way in which clinicians and prospective supervisors have been trained. A continual complaint that crops up from time to time is that of educational practices—those who teach and those who teach teachers. B. F. Skinner as far back as 1984, in addressing the educational crisis and proposals for school reform, then stated the following: "College teaching is the only profession for which there is no professional training. Would-be doctors go to medical schools, would-be lawyers go to law schools, and would-be engineers go to institutes of technology, but would-be college teachers just start teaching" (p. 950). I know that this has been true for many instructors in our fields for a long time. The problem becomes worse when one considers how much of our educational training is predicated on the use of adjuncts—the hiring of professionals in the field of study who may never have had a single class in how to teach. I feel fortunate to have come through a program of counselor education, where, as part of my training, I was allowed to teach, under supervision, classes in my program for those in both master's programs as well as doctoral classes. In addition, my course work in supervision included not only one semester of courses on pedagogy but a course in adult education and two supervised experiences in clinical supervision, in addition to a class I decided to take on how to supervise. Many instructors in higher education have nary had a class, let alone have been supervised. The supervision of those who are teaching as well as supervising, in many universities, is relegated to the chair of the department, in my experience; I think I have a great topic here for some research.

The concept of adult learning (Knowles, Holton, Swanson, 2005; Merriam, Caffarella, & Baumgartner, 2006), and the andragogy that is a part of it (Knowles, 1950; Knowles, 1968; Knowles, 1980; Merriam, 2001), introduce concepts regarding the training and educating of adults that add to education for adults and refute the typical training and supervision methods that have prevailed from start to hopefully this finishing touch. And although one can see education on a continuum from a pedagogy that is teacher driven to that of andragogy, which is more student or self-driven, the concepts of andragogy seem much closer to what is needed by adults, especially those who have had more experience clinically and as supervisors. Andragogy assumes, as we come to see later, that we exist in the Information Age, filled with lots of knowledge that is at our fingertips. Also, we learn because we want to and need to know, and we have motivations that are intrinsic to who we are and where we are in our lives. Knowles, Holton, and Swanson (2005) said that learning is related to our context as an adult, to the real world around us. It is important to look at our graduate students, and more importantly, those who are being supervised and their supervisors in the trenches of mental health facilities, as adult learners. Knowles et al. reiterated that our mission of training, educating, and supervising changes *because* of the stresses and context of adults who "spend at least eight hours a day working and often as many hours attending to family, household, and community concerns" (p. 61).

Andragogy as a way of thinking about adult education and learning has been cited in the literature of several other fields of study. Forrest and Peterson (2006), noting the flattening of hierarchical stances in the structures of business, have chided their own education practices, as well as put forth the notions of andragogy in business education. Stating that "Pedagogy is an archaic term that the ancient Greeks utilized to describe the education of children" (p. 131), they noted that pedagogy is about subject matter instructors attempt to impart to their students, while ignoring any and all ideas, strengths, and skills that they might currently have. On a personal note, while I was being trained in an independent training organization for family therapy by a prominent person in the field, our first class group of 10 clinical students was told that we would soon forget what we have known before and finally learn the correct way of doing family therapy. Many of us were seasoned clinicians, and I am sure I was not the only one who was put off by the arrogance of this statement. Had this person scaffolded the information, by suggesting that we were about to learn new, and perhaps more useful ideas, without bashing what we already knew, the class would have more readily taken in the information; I know I would have.

That andragogy has hit other fields in a big current way is evident by the literature. Hatcher and Cutler-White (2009), in their editorial, take

their human resource development group to task for becoming too theoretical in their training and admonish them to go back to what Knowles taught them years ago about real-world work experience and training. A bit closer to home, Jones (2005), in her editorial, suggested that those involved with the training of conflict resolution have been remise for not teaching the adult learning theories of andragogy. Noting that other fields such as "social work, business and medicine" (p. 132) have adapted their training and teaching with the ideas of andragogy, she suggested a change in practice so that those being trained can learn "real-world applications," the ability to control "what, how, why, when, and where details of their learning," and perhaps the most important when cross-culturally applying what she says to our field, "support from peers and to reduce the fear of judgment while participants are learning to apply new skills" (pp. 132–133). Even closer to home, Polloio and Macgowan (2010), in discussing the training of group work in social work education, suggested that an andragogical assumption— "that the learner is an adult, and is capable of participating in the educational process, rather than a more passive learning approach" (p. 203)— is imperative to their work. Basically, the ideas of andragogy are simple and forthright in their methods and values.

As we will see Chapter 6, it is believed that those in the Information Age—the adults we are supervising—have a different reason for their work. They are driven mostly by intrinsic motivations, because this is the field they chose to spend a great deal of effort and time with. Such is also one of the concepts of andragogy: Adults learn not because they are told to, or because they have to, as in the typical K–12 education system; their learning is for different reasons. Because they are adults, they want to know the reasons for what they are learning, and that learning has to make sense to them as Knowledge workers. In addition, the learning for adults needs to be immediately applicable to their lives in the world of work, and they need to be given credit for the bank of experiences they already have. Most of all, adults are self-directed and motivated to learn their subject on their own, and applications must fit their future or current work. Theories maybe nice, but applications are most important, and adult learners—our supervisees—need to see how what they are learning applies. In Heath and Storm's (1983) language, supervision needs to be useful to the supervisee in their applications with their clients.

In Chapter 6, we address the strengths-based makings of those larger organisms that utilize supervision strategies. But as long as we are addressing the andragogical needs of organizations, I would like to introduce a point. Organizational learning is critical to our concepts of andragogy, in that there is a synergy between what individuals learn and what the organizations put forth as important, and also recursively, what organizations learn. In citing Senge, Merriam, Caffarella, and Baumgartner quoted, "Organizations learn only through individuals who learn" (2006, p. 44). They all believed that in order for organizations to learn, the people of the organization need to shift the way they think from seeing parts to seeing the system, thus "from seeing people as helpless reactors to seeing them as active participants in their reality, from reacting to the present to creating the future" (Senge, cited in Merriam et al., 2006, p. 44). The ideas of adult learning—andragogy, if you will—assume that for adults in and of organizations, as well as the organizations themselves to continue to grow and learn, mechanisms need to be put in place and priorities prompted that allow for teams of committed employees at all levels to engage in continual learning and allow the feedback and thus the implementation of their new knowledge to the organization in order to adapt to new ever- changing challenges and ways of operating. We see in Chapter 6 how management theory and appreciative inquiry, an organizational development change process, contend these very same ideas. Organizations need to be strengths-based if they are to grow

and be vital in the workplace for their customers and constituents at all levels.

Later I begin to unpack all of the ideas discussed earlier, elaborating on these points in greater depth throughout the book. But for now, I think it is important that we look at what I found mental health agencies want from their therapists and interns (Edwards, 2001; Edwards & Pyskoty, 2004). Of less importance, but certainly supporting a move to more collaborative methods, was the interesting data regarding the types of treatment methods being used today and who is practicing them (see Table 3.1). Clearly, according to this data, there is a shift occurring by many clinicians away from the more problem-focused methods to those that emphasize collaboration and strengths.[1] Rather than seeing most of the problems human beings have as purely organic or chemical and biological, there is an emphasis on strengths and what is going well in people's lives.

Beyond Clinical Skills

My research of site supervisors, both in Illinois as a pilot study and later nationally, showed that the real need seemed to be a clinician's ability to work as a teammate (Edwards, 2001; Edwards & Pyskoty, 2004). Supervisors want clinicians who are not only skilled in counseling but who have maturity and good character. Comments from respondents ranged from "self-starters," "patience," "positive job attitude," "confident," and "good work ethic," to "ability to set boundaries," "adaptable," "good intentions," "creative," and "good self-care." Survey results stressed personal factors that indicated a mature, self-reliant, and highly capable person was what they desired. "Site Supervisors indicated that they want more than just well-trained people; they want clinicians who are of good quality, substance, integrity, and hold a positive attitude" (Edwards & Pyskoty, 2004, pp. 3–40).

---

[1]Surveys such as this one have been done before, always with evidence that the field shifts its models continually, showing a "next big deal" trend from year to year (see McKenzie, Atkinson, Quinn, & Heath, 1986, for further evidence of this point).

Table 3.1   Usage of Counseling/Psychotherapy Models

Types/Models of Counseling/ Psychotherapy	*A* Illinois N = 584 n = 186 31.84%	*B* National Aggregated Professions N = 1,660 n = 456 27.5%	*C* Professional Counseling N = 877 n = 241 27.48%	*D* Psychology N = 437 n = 94 21.51%	*E* Social Work N = 346 n = 119 34.39%
Adlerian	6	3	3	0	0
Behavioral	65	58	35	11	9
Brief Strategic	35	35	16	6	9
Client Centered	38	39	33	3	2
Cognitive	66	93	49	34	9
Family Systems	54	65	35	8	21
Jungian	1	1	0	1	0
Narrative	9	3	0	2	1
Psychodynamic	34	58	10	25	24
Reality	23	27	24	0	3
Solution Focused	82	82	51	4	25
Structural	5	3	1	0	2

Note. Table shows raw count usage of various models of counseling/psychotherapy as reported by internship sites from Illinois Counseling sites (A), aggregate from the United States (B), and by discipline in the United States (A, B, & C). Some sites indicated more than one model, thus percentages are not reported. Most all sites also report providing internship preparation for multidisciplines.

Data are from COR Grant research from a State of Illinois Survey (1999–2000) and a National Survey (2000–2001), by Dr. Jeffrey K. Edwards, Department of Counselor Education, Northeastern Illinois University, Chicago, IL 60625.

Supervisors of all the disciplines across the board—clinical professional counselors, couple and family therapists, psychologists, and social workers—all have the same desires. They are looking for maturity and team players over skilled clinicians. How then does this translate to how clinicians should be supervised? As clinical supervision is usually focused on techniques and interface issues (countertransference)—all clinically oriented matter—how does one go about increasing these human factors? Cutting edge management literature and strengths-based work provide the answer. Today's clinicians are Information Age works and have already been clinically trained exceptionally well. They may need case consultation with difficult cases on occasion, but most of all what they need are confidence and a collegial empathic supervisor who helps them to continue building their own strengths.

Because we are in the Information Age, our graduating students as well as our interns are better trained, have more information regarding appropriate treatment strategies, and have had better clinical supervision in their graduate training than ever before, in many cases having better training than their professors. Standards for every guild (clinical counselors, psychologists, social workers, etc.) are similar with respect to how we expect them to perform due to managed care policies. They have excellent university training and skill building as well as practicum and internship experiences and supervision. Yet, more is expected of them, and for the most part, they are supervised as if they know very little. I do not deny the good intentions of those who wield the power to supervise and manage their cases. However, I do know that the emphasis is most often on an outdated and pathologically oriented view of human nature that looks for problems rather than strengths and sees human beings as expendable and machine-like, operating on a level referred to as the Industrial Age (Covey, 2004; Drucker, 1968). Under this outdated model, workers are replaceable, can be controlled and suppressed (carrot stick), and their potential and creativity decreased in favor of one size fits all carbon copies (shades of early IBM!). But now, we live in the age of highly trained and competent Knowledge and Information workers, who want independence as well as an agreement to be creative. Clinicians are very creative and competent people. And the more we treat them as such the better will be the outcome for all stakeholders in the field—client, clinician, supervisors, and financiers.

When it comes to university teaching and agency leadership, we already know that site supervisors want something in addition to clinical skills. How does a university teach cooperative and team-enhancing skills? Are they really skills or are they more attitudes? I believe we need to develop a whole different set of attitudes, just as our guilds build in the need and importance of professionalization. Believe it or not, there are strengths-based ideas that can address these issues and help develop attitudes. In addition, the cost of replacing workers runs incredibly high, not only in the monetary fact agencies have in firing and then looking for a new hire as a replacement, but in human costs. How does one move on, after someone has just let them go? Strengths-based work is exactly what these new interns and employees need.

A FIRST GLIMPSE AT STRENGTHS-BASED CLINICAL SUPERVISION

Strengths-based clinical work has been around since the beginning of all of our guilds, in one way or another. There are many historical precursors such as the work of Gordon Allport (1983), Abraham Maslow (1971), Carl Rogers (1961), and Albert Bandura (1977b, 1997), from which the strengths-based orientation ideas flowed. Seligman (2002) documented how the early work of psychologists was not focused on pathology and mental illness but on curing mental illness, making the lives of people happier, fulfilling, and more productive, and identifying and nurturing children who have extremely high IQ's. Somewhere along the line, right after World War II, money from the Veterans Administration Act of 1946 provided financial aid to those who wanted to study psychology so that they may treat returning vets from the war, and the National Institute for Mental Health began to funnel finances into research grants for mental disorders; at this time any research on healthy individuals began to take a back seat. "Psychologists become almost synonymous with treating mental illness. Its historic mission of making the lives of the untroubled people more productive and fulfilling takes a back seat to healing disorders, and attempts to identify and nurture genius are all but abandoned" (Seligman, 2002, p. 19). Wellness and strengths seem to have been center stage up until the late 1940s. But each time, the homeodynamic nature of our interrelated fields would move counter to these pathologically oriented upstarts and take some of what they put forth as keepers, yet moving back to the model of medical science we know so well. No matter what the reasons, the medical model of diagnosis of deficits continues to be a force to be reckoned with, even if it makes little sense for the majority of people and supervisees we see and work with. I discuss strengths-based ideas, both in a clinical sense as well as an administrative sense, here as a taste and in Chapters 4, 5, and 6 in greater depth.

Clinical Work

In the middle to late 1980s, some of us thought a "perfect storm" of strengths-based change was coming, as several factors come together and gave us hope that the medical model might soon topple as king. Postmodernism and social constructivism came to the fields of family therapy and clinical counseling and began to spill over to the other guilds and fields in our family of helpers (Edwards & Chen, 1999; Efran, Lukens, & Lukens, 1988; Guterman, 1994; Krauth, 1995; Milne, Edwards, & Murchie, 2001). What is interesting to note is with the advent of these new models, changes in feedback, evaluation, and hierarchy also changed. Multiculturalism and cross culturalism also became an important change in the way we began to understand how we work with people (Smith, 2006), recognizing that our strengths do come from our cultural impacts. These influences are all part of the strengths-based supervision model.

Social constructivism and postmodernism.

In the middle to late 1980s, postmodernism and social constructivism was the new dog on the planet of many clinical enterprises. Most readily heralded in by the comic book hero cover of the *Family Therapy Networker* magazine, two caped superheroes announce to the world, "Holy Epistemology Reality Man! It's the constructivists and they're changing objective reality as we know it with just their minds!!" (Dale, 1988). And of course it was assumed that this would be a problem for psychotherapy, but it isn't. The concepts of postmodernism and social constructivism have been around in other fields for quite some time, but they were new to the fields of counseling and psychotherapy in the 1980s, following on the heels of a Batesonian ideology, both of which I delve into in the next chapter. This new to our field model did, however, spawn four unique new models for counseling and psychotherapy. I provide a basic unpacking here and a deeper understanding with applications of the concepts to the field of supervision in the next chapter.

Collaborative languaging systems. The first of our models is collaborative languaging systems therapy, which pays attention to ways of being collaborative with clients in their process in a respectful nonhierarchical manner. Believing that it is better to adopt a "not knowing" way of interviewing so that the client becomes the expert, not the therapist, and that language or the way we talk about problems are what makes them problems, makes this frame remarkably strengths-based (Anderson & Goolishian, 1988). Goolishian (1990) changed what therapists and supervisors do from "doing therapy or supervision" to "having a conversation *with* someone."

Solution-Focused Therapy. Also called brief solution focused therapy, this model's developers, Steven deShazar and his wife, Insoo Kim Berg, actually took the modernist, strategic family therapy MRI model and turned it on its head, by asking the question "when isn't the problem a problem?" rather than prescribing 180-degree changes. Thus they invited clients into a view of how the world could be different without the problem, as well as providing behavioral examples of how that might happen (Berg, 1994; de Shazer, 1988, 1994).

Solution focused therapists and authors Walter and Peller (1992), in making the model's premise clear to readers, reminded us that Chicago Cubs former Coach Jim Frey once told a slumping pitcher to go watch videos of himself when he was pitching really well, rather than watch hundreds of times when he did poorly, so he might "learn from his mistakes." Do you think Frey might have said that was not "valuable information"?

Narrative Therapy. One of the most written about therapy models (Nichols & Schwartz, 2001), Narrative Therapy, ensconced the field with the notions that people are not the problem, the problem is the problem, through externalizing the problem and finding examples when the person has gained control over the external problem, as well as seeing how the "problem" colonizes the person's everyday life. The stories of our lives can be filled with saturated examples of the problems in our lives, while there are also many examples of times when the problem was either "defeated" or ignored as part of the story line that gives us meaning and socially constructed views or maps of how we see ourselves (White, 2007; White & Epston, 1990). My colleague, Andy Young, after reading White's book, *Maps of Narrative Practice* (2007), came up with his own version of maps we have in our heads. He suggested that if McDonald's published all of the maps of the world, there would be notations of every McDonald's restaurant on each map, but no notations of Burger King or Wendy's (A. Young, personal communication, November, 16, 2009). The "colonization" of potential places to eat would be effected by the maps we have. So too are the views we have of ourselves, as told over and over by our families, teachers, and other significant voices in our lives. Our narratives are maps that most likely are missing lots of data, and in our field, the people we work with have data that is more often filled with failures and mistakes, rather than potentials, successes, and courageous times. The map in our head is the territory we believe, but the map is not always an accurate representation of the real territory (Korzybski, 1933).

Reflecting teams. Not so much a model of therapy as it is a method that may accompany other models, reflecting teams changed a few older ideas from the family systems models, namely the Milan Team's behind the one way mirror session breaks, and they now include the behind the mirror team, with the therapist and family in separate yet interrelated systems. The therapist and client(s) work together for about 45 minutes, while the team listens and watches, and then they switch, and the therapist and client(s) watch and listen while the team talks about them with mostly reflections of their own thoughts as well as positive connotations of the problem. This unrehearsed conversation by the team unfolds and unveils the usual chatter that occurs when colleagues watch a session from behind the mirror, so that the "client" may benefit. One of the main founders of the reflective team, Tom Andersen (1992), wondered, "Why did we hide away our deliberations about the families? Perhaps we should stay with the families and let them see and hear what we did and how we worked with the questions?" (p. 57). His own reflection is "perhaps by giving them access to our process, they would more easily find their own answers" (Andersen, 1992, p. 57). I have seen and used reflecting teams during narrative, solution focused, and collaborative language systems sessions. They work well and add an excitement, novelty, and several different positive perspectives to what the client gets out of each session. Also, colleague David Kleist from Idaho State University uses reflecting teams as a method of supervision for his interns as well as a way to increase diversity of opinion in the classes he teaches (Edwards & Kleist, 2007). I have begun using them in my own classes with interesting positive results.

Psychological thought.

From the roots of Martin Seligman's work with learned helplessness (1975) came his work on learned optimism (1991). His continued research emphases on prevention led him to believe that in addition to risk factors that were so often talked about, the need for protective factors—those conditions that work to prevent problems from occurring or reoccurring—must be ramped up in the voice of those who research, fund research, or practice prevention, calling it a subset of Positive Psychology (Seligman, 2001). The rest is history, and a whole lot of interesting supportive research followed.

Positive Psychology. Marty Seligman made it his 1998 APA presidency's crowning jewel to call the membership to begin using Positive Psychology (Seligman & Csikszentmihalyi, 2000), and so, in less than a decade, several university programs are dedicated to research and training in Positive Psychology, while the ongoing tons of research has produced solid evidence of its merits (Snyder & Lopez, 2005). My favorite Seligman quote is, "I do not believe that you should devote overly much effort to correcting your weaknesses. Rather, I believe that the highest success in living and the deepest emotional satisfaction comes from building and using your signature strengths" (Seligman, 2002, p. 13). Positive Psychology author, researcher, and teacher, Chris Peterson, using one of many interesting activities to demonstrate Positive Psychology intervention strategies, starts off his classes by asking the students to introduce themselves, by telling a story of a time in their life that shows them at their very best (Peterson, 2006). Of course, like any great professor, he tells his own story as an example. After reading this, I began to use this class opener in all of my classes, and the results were dramatic, just like Peterson suggests they might be. What is interesting to me is that students have a hard time beginning this way and need to be prepped. We are used to telling stories about our misfortunes but not about times when we were at our best. To me, this is our clinical/supervision culture in a nutshell. We are used to looking for problems but not for grace.

Living resilient systems.

Resiliency. Froma Walsh (1998) regaled the idea of resiliency, especially with families, by first utilizing the literature of child development and mental health theory and research. She stated, "This approach is based on the conviction that both individual and family strengths can be forged through collaborative efforts to deal with sudden crises or prolonged adversity" (p. 3). Walsh's work takes the large fund of resiliency literature from the child development work and converts it to the family systems model, providing the same sort of life correcting beliefs and exchanges that work so well with children.

Walsh's (1998) definition of resilience is "the capacity to rebound from adversity strengthened and more resourceful. It is an active process of endurance, self-righting, and growth in response to crisis and challenge" (p. 4). Endurance, growth, and resiliency are important characteristics in order to have the staying power needed to move through those 10,000 we talked about earlier (Gladwell, 2008). It is here that we begin to see some crossover with some of the clinically oriented fields of strengths-based ideas, as resiliency ideas begin to come together with Seligman's Positive Psychology ideas. The statistics of the past two decades of children who have come from highly dysfunctionally patterned families show that most tend to survive and also make good lives for themselves. Most of those who come from gangs, or were born to teenage moms, and experienced substance abuse or poverty experiences within their family structures, not only overcame their adversities but had good adult lives later (Benard, 1991; Werner, 1982, 1995). It seems that the protective factors that Seligman considers a part of Positive Psychology have even more of a profound effect on these children than the risk factors, leading researchers to believe that the medical model provides some of the mythology about resilient children (Smith, 2006). Smith points out that our traditional model of psychopathology leads us to a paradigm that forces us to see the glass as half empty and concludes that, "The strength perspective provides a corrective paradigm that allows psychologists to see the glass as half full rather than half empty" (p. 16). The glass as half full is an important view that supervisors must take as they work with clinicians and interns who see some of the most difficult to witness human conditions. If they are isomorphically going to help their clients change, they need the same strengths-seeking exchanges in their sessions, also.

Administrative supervision.

Organizational development. Patricia Henderson has provided us with an excellent source of understanding how to operate, manage, and supervise a counseling program. Her skills lie mainly in school counseling programs, but the work is true to all agencies and departments of human services delivery. I have no quibbles with her goals and ideas; they are geared in the right direction when she says that "the ultimate purpose of administrative supervision is to ensure delivery of the highest quality counseling services to the department's clients in alignment with the mission statement and goals of the agency by promoting the highest level of counselor professional development" (Henderson, 2009, p. 3). I believe, however, that her work and ideas are based on premises that are a bit outdated and not in line with modern-day strengths-based premises. Let me explore here, briefly, some additional and more useful ideas that align with the central concepts of this book.

Appreciative inquiry. In organizational development, David Cooperrider and others after him have brought forth a new, novel, and award-winning approach to help organizations look at themselves from a different perspective and reorganize around their strengths. Based on notions from systems thinking that a second-order change, a change in fundamental ideas, is what a real change in paradigms can bring to all organizations, appreciative inquiry (AI) looks for what is working already, much akin to the counseling and psychotherapies we mentioned earlier (Cooperrider & Srivastva, 1987). Devotees of AI, Willoughby and Samuels (2009), stated the following: "Appreciative Inquiry (AI) is a strategy for purposeful change that identifies the best of 'what is' in order to pursue dreams and possibilities of 'what could be.' It is a search for

the strengths and life-giving forces that are found within every system—those factors that hold the potential for inspired positive change" (p. 1).

Leadership.

Strengths-Based leadership. Leadership researchers Tom Rath and Barry Conchie (2008) asked the question, "What are the keys to being a more effective leader?" (p. 1). To arrive at their answer, they and other experts aligned with the Gallup organization looked at seven decades of data, finding interesting answers to their question. It turns out that the most effective leaders focus on the strengths of their employees, thus increasing their employees' engagement in the organization almost three-fourths over those who do not. One of the top executives made the point that, "If you focus on peoples' weaknesses, they lose confidence" (p. 14). They conclude from this portion of the research that it is more important to focus on our strengths, and not our weaknesses, if we want to build self-confidence (Rath & Conchie, 2008). Intriguingly, they point to solid research that shows that people with higher levels of self-confidence have a leg up on those who do not, especially in the areas of health and income, and organizations that focus on their employees' strengths reap the benefits with organizational growth potential (Rath & Conchie, 2008).

Finally, Stephen Covey (2004) summed it up what I think my job as a supervisor should be when he said the following: "Simply put—at its most elemental and practical level—leadership is communicating to people their worth and potential so clearly that they come to see it in themselves" (p. 98).

Management.

From early on in his research and writings, Peter Drucker has implored the field of management to stop looking at employees from the very ancient age of the Industrial-Age worker, where they are seen as expendable and focused on financial rewards, thus able to be manipulated by carrot and stick methods. Instead, he has suggested that what we have today is Knowledge-Age workers and Information-Age workers who know a great deal, have wonderful training, and are immersed in a time when information about everything is readily at hand and constantly changing. This changes the way employees and supervisees should be treated, as well as the manner and methods that should be employed to work with them. In addition, the literature is replete with the cost of using an Industrial Age mentality in terms of severance and retraining costs to the workforce.

The management literature is full of quality research that shows the use and encouragement of strengths produces better results, especially with creative people that are what we would now know as Information-Age workers (Florida & Goodnight, 2005; Quinn, 2005). Supervisors of both clinical work, as well as those who direct an agency, university, or other organization in our fields, would benefit greatly from the changes we explore in the next two chapters.

It is clear with the sheer numbers of strengths-based ideas that they have gained momentum and strength (pun intended) in multiple fields. What is interesting is how areas of work outside our clinical field have begun to adapt to these ideas quite readily and without the backlash of competing enterprises. All new ideas compete with "normal science" to gain acceptance. Strengths-based ideas continue to do battle for the privileged position, with the deeper pockets of the medical model that hold sway in our Western world. Homeostasis continues to exert its force with finance, power, and privilege, as there are large stakes in this game. It is sometimes a perilous, uphill, icy climb, without crampons and a belay.

The benefits of strengths-based supervision are enormous and well documented. Strengths-based supervision can help supervisees collaboratively rewrite the way they work and then isomorphically begin to use strengths with clients; students who go on to teach will include these models in their teaching, passing them on to the next generation as part of the fabric of our culture. Strengths-based clinical supervision, as with any good model, has an operating principle and an executive skill set. These are unpacked in later chapters, but for now, let me lay out the blueprints. Operating principles are cultural mores, values, or beliefs about how to behave and how to think. Operating principles can be a yardstick against which one judges his or her day-to-day living and working. Two central operating principles, working with people to elicit their strengths rather than searching for and dwelling on their weaknesses or problems, and working for personal agency—being agentic (agency building)—comprise the hub around which strengths-based clinical supervision operates.

Life can be punctuated in many ways. Our Western culture has adopted a problem-focused operating principle—30% chance of showers rather than a 70% chance of staying dry (Edwards & Heath, 2007). We talk about children that are "at risk," rather than seeing them as "at potential" (Bermeo, 2009). The problem-focused view is taken from the medically modeled view, left over from Newtonian physics that postulates that all of the universe, people included, is made up of parts that work together and when "broken" can be "fixed." Strengths-based work deconstructs that need for problem-focused theories, challenges that belief, and attends to an alternative theory or narrative, an operating principle that looks for and elicits strengths in people with whom we work. Clearly it is equally and perhaps more useful when applied to humans and their related systems. Helping the people we work with develop their own agency, their own voice in work, the ability to understand that they can succeed and have the skills to do so, is far more beneficial than to continue to attempt to correct problems. We have used the medical model as our metaphor for too long, and I believe it is time we change that metaphor.

4

STRENGTHS-BASED CLINICAL SUPERVISION PRIMER

Social Constructivism and Postmodern Influences

In this learning process we assume from the start that as long as you are breathing, there is more right with you than there is wrong . . .

—Jon Kabat-Zinn (2009, p. 2)

Froma Walsh (2003a) begins the second chapter of her groundbreaking book, *Normal Family Process,* by asserting that clinicians' work has been subjugated by the medical model, training them to look for deficits and problems. Positive Psychology founder Martin Seligman (2002) said, "I do not believe that you should devote overly much effort to correcting your weaknesses. Rather, I believe that the highest success in living and the deepest emotional satisfaction comes from building and using your signature strengths" (p. 13).

It could be argued that strengths-based counseling ideas have been around for decades (Maslow, 1971; Rogers, 1961). Maslow (1971) said, ". . . I hate the medical model that they imply because the medical model suggests that the person who comes to the counselor is a sick person, beset by disease and illness, seeking a

cure" p. 49). He goes on to talk about a process of growing that entails becoming the best one can be rather than fixing or remediating the person. Rogers (1961) also viewed the people he worked with as organic, ever changing, ever growing toward their real whole selves. He said, "It seems to me at the bottom each person is asking, 'Who am I, really? How can I get in touch with this real self, underlying all my surface behavior? How can I become myself?'" (p. 108). These are much different views than today's problem-focused view. But somewhere along the way psychiatry and the pharmaceutical industry captured and entrenched those of us in this field with a view consumed with a problem focus that some believe can be treated best by medicine and that gives limited access to talk therapy (Edwards & Heath, 2007). Yet the strengths-based models continue to push an optimistic head through the forces that wish to keep them down. The fields of human understanding have been moving from a problem and deficits focus to a strengths-based perspective, despite the continued struggles. It is most appropriate, then, that our models of supervision not just tag along but lead the way.

When I was being supervised as a supervisor of family therapy, I had to write a description of my beliefs and understanding of what makes for good supervision. Near the end, I summed up my views with a statement using an ecological metaphor, saying that my overarching belief was that I should "leave less footprints." I continue to believe that most clinicians have had excellent training and almost always err on the safe side, so that they "do no harm." We have many wonderful clinicians who are helping; but it isn't the clinicians who have a problem, it's the models of clinical training, almost all based on the medical model that looks for problems and insists that the clinician's (supervisor's) job is to remediate. Strengths-based thought provides the metatheories that shape what we do with this better model—one that doesn't leave so many footprints on the people with whom we work. It is far more respectful of their personal voices. With that in mind, let us take a look at what strengths-based work looks like.

STRENGTHS-BASED CONCEPTS

In this chapter, I address clinical supervision, as seen from the position of postmodernism and social constructionist ideas, and in Chapter 5, we look at how ideas from psychology have their own interesting strengths-based ideas. Then in Chapter 6, we turn to similar ideas that have been shaping the fields of organizational development, leadership, and management. It is my premise that supervisors are leaders and rather than being a separate part of our field, leadership within supervision is really part of a larger system. During the preview of this book by a cadre of academics, one of them wrote that she had not bothered to read the preview chapter that is about leadership and management, as she did

not teach that in any class. I believe that this sort of attitude is short sighted. As supervisors, we are seen as leaders, regardless of how we think of ourselves. Supervision requires the skills and knowledge that are discussed in Chapters 4, 5, and 6. Next, many of our former students will traverse and climb the ladder to positions where these skills and informed ideas will be useful, and as I have said many times so far, this book is for those folks who might choose to work in the trenches, rather than move on to doctoral work. As you review Chapter 6, you will find not only supporting data for the use of strengths-based ideas and techniques but confirming information that will add to your supervisory skills. So please do not skip over this chapter. As we adapt to these strengths-based concepts within the larger family of clinical disciplines, I believe it is important that our supervision also adheres to these ideas.

Smith (2006), in her article for a special issue of *The Counseling Psychologist* titled "The Strength-Based Counseling Model," pointed to seven specific professions or movements that have contributed to strengths-based foundations historically: counseling psychology, prevention research, Positive Psychology, positive youth movement, social work, solution focused therapy, and narrative therapy. Although I agree with her on many of the points she made, she has missed major components philosophically that lend the strengths-based supervision model incredible zest and solid researched legs to stand on, that being the social constructivist and postmodernist movements. Indeed, the narrative and solution-focused models are descendents of postmodern and social constructivist thought (Freedman & Combs, 1996; Walsh, 2003a). In addition, Smith folds resiliency into prevention, yet calls it a "center piece," while Walsh (1996, 2003a) has been using resiliency as a framework for clinical work for some time. Note also that there is a difference in what Smith and I call strengths-based work. I call it strengths-based, meaning that there are several coexisting interconnecting concepts, while she uses the singular form.

Any of the strengths-based models—collaborative languaging systems, solution-focused therapy, narrative therapy, reflecting teams, Positive Psychology, or resiliency—have a focus on an idiosyncratic collaboration between the clinician (supervisor) and the client (supervisee) regarding what will make life better, and an agentic perspective that facilitates instilling a belief with actions that increase clients' (supervisees') effectiveness. I present case vignettes of strengths-based work as applied to clinical supervision, with additional ideas of how to further the effect. I go over each of the models noting their underlying philosophical base, historical roots, objectives and methods, as well as application to clinical supervision. So here we go.

Social Constructivist and Postmodernist Informed Models

The first four models of strengths-based supervision—collaborative languaging systems, solution focused, narrative, and reflecting teams—all fall under the philosophical umbrella of postmodernism and social constructivism. Therefore, I think it best to try to unpack these intertwined concepts before moving into the different specific models of supervision. At this juncture, there is a division between clinical/supervisory concepts that line up under the modernist (some call it realism) frameworks and the postmodernist and social constructivist models. It is clear that many of the models in use today fall under an individual clinical and supervisory philosophy of modernism. It is equally clear that most marital and family clinical and supervisory work falls under the postmodern and social constructivist model. Although there are also crossovers, this categorization is generally accurate (Storm, Todd, Sprenkle, & Morgan, 2001). Thus, for many who practice their supervisory skills in settings where there is crossover with multiple clinicians and supervisors at work, it can seem as if they live in two distinct universes, yet we know that the world is really a multiverse after all, with multiple ways of understanding and

knowing. Nevertheless, it is important to our discussion of strengths-based supervision to understand the differences. As Becvar and Becvar understand it, when practicing from a postmodern, social constructivist position, the supervisor is not an expert but may have lots of stories in his or her head that can provide explanations and ideas for change. But they must be seen as the supervisor's stories that may or may not be helpful to the supervisee and that are shared tentatively. Unless the supervisee's client is present during supervision, all that can be known is the supervisee's story of the client's story (Becvar & Becvar, 2008). Even when listening to tapes, the tangled web of these stories is only a piece of the context that gives meaning to what is being discussed and worked on.

Postmodernism.

Postmodernism is a philosophy and a social age demarcation that literally means after modernism or modernity. One of the foremost views of postmodernism is that our own ideas about life are embedded in and by language, and they continually change with historical times. Thus, truth can be changed according to the context or cultural group defining it.

Postmodernism has had a strong foothold in literature, architecture, and the arts since the 1930s. Family therapy, counseling, and the like began to include postmodernist thought in their literature and practice in the 1980s. In art, music, and drama, there has been a turning away from older Victorian thought about how these disciplines should be defined, and a moving toward a self-reflexive, fragmented, multiple perspective and deconstructed artistic endeavor. Rather than seeming melancholy with life, it can present as life being meaningless (Klages, 2007). Quentin Tarantino movies, especially *Pulp Fiction,* with its pastiche and self-reflexivity, are considered prime examples of postmodern film. There is no central character but instead several, whose independent thick narratives are intertwined in a patchwork of meaning making that interplays with each other.

The musical *Wicked* is a postmodern deconstruction of the *Wizard of Oz* story (narrative) as told from the "wicked" witch Elphaba's narrative, demonstrating that there are always multiple understandings to stories, depending on who tells them. Elphaba has faced discrimination from the other witches because of her green skin color. By viewing the story this way, Elphaba's behavior is contextualized, and she is seen as the captivating main figure, while Glinda the good witch is viewed by Elphaba as ditzy, overexuberant, and "just . . . blond" (Schwartz, 2003). In literature, as with postmodern influenced clinical work, there is a focus on individual personal text and narrative and multiple perspectives. Skepticism of big T truths, universalism, singular causation, and rejection of the need for hierarchy in favor of laterality, are central features of postmodern thought (Lax, 1992). As it applies to clinical work, Lax makes several salient points. First, we might consider seeing the clients we work with (supervisees) as narratives in process rather than a person to be interpreted or objectified. In addition, the narrative of the client only comes about through the interaction with others, rather than as a singular entity we might call self. People's narratives are always being constructed and deconstructed as they engage in dialog with others. They are given meaning within the context they are in at the time (Lax, 1992).

Postmodernism sees meaning changing over time as new contexts and social constructs come about. Language and "truth/reality," thus meaning, although having the potential for multiple perspectives, can be colonized and marginalized by those who are in power as their views or current usages will be the ones that are privileged and presented as correct. Two examples will suffice, I hope. First, language can change in meaning; thus a chewing gum intended to help upset stomachs called Aids did quite well until the name became associated with the disease. Language creates meaning, and meaning can change context. Next, the use of talk therapy, shown time and again to be successful, has been marginalized by the medical community where primary care physicians prescribe medications rather than refer to nonmedical clinicians, and pharmaceutical companies have a vested interest in promoting medications. This is true even when medications have been shown to be less effective, maintaining the myth that they are the primary care for all psychological and emotional problems (Edwards & Heath, 2007; Kirsch, 2010). Hansen (2010) wrote that counseling and the traditional theories that have informed clinical practice have mostly come from a modernist perspective because of the overarching epistemology that was current during their development. He advocates for a serious examination and change to the postmodern perspective in the counseling fields, noting that a postmodern epistemology folds in concepts like multiculturalism because of the belief in multiple ways of being rather than a perspective of universalism (Hansen, 2010).

Critics of postmodernism have accused the movement of presenting a relativistic view of life, where meaning can be constructed in whatever way the maker sees fit—a situational ethic, if you will. The Christian Right, along with other fundamentalist groups, believes that postmodernism chips away at the Truths (big T) the group holds as dear and that moral relativism can cause the normalization of what the group considers deviant behavior. Postmodernism has also been called anti-enlightenment because the truths associated with that period of time, such as reason, empiricism, and the belief that all parts of the universe, including people, are constructed like machines with parts that can be fixed or replaced, are less ensconced with postmodern ideas (Sokal & Bricmont, 1999).

Postmodernism and social constructivism acknowledge that it is groups of people in conversation, in addition to the ways and directions in which they have these conversations, that create our reality. This creates a change in most traditional supervisory practices. As we witnessed this philosophical shift, new social constructivist models of counseling became fodder for the literature and models of therapy, and four relatively new models of therapy, initially associated with family therapy—collaborative languaging systems, solution-focused therapy, narrative therapy, and reflecting teams—became the new zeitgeist for many in our field.

Social Constructivism

Constructivism has been a philosophy of knowledge that is well over 300 years old in our Western culture and dates back 2,000 years as wisdom traditions in the East (Mahoney, 2005). The works of Kant (1724–1804), Vico (1668–1744) and Vaihinger (1852–1933) represent some of the earlier thinking on constructivism, while later ideas were illuminated by Jean Piaget, Alfred Adler, and George Kelly (Mahoney, 2005). During the early 1980s, another philosophical thread began to weave its way through the models of family therapy and counseling. Mahoney (2005) pointed out that since 1978, references in PsychLit searches of articles pertaining to constructivism have jumped exponentially. Today, and in other chapters of this book, you will see that social constructivism is important not only to clinical supervision but also to administrative and management supervision.

Norbert Wiener (1948), in his early work, Gregory Bateson (1972, 1979), Bateson and Bateson (1988), Margret Mead, Kurt Lewin, and William Ross Ashby (1952, 1956), Heinz von Foerster, (1949, 2002), Molly Harrower, and others who attended the Macy conferences during the 1940s and those who were interested in cybernetics (the use of feedback processes to effect control and learning) and the cybernetics of cybernetics, a higher level of feedback that controls the way in which the feedback processes itself, were among those developing theories during the beginning of modern-day constructivist thinking. Cybernetics is an information feedback process that provides either positive (continue doing what you are doing) or negative (stop what you are doing) feedback, regulating behavior and "appropriate" thought. Second-order cybernetics, the operations of mind (people in relationships) and feedback mechanisms set to keep systems and people on track with their

beliefs (worldviews), is central to this discussion. This concept, like epistemology, embodies the belief that we have preset ideas based on our learning and upbringing, informed by family operating principles and worldview, that are informed by culture yet potentially opened through exchanges. Bateson's earlier points were that mind could be used to describe a family's or culture's preset condition and did not solely reside within a person (Bateson, 1972). Thus, by structuring his concept of a "mind" in such a manner, he included all organisms which have a certain degree of autonomy in their own self-regulation but which have no clear boundary or outer "skin." "What is described here is something that can receive information and can, through the self-regulation or self-correction made possible by circular trains of causation, maintain the truth of certain propositions about itself" (Bateson & Bateson, 1988, p. 19).

Unconscious processes of "mind" allow certain basic premises regarding the relationship of the system to context, without critical examination, to be accepted as true (Bateson, 1972). Bateson suggested that if we were to understand and know how our perceptions were taking place, we would not believe them. Because of the fleeting time that it takes to perceive (the biological act of perception), we do believe in our perceptions, because from the time perception begins, to the time we are aware, there is a gap, ever so slight, and therefore we are always looking back in time.

Powers (1973) produced a major work on control theory using cybernetic-like principals to construct a model of brain functions using neural transmission to set up a model of a control system of living organisms. He pointed out that the nervous system's operation is analog and therefore provides a continuous representation rather than a discrete representation: "No one neural impulse has any discernable relationship to observations (objective or subjective) of behavior" (p. 21). The brain's processing of the neural transmission relies on perception as determined by a "network of contingencies" (p. 25), depending on how the brain determines what is necessary. He suggested that behavior represents a set of actions which has a specific range of characterizations by which we determine relationships or roles. Hitting a ball with a bat might be considered playing baseball, while hitting a tree with a bat would not. A certain range of behaviors constitutes what a society considers to be parenting, while behaviors outside those prescribed ranges do not. These roles are ascribed by values "that state of a controlled quantity one has accepted as good" (p. 26). The organism (and the mind) determines what is within the valued parameters that makes sense of difference.

This difference is interpreted through the neural network, by a series of loops of positive and negative feedback; positive feedback tells the neural impulses to continue firing until the input is past the receptors' setting, at which point it inhibits or stops behavior. "A perception is occurring if the neural current corresponding to that perception has a magnitude greater than zero" (Powers, 1973, p. 35). A perception is a current that is preset at some magnitude to reflect difference, as there is always neural current and input from all of the senses. Second-order perceptions arise from first-order perceptions entering and choice points depending on, not just the magnitude of the neural current, but the magnitude of some more general setting or variable " . . . temperature, for example, or pressure, rather than local flow of heat or local mechanical deformation" (Powers, 1973, p. 37). Control and perception are internal operations leading to an inevitable constructivist conclusion: "We may strongly suspect that there is a real universe out there, but our perceptions are not that universe" (Powers, 1973, p. 37). Reference conditions could be hunger, sexual desire, beliefs, personal goals, belonging, status, control, fatherhood, knowledge of how to be a teacher, or any behavior. "It is not the actual environmental situation that leads to responses, but that situation *as perceived by the organism*" [emphasis added] (p. 48). This brings us to a constructivist point of view suggesting that "what we experience are not passive reflections of reality, but active constructions by the subject" (Heylighen & Joslyn, 2001).

What we have is a self-correcting second-order cybernetic system within a system, or as Heylighen and Joslyn (2001) stated, "As quantum mechanics has taught us, observer and observed cannot be separated, and the result of observations will depend on their interaction. The observer, too, is a cybernetic system, trying to construct a model of another cybernetic system" (pp. 3–4). Or as Einstein said, "Your theory determines what you see." Put another way, we might say your family/culture/religion/nation/worldview and the language you use determines what you "see" and believe. Thus, there is no objective reality, and we have preconceived ideas about the world that are hard to shake that keep us from seeing things from other perspectives. Supervisors must understand that the observer (supervisor) is part of the system, and that together with our supervisees, we create a socially constructed reality. As the folks from the Taos Group said, "The meanings we assign to the world are not our private inventions. They do not originate in minds cut away from others. They are created within our history of relationships—from our early childhoods to our most recent conversations" (Anderson et al., 2008, p. 14). Thus, even when we probe or question how someone is making meaning of an event, feeling, or thought, we should be cognizant that "mind" has contextualized what is *in* conversation *during* conversations with others from their past or current situations and that "mind" informs us during our conversations. Mind and how it is informed is a communal process.

Newer brain science supports these ideas of constructivists. Brain researcher and psychiatrist Dan Siegel (2007) posited that we all have a "top-down" way of operating, meaning that our brains are already encoded with preset conditions or values. Siegel referenced the work of Engel, Fries, and Singer (2001; cited in Siegel, 2007) who, in discussing cognition, said that more recent research of how perception is constructed is far more active and selective. "Indeed, there is ample evidence that the processing of stimuli is controlled by top-down influences that strongly shape the intrinsic dynamics of the thalamocortical networks and constantly create predictions about forthcoming sensory events (Engle et al., cited in Siegel, 2007, p. 134). Siegel called what happens with these neurological events "enslavement," meaning that our pre-set values stop us from being truly open to input from the outside. "The ways in which our narrative function is shaped by the context of our telling (to others or ourselves) reveals a profound influence of top-down process which can obscure direct experience" (Siegel, 2007, p. 99). He said that culture is the conduit that transfers meaning to individuals and through the generations. Our narratives are a function of the shaping of prelanguage neural processes that are organized by the contexts that are prescribed by this top-down process. And although Siegel called this process by another name, it is in essence the "mind" we know of from second-order cybernetics and social construction informing us of how to narrate (give meaning) to bare awareness of our perceptions. So much of our field's focus has been on brain chemistry, and here we have strong research of the brain concurring with the work of earlier theorists (Bateson, 1972; Keeney, 1983; Powers, 1973; Watzlawick, 1984) and also with those social constructivists of today (Andersen, 1991a; Anderson & Goolishian, 1988; Gergen, 1994, 2001a, 2001b, 2006, 2009a, 2009b; McNamee & Gergen, 1991, 1999).

We hear someone talk and we make our own meaning of it influenced by preconstructed learning encoded in the brain—top-down enslaved. We are socially constructing meaning-making creatures that continue to hold on to what we believe, even in the face of new "facts" and "truths." The enslavement of our thoughts, truths, and beliefs are encoded into our minds through language; the way it is said (meta), the person that says it (authority), and the meaning we make of it (personal reediting via our own top-down processes). As you read these ideas now, you are taking them in and making your own sense of what you read according to your own present top-down narratives. If you understand these concepts and like them and agree with them, or they add to previous narratives you have, you will shake your head yes. If you understand this differently and disagree, you could shake your head and say to yourself, "Boy, that isn't the way I understand it." If you "know" something about what I am saying but have rejected it, you will most likely put the book down or throw the book at a wall, vowing to burn the book next chance you get. The crux of it all is that language becomes *the* important component of how we begin to understand (epistemology—how we know what we know) and encode our knowing.

Postmodernism tells us that our narratives are also informed by the historical context in which we are living. Rather than seeing grand narratives and truths about people's lives, postmodernism sees them as imbedded in the history of the telling and understands that who is doing the telling is equally important. For instance, take the history of the Vietnam War. Even the meaning of its name can vary due to the person doing the telling. I came upon this recently during a class I was teaching. A young Asian woman looked fascinated and excited as I talked about how the victors of wars always get to claim the "Truth" written in history books. She gleefully began to describe the "American War" during the 1960s in her country of Vietnam. "Why do you call it the Vietnam War? It was Americans who came into our country," she said.

Language maps our territory, giving us sign posts we use to describe reality. The language we use to describe people changes over time, spinning different tales about them, from problematic to heroic. Native Americans were once described with derogatory names that described their color, "red skins," and their behavior as "savages," seen by the dominate culture pejoratively, thus "enslaving" and marginalizing them by those who maintained and used this language. Today, they are called Native Americans or First Nation People. Language changes the way one perceives, the way people perceive themselves, and the way others may act toward people. Dominant groups marginalizing or colonizing language can take away a person's ability to see things without the top-down influence. Any teacher worth his or her salt can also tell stories about a child's road to a problem-saturated life, as files from early or singular experiences get passed on up from year to year, telling narratives that add to the ongoing negative evaluation of the youth. Almost all organizations have this capacity, where members tell stories (their views) about someone who disagrees with the status quo or who doesn't share the same view. These socially constructed narratives are spread throughout the organization, marginalizing and giving a negative problem-saturated story to someone who has a different, more personal story of the situation. In a similar vein, Janis (1972) conducted an extensive study of a phenomenon called Groupthink, where members of a group minimize one or more of the members' ideas, sometimes with great consequence, like during the lead-up to the 1986 destruction of the space shuttle Challenger that killed all seven of its crew. Several engineers and members of that team had critical information and doubts regarding O-ring functioning at a lower launch temperature that could have saved the mission, while others denied those facts and insisted on the launch and the ensuing tragedy. Critical to group think, or, for our purposes, how social construction can create or become problem saturated, is the way that constructed stories without base or regardless of other information can be created in good faith, ignoring more realistic alternative narratives by one or more persons or groups whose views are marginalized. Reality is not static, but it is created through language by groups of people with collaborative views, sometimes to the detriment of others.

You will remember that "the map is not the territory" in reality (Korzybski, 1933). However, it *is* the territory we keep in our heads that directs how we see ourselves and others and how our narratives guide us. As we move into the four models that use postmodernism and social constructivism as a philosophical base of understanding, it is important to note that supervisors using these models also understand that what they are doing is evolving, and therefore, these are not definitive models or ways of understanding and finding objective truths. From this position, as language is continually rehashed, it is continually

reshaping our understanding, and thus reality changes over time (Philp, Guy, & Lowe, 2007).

Collaborative languaging systems.

As collaborative languaging systems authors Harold Goolishian and Harlene Anderson (1988) tell the story, their thoughts and practice of this model came about from their work and thinking about chronic failures in their treatment process. As they struggled to understand and work with more divisive and challenging clients, such as those involved in sexual and domestic abuse, and mandated clients from adult and juvenile probation agencies, their conversations among themselves, with trainees and supervisees and others in the field, led them to question what constitutes therapy and a realm of related topics. They understood that the social group they worked with in therapy was a system of language distinguished by the way group members talked about a problem and not an arbitrary, predetermined concept such as a diagnosis.

Anderson and Goolishian (1988) agreed on several premises about human systems and their ability to work with them that I now transpose into supervisor premises from this perspective. They are in brief: Human systems use language to make meaning, and realities are constructed socially. This means that their clinical work comes together around what people believe to be the "problem" in a linguistic situation, where both the clients (supervisees) and the clinicians (supervisors) are mutually looking for ways to exchange ideas about "dissolving" the problem.

Rather than being an expert at problem solving and other typical supervisory behaviors, the role of the supervisor is of a "master conversationalist" who attempts to create space where dialogue is opened up, rather than closed down (Anderson & Goolishian, 1988). Anderson and Goolishian (1988) said, "In the therapeutic conversation, these are opportunities to initiate dialogue, and they are offered in such a way that conversation is continued rather than closed" (p. 383). Atkinson and Heath (1990), in acknowledging that the views of clinicians are their own and thus not objective, believed that clinicians should share their ideas with those with whom they work. They stated, "Second-order family therapists will recognize that their ideas and suggestions may be helpful if heard, and they will not hesitate to share them" (p. 152).

Anderson and Goolishian (1992) have several ideas they see as central to a therapeutic conversation that applies to supervision. I do believe that good supervisors are always involved in therapeutic conversations, as clinicians should be. First, from this model's ideals, supervisors maintain the dialogue and questions within the parameters of the problem being presented. Their objective is to expand the options of making new meanings for the "problem" under consideration. Supervisors must hold contradictory and multiple meanings within the conversation. Rather than a "yes, but" response, "yes, and" will expand rather than stifle options. Cooperative language is used in conversations, because preset options within the mind "can reject what is perceived as uncooperative language, yet is not used strategically, but as respectful. Using the supervisee's language helps to continue that which she or he already understands, and honors it. Supervisors are respectful and listen with a 'not knowing' mind" (p. 28). This Zen-like condition, also called a "beginners mind" (Kabat-Zinn, 2009), means to listen with no preconceived ideas, which is very difficult. Next, supervisors ask questions that also require new, more focused questions from the supervisee. Not unlike a Zen kōan, these questions are meant to be answered and informed by the views of the supervisee, and perhaps they are not to be answered by rational or logical thinking. They just are, and the answers just are, but they make sense to those involved. Finally, as was said before, rather than being an expert with knowledge of the supervisee's dilemmas, the supervisor is the one responsible for the conversational context, aware of cocreating the problem-defining space. To do this in a way as not to impose their own creations, supervisors must maintain an internal dialogue that allows for the multiple views talked about earlier, yet with a tentativeness regarding the "truth" of any and all.

Supervisors who understand and use this framework believe that their views are not better or expert with regard to their clients (supervisees). I, for instance, believe that often my supervisees have a better grasp of their clients' dilemmas than I do because they are the ones working with them. I have thoughts and ideas I may share, informed by the training and the 43 clinical years I have had, but unless I am in the room with them—over time—and have a good grasp of the client's and my supervisee's situation, my ideas are only that. But I can add to the conversation. And that is as it should be. I understand that when my supervisee and I begin to talk about cases, I am as concerned about their growth as a clinician as I am concerned about their clients. As I discussed in Chapter 1, I trust that my supervisees have already had excellent training and know a great deal about the therapeutic process. My job is to help cocreate new options with them and help add to their fund of clinical experiences. I have passed that magic 10,000 hours mentioned in Chapter 1, so I have a great deal to share. It is the supervisee who has to make the bridge between what we talk about (shared conversation in socially constructed ideas) and how his or her time is spent with clients in a shared conversation. Finally, rather than thinking about the supervision process as an opportunity to intervene and make needed changes in my supervisee's clinical work, I believe we share and cocreate a unique set of understandings that fits where the supervisee is now with the client(s) we are discussing, while understanding fully that time marches on, and the supervisee may change his or her clinical views several times over; I have—from psychodynamic to client centered, to cognitive behavioral, to problem-focused systems, and on to strengths-based systems.

Gleaning Useful Supervisory Concepts

To date, there are no publications regarding collaborative languaging systems supervision, which sort of surprised me, given the overarching use of the philosophical base in clinical work. I am truly enamored of the concept of "not knowing" as it relates to what supervisees tell us about their clients. I would think that even with the audiotapes that so many modernist supervisors believe to be important and some accreditations require, the focus would not be one of telling supervisees what they might say differently or what they are missing but rather discussing meaning and personal perspectives of the supervisees—helping them find their own "voice" and refining it. I would want to be a part of coconstructing new ways of understanding what they have been involved with during their clinical work.

I also resonate with the idea that supervision is a dialectic collaborative process, rather than an opportunity to set supervisees straight and fix their mistakes. Seeing meaning (thus reality) as being made through discussion seems a much better fit for a relational activity filled with so much potential. Supervisees, like clients, make far more progress when they are the ones who make the decisions for themselves (Lambert & Bergin, 1994). Sharing ideas with the belief that supervisees can take or leave them because they are *my* ideas or experiences that *may* or *may not* fit for their particular situation or need allows for choice and encourages supervisees to think for themselves and be responsible for outcomes and course corrections of their clinical work. There is a core of ideas from this model that is really useful, not as techniques, but as a way to think about this job of clinical supervision. The not knowing reminds me that we all have thoughts, but that they are not real, only thoughts (Kabat-Zinn, 2009). The issue of evaluation is not something that would come up in a socially constructed postmodern clinical frame (Turner & Fine, 1995).

SOLUTION-FOCUSED SUPERVISION

Using the work of the Mental Research Institute's brief therapy model as a backdrop, Steve de Shazer and Insoo Kim Berg developed Solution-Focused Therapy. Realizing that most therapy models are problem focused, de Shazer and Berg flipped the Mental Research Institute (MRI) model on its head. Rather than asking clients what their attempted solutions were and requesting that they try something completely different (a 180-degree change of behavior), their solution-focused model went straight to the heart of the matter. Based on the premise that language and attempted solutions create the context that keeps us stuck, they begin to ask the question, "When is the problem not a problem?" De Shazer's (1984) *The Death of Resistance* put forth the idea that the language we use as we talk with our clients might be important in attaining a working alliance. Also, assuming that people's problems don't always occur continuously and that there are exceptions to every problem sequence, solution-focused therapy focuses people's thoughts and behaviors on doing more of what goes well in their lives. Once upon a time, people questioned the use of solution-focused work, calling it solution forced. Early on in the model's use, it was assumed that clinicians using the model should be bold in avoiding feelings and quick to refocus clients on the exceptions when they wanted to talk about problems (Nylund & Corsiglia, 1994). Today, of course, it is one of the darlings of the managed care companies and one of the most taught and used models around (Edwards & Heath, 2007). Easy to use with clients, questions such as, "Are there times during the week when your situation is going better? What is different about those times?" and "Could you do more of that?" are the usual mode of focus with clients.

Seeing each person who presents for clinical work—clinician or supervisee—as either a customer, a complainant, or a visitor, solution-focused practitioners skirt the issue of diagnosis and lump them into categories related to their readiness and willingness for change. In our case, supervisees are our clients, the ones we are engaged to help. At any time, supervisees can be in one of these three categories. Customers are those who come to session with a ready set. They know what they want out of supervision, are not afraid to take advice, as most often ask for it, and integrate the advice we provide with their own thoughts and directions for clinical work as it fits. Complainants are just that; they complain about their agency, their clients, their workload, and their lives. Complainants should be helped to see their own locus of control over their lives and their part in relationships that are not working out to their own satisfaction. Visitors are those supervisees that come because they have the time scheduled in their calendars but may not have anything to talk about . . . they are visiting. There are specific tasks that solution-focused clinicians and supervisors have for each of these sets. A supervisee's set may be part of his or her own developmental stage or temporal; in either case, the supervisee's inability to see possible solutions that will change problematic sequences is what is most likely getting in the way of better progress. Scaling questions, such as "on a scale of 1 to 10, one being the least and ten being the most, where would you rank your 'problem' right now?" are used to gage severity or persistency. Finally, the use of the miracle question, an offshoot of Adlerian's individual psychology "question," was once a unique and carefully prescribed technique of solution-focused therapy: "If a miracle happened tonight, and you awoke to find the problem was gone, how would you be different?" But others have replaced it with "movie making" or other interesting vehicles to propel the client into a view of self without the problem hanging around (Walter & Peller, 1992). Once a supervisor understands the basics of this relatively simple model, it is quite easy to envision how one might use this with supervisees.

What is interesting but not unexpected is that a model as simple as Solution-Focused Therapy would have so few publications on Solution-Focused Supervision (SFS). There are publications spanning 17 years, starting in 1990 and ending with one published in Chinese in 2007. Wetchler (1990) suggested that supervision from a solution-focused position requires both a good grasp of what the model requires clinically, as well as an educational component. From that point on, others added to what was already put forth. For instance, Marek, Sandifer, Beach,

Coward, and Protinsky (1994) reminded us that the model of supervision centers on strengths and resources rather than deficits and problems, using what has been found to be successful solutions to the problem in the past. The cocreation of meanings or views of the situation can expand the range of alternatives available through the use of concrete behavioral goals, evaluation through scaling questions, and the questioning of supervisees to talk about life without the problem. Selekman and Todd (1995) stated that they wish to "push even further the implications of the assumptions" (p. 21). Although the use of SFS provides maximum benefits to those who are learning or currently using solution-focused therapy, they also believe it to be of benefit to those who do not. They find the use of self-disclosure regarding the supervisor's struggles with learning new models to be beneficial. They also begin to cross-pollinate their solution focus with concepts from narrative work, that is, externalization of less useful clinical behaviors: "The problem with anger in these situations is that it is controlling you rather you controlling it. So what are you going to do to stand up to anger . . ." (Selekman & Todd, 1995, p. 27). Juhnke (1996) provided us with a model for supervision of entry-level counseling students working with individuals, rather than for students of marriage and family therapy. His thesis is that solution-focused supervision can increase the level of skills and confidence of supervisees. He uses a presession questionnaire to assess where supervisees are with respect to their skills, their ability to be present, and how they can promote their own self-confidence.

Thomas (1996) believed that much like narrative and collaborative languaging systems, curiosity and respect are implicit in the model. Thomas used the themes presented by Heath and Tharp's (1991) examination of the supervisory process to understand what therapists need and want in order to demonstrate how solution-focused supervision fits. They are as follows: (a) Base relationships on mutual respect; (b) you don't have to be a guru; (c) supervise us or evaluate us, not both; (d) assume that we're competent, as we are hard enough on ourselves already; (e) tell us what we are is doing right, affirm us, empower us, and listen to us; (f) make the supervision a human experience. Thomas also reminded us that there is not an assumption of symptoms or underlying problems in Solution-Focused Therapy and that to look for cause or function of symptoms perpetuates the belief that there are such phenomena (Heath & Tharp, cited in Thomas, 1996).

Triantafillou (1997) reminded us that amplifying small changes and punctuating the exceptional behaviors of supervisees with sincere compliments is very useful. Of use are his "Guidelines for Solutions-Focused Supervision," which frame the work that is included as an appendix. Presbury, Echterling, and McKee (1999) said that solution-focused supervision can help provide an inner vision for supervisees, so that the real goal of supervision is to help them develop their own clinical identity. Noting that supervisees really want a collaborative relationship, they share Cresci's belief that the ideal relationship in supervision is more collegial, not hierarchical (Presbury, Echterling, & McKee, 1999, p. 3).

Pichot and Dolan (2003) demonstrated the successes and lessons they learned from implementing a solution-oriented model in a substance abuse treatment facility, as did Powell and Brodsky (2004). Koob (2002), using information from his dissertation work, posited that clinicians can experience burnout, which can be traced back to ineffective supervision, and more traditional supervision models have not demonstrated a solid base of supervisee self-efficacy. He pointed to his research, which showed that a solution-focused style of supervision can produce clinicians with higher levels of perceived self-efficacy, which will increase their ability to sustain a clinical profession. Trenhaile (2005) developed a solution-oriented worksheet to help students analyze their own performance. Showing the need for solution-focused supervision, Wheeler (2007) discussed a situation where the supervisor addressed a supervisee's problems in his or her clinical work and noticed that as he did so, the supervisee began to make little progress and the family also began to show signs of regressing. This led to the self-correction of the supervisor, back to solution-focused supervision.

Gleaning Useful Supervisory Concepts

The use of scaling questions is valuable when helping the supervisees place their clients' situations in a context. Futuring is a method that helps supervisees see how a change in thinking or behaving, in my opinion, is a good replacement for the solution-focused concept of the miracle question or the newer concept of movie making (Walter & Peller, 1992). Seeing supervisees as customers, complainants, or visitors has always been a useful frame for me. What it does is inform me about how I might use language to engage what some call resistance. I am aware that when I notice their difference in epistemology, I can say things to them in their own language and be patient and respectful of their own views.

The use of exceptions helps to redefine and enlarge the scope of what they are seeing and how they understand their situation. It provides alternative views of a problem and options for future work that I think is particularly useful. I like the belief that supervisees have all of the resources needed to solve their own problems, with one caveat. We all make meaning, thus learning new information from the interchange of dialogue, especially when learning something new like clinical work. It may go against the solution-focused ideal to provide alternate ideas and even to share personal stories and ideas, but sometimes supervisees want examples and a different way of thinking about a problem. To stay with a model when someone is fumbling is not, in my opinion, a good alternative when I can be part of coconstructing new pathways of clinical work. My assumption, based on over 40 years of supervising, is that supervisees take what I suggest and change it to be their own anyway. In fact, I encourage them to do so.

TWO TEACHING VIGNETTES

Sara was a bright, energetic student who very often said things that undervalued her. Although her papers were always done on time, with good solid research and writing, she never seemed to go the extra mile, and during group supervision she lacked the same eagerness of expression as her student colleague when we talked about cases. One day during individual supervision, I asked her if she would present a particularly interesting case we had been discussing in individual supervision, the next time we had group supervision. She paled and said that her cases were not as important or interesting as the others. She was a midlevel manager in a rehabilitation center for the developmentally challenged where she also was doing her internship, and she was quite good at what she did, according to her immediate administrator and supervisor.

"I'm really curious why you might say that, Sara. Are there ever times when you feel like your work and your training are really useful to those you are serving?" I asked. She answered that indeed she did think her work was very important, and she began a long, meaning-filled description of how she had learned to be so good at it. It turned out she was the only one in her family that had a good relationship with her middle brother who was developmentally challenged. In her family, two other brothers had excelled at math and science, as did her mother and father, and both older brothers went off to their parents' alma mater, a prestigious east coast university. Sara went to a smaller Midwestern university and was considered the caretaker of her challenged brother. I asked how she was able to do that, given that she thought her brothers were so much smarter. "Well," she said, "I guess I have more social intelligence than they do." We both agreed that she was different from her brothers and family for a good reason and that she was in the right field of study and work.

It was no surprise to me that her input in group supervision increased, as did her demeanor. It seemed to me that her efficacy was raised several notches also. Solution-focused ideas along with coconstructed meaning making during supervision provided a way to increase her level of confidence in her work and hopefully in her life.

While supervising Amy, a new, young supervisee who didn't have much confidence in her ability, all of my compliments seemed to fall on deaf ears. She was discussing a 16-year-old girl, who came of her own volition, and related well to my 20-something student. After punctuating several instances of what I thought was very good clinical work, and complimenting her ability to form a relationship with this young client, she finally said to me, "Oh, that's just all that positive stuff you are using." I had to reaffirm that my compliments were sincere and I wouldn't say so if I didn't mean it. She took that well, but there can be a tendency for students who are learning about strengths-based work to assume that they are techniques and strategies, rather than sincere positive comments.

Narrative Supervision

Narrative therapy stems from the work of Australian Michael White and colleague David Epston from New Zealand. White, who had a bachelor's degree in social work from the University of South Australia and an honorary doctorate from John F. Kennedy University, first came to major prominence after he wrote an article for *Journal of Family Systems Medicine* in 1984 called "Pseudo-Encopresis: From Avalanche to Victory, From Vicious to Virtuous Cycles" (White, 1984). Here he used second-order cybernetics to explain a unique treatment for a serious condition of children. It is interesting to note that White made it a point to call his article that was published in a medical journal "Pseudo-Encopresis," thus avoiding an affront on the medical community who firmly believe the condition to be biological.

His method of work was to externalize the problem so that the person involved with the treatment could get a hold on it and take steps to defeat the problem. His externalization in the case he presented took the form of "Sneaky Poo and Sneaky Pee," a frame children readily understood and embraced. He asked questions regarding how the problem (Sneaky Poo or Pee) had forced the clients into a situation where the child believed there were no alternatives to the problematic behavior. He would then ask questions regarding times the child had overcome this Sneaky Poo and even defeated it. They would then figure out ways that they could continue to put down this rapscallion, such as running faster to the bathroom than the child could. They also included the parents and rest of the family in the child's efforts, so that they became victorious in their defeating cycles. Thus began a technique, and to the social constructivist informed narrative therapists, an attitude, about problem construction and treatment (Whiting, 2007). The new treatment cry from narrative therapists was that people are not the problem, but the problem is the problem. But that was not the end point of narrative therapy's ideals and goals, and a host of novel jargon ways of describing their techniques and attitudes became commonplace, if not perplexing to those outside the circle.

Language again in this model is an important part of the narrative movement, in that in keeping with the social constructivist model, reality is understood to be constructed by the interactive dialogue of people and the words we use. Freedman and Combs (1996) demonstrated how the simple act of changing a word from an adjective to a noun, for example from "People say I am always angry," to "Anger gets the best of me," allows the state of anger to be externalized. By externalizing the problem, those who come for sessions can understand how someone else, or their culture, family, workgroup, and even place of worship, contributes to their socially constructed view of who they are, and therefore it can give them options to fight against those who would seek to define them. There is a heavy influence of social justice, ethics, and personal narratives because majority groups can attempt to position the labels of who or what people are thought to be, thus capturing and colonizing personal self-definitions. The question is always, who makes the rules or assessments, and how has it come about that they get that sort of power over others?

It is interesting to note that of the many articles written about narrative supervision, some are written as generalists—narrative supervision for the masses—while the others are written as supervision for narrative therapists (see, e.g., Carlson & Erickson, 2001). I guess there is a difference, and I will try to make my own meaning out of what comes next. I was reminded of how I first felt when I began to see problems as being imbedded in systems instead of seeing them as personal problems and then later as being socially constructed. It is disconcerting for sure. Narrative supervisor Jason Whiting said it this way: "I have felt like a dog chasing its tail, skeptical about all-encompassing stories about what supervision is, yet desiring clear ideas to guide my practice" (as cited in Behan, 2003, p. 29). I think I know what he means . . . sometimes.

Whiting (2007) suggested that when clinicians present a case that seems hopeless as described in pathological terms, the supervisor can resist the way the case is presented and help to expand the story. This would be thickening the description to include alternatives and a more complete story line, so that the clinician can begin to restory the version with these possible alternatives of richer descriptions. Using externalization, supervisors might also help supervisees (stakeholder) talk about and experience how the power of their culture has captivated and constituted their worldview, to the point where a person's subjective experiences are part of the fabric of their reality. This has political ramifications and affects those who are in the minority in a particular discourse or story, because it can marginalize their own subjective story (Neal, 1996).

Narrative clinicians and supervisors see the use of supportive groups as key to making new meanings and perhaps solidifying new socially constructed views of those with whom they work. Carlson and Erickson (2001) discussed their use of what they called "fostering communities of concern" (p. 208). Their point was that during trainings of a new way of counseling, and sometimes a foreign way of thinking, it is important to develop these communities so that there is a supportive environment that can hear their voices and personal stories. This is an offshoot, for a narrative therapist, of the many community groups that help in the reauthoring of shared meaning for a person in the group so that it is performed (behavior) and becomes real and understood. These witnessing groups have been used by narrative therapists for all sorts of retelling and reauthoring of personal stories (see, e.g., Reynolds, 2002).

Narrative supervision is more an attitude than a method, according to those who practice it (Whiting, 2007); it is the reauthoring of supervisees' stories from experiencing unexpected difficulties with clients to becoming victorious and strong as a clinician resonates with me as being from a strengths-based perspective. In addition, the role of expert that is so much a part of modernist supervision is abandoned, and instead the attitude of being curious about intentions in the supervisory sessions, or expectations

for the client's outcomes, rather than making pronouncements, is intended to provoke thought rather than create insecurities (Whiting, 2007). A narrative clinician would most likely never talk about diagnosis or other like discourse, preferring to discuss multiple perspectives and preferred outcomes instead.

One of the things that kind of itches my sensibility is the way narrative therapists try really hard not to privilege specific language but have their own vernacular that is hard for others to relate to. "Privileging," "situating," "marginalizing," "colonizing," "externalizing," and "deconstructing" all have a privileged sound to me, the language of those who speak "narrativeese." Preferred outcomes is certainly a strengths-based idea, and we see later in Chapter 5 how a group in the leadership and organizational development fields uses the same ideas but with different, easier to understand language. What got me thinking about the dichotomous nature of narrative supervisors and clinicians was an article by Carlson and Erickson (2001) called, "Honoring and Privileging Personal Experience and Knowledge: Ideas for a Narrative Therapy Approach to the Training and Supervision of New Therapists." The key concepts from this article are all about honoring personal experiences and then anchoring this with the following quote from Michael White regarding more traditional supervision: ". . . a culture that produces particular, highly specialized, and formal knowledges that constitute systems for the analysis of persons' expressions of life, which are constructed in terms of behaviors" (White, 1997, cited in Carlson & Erickson, 2001, p. 202). They then begin to use a non "average Jane" narrative jargon that one can only understand from further exploration and adaptation to the narrative way.

Gleaning Useful Supervisory Concepts

Thinking about people as stories that have been told and internalized, rather than as people with diseases or conditions, is a more useful concept as we work with supervisees. The way we make meaning of events and the people in our lives is a lived and shared experience and has impact on those we serve. Reauthoring supervisees' lives is an ongoing process of coauthoring and helping shape their forward direction. I like much of what narrative supervision does. I do prefer the concept of reediting to reauthoring or restorying, as it also includes the supervisor in the mix as understood by social constructionists. It is through discussion with other individuals, past or present, that we begin to thicken, try out, and retell our stories. The use of supportive groups or "communities of concern" (Carlson & Erickson, 2001) is extremely useful because it gives voice to the supervisees, while their colleagues stand ready to witness and testify together to the challenges, growth, and strengths they all have. They also begin to live out their reedited narrative as more confident clinicians. During the 20-plus years I have taught clinical internships, I have used the power of an intentional community group that stands ready to witness the struggles and the successes they all have experienced. During those 20-plus years, several of them have remained friends and colleagues even at a great distance. E-mails appear every so often to ask the question, "Hey guys, let's do check in. How are you guys?" That says it all to me.

I connect narrative supervision (therapy) with the Pygmalion effect, which has been demonstrated successfully both for organizations (Cooperrider, 2000) and human interaction in the classroom (Rosenthal, 2002). That is, the way individuals make meaning of those they interact with has influence with respect to positive or negative outcomes. Evidence shows that educators who have positively constructed views of their students have more successful students, and leaders that have positive views of their organizations have successful outcomes within that realm (Cooperrider, 2000; Rosenthal, 2002). This sounds like strengths-based saturated stories to me. Our socially constructed realities have an effect on those with whom we interact, a phenomenon that is most certainly useful in supervision and direct clinical work. The combination of narrative supervision and clinical work, for all its privileged jargon, has the right idea.

TEACHING VIGNETTE

Hanna was a second semester intern in our Community Counseling Program, doing her clinical work at an agency for the severely mentally ill. One of her clients, Tom, was a young man in his mid-20s with a diagnosis of schizophrenia. His medication was always an issue, and although he was living in a Self-Contained Independent Living Arrangement (SCILA), he continued to become more and more verbally abusive and hostile in his work with Hanna. Hanna was good natured and had formed a good relationship with Tom, and as part of their weekly work, she took him on public transportation to get groceries and attend to other daily living tasks. Hanna had talked in supervision about the steps she had taken to help Tom move from being a young man who did not do much for himself to one who now could, with help, shop, figure out living needs, make lists of what he would need from stores, and budget for the purchases. She also reported that during the 12 weeks she had been working with Tom, he became more dependent on her, wanting more and more time and sessions, which Hanna did not provide as it was not contracted for in his service plan. It was evident that this relationship was important to both Hanna and Tom, but for different reasons, and Tom's way of dealing with the limits set was to become verbally angry with Hanna.

Hanna, at one point, told her site supervisor that Tom was becoming more hostile and that she wondered what to do. Her supervisor, out of her own frustration and a desire to protect Hanna, changed Hanna's assignment and removed her from further work with Tom, giving her a new client that was a higher functioning female.

By the time I heard about this, a week had already passed, and Hanna was very unhappy about the new arrangements. As she talked about the situation during group supervision, she began to cry softly and said that nothing about this situation was fair, and from her point of view, she wished her supervisor had not made such an arbitrary decision without her input. I asked her how she experienced the situation as she had described it—how was she ascribing meaning to the event. Then the tears flowed, as she said she felt like a failure, and that all the long weeks with this client seemed to be for naught. My concern was mostly for Hanna and her personal agency at this point, so I asked if she could think of alternative ways of, first having a talk with her site supervisor that might make space for an alternative ending to this client relationship, and second, if she had thought of alternative ways of thinking about what had just happened. She said that the first point was out of the question already; the termination of this relationship was taken care of by her supervisor, who had called Tom and the staff that worked with Tom, but she had learned that her voice was important to her, that her opinion should have been taken into consideration, and that in the future she would speak her piece, regardless. I asked her that now given how it had been handled, what did she think she will tell herself? She quickly answered as follows: "When this internship is over, and I have some years under my belt, I know that I can work well with difficult clients, and I am going to be one helluva clinician."

Her chums in the "intentional support group," aka, group supervision class, then provided her with many examples of her strength and growth as a clinician. Hanna smiled.

Hanna's experience is somewhat atypical for the sites at which we have students, and I am sure that her supervisor's concerns were more about liability than Hanna's learning. Still, narrative and social constructivist thinking, and really common sense, all have the possibilities of multiple endings that could be coconstructed. Hanna's voice, and the marginalizing of it, had repercussions for a client also, as the systems' problem construct enlarges. How does Tom make meaning of this situation? How does the removal of Hanna without a chance to talk and make sense of it all affect his life in the future? How does the change of assignments construct meaning for the site supervisor? Hanna's tenacity and ability to move on regardless of the situation shows strength and resiliency and an alternative way of working that has more opportunity and potential for her growth than the way it was left at her agency. Our "voice"—the ability to speak our mind—is important to our belief in our selves.

Some may wonder if this supervision had anything to do with the client, Tom. Well, yes and no. Let me give you my thinking. As a university supervisor in a big city, I do not believe that I have the right to change the way a site operates, especially for a onetime event. In supervising students and postgraduates, I have experienced clinical supervisors who are absolutely wonderful and a few who don't get it, from my perspective. However, I don't believe that my intervention into a site's business is appropriate, unless I am asked or if there is a serious ethical issue involved. There are several other avenues of intervention that I would pursue, like having the student discuss her concerns first, all the way up to my talking with agency personnel. It is a continuum, and after the fact in a situation where the supervisor is doing what could be construed as protecting both intern and client, I do not think it appropriate. Of course, at our university, this sort of information is logged and documented for the next round of interns, and it also informs me what our next round of interns may be up against at that site. But negotiating the vagaries of highly competitive sites in a large metropolitan city is interesting. The fact that there are too many universities training too many clinicians is a problem, and one that we will have to tackle eventually. There are many Toms out there, and if I can help Hanna understand to have her own voice—her growing self-efficacy as a clinician—then I believe I have done my job.

REFLECTING TEAM SUPERVISION

I have had the privilege of meeting, watching, and participating with the master of reflecting teams, Tom Andersen from Norway, while I was in my doctoral program during the late 1980s. The usefulness of the reflecting team is that, as Andersen understands it, reflecting teams level the playing field so that clients can actually hear what a group of other clinicians has to say about them (1991a, 1991b). In our case of supervision, supervisors and supervisees can hear what a group of clinicians and clinicians in training has to say about their work. Actually some of the collaborative language folks, those who first invented the reflecting team process, are concerned that clients are often not really "heard because therapists are doing therapy *to* them rather than *with* them" (Nichols, 2009, p. 231). Reflecting teams replaced the brief strategic model's use of a team session break, where

around the midpoint of the clinician interview those observers behind the mirror would consult with the clinician alone to either provide feedback or an invariant prescription to the client(s) (Selvini Palazzoli, 1986). Andersen began to experiment with the use of what he called reflecting teams as a method of opening up the space between clients and clinicians, to empower the voice and views of the clients with which they consulted (Andersen, 1991a, 1991b). The team's job was to watch the therapeutic system (clients and clinician) for a time and then to comment on what team members "saw" using collaborative, supportive, open, and positively connoted language. The purpose was to be true to the social constructivist ideas that provided the philosophical stance they wanted to provide. After the team, usually three or four clinicians, had observed the therapeutic system, it would then provide reflections regarding what the clinicians had just witnessed. These reflections were in keeping with postmodern, social constructivist thinking, and they were collaborative, strengths-based, and from multiple perspectives (Brownlee & McKenna, 2009). Then the therapeutic system would turn toward the clinicians themselves, and having been invited to discuss what they had just observed, they would comment on and punctuate what they found useful and sometimes not useful.

The jury is still out on the usefulness of reflecting teams for clinical use, because some research has shown positive effects (Cox, Banez, Haley, & Mostade, 2003; Janowsky, Dickerson, & Zimmerman, 1995; Smith, Jenkins, & Sells, 1995), while other research has shown negative effects (Griffith et al., 1992; Lax, 1995; Lever & Gmeiner, 2000; Young et al., 1997). However, most outcome studies have indicated satisfaction from clients who were involved with reflecting teams (Brownlee & McKenna, 2009). Although these studies were for clinical applications, the use for training and supervision is positive. Monk and Winsland (2000) presented a reflecting team model for counselor education internships by applying the concepts in the early training of students during their skills classes. The team is rotated around so that all participants including the instructor can get a turn. The job of the team is to expand on the interview with personal reflections and to help in developing the students' listening skills. Lebensohn-Chialvo, Crago, and Shisslak (2000) described the use of reflecting teams for the training of family practice residents. Their work included a longitudinal research with a small sample (18) of residents for the purpose of teaching listening and interviewing skills, systemic-oriented psychosocial interventions, and behavioral consultations. Stakeholders indicated that they found the reflecting team to be a useful method for training. Finally, Fine (2003) gave an interesting perspective regarding his concerns of using the reflecting team in academic settings by making the fine distinction between "power with and power over" in reflecting team training and supervision. Using the constructs of Bishop (2000) and Starhawk (1987), Fine applied the concepts of "power with," where power is shared equally among equals, and "power over," where the use of power is to be competitive and dominate others. Fine's concern was that in a training context, such as in the use of reflecting teams, the natural inclination is to be competitive. This is contrary to the intent of a reflecting team's purpose of providing multiple perspectives, collaborative

intents, and spontaneity (Fine, 2003). This has not been my experience, however.

Gleaning Useful Supervisory Concepts

My own experience with reflecting teams has been very positive, and I really like the idea of expanding the possibilities that constrict and give tunnel vision to clients. Multiple perspectives given by other clinicians state loud and clear to both clients and students that there is not one right answer to people's dilemmas. In addition, multiple perspectives demonstrate that we do not all think alike, and we all have various ideas that can have a grand range of possibilities. Reflecting teams help supervisees begin to see the usefulness of using strengths-based language that can be spoken in normal language. On the other hand, I have seen students become confused with the entire vernacular and characteristic words clinicians and supervisors use to hide behind in order to sound proficient, rather than speaking the language that comes naturally.

Using teams in supervision groups demonstrates to the members that there are multiple ways of understanding and practicing clinically, and when this is done with skill and practice, it can help those who are being reflected on feel really heard and understood.

TEACHING VIGNETTE

During a training I recently gave demonstrating strengths-based supervision for a recertification of AAMFT approved supervisors, I used a reflecting team. As I worked with one of the attendees for a brief time, she began to talk about her concerns with a couple with whom she was working on sexual issues and her frustration with feeling as if she did not know enough yet to move them forward. My strengths-based supervision worked to help her develop some agency, but it was not until the team rolled out their reflections and I processed the supervisee's experience that she stated with great awe and respect, "I felt really heard and validated from the comments of the team! This was so helpful. This was great."

A Glasnost Look at Postmodern/ Social Constructivist Supervision

Early in my doctoral training, when I studied and trained to become an AAMFT Approved Supervisor Designee (ASD), I all but abandoned my training from several years earlier while at the Family Institute of Chicago, where I was taught a problem-focused systems therapy model (Pinsof, 1995). My two astute and inform- ing AAMFT trainers saw a glimmer of interest and hope in my eye whenever we talked about constructivism and postmodernism, and yet they also worried about the newer models that fell within this category, as I remember it. Narrative, solution-focused, and collaborative languaging therapies were coming into the fold, and I too worried that these methods would dilute, or worse yet, manualize the purity of an idea that changed my life. As a problem focus dropped away for me, and a magical view of life where possibilities were not only envisioned but could become reality developed, I learned the simplistic notion that therapists' words and their thorough involvement with clients could change lives; they did mine. My personal agency grew, and as I willingly took those steps to act as if I was competent, I became what I wanted to be. Although I learned the offshoot models well enough to teach them in classes and to explain or demonstrate them with enough knowledge that students became drawn to them, I still was never a purist of any of them. Instead, I began to see ways that I might act in a manner that cocre- ated the potential for change in most of those with whom I worked. It should be apparent throughout the discussions of these models that many writers have suggested that clinicians should see these as ways of understanding and being—an attitude of life rather than as methods or techniques. I agree. And so I have adopted their ideas as ways of understanding. I come back to this again at the end of this book. Unlike the many models that inform individual counsel- ing, or even family counseling, I really believe that our old-fashioned problem-focused way of thinking about people and ourselves—and our supervising of clinicians—is informed by a broken view of human nature.

TWO TEACHING VIGNETTES

Anna and Susan were two student interns (not at the same time) who informed me that they had experienced serious depression in the past and were currently on medication. With both of them I noted that they were working with clients who had a similar diagnosis and that they had a keen sense of wanting to help their clients manage their "depression." I began talking with them about maps and used the notions that Andy Young had taught me. If you remember from Chapter 3, Andy suggested that if the McDonald's company was in charge of the map making for the entire world, it might place McDonald's restaurants exclusively on all the maps it made, to the exclusion of other restaurants. He went on to say that, narratively, that is how we construct our own internal maps about ourselves; we pay more attention to the stuff we have done wrong and not enough attention to the really good stuff we do or even to the everyday stuff. Our map, like that McDonald's might con- struct, is not really an accurate representation of where to go for a good meal, and our own internal maps do not represent us well either, failing to show the times we succeeded, did well, or behaved rather kindly and graciously (Andy Young, personal communication, November 16, 2009).

Now, I am always a bit skeptical about the way the industry, media, and the public at large throw around the "depression" label. In fact, I know all too many clinicians who are thoroughly indoctrinated with the medical model usage of depression. Too many other factors show that not all people who are seriously sad have clinical, chemically involved depression (Seligman, 1975). As I talked with these two women, at different times, about the "McDonald's" version of a map and how that is like humans who have their own maps and unthickened spaces of victorious times, they both began taking lots of notes on what I was saying. I thought it curious a few years ago, when Anna began her note taking, but when Susan repeated the scene years later, I began to reflect on the concept of how isomorphs are repeated patterns in interconnected systems. When the concept is used in supervision and training, it means that two interconnected systems have components, or in this case, minds that are reflected and almost identical in all parts of the system (Liddle & Saba, 1983). As I reflected also on the less problem-saturated idea of maps, I also assumed that both of these women were connecting with my thoughts about depression and would connect with their clients in their own idiosyncratic way, using the concept of maps as they saw usefulness for their clients. The meaning making will be "transferred," rehashed, remembered, and reconstructed, as Anderson et al. (2008) suggested, occurring along a continuum from the volume of notes they both took, to their discussions elsewhere, perhaps making a new difference that will make a difference for all.

Rita was a master's degree student in our family program. She had been a midlevel manager in a resident center for severely mentally ill patients. She had many years of experience and was interning at her job where she needed to add components of counseling activities she did not usually do during her customary workday. Doing family work with the severely mentally ill at her site was not a typical treatment method, but she dove right in, working with the administration to drum up clients. She also had an "old-timer's mind" rather than a "beginner's mind" (Kabat-Zinn, 2009, p. 35), which can present challenges to some supervisors. Old-timers have been around for some time, practicing in a different way than what we may be trying to teach them. In Rita's case, she had been a bachelor's-level mental health aide who had learned some very good techniques and had a great attitude for the work. She was, however, in our family program, which required her to master some newer ideas, like strengths-based work. And although she may have gathered the educational book learning, when it came to application, her problem-focused "old-timer's mind" sometimes got in the way. She needed an epistemological shift.

As she began to discuss a case she had questions about, the situation had similar dynamics to circumstances that longtime couples researcher and clinician, John Gottman, discussed in his articles and books. There was one in particular I knew she had read the previous year (Gottman & Silver, 2000). She described a couple's problem involving one partner who was pushing for more discussion and conclusion while the other partner was shutting down, being perceived as stonewalling the partner. In reality, according to Gottman's research, the partner

(Continued)

(Continued)

is having a physical meltdown as recorded on sophisticated physical monitoring. Rita called it a repair attempt, which was not accurate, but I seized on the moment to congratulate her on remembering the Gottman sequence she had studied at least a year earlier. She smiled as I praised her, and then we began to discuss what Gottman might do in this situation. I saw no need to correct the name of the technique at this point but took the time to congratulate her on remembering some hours' worth of discussion in a sea of other often conflicting, and as yet to be practiced, techniques. She was now fully involved with me as her supervisor, knowing that I was on her side and was not there to criticize, only to help. She jotted down ideas as we brainstormed, coconstructed, and applied more ideas to her knowledge of the severely mentally ill population with which she worked and our combined knowledge of Gottman's work. Later on during supervision, we discussed the usual concepts of repair attempts and gave it back its proper context, all without having to embarrass her during our first supervision session. There is a time and a place for everything. Rita saved face, and the narrative of herself remained intact.

This completes the first part of fully appreciating and understanding strengths-based clinical supervision as seen through the lens of and informed by social constructivism and postmodern thought. Chapter 5 takes a look at those ideas from psychology that have moved the dialogue and thought forward in a strengths-based manner. The concepts of negating the completeness of the medically oriented, problem-focused model have clear parallel roots in the field of traditional psychological thought and theory.

5

STRENGTHS-BASED CLINICAL SUPERVISION PRIMER

From the Roots of Psychology

Many of our fears are tissue paper thin, and a single courageous step would carry us clear through them.

—Brendan Francis Behan (1923–1964)

POSITIVE PSYCHOLOGY

There are many historic leaders of Positive Psychology such as Abraham Maslow, Carl Rogers, and Albert Bandura, and psychology's emphasis on wellness and strengths seemed to have been center stage up until the late 1940s, when the emphasis shifted to the treatment of "diseases" during World War II, as veterans came back from the war, needing attention. Positive Psychology, as we know it today, was first mentioned in former APA president, Martin E. P. Seligman's, inaugural address (1998). Later Seligman and colleague Csikszentmihalyi wrote an article in the *American Psychologist* called "Positive Psychology: An Introduction" (2000). Thus began the modern-day movement of Positive Psychology.

Positive Psychology Premises

A strengths-based strategy, Positive Psychology is also a scientific study that looks at what goes right in life (Peterson, 2006), as well as a specific protocol for Positive Psychotherapy (Seligman, Rashid, & Parks, 2006). Like some of the other strengths-based models, Positive Psychology challenges the medical model as the only manner to work with mental health issues. But unlike the other strengths-based models, it is not a treatment modality as much as it is a prevention model and a series of well-researched protocols that work to increase the factors associated with happiness and an authentic life. That there has not been an accompanying Positive Psychology supervision will undoubtedly be short lived, and I will give it a beginning try here. As one of the creative researchers and authors of Positive Psychology, Chris Peterson informed me that there is no direct supervision process that is the result of the Positive Psychology movement. He said that it "can inform goals (expanding them), provide assessment beyond the zero point, and suggest some strategies and techniques" (C. Peterson, personal communication, March 1, 2010).

The roots of modern day Positive Psychology began from Seligman's work on optimism, starting with his efforts to understand depression. Seligman's early work on learned helplessness (Seligman, 1975) stemmed from his interest in depression, and it is highly regarded in the profession. It is the basis of a psychological theory that demonstrates how one's perceived inability to control the outcome of a bad situation can lead to the mental illness called clinical depression. Seligman later decided that if helplessness (and thus depression) could be a learned phenomena, one could also learn to be optimistic (Seligman, 1991, 1996), and his book is filled with evidence regarding how optimistic people, as opposed to pessimistic people, have developed the ability to have better, longer, and more successful lives. His call for a positive psychology (Seligman & Csikszentmihalyi, 2000) was followed by an article in *Prevention and Treatment* where he took to task the National Advisory Mental Health Council's report on prevention for its continued overemphasis on the disease model and a lack of commitment to protective factors, which he named a "subset of what I call positive psychology" (Seligman, 2001, p. 2). Next Seligman published his book, *Authentic Happiness: Using the New Positive Psychology to Realize Your Potential for Lasting Fulfillment* (Seligman, 2002), demonstrating the power of happiness along with the growing research on what effects happiness has on people. This heralded a robust gathering of like-minded researchers who were tired of the medical model as the only way to understand and treat the growing list of *Diagnostic and Statistical Manual of Mental Disorders* (DSM) categorizations (Maddux, 2005) and the status quo of a medical model for understanding human beings (Keys & Lopez, 2005; Wright & Lopez, 2005). A growing list of research efforts aimed at improving human beings began to broaden, as this hearty band began to take back what had been a large part of psychology's original aims of making the lives of people happier, fulfilling, and more productive (Seligman, Parks, & Steen 2004).

Positive Psychology is about living life fully with a good deal of happiness; when it is engaged in human living, Positive Psychology can move mountains of depression, anxiety, alienation, and despair. Knowing that happiness is a subjective phenomenon that has been discussed in many contexts, Positive Psychology proposes to scientifically investigate the components of happiness and what contributes to those components (Seligman et al., 2004). These components are a pleasant life, an engaged life, and a meaningful life. We can, it turns out, increase the pleasantness of our life (positive emotions) through a series of activities (interventions), such as working to recognize and increase our gratitude for those in our life who have been kind or helpful and by entertaining forgiveness for those who have done us harm. The pathways are, however, limited (Seligman et al., 2004). Another path to happiness is through gratifying activities, such as engaging in work we like, or in discussions with others about things that matter to us, or involving ourselves in activities that provide us with a sense of our creativity, perseverance, love of beauty, or other character strengths—those things in life we can readily be fully engaged with and enjoy. They do not necessarily have to be pleasant at the time of their doing, but in retrospect, they give us a sense of accomplishment or enjoyment; training for a sports event or writing a long and well-documented article or book may not give immediate pleasure, but in looking back, the activity provides a sense of great accomplishment. A third path to happiness is to involve ourselves with something that is outside of our local self, connecting us with something greater, such as providing service to others, and it can include learning something new, doing something for someone else or for our family or community, or developing spirituality. All of these are examples of a flow experience that can be larger than ourselves, which can be gratifying (Csikszentmihalyi, 2008). Thus, PP has become a defined, well-researched set of activities that is aimed at increasing human beings' enjoyment of their lives, which can enrich our lives and provide protection against the unhappiness and despair that can become problematic.

It has been no secret that in impoverished areas of the world and individual lives, where despair and alienation live and breed, epidemiological studies show that mental illness thrives (Albee &

Ryan-Finn, 1993). Finding ways to increase the happiness of the average human being is a worthwhile endeavor. Therefore, an emphasis on study and work in areas of people's lives that act as protective factors and lead to a greater focus on what leads to happiness brought about the pillars of Positive Psychology (Peterson, 2006). The pillars, as outlined by Peterson (2006), are as follows:

a. positive subjective experiences (happiness, pleasure, gratification, fulfillment)

b. positive individual traits (strength of character, talents, interests, values), and

c. positive institutions (families, schools, businesses, communities, societies).

(p. 20)

In the beginning paragraph of chapter 4, I quoted Seligman's (2002) battle cry: "I do not believe that you should devote overly much effort to correcting your weaknesses. Rather, I believe that the highest success in living and the deepest emotional satisfaction comes from building and using your signature strengths" (p. 13). So just what are character strengths? Peterson and Seligman (2004) have put forth a classification system they hope will become a companion to the American Psychiatric Association's current edition of the DSM (DSM-IV-TR). The book, *Character Strengths and Virtues: A Handbook and Classification* (Peterson & Seligman, 2004), is a monumental work that documents the well-being of humans by describing and classifying strengths and virtues that enable human thriving. These signature strengths are organized into six virtuous types valued by all of the major moral philosophers, as well as the signature strengths one can have (see Table 5.1). At present, there is a growing research effort, and information can be obtained at any of the university sites with degreed programs for the dissemination and study of Positive Psychology in the United States and Europe. Positive Psychology's grasp grows wider every day. There are several websites where one can obtain further information regarding Positive Psychology (see http://www.positivepsychology.org/,

http://www.reflectivehappiness.com). There is also an online Positive Psychology voluntary research site for anyone wanting to participate in this research (see http://www.ppresearch.sas.upenn.edu/). This last site includes activities for participation and reporting. For those interested in how Positive Psychology can be useful for larger venues, such as organizations, see http://www.bus.umich.edu/Positive/. The mother of all their information and ongoing repeatable questionnaires that will measure, among other factors, your signature strengths, can be found at http://www.authentichappiness.sas.upenn.edu/Default.aspx.

The study of Positive Psychology provides information regarding what makes one happy, thus less symptomatic, while Positive Psychotherapy uses the information and interventions to provide an integrated treatment strategy, especially for depression. But as you will see, those who practice Positive Psychology believe it can be generalized to other human problems typically treated with problem-focused therapies.

Positive Psychotherapy

Modern-day Positive Psychology has grown exponentially, and the first aim at having a model of Positive Psychotherapy arrived on the scene in 2005, when Seligman (2005) wrote a chapter entitled, "Positive Psychology, Positive Prevention, and Positive Therapy." This was followed by an article in the *American Psychologist* (Seligman et al., 2006), which outlined the beginnings of this model using interventions aimed at increasing positive emotions and engagement in life, rather than using a deficit-based remediation or repair treatment approach. Their model demonstrates solid evidence for reducing depression, and it is aimed at using the three scientifically researchable components discussed earlier that help to develop happiness. They are a pleasant life, an engaged life, and a meaningful life. The techniques used in Positive Psychotherapy to attend to these areas have solid research behind them aimed at bringing about a happier life, and they outline a treatment plan that progresses through a series of these interventions that are manualized in a protocol (see Table 5.2).

Table 5.1   Classification of 6 Virtues and 24 Character Strengths (Peterson & Seligman, 2004)

Virtue and strength	Definition
1. Wisdom and knowledge	Cognitive strengths that entail the acquisition and use of knowledge
Creativity	Thinking of novel and productive ways to do things
Curiosity	Taking an interest in all of ongoing experience
Open-mindedness	Thinking things through and examining them from all sides
Love of learning	Mastering new skills, topics, and bodies of knowledge
Perspective	Being able to provide wise counsel to others
2. Courage	Emotional strengths that involve the exercise of will to accomplish goals in the face of opposition, external or internal
Authenticity	Speaking the truth and presenting oneself in a genuine way
Bravery	*Not* shrinking from threat, challenge, difficulty, or pain
Persistence	Finishing what one starts
Zest	Approaching life with excitement and energy
3. Humanity	Interpersonal strengths that involve "tending and befriending" others
Kindness	Doing favors and good deeds for others
Love	Valuing close relations with others
Social intelligence	Being aware of the motives and feelings of self and others
4. Justice	Civic strengths that underlie healthy community life
Fairness	Treating all people the same according to notions of fairness and justice
Leadership	Organizing group activities and seeing that they happen
Teamwork	Working well as a member of a group or team
5. Temperance	Strengths that protect against excess
Forgiveness	Forgiving those who have done wrong
Modesty	Letting one's accomplishments speak for themselves
Prudence	Being careful about one's choices; *not* saying or doing things that might later be regretted
Self-regulation	Regulating what one feels and does
6. Transcendence	Strengths that forge connections to the larger universe and provide meaning
Appreciation of beauty	Noticing and appreciating beauty, excellence, and/or skilled and excellence performance in all domains of life
Gratitude	Being aware of and thankful for the good things that happen
Hope	Expecting the best and working to achieve it
Humor	Liking to laugh and tease; bringing smiles to other people
Religiousness	Having coherent beliefs about the higher purpose and meaning of life

Table 5.2   Idealized Session-by-Session Description of Positive Psychotherapy (Seligman, Rashid, & Parks, 2006)

Session and theme description	
1. Orientation	*Lack of Positive Resources Maintains Depression* The role of absence or lack of positive emotions, character strengths, and meaning in maintaining depression and empty life is discussed. The framework of PPT, the therapist's role, and the client's responsibilities are discussed. *Homework:* Clients write a one-page (roughly 300-word) positive introduction in which they tell a concrete story illustrating their character strengths.
2. Engagement	*Identifying Signature Strengths* Clients identify their signature strengths from the positive introduction and discuss situations in which these signature strengths have helped previously. Three pathways to happiness (pleasure, engagement, and meaning) are discussed in light of PPTI results. *Homework:* Clients complete the VIA-IS questionnaire online, which identifies clients' signature strengths.
3. Engagement/pleasure	*Cultivation of Signature Strengths and Positive Emotions* Deployment of signature strengths is discussed. Clients are coached to formulate specific, concrete, and achievable behaviors regarding the cultivation of signature strengths. The role of positive emotion in well-being is discussed. *Homework (ongoing):* Clients start a Blessings Journal in which three good things (big or small) that happened during the day are written.
4. Pleasure	*Good Versus Bad Memories* Role of good and bad memories is discussed in terms of maintenance of symptoms of depression. Clients are encouraged to express feelings of anger and bitterness. Effects of holding onto anger and bitterness on depression and well-being are discussed. *Homework:* Clients write about three bad memories, anger associated with them, and their impact in maintaining depression.
5. Pleasure/engagement	*Forgiveness* Forgiveness is introduced as a powerful tool that can transform anger and bitterness into feelings of neutrality or even, for some, positive emotions. *Homework:* Clients write a forgiveness letter describing a transgression and related emotions and pledge to forgive the transgressor (if appropriate) but may not deliver the letter.

(Continued)

Table 5.2 (Continued)

Session and theme description	
6. Pleasure/engagement	*Gratitude* Gratitude is discussed as enduring thankfulness, and the role of good and bad memories is highlighted again with an emphasis on gratitude. *Homework:* Clients write and present a letter of gratitude to someone they have never properly thanked.
7. Pleasure/engagement	*Midtherapy Check* Both forgiveness and gratitude homework are followed up. This typically takes more than one session. Importance of cultivation of positive emotions is discussed. Clients are encouraged to bring and discuss the effects of the Blessings Journal. Goals regarding using signature strengths are reviewed. The process and progress are discussed in detail. Clients' feedback toward therapeutic gains is elicited and discussed.
8. Meaning/engagement	*Satisficing Instead of Maximizing* Satisficing (good enough) instead of maximizing in the context of the hedonic treadmill is discussed. Satisficing through engagement is encouraged instead of maximizing. *Homework:* Clients write ways to increase satisficing and devise a personal satisficing plan.
9. Pleasure	*Optimism and Hope* Clients are guided to think of times when they lost out at something important, when a big plan collapsed, or when they were rejected by someone. Then clients are asked to consider that when one door closes, another one almost always opens. *Homework:* Clients identify three doors that closed and three doors that then opened.
10. Engagement/meaning	*Love and Attachment* Active-constructive responding is discussed. Clients are invited to recognize signature strengths of a significant other. *Homework 1 (ongoing):* Active-constructive feedback—clients are coached on how to respond actively and constructively to positive events reported by others. *Homework 2:* Clients arrange a date that celebrates their signature strengths and those of their significant other.
11. Meaning	*Family Tree of Strengths* Significance of recognizing the signature strengths of family members is discussed. *Homework:* Clients ask family members to take the VIA-IS online and then draw a tree that includes signature strengths of all members of their family including children. A family gathering is to be arranged to discuss everyone's signature strengths.

Session and theme description	
12. Pleasure	*Savoring*
	Savoring is introduced as awareness of pleasure and a deliberate attempt to make it last. The hedonic treadmill is reiterated as a possible threat to savoring and how to safeguard against it.
	Homework: Clients plan pleasurable activities and carry them out as planned. Specific savoring techniques are provided.
13. Meaning	*Gift of Time*
	Regardless of their financial circumstances, clients have the power to give one of the greatest gifts of all, the gift of time. Ways of using signature strengths to offer the gift of time in serving something much larger than the self are discussed.
	Homework: Clients are to give the gift of time by doing something that requires a fair amount of time and whose creation calls on signature strengths, such as mentoring a child or performing community service.
14. Integration	*The Full Life*
	The concept of a full life that integrates pleasure, engagement, and meaning is discussed. Clients complete PPTI and other depression measures before the final session. Progress is reviewed, and gains and maintenance are discussed.

Note. PPT = Positive Psychotherapy; PPTI = Positive Psychotherapy Inventory; VIA-IS = Values in Action Inventory of Strengths.

Referring to their methodology as it was applied to work with depression, the authors noted that even though the use of PPT produces both "clinical and statistically significant decreases in depression, we view these results as highly preliminary, and we urge caution on several grounds" (Seligman et al. 2006, p. 785). These cautions are related to sample size, even though, as they mentioned, they are in the same ballpark as most outcome studies, to which they concluded, "We doubt that the effects of PPT are specific to depression, and we expect that increasing positive emotion, engagement and meaning promote highly general ways of buffering against a variety of disorders and troubles" (pp. 785–786).

The Positive Psychology method is really not that dissimilar from the social constructivism presented earlier. Mahoney (2005), in comparing the two, made the case that, "Learned optimism, learned resourcefulness, and hope, for example, are expressions of such engagement. Constructivism maintains not only that living systems are active

but also that their activity is primarily directed toward self-organization—toward establishing, maintaining, and elaborating a patterned order" (p. 747). He stated that this ordering of patterns that people integrate because they are working become their own personal realities, as they put them to use through actions. As clients begin to use the interventions and act to incorporate parts of Positive Psychotherapy in their lives, they will begin to adapt and create new meanings based on their performance successes.

Gleaning Useful Supervisory Concepts

As Positive Psychotherapy could be applied to clinical supervision, I have used several of the "intervention" components with student interns and in workshops discussing and demonstrating strengths-based supervision. The first exercise I used was one that Peterson (2006) addressed, where students in their Positive Psychology classes are asked to tell a story about themselves where they describe a time in their lives when they were at their very best. After reading about this exercise, I decided to begin each of my classes with a similar request, first telling a story about my son when I experienced the best of him. I include that story here.

THE BEST OF THE BEST

My two young teenage sons came to live with me and my second wife during our first year of marriage—actually after three months. I had been single for 5 years after their mother and I divorced, seeing the boys on weekends and long summer breaks. This continued when I remarried, and my sons, who had met several new friends in the neighborhood, asked if they could live with us. There was no honeymoon the first year for us; the events surrounding two high-strung adolescent boys who were not thrilled about their father's recent marriage began with broken windows, paintball gun marks (presents from their mother) around our house when we were at work, and so forth. Their subtle anger and uproarious actions became routine, and yet through it all we survived. Both are now grown men, owners of master's degrees in education, and they are wonderful teachers and wrestling coaches in a high school with wives and children of their own. My wife and I have now been married for 30 years. Is this a miracle? Through it all, my wife graciously took a backseat to many things, but she provided love, nurturance, and food to teenage boys, and she also bought my youngest his letterman's jacket, when I was in my doctoral program with limited funds. The problems did not stop soon, as during their late teens and early adulthood we had many false starts as they left home, only to return months later asking for a second, third, or fourth chance, which were always greeted with love, forgiveness, and a place to eat, sleep, and try their education and launching again.

When my youngest got married in his mid-20s (and here comes the best), during the reception (which was paid for by their mother and my wife and I), he and his wife did their dance together as a newly married couple, and then as is typical, they both went off to ask their respective opposite gender parents to finish the dance. Somewhere in the midst of that, my son escorted his mother back to the edge of the dance floor where all the guests were circled watching, gave her a kiss and said something to her, and then he proceeded directly across the floor to where his stepmother and I were tearfully watching. He stood in front of his stepmother and asked her to finish the dance with him. We were not suspecting this, and we were struck dumb. Even now, as I write this story, tears well. After all those years of trouble, consternation, and heartache we saw before us a humble, loving, grown man who was willing to admit, at least in deed, that his stepmother meant a lot to him. We all cried, knowing that we were family at last.

Whenever I tell this story in class it is met universally with the same sort of emotions, as women cry and men look shaken. But they know what I am asking them to do, and their stories pour out like a cloudburst that has been waiting for the right time to soak and nurture the soil of their beings. The more I tell the story, the more the narrative thickens and creates new, better, and stronger meaning for me and my son.

What is most interesting to me is how we have been conditioned to talk about our problems; we talk about them with almost anyone. On a plane recently, the man in the seat next to me asked me what I did for a living and thus began his life story for the next hour and a half of the flight. But when I ask students or workshop participants to talk about their "Best of the Best," they are shy, stymied, and not ready to push forward. Some think it is bragging; others just mention how different it is to talk about something that was exceptional in their lives. Our culture has indoctrinated us to dwell on the negatives.

I have used this method successfully with supervisees and students in my classes many times over the past few years, but with a twist: I ask them to get into pairs and then tell a story about a time when their clinical work was what they might consider their best. On trial and error, I have found that it is easier for them to do this in pairs first rather than to tell it to the whole class. It puts front and center their ability to do well—their self-worth—during a time when they might not experience themselves as totally competent. By punctuating their best, they are reminded that they are in a process where they are quite capable.

The second Positive Psychology intervention I have used is also from Peterson's (2006) book as well as an activity/intervention from the book, *Character Strengths and Virtues: A Handbook and Classification* (Peterson & Seligman, 2004); it is called savoring. Savoring is an activity that people can cultivate, and those who learn to savor on a regular basis are happier and more satisfied with their lives. It is also a meditative technique to help one become mindful, which is described by Kabat-Zinn (2009). Bryant (2003) stated the following:

> Beliefs about one's capacity to savor have important implications for understanding positive well-being. Just because one experiences positive events does not mean that one feels capable of savoring these events, that is, of generating, intensifying, and prolonging enjoyment through one's own volition. (p. 175)

Savoring is an important part of life that we don't often take the time, or believe to be appropriate, to enjoy. Yet it can be a very important part of making positive meaning of experiences and overcoming challenges in life. I have found it an exciting component of helping supervisees become aware of their own abilities and perhaps add to their own agency.

SAVORING

When working with Sue during supervision, we began to talk about her clinical work with a couple who were working on their sexual relationship that was giving her some concerns. The couple had presented with a fairly complicated experience involving their hypo sexual desire, and Sue had done the usual sensate focus training, but the work was going rather slowly, and she had hoped that they might have shown a few signs of rapid recovery. Rather than looking for exceptions as I might have done before I studied Positive Psychotherapy, I asked her to recall a time she had a very good experience working with this couple and to take her time thinking about it, savoring the event in detail, and then to talk about it with me. All of a sudden she beamed and began to chuckle. I commented that her face lit up like a Christmas tree when she started to savor this memory, and we began to talk about the good experiences she has had with them and what made it so good. Of course, it was mostly

(Continued)

(Continued)

that she liked them and they obviously liked her, and that made a big difference. Rather than wanting to find a speedier outcome that might be short lived, she decided to focus again on their relationship issues, within the context of their sexuality. Again, she beamed and we both could tell that techniques are great but only up to a point. Further strengthening of their relationship might provide a more lasting outcome.

The idea of signature strengths is a positive influence in my life, one that has helped me find better balance. As I discovered that creativity, curiosity, love of learning, wisdom, perseverance, and appreciation of beauty were high on my list of signature strengths, I was able to adjust some of my own thinking. As I did repeated measures of my signature strengths over time, I was able to see that there were also areas—prudence, bravery, leadership, and kindness—that scored lower, and I vowed to work on these even to the extent of running for the office of president of a state branch of the ACA, which I won. As beauty and love of learning are repeatedly high on my list, I have included those as regular parts of my life; playing my guitar and singing with a friend for events also are a regular part of my life, as well as listening to all sorts of music, taking the opportunity to learn new things like taking photography classes, and staying involved in research and writing at a time when I could, academically, slack off. This has made me a better and more engaged professor. I work hard at using my higher signature strengths as part of the way I provide and work in leadership, and I have received high praise from other fellow leaders and members.

I am beginning to ask students to take their own examination of their signature strengths and consider ways that they could use the feedback to enrich their lives. With supervisees I encourage them to use the information to provide a balance in their clinical work and to combat potential burnout. I am positive on Positive Psychology.

I think it will take a while to begin to see how the use of Positive Psychology and Positive Psychotherapy in the context of clinical supervision can be useful. The methods of intervention are so different from what most clinicians perceive as clinical work that there could be dissonance preventing their use. And yet, I find their use to be an interesting and novel adjunct to my work as a supervisor.

RESILIENCY

Resilience is a well-researched, predictable event in people's lives, when they have come on hard times. Resilience is not something that requires special skills. Resilience has stages and conditions that we all can call upon, if we are willing. We use resilience in the care and therapy of our clients, or in our case, our supervisees. It is not a technique; it is an attitude about life and one I want to talk about here. I have used resilience in my own work, clinically and as a supervisor, but what is more interesting to me is that a lot of folks already know the secret. Following is a ministry about resilience that really surprised me.

I am presenting a workshop on strengths-based supervision at a family therapy conference. We get to the point where I am going to launch into a short piece on resiliency, and I decide to be collaborative and use the existing knowledge and strengths of the group. I ask if anyone has ever studied or worked with Froma Walsh (1996, 1998, 2003b), and three hands shoot up—well, we are in the Chicago metro area, where Froma lives, so I am not surprised, as this is a reasonable question for family therapists. She is, after all, a very well-known family therapy teacher and trainer and she was my supervisor for a year. I ask them what they learned about resiliency from her, and in unison they say, "It's not a technique; it's an attitude." Of course, they are right; as I said before, Walsh was not the first to study and put forth the ideas of resiliency, even in the field of family therapy studies. As resiliency became a studied and useful concept, not only for individuals but as applied to families, the research began to blossom, reaching out to all sorts of family types and different situations. The discussion of resiliency has taken several different turns over the years until finally we come to an interesting conclusion. As one of the leading researchers on resiliency stated, "Resiliency appears to be a common phenomenon arising from ordinary human adaptive processes" (Masten, 2001, p. 227). No wonder she called it "Ordinary Magic." But if it is not so special, and it is not about techniques or special ways of working with clients—in our case supervisees—what does it take to work from a position of resiliency? Let us take a gander at what the research tells us about resiliency.

Smith (2006) used the work done with at-risk youth as a central piece of her work on a strengths-based counseling model, noting that the concept of at risk can be a bit of a misnomer. Affluence, coming from a good family, doing well in school, and so forth, are not total protections from being involved in risk-taking behavior; in fact, at one time or another most of us are at risk for some type of problem during our lives. The converse is also accurate. Despite living in very problematic families and neighborhoods, doing poorly in school, or engaging other at-risk behaviors, resilience research has found that most children come out the other side having decent adult lives (Benard, 1991, cited in Smith, 2006). Resiliency is such a remarkable human quality that it is hard to pin down exactly who is at risk and who is not. But we can look at the factors and conditions that are involved in resiliency.

Starting in the 1970s, social scientists began to study in earnest resiliency in children and youth who have typically been considered at risk for psychopathology (see, e.g., Rutter, 1979, 1990).

The study of resiliency in children has been an upstart process for the deficit-based mentality of how disadvantaged children might grow up, and early studies categorized the resilient as invulnerable and other words setting them apart. Yet, it seems that in most cases, resiliency is a normal adaptive process that, when in good working order, is available to most, "even in the face of severe adversity" (Masten, 2001, p. 227). In one of the earlier studies, Garmezy (1991) showed that the effects of poverty, although horrible in the aggregate, are not necessarily devastating to all who live within it. The same sort of protective factors that are available and normal for others are alive and well here. For instance, the cry that urban schools are hotbeds for gang violence and drug problems fails to recognize that many children succeed with the help of teachers and significant adults who are able to motivate children past their conditions. The problem may not be the schools themselves but the districts' inability to reassign so that there is not an overloading of particular schools with the least able students who may bring others along with them down the slippery slope (Garmezy, 1991). Praising the work of urban schools, Garmezy stated the following:

> What is apparently needed by school personnel is the proud awareness that by putting forth the best effort in their classrooms and schools they are engaged in the most worthy of social enterprises— the enhancement of competence in their children and their tailoring, in part, of a protective shield to help children withstand the multiple vicissitudes that they can expect of a stressful world. (p. 427)

Moving on to other areas, Bonanno (2004) deconstructed our usual assumptions of several intersecting human problems with respect to recovery versus resiliency. He showed that in situations where loss or trauma has occurred, a goodly number of people show signs of resiliency, the ability of humans to weather the storms of life, rather than needing interventions for what clinicians usually consider recovery. In fact, the usual assumption that people need to have significant interventions postevent is not accurate and cannot be defined as abreactions to the event. Solid research shows that a fairly large portion of people having undergone grief work or trauma counseling actually get worse (Bonanno, 2004). Resiliency to loss or traumatic life-threatening events is common and "does not appear to indicate pathology but rather health adjustment" (Bonanno, 2004, p. 23). Resiliency is a remarkable and underrated human condition that professionals and the population at large tend to dismiss.

Some of the variables that seem to matter most and those we naturally think of as important include being connected with caring, competent adults, having adequate cognitive skills and the ability to self-regulate, and having a positive self-image, as well as the motivation to do well (Masten, 2001). The interventions coming from this research that can enhance protective factors are simple enough, including promoting competencies and prevention of symptoms or risks. The synergy of these conditions is key to producing well-developing children and youth and points to the environmental factors that could be controlled. Investing in the development of self-confidence and educational skills, as well as good parenting and adult support, is key, and working together provides a cumulative effect. And yet, because the human spirit and makeup is such that adaptation to adversity is so great, a youth that lives in a home where there is great distraction and multiple problems can thrive because of a committed significant adult—be that a relative, school counselor or social worker, teacher, or coach.

Masten and Curtis (2000) made the point that our current classification systems for psychopathology "need an overhaul to address more effectively the salient role of competence and adaptive functioning in defining and treating disorder" (p. 234). To begin with, Masten (2001) suggested that all of the research on resiliency point to the central themes of positive psychology, because the traditions of psychology have failed to address specific information regarding the strength of human beings.

Walsh (1996, 1998, 2003b), although not the first to put forth the notion of resiliency as a family affair, was one of the first to write about it in the context of a treatment consideration. By looking at the common traits associated with individuals, and then applying them to families, she offered clinicians a new way of working and viewing the families with which they work. Noting that in many cases families have been seen as potential risk factors, she made the same systemic shift people who use family systems thinking did some decades ago, by suggesting that (and here is the attitudinal shift I spoke about earlier) families can be seen as protective factors, serious influencers of success and promotion of well-being. Her promotion of families suggests that, "In building family resilience, we strengthen the family as a functional unit and enable the family to foster resilience in all its members" (Walsh, 1996, p. 263). Using a systemic view of resilience, Walsh noted that it is a relational event that can influence and create resilient individuals. Children and adolescents learn their views of themselves (self-reliance and efficacy), how to view their outside world (worldview as a struggle or a place that provides sustenance), relationships (affirming or constricting), and resiliency (picking oneself up and moving on or succumbing to adversity) from significant people in their lives. It is these attitudes that they can then bring forward to their own adulthood and then pass on to their own offspring. Relational resilience means a change in how we view families, from damaged to challenged (Walsh, 1996, 1998, 2003b). How we as clinicians and supervisors function also depends on our own views, because our view of family "normal" is usually associated with the typical bell-shaped curve that places normal within the scope of variables between standard deviations. Those families that do not fit within those parameters, but instead are within the tails, can be pathologized when they might be living within cultural norms or personal events that are dictated by their current context. Normality is a social construct that we have come to believe is real and true for all. "The very concept of the family has been undergoing redefinition as tumultuous social and economic changes of recent decades have altered the landscape of family life" (Walsh, 2003a, p. 4). Our views of family life have been constructed through social political and media events, and as family historian Stephanie Coontz (2000) demonstrated in her book, *The Way We Never Were: American Families and the Nostalgia Trap,* our concepts of the family are not what are projected by any of them, and they never have been. We do not live in a Leave it to Beaver, Cliff Huxtable, or Brady Bunch world. Our families have never really looked like those historically and they certainly do not now.

As Walsh (1998) pointed out, there are several key family processes that are part of a resilient family life, including a shared belief system—an organizing principle or worldview for living one's life and the meanings we ascribe to events, bad or good. Families also provide processes she called "shock absorbers," which include flexibility, connectedness, resources both social and financial, that provide stability as well as efficacy in living. Flexibility during transitions and developmental stages can be extremely important as to whether a family succumbs to stress or the members move on with their lives. Finally, as I mentioned at the beginning of this section, resilience is an attitude about working with and viewing families and individuals. It is important to remember that, "Resiliency does not come from rare and special qualities, but from the everyday magic of ordinary, normative human resources in the minds and brains and bodies of children, in their families and relationships, and in their communities" (Masten, 2001, p. 235). Observing that treatment and healing are different phenomena, as one is applied while the other comes from within, Walsh suggested that many of the newer strengths-based concepts have come about because clinicians have finally recognized that families do have their own sources for healing. So we have come full circle. By the way, Walsh (2006) has an incredible set of resiliency practices that any clinician can use successfully. One of these practices has become commonplace in clinical work. I remember Walsh talking to our supervision group at the Family Institute of Chicago (a part of Northwestern University) and stressing that we should normalize people's stresses, thus putting them in a context of strengths. At first, it made no sense to me and my "pathology" trained epistemology, but she was teaching us to help heal families and their members, not diagnose and label them with irreparable iatrogenic language.

Gleaning Useful Supervisory Concepts

Resilience concepts are a welcome addition to the ideas of strengths-based supervision. Again, I must emphasis that much of the clinical supervision literature is from a medically modeled view, and it is sorely out of date. As the resiliency researchers suggest, the focus on deficits is problematic and not in tune with the reality of those with whom they are working. Supervisees come to us wanting help with cases in which they are feeling stuck or fear they lack the necessary skills. Yet, as I have said before, they are some of the most well-trained, capable people to come out of graduate schools. Resiliency concepts work to empower supervisees to work more effectively and to believe in their own abilities. Just as children and adolescents learn from their families and other significant people in their lives, our adult supervisees learn from us their views of themselves as clinicians, how to view their outside world of colleagues, relationships, and resiliency. They learn that view from gentle collaborative relationships, not from experiences where they are taught to limit their imagination, alternatives, and possibilities.

Sum of gleanings.

The first thing that jumped out at me after writing and rewriting this section was how attitudinal strengths-based supervision purports to be. Even though several of these ideas come from different philosophical positions, they have the common thread of being against a deficits model and for an agentic perspective as the most important quality with which to work. The status quo of the medical model is intellectually struck down as king, and in its place are put several ideas of how to work with folks from a strengths-based position. Agency, the ability to help empower the people we work with so that they believe that they can succeed, is the most powerful force among humans, other than love. But it is not enough just to believe that you can succeed. People must then be willing, with some sort of social support, to begin the performance; they must step into that belief with everything they have at their disposal to practice, and practice until they know the feelings and behaviors of success—which also includes knowing that there will be times when they need to persevere and to get up when they have been knocked down. This sort of attitude can come from one's family of origin, one's chosen family or group of supporters, or a clinical experience including supervision.

> When my daughter Zoë was in kindergarten, she came home one day and as we talked, she told me she couldn't do the monkey bars. She looked sad and said that a lot of the kids could already go hand over hand from the first to the last rung. She could only do one or two and then had to jump to the ground. I asked her what she thought she could do to increase her ability so that some time down the road she might be able to complete the whole set of bars. She pondered this question, as only a 5-year-old can, complete with faces to show she was thinking, and then she said those wonderful words that would last her a lifetime: "I guess I will have to practice, but first I have to believe that I can do it, Dad."
>
> Every day from that point on, I got a report of progress, and every day we celebrated with smiles and encouragement and sometimes a snack, until she had completed the task. She moved from having a goal, to believing she could meet that goal, to moving into the behavior and practice that made her succeed. But she learned something far more important during those weeks—that she can do almost anything she wants, if she puts her mind to it and practices. She learned agency.

ENFOLDING STRENGTHS-BASED SUPERVISION

I have made the case throughout this chapter, and as a central theme of this book, that personal agency is a critical part of what clinical supervisors of any stripe do to help the growth of themselves as supervisors, as well as in their work with their supervisees. Zimmerman and Cleary (2006) reminded us that, "Personal agency refers to one's capability to originate and direct actions for given purposes. It is influenced by the belief in one's effectiveness in performing specific tasks, which is termed self-efficacy, as well as by one's actual skill" (p. 45). Our supervisees need to believe that they can do this very difficult job of working with people who are having difficulties. The different sorts of clients our supervisees see will lead many of them to places they have never experienced before, situations that can be unfathomable—abuse, crisis, violence, and despair. They need to understand that they are not alone in this process and that they can do this work. They need to have the belief in themselves, know that they can originate actions to be helpful, and act on their understandings. Personal agency is more than just believing; it is moving into that unknown space and acting on the belief to succeed and having the resiliency to get back up again when our best intentions do not work.

I will not belabor the point, but one must at least acknowledge that traditionally we have been indoctrinated with the view that supervisors know best and that our job is to make corrections, remediations, and fixes so that they resemble "our perfect" clinical work. Those ideas we may put forth, no matter how kind and gentle, can still have implications for what they can do to perpetuate the system and to make clear that those with whom we work will only come to near perfection with our help, at least in our minds. What a change comes from the narrative in which the hierarchical and egotistical view of an all-knowing supervisor is changed to one of a supervisor who really listens. Jill Freedman, in an interview with Schwarzbaum (2009), answered the question, posed about who were the influential shapers of her work, this way: "I hope that the people I work with as clients influence my practice" (p. 161). This response is the sort of "one-down, not knowing" attitude I would expect from strengths-based supervisors. I hope that all supervisors learn tons from their supervisees.

The next thing that was evident is that there are many roads to good work with people, both in clinical work and supervision. Our traditional lock on listening to tapes to hear if our supervisees are making what *we* believe to be adequate responses is not always the most useful tool in our shed, after all—responses to what? Which model are we using, and what are the circumstances of the client/clinician working relationship at the time? Context and intuition are always important, and listening to a tape provides us with only one variable that constitutes a clinical session. If we only assume that a client-centered response is accurate, we delimit other models. One only has to watch tapes of some of the so-called masters to realize that there are many different possibilities of interaction. And so it is with supervision.

Finally, all seem to imbue an attitude rather than a set of techniques at the metalevel. Oh, yes. There are protocols of activities (Peterson & Seligman, 2004), and formulaic responses (Walter & Peller, 1992), and jargon that, well, I don't know what it does, and techniques

(Freedman & Combs, 1996; White & Epston, 2000) that may all have ways of operating, but the soul of them all seems to be to change the prevailing attitude about the people with whom we work, from a deficit-based model to a strength-finding model. I love that and have seen it work wonders, both clinically as well as with supervisees. All of the models presented earlier have an agentic flare, with encouragement to performance so as to enhance and train our neurons in the ability and knowledge of resiliency and perseverance. From the solution-focused mantra of looking for exactions coupled with the request to try more of that, to the simple positive psychology intervention of finding signature strengths and doing more of those and enjoying the moments (flow) we are living, all are agentic, rather than deficit based.

Every form of these new ideas opens up possibilities for also providing multicultural, cross-cultural approaches to supervision. Smith (2006), in her seminal article on strength-based clinical work, suggested the thought that "a core component of the strength-based theory is that culture has a major impact on how people view and evaluate human strengths. All strengths are culturally based" (p. 17). Narrative work with its focus on social justice through a flattening of hierarchical positions (Freedman & Combs, 1996) is certainly an ally of cross-cultural and multicultural perspectives, as are reflecting teams and languaging efforts. In fact, strengths-based supervision is a grand narrative positing equality and understanding at deep levels of difference and similarity of people regardless of who they are or where they come from, figuratively or literally.

I come back to this again, but the issue of evaluation becomes moot when one is looking for and mining strengths in people. The literature throughout this book has statements from several different points of view that are alternative ways of making an assessment, if that needs to be done. But a far more radical approach might be to do what we are supposed to do in our training of group work: split the functions if one must make judgments about others' social constructions. But of course, I also agree with Turner and Fine (1995), that I can do both quite well with transparency, solid expectations that we both agree on—one for their own growth and potential and another about what administrative expectations are with respect to their work. When I discussed this with one of my colleagues, Andy Young, with whom I do workshops, he said, "When you are telling them what they are doing well, aren't you providing solid evaluation? Where does it state that you have to do otherwise?" (A. Young, personal communication, November 16, 2009). And of course, Andy was right. I have tried to address these issues throughout the book, because they are concerns of us all in today's world.

I have placed these ideas before you in these rather long, and I hope interesting, two chapters, but I would like to end with a few more overarching thoughts, to finally put the nail in the coffin of what has become, in some circles, the way of doing "appropriate" supervision.

The World is Flat and We Are Not

Thomas Friedman's (2005) book, *The World is Flat,* clearly puts forth the notion that because of the changing face of the world's media and technology, there is no longer such a grand need for overseers and managers. At one point in his book he tells the story of accompanying General Richard Myers, chairman of the Joint Chiefs of Staff, on a tour of U.S. military headquarters in Baghdad, Iraq. As they walked around, Friedman was taken by the media technology that is helping our troops. He watched in awe as a soldier monitored the situation from his laptop attached to a camera on a Predator drone that was flying overhead, and Meyers reported that, "technology had "'flattened'" the military hierarchy—by giving so much information to the low-level officer, or even the enlisted man who was operating the computer, and empowering him to make decisions about the information he was gathering" (p. 39).

There are three points that this quote exudes when placed in the context of clinical supervision and clinical work. First, technology has given us the tools to do more, know more, and work smarter than ever before. As I have stated repeatedly throughout this book, in our field of clinical work, our students are taught more, supervised more, and know more about working with clients than ever before. By the time they have graduated from their various programs, they have been taught several different models of counseling, have been recorded via audiotape and videotape for feedback purposes, and have absorbed a number of models to use in their work. Second, the operative word to sum up the previous paragraph is "empowering." Although I am sure that most clinical supervisors believe their work is empowering their supervisees, I have heard many horror stories about clinical supervision gone bad. Many of the models of supervision are reflective of our models of clinical work—mainly problem focused or remediation focused, attempting to solve or correct the problems presented—and it is an attitude we need to rid ourselves of. These models focus on a top-down hierarchical model where the supervisor is supposed to remediate or solve the supervisee's problems and teach the correct way. This is not empowering. According to the Cambridge dictionary online, empowering is (verb) "to give someone official authority or the freedom to do something," or (adjective) "something that is empowering makes you more confident and makes you feel that you are in control of your life" (see http://dictionary.cambridge .org/dictionary/british/empower?q=empower). Nelson and Friedlander (2001), while researching conflicts among supervisors and supervisees, found that conflicts occur on a wide continuum, from the supervisor being too distant and unavailable to being too familiar with supervisees. However, many power struggles between supervisors and supervisees include the disempowering or devaluing of supervisees past clinical experience, as well as supervisors imposing their own model of clinical work on their supervisee, among others. I believe that empowering supervisees is key to excellent supervision. Finally, if the U.S. Army sees the sensibility of giving up the rigidity of a hierarchical organization during war time, what makes clinical supervisors believe they cannot do this? Historical contexts still inform us, and ancient views and timeworn practices are just that. They are worn thin, and I believe it is time to move to a truly empowering model that shares the same philosophy as the newer clinical models.

Just Try and Make Them

The thought must occur to all supervisors at some time during the course of supervision that when supervisees are alone and not being taped or watched—alone behind closed doors—they probably practice clinically using ideas other than what their supervisor might do or even approve of. Most clinical work occurs with such nuanced differences in each session that to believe one or two models might be enough to help when the client's situation hits a crisis or is seriously wrong headed. We cannot force our supervisees to practice as *we* would like them to, and we should want them to be able to react with grace and transparent therapeutic efforts that are applicable to the moment, rather than on some basis of theory. Those who have practiced clinically and as a supervisor for any length of time have to look back over their career and take stock at the many changes they have had with respect to how best to work with our clients, be they clinical clients or supervisory clients. Cookie cutter counseling just does not work outside of the laboratory.

Wisdom and Truths: Guiding Principles and Systemic Logic

I have been a cook throughout my life. I love to putter around in the kitchen, making good, solid food for my family. My eggplant parmesan was the final straw that convinced my wife to marry me, I think. I love to make bread also, and I will make both loaves of whole wheat and white at the same time. When my oldest son was about 12, he asked me if he could cut a piece of bread to eat, and I said, "Sure; make sure you don't cut your finger off!" Then it hit me; I was

telling him what I did not want him to do, rather than what I would like him to do. It is a simple thing; I have heard it before from experts, but we are always more focused on the negative, rather than the positive. So I corrected myself and said, "It works better if you use the bread board, and cut with the bread knife straight down, with a sawing motion, and keep your fingers back and away from the blade." To which he responded, "Got it Dad, I've done this before, you know." But at least it was not the response, "What do you think I am, an idiot?" Now, more times than not, I am clear that the issue of strengths-based ideas is more about an attitude than it is about techniques. As I pointed to earlier in Chapter 1, attitude changes our view when seeing clients who are thought to be "at risk," to see them as "at potential" (Bermeo, 2009). I now come back to reiterate those six elements of strengths-based clinical supervision skills:

- See the glass as half full more times than not.
- See every stakeholder as capable and having unique contributions.
- Help covisees (stakeholders) develop their personal agency (self-efficacy).
- Help stakeholders begin the process of strengths-based forethought.
- Help stakeholders find and use their voice.
- Encourage stakeholders to pass it on to others.

It is, for some, a major stretch to see both supervisor and supervisee on the same level playing field, both with hopes and dreams of what is to come and what the ends are of their journey. But if we truly believe that we are both stakeholders in the process, it changes the way we approach, respect, and treat each other. It is startling for some and comforting to others to realize the scientific fact that our brains can have such a powerful effect over us, to provide us with a top-down view of what has been socially constructed as truths. Our learning from family, culture, and education has provided us with a road map so we do not have to think too critically about much of life, and we can be on auto pilot for much of our life, rather than savoring and paying attention (Kabat-Zinn, 2009; Siegel, 2007). So, if some of the information

I have provided is not according to your epistemological understanding, step back and ask yourself this: "Why am I so set in my ways about this? Where did I learn what I know, and is it still a relevant understanding of life? Why do we look at problems in such a medically oriented set of realities? And what is it about the ideas in this book that affect me so positively or negatively?" And then, after opening yourself to new ideas, ask what fits about these concepts and what does not. That is openness, and we can both be all right with your final conclusions—that our work together here has been a social construction of ideas, out of which you will then make your own meaning. Then we can agree to disagree or add to each other's beliefs in a new way of supervising.

6

THE LARGER PICTURE

Strengths-Based Management and Leadership

There are no leaders unless others are willing to work collaboratively with them, and there are no follow-ers unless there are leaders who are willing to serve as the relational conduit for inquiry and action.

—Harlene Anderson et al. (2008, p. 34)

Edmund Burke, a member of the British Parliament during the 1900s, who offered what has become a classic definition of leadership, said he would give great weight to his constituents' wishes, high respect to their opinions, and constant attention to their business, but he would not abandon his conscience or independence: "Your representative owes you, not his industry only, but his judgment; and he betrays, instead of serving you, if he sacrifices it to your opinion" (Burke, 1774, p. 6). Leadership, according to him, is doing the right thing.

As we explore leadership and organizational development both in agencies and training facilities, I wanted to put forth from the beginning, my position that we are working with complex, living, breathing, and feeling people. Their inclusion in the equation and our care of them is center to what I believe is important. Leaders must have vision and be able to see the larger picture of their influence and responsibility. Leaders must try to gauge what the consequences

of every decision made will have on the whole of the organization and hold all stakeholders up as equally important, while at the same time make decisions that are important to the whole, but in the end, decisions are solely the leaders' to make.

This book is about supervision and leadership, and this chapter is about the larger picture of supervision and leadership. Every book I have ever read about supervision, including the early and current works of the ACA's book on administrative supervision (Henderson, 2009), was written for doctoral students training at a university. West Russo's (2010) research led her to believe that, "While much of the formal training in supervision is occurring in university settings with graduate students, there are also informal workshops for practitioners who are already working in the field as supervisors" (p. 22). I have produced and attended many of these formal and informal workshops on supervision for over 15 years, and they were all about clinical work, not about the running of an agency. Suffice it to say that administrative supervision at the graduate level, or anywhere else, is lacking. We are clinicians by training, yet there are large numbers of well-educated professionals directing, administering, leading, managing, and running agencies of all sorts who have never thought about or read the information from the actual fields from which this work comes. It is not enough to know the typical executive skills, so this chapter gives some directions. A basic assumption of a strengths-based model of managing, leading, and supervising is to begin seeing in a new light those with whom we work. Drucker's (1968, 1985, 1990, 1998, 2004, 2005) concepts of management changed the workforce from "Industrial Age" workers, to "Knowledge Age" workers, and finally to "Information Age" workers, who have a great deal of knowledge, integrity, and ingenuity, all of which should be honored, encouraged, and given voice. In this chapter, we explore the inner workings of organizations, comparing and contrasting a more traditional perspective with a strengths-based one. Typically called administrative supervision, I call it what it is: leadership and management. "Administrative supervision in counseling is a process—a sequence of activities—based on principles of supervision, leadership, management, and administration" (Henderson, 2009, p. 3). By now you understand that one of the premises I adhere to is that good supervision has a large dose of good leadership qualities— strengths-based supervision and leadership. In Chapter 3, I touched on some of the topics that I think great leaders and organizational managers should pay attention to and where they come from, but here I attempt to flesh them out. Leadership is one of the most relevant aspects of any organizational context. However, defining leadership is a challenge, and it has changed in style and concept along the way. Finley (1994) said that, "The industrial paradigm of leadership which equates leadership with good management and implies a hierarchical relationship between leader and follower, associated more with mechanistic forms of organizational structures and

relationships, is a concept of the past" (p. 57). It is a concept from the past that needs to change.

First of all, let us differentiate between leadership and management. Managers usually have subordinates called "reports," because they report to the manager for all of their actions and doings. Managers give out directions and tasks for these reports to follow and complete. Managers have their authority because the organization they work for says they are in charge of something, and their reports do what is asked of them in a very hierarchical system. Managers get paid to get things done, as they too are reports to someone, most often a director, vice president, CEO, and so forth. They have to pay attention to a bottom line, making sure that they stay on budget and get the work done without problems and on time. Their work is usually parsed out to their reports to take care of, and then managers can pay more attention to supervising their reports, improvising better ways to get their goals and financial concerns met. Managers are most often risk aversive, do not like conflict among their reports or from above or below, and want to run a smooth department or subset of an organization. Managers are the hub of all activity in an organization—middle management—that when included in the planning can move a company ahead, if the leaders above are skilled at listening past their own vision and voice. Managers have the pulse of organization close to their job. But the same can be said for managers who isomorphically do the same with their reports. The most successful managers are those who include their reports in the planning and programming, helping them to speak and follow their own voice and sharing that voice with those in their work group. Managers can be leaders too, and they need to have leadership skills to make their department run well. What I am describing is a less hierarchical organization, where being a boss is not about bossing reports around but including them in the process at every step of planning and implementing; this is a huge change in the way some leaders behave and think.

Most often leadership is associated with those at the top, but this is not always the case. Leaders have followers and may or may not have reports unless they are in an organization where they do both. Leaders do not necessarily have formal authority, and not everyone will follow a leader. This is a very important point of leadership, because as Anderson et al. (2008) pointed out, "There are no leaders unless others are willing to work collaboratively with them, and there are no followers unless there are leaders who are willing to serve as the relational conduit for inquiry and action" (p. 34).

LEADERSHIP IN PRACTICE

Leadership has been considered and studied for a long time. Some defined behaviors they think make a good leader, others point out what they believe are the qualities of a good leader, and some try to define leadership styles. An interesting perspective on leadership comes from John Man's (2009) book, *The Leadership Secrets of Genghis Khan: 21 Lessons From History's Most Successful Conqueror.* Man pointed out that, "One thing most agree on is that 'true' leadership differs from both the exercise of power and the art of management" (p. 7). He observed that regardless of the advantages one has, be they strength, wealth, or status in an organization, they are not necessarily the same as having good leadership abilities. One must have a good sense of persuasion in order to help others get on board with where the leader would like his or her people to follow. But it is not, as Kahn was, about being a conqueror. It is very much to the contrary.

We all know the charismatic leaders such as Chrysler's Lee Iacocca, Walmart's Sam Walton, and even the 35th president of the United States, John F. Kennedy. By what seems to be the sheer force of their personal charisma, they have been able to move people to do remarkable feats. But charisma alone has a tendency to fall apart without substance and action. Today, the charismatic leader has morphed to an action-centered leader (Adair, 1987, 1996, 2003, 2005, 2007) and a service or servant leader (Grönfeldt & Strother, 2006; Walumbwa, Hartnell, & Oke, 2010), in

order to make change happen and create lasting organizational success. Both of these models have one thing in common: They focus on taking care of the needs of those for whom leadership is a leader. So, our new model must take the best of a Nelson Mandela, who knows that success is achieved by meeting the needs and bringing together all who are in the system.

Servant Leadership

Service or servant leadership styles are most like the strengths-based approaches I have been talking about, both in philosophy as well as pragmatically. Greenleaf describes servant leadership as placing the good of those who are followers (supervisees, employees, or students) over the self-interests of the leader (Greenleaf, cited in Hale & Fields, 2007). In addition, leadership focuses on the development of and well-being of those the leader has as "reports" and de-emphasizes the successes and glory of the leaders themselves (Barbuto & Wheeler, cited in Hale & Fields, 2007). Servant leadership was first formally described by Greenleaf (2002), who put forth the first description of what a servant leader portends to do: "The servant leader *is* servant first . . . It begins with the natural feeling that one wants to serve, to serve *first.* Then conscious choice brings one to aspire to lead. That person is sharply different from one who is *leader* first, perhaps because of the need to assuage an unusual power drive or to acquire material possessions" (Greenleaf, 2002, p. 352). And, of course, it follows that if you take care of your employees, they will take care of you.

More key factors that are associated with servant leadership are increasing the capacity of followers to be creative in their work, creating team building among followers, encouraging followers to take on greater responsibilities that suit them, and providing them with satisfaction on the job. The servant leader remains concerned about the followers' taking the credit and focuses on how a group of people can develop more creativity and responsiveness rather than chest thumping and looking good themselves. Interestingly, Hale and Fields (2007) noted that this sort of leadership is not cross-culturally recognized and that it does seem counterculture to much of the United States. Remembering that culture and personal constructs of worldviews are socially constructed, it is easy to extrapolate and infer that our top-down perspective of leadership in the United States is also socially constructed and a holdover from management that fits an industrial-aged worldview. But is it necessarily a good fit for who we have become? Top-down enslavement of a socially constructed ideology from the past may also be a relic whose time has come and gone.

My wife Betsy is the manager of operations for a large, international, horticultural company, and she is an excellent servant leader. One of the many things she has done for her "reports" is to lower the hierarchy and truly work to empower and provide for them. A great example is how she worked with a woman who had been at the same job for years. This woman did her job well, but as will happen, she started getting bored and stagnant doing the same old tasks, as the company structure does not provide many opportunities for advancement with longevity. During a review, Betsy asked her about her likes and dislikes and found that the woman liked taking photography with her small digital camera. A recent reorganization had left an open spot for the company photographer, so Betsy inquired if that job was already taken, and then, with the woman's excited agreement, they made the recommendation that she fill this part-time adjunctive job, taking pictures of all the new branded flowers, among other things. Betsy also arranged for her to use a new camera both professionally and personally, and the woman began taking classes and lots of pictures and entering local contests. She began to win contests, and her self-esteem received a much-needed lift and motivation, and she actually won a really nice, expensive camera as a prize one time. This act of empowerment and placing reports' interests first is not only an example of great servant leadership, but it shows that the cost benefit is tremendous. Betsy's loyalty and dedication to her job and company was evident many times

over. In an economy where people jump from job to job, the cost of retraining and hiring new employees is staggering.

What I have presented here is very prevalent in social service agencies. Fitz-enz (2001) demonstrated that the cost of losing one professional employee can be over $100,000 when you factor in the cost of termination, replacement factors, lost production, and the learning curve for a new hire. Better to keep their interests in mind and help them grow and contribute to the organizational development. But most servant leaders do not take this form of leadership to help the bottom line; they do it because they believe it is the right thing to do.

When I was a few years into a job as a child and family therapist at a well-known residential treatment center, my supervisor and the director of the agency I was working for offered me the opportunity to attend and have two-thirds of the fees paid for so that I could attend the Family Institute of Chicago, a prestigious training facility for instruction in family therapy. I became a better clinician and a loyal employee. I will never forget the director's comments to me, when he said, "This will probably be your exit papers from here, when you find that you will be more marketable elsewhere. But in the meantime, we believe it will be helpful to the children and their families you work with." Here was a real servant leader.

Service Leadership

Although there is sound support for the idea of empowering employees, leadership has also been described as a process by which a person is able to influence others to accomplish a common goal or task (Chemers, 2002). Today, in order to accomplish this, a leader must be seen as someone who has his or her followers' best interests at heart, while creating a culture of success—a cultural climate that both takes care of and includes employees in the outcome, as well as making sure the cultural climate defines success for all stakeholders, employees, customers, and community. Alan Keith of Genentech said, "Leadership is ultimately about creating a way for people to contribute to making something extraordinary happen" (cited in Kouzes & Posner, 2007, p. 3). A variation of leadership that continues this direction, service leadership, postulates that an organization that has best-in-class operations needs to "encourage prudent risk-taking and creativity" (Grönfeldt & Strother, 2006, p. 1). This sounds a lot like the concept of "leading-edge practices" instead of "best practices," to me. To do this, Grönfeldt & Strother (2006) suggested that the culture of the organization must have core values that every employee buys into and understands. It is here that key members of the leadership team need to be involved with the core values (corporate culture) that are then disseminated to the rest of the employees to engender in all they do (Grönfeldt & Strother, 2006).

Service leadership, at the same time, entails making sure that members of the organization have their customers' best interests at heart and continues to make it clear to their customers through everything they do. Today, in agency work as well as university training, that means improving how the organization deals with and keeps customer service at the forefront. This can be a far more complex endeavor in clinical practice and training than it is in the corporate world, as there are far more stakeholders because of the nature of the intended product. Our stakeholders are not only clients, but funding agencies, interface relationships between both universities where the early training occurs and the agencies where the interns and employees come from, and the community at large. This is really a task straight from community counseling strategies, with needs assessments that include the whole of the community, with members who are interrelated and interdependent with each other (Lewis, Lewis, Daniels, & D'Andrea, 2010). According to community counseling standards, a needs assessment must include, or at least try to assess and gather as stakeholders, all parties involved. Later in this chapter, I introduce the concept of a 360-degree evaluation process (Church, & Bracken, 1997; Hazucha, Hezlett, & Schneider, 2006; Ward, 1997) that should be the

leading-edge component in a circular process of change and evolution to stay sharp and relevant.

To corroborate this position of servant leadership that works to help employees (stakeholders) feel empowered, Florida and Goodnight (2005) noted that creative people are motivated by intrinsic rewards rather than extrinsic ones and employees do their best when they are engaged intellectually. I am intrigued by their notion that if we wish to help our stakeholders become great, we need to provide them with greater personal challenges, like solving riddles, and so forth; these types of people—those who thrive on their own creativity—are able to handle their own workload rather than having it dictated to by someone else. Florida and Goodnight's suggestions for supervising these creative "Knowledge-Age" workers" and/or "Information-Age" workers are to help them build collegial relationships where collaboration, trust, and teamwork are most prevalent. This is very similar to what my information from site supervisors (Edwards, 2011) said they wanted. We only need to put this into practice in order to make it work well. Or again, as Covey (2004) said, "Leadership is communicating to people their worth and potential so clearly that they come to see it in themselves" (p. 98).

Strengths-Based Leadership

As I mentioned in my opening chapter, Rath and Conchie (2008) have gathered together five decades of research data from the Gallup organization on the topic of good leadership, and they then began a study of over 10,000 followers to investigate what, from a followers' point of view, makes for excellent leadership. What they found provides us with an interesting look at what it takes to be an outstanding leader, an outstanding manager, an outstanding supervisor. Is it intrinsic qualities of a leader that make them great, or is it the outcomes that they seek? Is it what they do to engender followers to follow, or is it a match that fits the circumstance? Is it the "take over" attitude of a Genghis Kahn or the optimistic force of a Winston Churchill?

Is it the strengths of the leader or how the leader finds strengths in those he or she leads?

To begin with, let us look at the factors that come out from Rath and Conchie's (2008) research. Central to the thesis of this book and quite compelling is that they found effective leaders are always invested in strengths. When "leadership fails to focus on individuals' strengths, the odds of an employee being engaged are a dismal 1 in 11 (9%)" (p. 2). But that changes drastically, "to almost 3 in 4 (73%)," when leadership focuses on their strengths (p. 2). Gaining strength (pun intended) for the use of strengths, they showed that this means there is an increase of eight times over from those who do not punctuate strengths, to those who do! Their conclusion on this point makes one a believer, when it is realized that this also increases the organization's bottom line, be it financial or expected outcome, as well as increasing every employee's well-being (Rath & Conchie, 2008). Next, it seems simple to say, but great leadership surrounds itself with great diverse teams, maximizing their strengths. As Rath and Conchie and their team examined their data over many times, they found that there are four dominant strengths or traits, that when placed together purposefully can maximize the team's outcome. We have come upon this concept of strengths domains before in the work of Seligman and his collective group, studying and implementing signature strengths in Positive Psychology (2002), and here it is again as components of leadership. So, not only do great leaders develop and punctuate the strengths of their supervisees, but they also utilize their own strengths and those of their teams. The dominant domains for leadership strengths are (a) executing, (b) influencing, (c) relationship building, and (d) strategic thinking. No one person can have all four of these, but some team members may have more than one. Each of these four strengths also have several themes that fit within the strengths, such as executing themes which include (a) achieving, (b) arranging, (c) believing, (d) being consistent, and so forth. "Instead of one dominant leader who tries to do everything or individuals who all have

similar strengths, contributions from all four domains lead to a strong and cohesive team" (Rath & Conchie, 2002, p. 23). The diverse nature of these leadership strengths makes for a synergy of effectiveness, that when combined with a lowering of the hierarchical bar and included with input and encouraging voice from all employees, can maximize the organization's potential. Leadership teams need not be stagnant or static, but they can and should change up according to the task. Using the community counseling model, a diversity of stakeholders from within the community can provide input that is relevant and broad based also. Warren Buffett has suggested that, "A leader is someone who can get things done through other people" (cited in Rath & Conchie, 2002, p. 79). What all of this means is that effective leaders bring a diverse group of common purposed people together using the organization's mission and objectives as a starting operating principle, and then together they move forward collectively to achieve solid outcome objectives. And they do this by honoring strengths of the organization's biggest resource, the people who work there.

ORGANIZATIONAL EVALUATION AND CHANGE USING POSITIVES

As I write this, my wife Betsy is going to work ready to be a trim tab for a change. As I mentioned earlier, she works as the operations manager for an international, multimillion dollar company, that like many other companies around the world these days, has met with difficult times. No, it isn't a counseling program or agency, but the similarities between how organizations operate are clear. They are systems, and systems are a series of other systems, which have operating principles that guide them, having usually have been handed down from the days of the Industrial Revolution when people did not have the same level of education or training they do today. Times have changed and so have the qualities and education of the people who work for these companies, as I have stressed throughout this book. Companies that understand this are usually more sustainable through hard times, and as systems they can evolve to the next higher level of evolution when stressed, as Nobel laureate Ilya Prigogine (1997) has shown. The word organization comes from the word organism, meaning alive. Organizations are alive, changing, and growing entities and systems. They are capable of change and also of being stressed and becoming stagnant due to out-of-date operating principles. Later in this chapter, I present the ideas of a revolutionary model of change using an organization's strengths, called AI (appreciative inquiry, as noted in a previous chapter; Cooperrider, 2000; Cooperrider & Whitney, 2000; Cooperrider & Srivastva, 1987).

In any case, Betsy's leader summoned all members of the leadership team together to evaluate where they can make changes to improve their production and cost cutting; it is an evaluation session. He requested that they come prepared to talk about each of their group's opportunities and challenges, a usual problem focus—where they have made mistakes this year and what they plan on doing about it.

This is a typical way of making evaluations, also called assessments or diagnoses. This way of operating is based on a medically oriented view, left over from the days of the Enlightenment Era and Newtonian physics. Medicine works on a basis of looking for the problem and then setting out to fix the symptom or the actual problem itself. For instance, if a bone is broken, or another easily diagnosed physical problem, it is possible to figure out what is wrong and provide a remedy. With other medical conditions, it can be a trifle more difficult. Take the common cold. There is not one single cause and effect correlation, so physicians take a symptom relief tack to lessen the suffering of the patient. The same is true when we talk about more complex human conditions. There is not direct discernable cause and effect between most psychiatric conditions. In fact, "In the DSM there is no assumption that each category of mental disorder is a completely discrete entity with absolute boundaries dividing

it from other mental disorders or from no mental disorders. There is also no assumption that all individuals described as having the same disorder are all alike in all important ways" (American Psychiatric Association, 2000, p. xxxi). They are called disorders or syndromes that have no bearing on a specific biological condition. One only has to look at WebMD to find that something as pervasive as depression has many contributing factors and that there is no common biology, other than the way it ends up feeling to people. So too, are other human conditions or situations. We are, after all, bio-psycho-social-spiritual creatures who also make meaning out of our situations that are socially constructed. All of this is to say that our usual vehicles for changing or developing human organizations have been influenced by out-of-date methods. Let us usher in the new.

Betsy, in her best organizational change plan, is going to be prepared to talk about what she and her team have done really well this year and what they see as options for increasing their productivity and cost cutting—options for change, not attempts to fix a problem. I like it and cannot wait to hear how her trim-tab mentality works. A trim tab is a smaller part of an oceangoing ship's very large rudder that can cut through the water first, making it easier for the rest of the rudder to follow. The same principle can apply in organizations to effect change.

Evaluation

Every idea from strengths-based work has at its core, the element of how language can be used to create positive contexts. Language can either open up possibilities or shut down future conversations and actions. Giving feedback or evaluation is the part of the job that can be the most frustrating or the most interesting because of the possibilities of empowering, creating contexts for change and growth, and demonstrating attitudes that can make an agency or a clinical supervisory session rich and rewarding. Both the supervisor as well as those who are engaged with us in the process can either benefit or be devalued.

Providing evaluation, however, means something different for most people, and it is here that strengths-based work is most effective. Understanding the roots of most strengths-based work provides a different means to how this work can enhance all we do. As I struggled to think about how evaluation can be a part of strengths-based work, my friend and copresenter, Andy Young, said the following: "You know, Jeff, giving people examples of those activities they do well, *is* evaluation" (A. Young, personal communication, November, 16, 2009). Really, so there you go. Where is it written that evaluation is about providing negative feedback? And in fact, in Chapter 2, I presented the situation of Jeff Zeig (1987), who was told by Mary Goulding that telling someone what they have done wrong is useless information. And I really believe that in most cases. But first, what is evaluation?

According to the Online Research Methods Knowledge Base (2009), "The most frequently given definition is: Evaluation is the systematic assessment of the worth or merit of some object." The knowledge base admits that no definition of evaluation can be perfect as there are many types that do not end up with assessment of worth, such as descriptive studies, so it suggests a definition that addresses the feedback process of any given evaluation. Thus, a second, more appropriate definition might be this: "Evaluation is the systematic acquisition and assessment of information to provide *useful* feedback about some object" [emphasis added] (n.d.). Ah, I am already feeling much better with this definition, as nowhere does it say that effective feedback or evaluation has to have any part of negativity. So, what might be better ways of providing this assessment or feedback? Two come to mind as appropriate. But just to reiterate, the usual notion that evaluation needs to point out the negatives, or what needs to be changed, is inaccurate.

Two better methods of providing evaluation are (a) 360-degree evaluation and (b) AI (Cooperrider, 2000; Cooperrider & Srivastva, 1987; Cooperrider & Whitney, 2000; Srivastva & Cooperrider, 1990).

360-Degree Evaluation

According to McCauley and Hezlett (2002), a 360-degree evaluation is a process of evaluation where employees (or supervisees) receive systematic feedback from multiple sources so that one individual does not hold all the cards, thus providing greater objectivity. "The groups providing feedback may include the employee's supervisor, peers, subordinates, and occasionally, clients. Upward feedback involves supervisors receiving feedback from their subordinates" (p. 318). Ward (1997) also included the person being evaluated in the process, with a self-report.

The nature of the feedback can vary depending on the organization's needs or process, but it can include personality traits, the ability to live up to the values of the organization, or productivity. Most often 360-degree evaluations are utilized for development rather than for performance evaluation. "Some recipients are advised to work on their development, while others are held accountable for their results (McCauley & Hezlett, 2002, p. 318). The reason for using a 360-degree evaluation is demonstrated elegantly by Ward (1997), with a quote from Adams (1991) he uses that follows:

> [Horses] have always understood a great deal more than they let on. It is difficult to be sat on every day by some creature without forming some opinion of them. On the other hand, it is perfectly possible to sit all day, every day, on top of another creature and not have the slightest thought about them whatsoever. (p. 6)

The point, of course, is that employees notice and have opinions about those above them, perhaps far greater than those who are on top may have of those who are reports. How we are treated by those in charge is always understood. That is one of the reasons I have tried to move to a level hierarchy, rather than a top-down format. Attending quickly in his book, Ward (1997) suggested that the two words found in regular evaluations that are omitted in his version of a 360-degree evaluation are confidential and anonymous; he noted also that in his opinion, nothing can ever be totally confidential in any organization. He argued that in many organizations, people are "happy to be identified with what they have said" (p. 6). Remember, my point has always been that evaluation does not have to be negatively framed, and when used for the development of those being evaluated, why wouldn't someone be happy to provide their perspectives on a person's strengths and performance? Having this type of evaluation has also been associated with increased improvement in productivity (London, Wohlers, & Gallager, 1991). An interesting add-on is that when structured for development, and including employees in the process of evaluation as well as design of the instrument, elements of value not usually thought of in traditional assessment can emerge (London & Beatty, 1995). I am reminded of my qualitative data from the national survey I did on site supervisors, where teamwork and self-care were indicated as important factors they would like to see when taking on new interns—something I never would have guessed (Edwards & Pyskoty, 2004). Ward also suggested that a multirater or multisourced evaluation has uses beyond those usually associated with evaluation, such as personal self-development, organized training and development, and team building.

Methods of data collection can be done formally by handing out a survey-type form that includes both rating scales as well as opportunities for open-ended questions that provide qualitative statements from the raters about specific components that they believe to be important when directed at either development or evaluation. Remember that evaluation is not theoretically geared toward providing negative comments or positive comments, as a requirement, unless the creators of the instrument deem them necessary.

Most interesting to me is how technology has interceded, and there are now online 360-degree evaluation sites that will provide organizations with a platform for doing multirater evaluations. These for-profit sites allow for input from multiple sources, and the feedback is collated and provided in a standardized form. This also allows for an anonymous feedback process.

Bell Curves as an Epistemological Framer of Evaluating Success

Our university utilizes a back and forth evaluation process where the site supervisor and the intern both fill out a likert-type scale evaluation on several dimensions, in addition to a few open-ended questions, and then both parties are asked to share them with each other. Quite frankly the ratings are like an A to F typical grading scale, but the way the evaluation form and process are structured leads to a situation where students are stuck in a perceived double bind. If they have negative comments to say about their site supervisor, they fail to indicate them. An interesting outcome of this process is that all too often site supervisors provide feedback ratings, in the middle to upper middle ranges, stating that they want to leave room for improvement later on. Although this type of attitude about rating is common, it leads, in my opinion, to a standard bell-shaped curved evaluation process, and it leaves little room for talking about strengths. Our notion that interns are midrange does not allow for the expectation of excellent evaluations, and it also does not take development into consideration. What may be excellent in the early stages of learning should not be the same during later stages, but the ratings do not take this developmental perspective into consideration.

A change is necessary, I believe, related to a change in quality of education and training, and our understanding of how expectation can create potentiality. We have been using the bell-shaped curve in education since the middle of the 19th century, again based primarily on a statistical assumption and expectation that all educational endeavors need to be laid out in such a way that only a few students will achieve at a high rate, and some at the lower rate, and most will end up in the middle. This expectation leads us to conclusions about people under evaluation that is not true, providing a self-fulfilling prophesy that also leaves out the potential efforts of those instructing or supervising. It also drives administrators of educational programs to worry that their classes are too easy or too tough—those situations where there are a lot of A and B type evaluations must be too easy, and vice versa, for those perceived as too tough. Expectation is a mighty informer of our reality. This mentality also leads to the false conclusion that some teachers or examiners must inflate the grades or evaluations, thus average students are the norm. Associated expectations when using the bell curve as a method of evaluation are that only those with certain skills or natural ability can succeed at the higher level and it is the evaluator's job and responsibility to sort out specific people into either the higher level or the lower level. This also leads to the limiting of those who can achieve at the highest level. Let me say that again: The use of a bell curve mentality limits those who can succeed at the upper levels. It is not necessarily the people being evaluated who are limiting themselves based on intelligence, efforts, or ability, as this can also be attributed to the evaluation method—our instrument of evaluation—which can limit success by limiting first our perceptions of them but also their own self-perceptions. Most often these factors are favored toward more privileged people at the high end and less privileged groups at the lower end—or as I have discussed before, seeing certain people as being at risk rather than at potential. Henry Ford said, "Whether you think you can, or whether you think you can't, you are right." Our epistemology and beliefs shape what we construe as correct, and this includes how we see those we have as reports or stakeholders.

The J-Curve as a New Normal of Evaluation and Success

In addition to our beliefs as a shaper of success, the implementation of conditions that can do a better job of encouraging and accounting for success,

along with increasing that self-efficacy—personal agency—with improvement of supervision and leadership, can lead to better outcomes of all or almost all within our professional reach. Hundreds of schools around the country have moved to a J-curve model that changes the deterministic mentality to one of hope and accountability for both students as well as teachers. The J-curve, when applied to education and schools, "does not limit the percentage of students capable of succeeding. This model is built on the conviction that with proper instructional practices over time, there is an unlimited capacity for successful students" (Mikels & Sartori, 2009).

Changing that old saw, which intimates that most people should never be graded high on every variable, to allow for growth later no matter how well the person under evaluation turns out, to one that *expects* high performance from the players, also puts some of the responsibility on those who are in charge—supervisors, chairs, administrators, and directors. Many schools that have changed this bell curve mentality to j-curved possibility have seen drastic increases in their student competencies. Strengths-based agencies are doing the same sort of evaluation of their interns and employees because it is part and parcel of strengths-based administration and supervision.

One of the most productive and coveted community mental health agencies I know of is the Schaumburg Family Counseling Center, in Schaumburg, Illinois. Students from all over apply for the three or four internship spots that are available every year; I have had a great working relationship with the center and feel fortunate that over the past 20-plus years, many of our students have interned there. I have watched it move from a mostly MRI strategic model to refined Solution-Focused and Narrative (both strengths-based) models of clinical work and training. It is mandatory that interns are there on Tuesdays and Thursdays from 10 in the morning until later in the evening. This completely strengths-based center provides months of collegial-based training and uses a one-way mirror and a reflecting team (Andersen, 1991b).

One of my former students, who did his internship at the Schaumburg center, told of a situation where a student from another country who was here on an educational visa didn't seem to get the model at first. My student was flabbergasted, although he was so well indoctrinated by this time with strengths-based ideas that not once did he ever hear a supervisor say a negative word or a critical comment or evaluative statement, but instead they pointed out—punctuated—everything this student did well and insured themselves that there were lots of opportunities to talk about the philosophy of their model, complete with literature to study. Eventually, this intern became highly competent and did extremely well with clients. The agency supervisors were true to their strengths-based model in clinical work as well as supervisory work.

The J-curve changes the expectation—a social construction—from one where it is expected that only some may produce well and most will perform in the middle, thus absolving those in charge and the learners of putting forth extra effort. As stated earlier, bell curves dictate that the outcome has already been predetermined in a specific direction with a specified percentage of outcomes within the normal part of the curve, thus limiting those who may succeed. J-curves also dictate the outcome, but as an expectation that higher performance and greater commitment to do what it takes will make it happen—by those in administrative, supervisor, and instructional positions, not by the learner. Learning is not a static, personal event, but like socially constructed change, it is an ongoing process that needs to be done in relationship. Those from the Taos Institute (Anderson et al., 2008) continue to remind us that, "It is through our relationship—through talking, gesturing, and acting together—that we determine what is real and valuable for us" (Anderson et al., 2008, p. 14). And thus, we must finally admit that "meaning is born in the act of affirmation" (Anderson et al., 2008, p. 15). The relationship between outcome and the work that students and teachers put into the process, as expected by the outcome, puts the ownership on both to do what it takes to accomplish the goal,

short of grade inflation. Our perception of what is possible, along with the tool we use to measure, have an effect on outcome. "Making meaning is something we do with each other" (Anderson et al., 2008, p. 25). We come back to this and the Pygmalion effect when we discuss AI later in this chapter.

Back to 360-Degree Evaluations

The use of multisourced evaluations with a frame to look for positives may be the one step to increasing personal agency and organizational competency that has yet to be tried or proven. It is highly unlikely that an agency where clients, coworkers, agency directors, clinicians, and clinical supervisors (multiple source evaluation) engage in 360-degree evaluations where there would be an incorrect evaluation of any employee. Using 360-degree evaluations does mean an additional level of commitment to the people who are in the organization, but the use of electronics can provide a simple and effective method for gathering, collating, and analyzing the outcome. I had set up a system like this years ago, when I was the clinical director of our practicum and internship experience. It worked great and had potential for providing quick and accurate responses for student evaluations, but it did take some work to get everyone committed to using it. In retrospect, training of site supervisors would have helped a great deal, but it was over a decade ago, and perhaps it was ahead of its time. Students' evaluation of their site supervisor was done in two phases, one that was shared and one that only the clinical coordinator saw, thus allowing our faculty to evaluate the site and site supervisor for decision making of site use in the future. One of the ongoing problems I see with sites is the use of rather new clinicians as supervisors. But the integration of fair and positive 360-degree evaluations by sites might add a layer of accountability as well as directionality of development as intended by the method anyway. In addition, as we see in the next section on AI, the use of finding and looking for strengths can produce incredibly powerful change for an organization.

APPRECIATIVE INQUIRY

Originally conceived of by David Cooperrider and Suresh Srivastva (1987) at Case Western Reserve University, AI (appreciative inquiry, as noted earlier) is an organizational development process of change, filled with the same philosophies and focuses that underpin strengths-based counseling and supervision. "Appreciative Inquiry is a way of thinking, seeing and acting for powerful, purposeful change in organizations. Appreciative Inquiry works on the assumption that whatever you want more of, already exists in all organizations" (Hall & Hammond, 1998). AI has been described as a way to bring about change by identifying the "best of 'what is' in order to pursue dreams and possibilities of 'what could be.' It is a search for strengths and life-giving forces that are found within every system—those factors that hold the potential for inspired, positive change" (Willoughby & Samuels, 2009, p. 1). As the postmodernist and social constructivist movement trounced through other fields such as literature, history, social justice, social science, counseling theory, and family studies, organizational development people at Case Western Reserve University led the way in applying their newfound philosophy and collaborative methods to their field (Barrett & Cooperrider, 2002; Cooperrider, Barrett, & Srivastva, 1995; Cooperrider & Dutton, 1999; Cooperrider & Sekerka, 2006; Cooperrider & Srivastva, 1987; Cooperrider, Whitney, & Stavros, 2008; Watkins & Cooperrider, 1996; Whitney, Cooperrider, Garrison, & Moore, 2002). AI moves the usual action research forward, from a first-order change (change in specific behaviors) to a second-order change where operating principles and paradigms give way to a discontinuous change. First-order change is where a social system changes behaviors but does not change the system's structure, while second-order change affects the rules of the system itself (Watzlawick, Weakland, & Fish, cited in Nichols, 2009). The movement from a problem-oriented perspective to a strengths-based perspective not only changes the behaviors but the rules (epistemology) of the organization with respect to change principles.

AI has been implanted into many other social organizational situations such as medical pedagogy (Quaintance, Arnold, & Thompson, 2010), organizational development, management pedagogy (Conklin, 2009), couple counseling using Positive Psychology (Perloiro, Neto, & Marujo, 2010), work to improve services for children and families (Onyett, 2009), and drug abuse among young marginalized people (McAdama & Mirza, 2009), to name only a few out of hundreds. To say that AI has taken the field of social sciences by storm would be an understatement. But perhaps, as we come soon in this chapter to the ideas put forth in Malcolm Gladwell's (2000) book, *The Tipping Point,* AI stands on the shoulders of other previous giants and perhaps can be the back door of change around the deep, deep pockets of the health care industry's marginalizing effects on other strengths-based therapies (Edwards, Chen, White, & Bradley, 2001).

What is AI, and how does it work? Like all of the other strengths-based concepts in this book, I can only whet your appetite for more. But those of you who have seen the need, either prior to or after reading this book, will find ample examples and clearer instructions to increase your understanding in many of the citations I have provided. At its most basic form, AI changes the usual paradigm of change, from one that looks for the problems and then fixes what is broken (a medical model), to one that searches for what works, and, through a series of conversations at every level of the organization, begins to define what those who are involved in the process like best and what is working well. Those involved then envision how the organization could produce more of that which is working well (Hall & Hammond, 1998). Cooperrider and Whitney (2000) described AI as a "co-evolutionary search for the best in people, their organizations, and the relevant world around them. In its broadest focus, it involves systematic discovery of what gives 'life' to a living system when it is most alive" (p. 5). At its heart, AI uses a 4-D model for moving an organization to new heights. Nobel Prize winner for dissipative systems, Prigogine's (1997) concept of how stressed systems can move to a higher level of organization is similar to the flow patterns of inquiry used in AI: discovery, dream, design, and destiny. An amazing, transformative process that is very similar to those I talked about in Chapter 3 is apparent. During all of the four cycles, from the discovery process to the destiny cycle, AI is consistent with the ideas of what we have been investigating together already, especially the idea of resiliency, which is a natural process in which we all participate. "Affirmative topic choice" is the core of any AI process, according to Cooperrider and Whitney, and the very seed of any change begins with the language and first questions that start the process. And though Cooperrider and Whitney's language is different, it has the very same intentions that our understandings of people or organizations (how we talk about them) are what shape the way we see them—our theories *will* determine how we know and see those with whom we work. And so, from the very first coming together, the very first expectation, the first words we speak to each other, this begins to create the future of our outcomes.

Discovery brings people together to begin, and rather than talking about what is broken, which focuses the conversations on broken parts and remediations—the usual methods of intervention–AI begins the conversations with many people coming together to discuss what it is that they like about the organization and what works well. Many iterations of the process happen, as pairs begin to look for those life-giving events and phenomena that they would like to increase and continue. Then the pairs may become four, or they may switch, always focusing on what gives life and success, rather than what breaks down. The methodology is fixed on successes and strengths, and during each iteration, as the process expands and doubles and moves to exponential possibilities, the groups keep notes on what it is that they would like to see continue because it is creating a healthy organization.

When introduced to new people, their questions are the usual ones: "But what about the problems? How will we fix the problems?" And sometimes, people's own top-down epistemological view is so

set, that it is difficult to get the change in the direction one wants. I taught a class on family therapy to a group of soon-to-be psychologists recently and although there were many in the class who resonated with the strengths-based ideas I presented, there were several who were so indoctrinated with the notion of pathology, that even when I demonstrated the techniques, they had grave doubts. Some said, yes, that is nice, but I do not think it would work with people who have been abused or with substance abusing people. They just had it in their heads that it would not work with these groups that they themselves were affiliated with—both clinically and personally. Our top-down enslavements can keep us from seeing possibilities, as some continue to believe that the only method that will work is the old, medically modeled one. Whitney and Trosten-Bloom (2010) answered this question by saying the following: "We are not saying to deny or ignore problems. What we are saying is that if you want to transform a situation, a relationship, an organization, or community, focusing on strengths is much more effective than focusing on problems" (p. 18).

Dreaming is the next phase, and it comes out of their discovery of what Cooperrider and Whitney (2000) find to be working well. Participants dream about what might be, what is possible, and what they appreciate about the organization. They use the interview narratives (yes, they call them narratives, too) to begin the process of listening to each other for what might be possible—dreaming of possibilities and amplifying what is already working, that could be useful in their future. But dreaming also puts the draw of a future to their narratives and thoughts and sets goals and directions. Dreaming also includes seeing where they all believe they fit in the grander scheme of things. Some organizations want to know what the world wants of them, using global notions, but imagine people in counseling spending time to see where they fit in their community, in their world. It gets them outside of themselves, and as Positive Psychology asks, helps them to see their interrelatedness with others. Helping others—being with others—has a positive effect on their joy and happiness and provides a buffer for their problems. So too, can this fit with organizations.

Designing the focus or dream and making it into a viable strategic plan can include going back and forth between the dream and the strategy to how it will be implemented; this dream requires sequencing the dream first, rather than beginning the design process. Putting the cart before figuring out what sort of power is going to run it would provide a potentially faulty construction process. Agencies that have not done their own process of making the dream fully understandable would not have a completed plan to follow. For some, this might mean redoing their community needs assessment and preparing for a revision of their mission statement and goals.

Destiny is seeing and envisioning where the organization is really headed. Destiny makes the entire process imperative and shows how the preferred outcomes (like with Narrative Therapy) provide a future pull that will guide the organization on to where it belonged all along. Destiny gives impetus to action, and like we have covered before, whether it is an action, a performance (narratives), a case of doing more of the same things that worked before (solution focused) or destiny, it propels the dreaming into the reality of what should be. As social constructivist models, we know that it is language that creates what can be real, but it is the behavior combined with belief that makes it come alive. Practice and performance makes it real.

While I was writing this section on AI, my wife picked up the movie *Invictus* (Eastwood, McCreary, Lorenz, Neufeld, & Freeman, 2009) for us to watch one night. *Invictus* is about the leadership of two intertwined people, South Africa President Nelson Mandela, and the team captain of the South African Springbok rugby team, François Pienaar. The team had been a symbol of apartheid but became a turning point of the country's change as the two men coevolved as their leaderships intersected. At one point in the film, Pienaar, in one of the best short motivational speeches, tells his team that winning this final World Cup match was "their destiny." I got goose bumps as I recognized the intersection of

AI today and that these two amazing leaders from 1995 postapartheid rebuilding of the country used AI concepts perhaps unwittingly. Central to the movie was Mandela giving Pienaar a copy of a Victorian poem called "Invictus", Latin for unconquered, that had kept Mandela alive during his 27 years as a political prisoner. The poem ends with this:

> It matters not how strait the gate,
> How charged with punishments the scroll,
> I am the master of my fate:
> I am the captain of my soul.
>
> —William Ernest Henley (1888, p. 4)

Several points of interest undergird the notions of AI. First is the principle of anticipation, that humans have unlimited resources for generativity and that our positive images of what is possible will lead and propel our future actions. This has been documented in placebo affects that allow us to believe situations are getting better because of a sugar coated pill, because we want them to get better (Kirsch, 2009; Kirsch & Moncrieff, 2007). In addition, how we view others, in fact, how we view anything it seems, can change based on our interpretation of the data we get from our senses. The Pygmalion effect demonstrates that when a group of teachers are led to believe (perceive) their classrooms are filled with underachieving students but are told that the students are gifted, this leads to amazing achievement and outcome, simply because those who work with them are led to believe (perceive) that they are quite capable (Rosenthal & Rubin, 1978).

In 2009, during my presidency, the Illinois Counseling Association began a Leadership Development Academy (LDA) to train new, interested leaders. The LDA was the brainchild of a past president and a president-elect who saw a need to increase and prepare new leaders in our organization. Held two days before the annual conference in Springfield, Illinois, our trainer was Neil Samuels, an organizational development specialist with ties to AI. The workshop training lasted one evening and one full day and utilized the concepts of AI. Samuels began the process by talking about the premises of AI and then jumped right into having participants get into groups of two to discuss what they liked about the organization, what, in their opinion made it work well, why they were members, and how they came to be interested in leadership. The process impressed even those who maintained a typical mental health view of problems. But by the end of the training, we had a well-versed and ready group of new potential leaders who had begun to take their place in the organizational leadership table. This is scheduled to happen every 2 years, and from my point of view, it will increase the likelihood of providing good leadership in an already overworked, volunteer organization. I was deeply impressed, and this is part of why I think it is such powerful tool for organizations. Just think how we might amplify the continuing strengths of our organization. Just think how encouraging it is for every member to see his or her worth and to know that the leaders want to encourage that strength for their own and the association's growth and potential. It is amazing.

One final point on Cooperrider and Whitney's (2000) views of strengths and change is really neat. They believe, and now I do also, that looking for strengths is heliotropic. Sunflowers are heliotropic, and Leonardo da Vinci first noticed and wrote about it in plant life. The tracking of the sun—of that which gives life—is heliotropism, and humans track that which gives us life, that which affirms life, that which appreciates life forces—our strengths. We believe that all organizations are heliotropic, searching for and growing in the direction of positive imagery. It sounds so much like Rogers and Maslow that I just can't help but wonder how it got lost in the muddle of the medical model we later ascribed to. Noticing and punctuating and amplifying strengths, rather than weaknesses, are what sustain us. And like green physician Larry Dossey (1990), who tells us how interconnected we are with, not only each other but the whole cosmos, it suggests that we are "recycled through lifetimes of several stars before becoming localized on our planet. Thus, not only are our roots in each other, they are also in the stars. We are, literally, star stuff" (p. 79).

No wonder we keep looking for the sun!

THE TIPPING POINT OF CHANGE

Malcolm Gladwell's (2000) writings and research from his best-selling book, *The Tipping Point* (another book which all should read), indicate that change can occur very rapidly or at least it appears that way. In fact, change has been building all the time, and then like a deck of cards, it comes tumbling to a new form. I know that the change from problem-focused counseling and supervision has been occurring over several years, and now is the time for the leaders to begin supervising this way. But what will make strengths-based clinical work become the usual way of working? Many supervisors are already using strengths-based ideas, hoping that we will prevail, and Gladwell tells us how it just could happen.

The tipping point is an excellent idea, with solid research cited to demonstrate its cause and effectiveness. It is, according to Gladwell, the best way to understand how trends in any phenomena sweep through culture like an epidemic. Using historical and current narratives of social events—from Paul Revere's ride that called men to fight the British, to the Hush Puppy shoe craze, Gladwell (2000) demonstrated how a few factors can be found to be the creators of change. Epidemiological evaluations of phenomena change demonstrate that there are three factors, each with component parts, that can be found in all cases of rapid social change: (a) the notion of contagiousness, (b) the notion that little causes can end up having large effects, and (c) the notion that final change will happen at a dramatic moment rather than gradually, at a tipping point when everything falls into place.

Gladwell (2000) broke these down into three rules for epidemic change, each with subtle smaller component pieces that make sense for those of us who would like to tip the medical model over to a strengths-based model in our fields. It seems that when Gladwell looked at all the facts, these three factors began to emerge in every case where there was a raging epidemic of social change, as well as disease epidemics.

The Law of the Few

In every case of social tipping point change, there are those who have the ability to disseminate to many others the idea of what will be changed. These few people have many contacts and through their enthusiasm, knowledge, and personal charm, they are able to spread the word so that others get on board with the new idea. Paul Revere knew many people and who to go to in order to spread the word. But for this to happen, there are several types of people that contribute to the epidemic of social change.

Connectors are those people who just like to be with many people. They know everyone within and outside of their field and are connected to the right people with influence and access to other contacts. This is a multiplier effect to move the social change to others, making it grow out from the hubs like a spider web. But unlike a spider web, a connector's influence runs in many directions and with many different types of people. These people are very well connected.

Mavens are people who gather knowledge from around them, all sorts of knowledge. And according to Gladwell (2000), they are more than absorbers of knowledge; they share their knowledge with others altruistically. They share their knowledge because they want to help others with what they know. They willingly tell others of their newfound knowledge because they want to help others with it. Most of all they are educators, sharing their knowledge with those around them who will listen. Their knowledge is legion and they are more than willing to share it with those who want to know.

Salesmen are the third type of people who fall within the law of the few. They have the ability to share their knowledge with many different people and convince them that what they are selling is good for them. They make them want to take part in the new epidemic, the next big thing. Gladwell (2000) has many narrative stories about these three types of people and how they are part of the contagiousness of tipping point social change.

As I looked at the host of strengths-based ideas and the proliferation of each of their ideas, the law of the few makes sense. The father of Positive Psychology during its current iteration is Martin Seligman. He was a past president of the APA and he made it a point to make Positive Psychology his signature for the year of his presidency. Because of his scope of influence, first with his learned helplessness work (1975) and later with the momentum of the growing field of Positive Psychology, he has an ever growing cadre of friends and the knowledge of the field of mental health that can spread the word. And, if one were to track down the literature on Positive Psychology, a running thread is the attachment of Seligman with almost every research project about this "new" idea. He is the ubiquitous constant who almost single-handedly made it a force to be reckoned with in our field. More than that, Seligman also saw the writing on the wall, that evidence-based models were becoming important, and having research in his blood, he has backed up his work, insisting on both qualitative and quantitative work to follow the PP line of reasoning. What is more important is that he has garnered a cadre of the faithful, who have been sick and tired of continuing down the pathological path and are ready to move into the next force of psychology, past what those forefathers like Rogers and Maslow were able to do. Seligman has used the few to push forward into a new, emerging science of human beings . . . looking for health, and what creates wellness, and now using it to produce evidence-based treatments that still fit within the model of health care. The amazing thing is that David Cooperrider has done the same thing for AI, and in fact, he has also hooked up with Seligman to make Positive Psychology and AI common household words in the field of strengths-based thinking and the lucrative education that will train others who are clamoring for change. Those involved with this movement have been collaborative and collectivist by not excluding other disciplines, and in the end, they may be the saviors of a field that has been mired in a problem-saturated view of human dilemmas.

When one looks at the other models, like solution focused, narrative, and so forth, it is apparent that they started out with one or two clinicians who had great ideas and spread out to many other clinicians, but they missed the chutzpah and large connections with others like a Seligman or a Cooperrider. Of the strengths-based models mentioned earlier, Solution-Focused Therapy has a lead in Illinois and comes in second nationally. This can be attributed to one factor alone; during the years preceding this survey, three Solution-Focused Therapy trainers, Scott Miller (see, e.g., Miller, Hubble & Duncan, 1996), and husband and wife team John Walter and Jane Peller (1992), made a major campaign of Solution-Focused Therapy training around the state. It cannot be only as some suspect, that the idea caught the attention of managed care groups, or it would be represented across disciplines too. Narrative therapists were eager to show off their wares too, but riding on the heels of the grand illusions of the golden years of family therapy, with its many schools and models, that is, Murray Bowen, Jay Haley, Harry Goolishian, or even Michel White, the time was not ready for a major epidemic, and they were not ready to move their ideas into a grand researchable arena. They may be used with great style within the arena of family therapists who ascribe to the usefulness of the model, but they have not crossed over to the masses of the mental health field with the full force of a Positive Psychology. And they lacked one of the powers of epidemic force, that of stickiness.

Stickiness is a quality or ability of an entity to persevere and stay in the mainstream of ideas. Gladwell (2000) moved the law of the few further along, noting that if it were as simple as having a few well-connected, knowledgeable salespersons spreading the word, marketing would be doing better for all products and, in our field, models. Remember that in Chapter 3, I mentioned that

there are over 400 clinical models and more sprouting up every day as academics and quick-thinking individuals invent and try out new ways of clinical treatment. Stickiness is what makes a few of them stay around for a while. They have appeal. It isn't just that they have been proven to be evidence based. And now, even though the National Institute for Mental Health has included efficacy research in limited ways, it still isn't enough to make some of them stick like a Positive Psychology or even a Solution-Focused model. Stickiness is something beyond logic and beyond typical marketing. As Gladwell (2000) said, "We all want to believe that the key to making an impact on someone lies with the inherent quality of the idea we present" (p. 131). But it isn't enough, apparently. Your agency, or a counseling model, can have all of the right bells and whistles, all the right contacts, all the right clinically trained staff, and excellent leaders and salespersons that have long and broad reach to all the right people, and still stumble. The answer is easy yet illusive. "There is a simple way to package information that, under the right circumstances, can make it irresistible. All you have to do is find it" (Gladwell, 2000, p. 132). And you can find it to make it stick. Most of the ideas that cause social epidemics to stick are due to idiosyncratic and novel ways of making them appealing to larger groups of people. This leads us to the last point of what embodies the tipping point of change—that of context.

Context provides a historic place in which the idea being present makes sense. It gives that idea a place that fits conditions and current thinking of the times. During one of my presentations on the concept of context being a huge part of understanding human dilemmas from an alternative view, I show a picture of a turtle with a snail on its back. The caption reads, "What does a snail say when riding on a turtle's back?" When the motion begins and the next sentence is revealed, the answer, of course, is "Weeee!" To the snail, the turtle is traveling really fast. All things are relative to something else. And the principle that adds fuel to the making of an epidemic is how powerful context can be, because it depends on time and place for the circumstance to have an effect on others. Gladwell (2000) pointed to broken window theory, created by criminologists George Kelling and Catherine Coles, as evidence of small significant events of context creating change (cited in Gladwell, 2000, p. 141). According to their theory, small changes create bigger outcomes; this was demonstrated when the New York crime spree ended because the police chief followed their advice and began to focus on cleaning up the high crime areas so that they no longer appealed to criminals, thus leading to the lowering of the epidemic. The same phenomena and intervention were used in the New York subway system, as police fought crime by cleaning up the graffiti on the trains. The compounding effect of small changes makes it a dangerous-looking place for criminals to ply their trade. The context of keeping both of these places clean and uninviting to criminal behavior had an overwhelming effect on reducing crime (Kelling & Coles, cited in Gladwell, 2000). Epidemics of social change can be reversed, it seems, through contextual interventions that provide a tipping point for change. Gladwell (2000) made the point that for an idea or phenomena or even an attitude change, the audience that you are playing to needs to be swept up, infected, and changed in critical ways. The stickiness factor needs to grab onto those who are to be changed and make them believers. This can be done by the way the message gets to them or by the importance that is attached from the audience to the giver of the message. When a very familiar face of a Marty Seligman begins to talk to those in his field, and even outside his guild because he is well known, people listen and put faith in what he has to say. The same is true about a David Cooperrider, but not nearly to the extent of a Seligman. For an agency to take shape and become well known it takes just a few people who are well connected and well informed—trusted and skilled at getting their message across—to infect a field heavily entrenched in a problem-focused view of life and helping into the possibility of a Positive Psychology. What seems to matter most, however, is that groups of collaborators who are already on the bandwagon then move the idea to a higher level through their own dedication and involvement. For an agency to do well, for a training facility to be enriched and enriching, for a strengths-based model to take hold, a few well-known, highly motivated, and connected individuals need to take the message to the group, know a great deal about it, and sell it to many other people. The dedication of a few can tip an idea to change what seems unchangeable.

SOLIDIFYING CHANGE

What fascinates me the most from Gladwell's (2000) work is how closely related the ideas of what creates a tipping point for change are to the notion of socially constructed problem-saturated stories from the postmodern models we have talked about. It doesn't take much to begin an epidemic of problem-saturated stories or of positive change. A few connectors, a handful of mavens, and good salesmanship can create a social epidemic that, when spun right, will stick for a long time. It becomes hard to combat against, in either direction, and we are likely to create a change that will be around for a long time.

There are several ways, from what we have discussed so far, that will help anyone make a change to a long-lasting, strengths-based model, especially in a culture where managed care and the medical model are still in charge. One idea belongs to Stephen Covey and the others are from Gladwell, as we discussed earlier. First, as I mentioned earlier in this chapter, my wife always tries to be a trim tab for change. She works for a company where plant specialists, greenhouse management professionals, and those with doctorates in biology rule the roost, as might be expected. Sometimes her MBA ideas don't fly well. She sees and understands how problems in her industry come about and can suggest proactive fixes (I know this isn't about fixing things) and yet, her ideas sometimes do not go over as well as when presented by someone within the fold of the industry. It is a different corporate culture, but Covey (2004) said if you want to create permanent change, paradigms need to shift, and one way to encourage that is by being what he called a trim tab. A trim tab is a smaller part of a large sailing vessel's rudder that is more easily turned, due to size and mass. Once the trim tab begins to move, it causes enough of a shift in direction that the rest of the rudder can then begin to follow; it works on the inertia of the ship to more easily change course. Inertia is a great word to use for the reluctance of change among humans who are top-downed with the way they believe things are. And if you are a trim tab for change, and you have connections and are a maven and have salespeople, you can have a tipping point. So, when you are filled with the force of strengths-based ideas and you feel like you have all of those ancients working against you, remember to be a trim tab. Reach out to those around you and state your case and bask in the knowledge that your clients are getting the best sort of experience that they can get from anyone. And all of this can happen without pointing out a single problem.

Leaders need to be focused on the strengths of those with whom they work and also the strengths of themselves. Seligman and the strengths-based ideas are correct, in that leaders need to hone their own strengths, and use them, as well as encourage the strengths of those who work for them. Leaders cannot do it all themselves and need to have dedicated teams who are in tune with and carry the message to the masses. They need to have teams that have members with diverse strengths. And the masses need to be infected with the mission of the culture in which they work. The masses need to know what it is that drives them and feel as if they are part of the larger whole, with a voice that matters.

Gladwell (2000) noted that research also shows that small groups, with diverse and complementary skills, prove to be far more workable, creative, and productive. Their autonomy and knowledge of their own needs and abilities remind me of what Florida and Goodnight (2005) found. Information-Age people are quite capable of working for rewards that are geared to their intrinsic needs rather than traditional carrot and stick rewards. Something happens to Information-Age workers when leadership focuses on their strengths and trusts their judgment. Look at Google or Apple for confirmation of my point. To think that a group of dedicated, interested, clinically trained and dedicated people cannot do the same is simply wrongheaded.

Finally, I have a few thoughts that I think might be useful to the whole field in general. With respect to clinical supervision, I have noted in the state in which I live, that all too often interns are given the newest licensed kid on the block as their clinical supervisor. I think this is clearly wrongheaded. In addition, doing workshops on supervision and talking about supervision with interns, I find that sometimes sites and site supervisors are focused more on themselves and the clerical needs of their agencies. They use interns to fill in for clerical staff; these interns can be used inappropriately, in general, rather than being trained as good clinicians. What our interns need are skilled and willing seasoned clinicians who also have understanding of supervision in all its shapes and sizes. Interns need to work with their supervisors on cases to get a sense of how to integrate their book learning with what is really happening in the trenches. Our field owes those who are coming into the field the best they can offer.

In addition, I truly believe that in many parts of our country, we have a glut of clinicians, while in other areas there are too few of them. The disproportionate glut is caused by universities and free-standing graduate programs filling student spaces rather than adjusting the limits of students to need. Nationally, ratios of students should be lowered where the numbers of clinicians who are coming into the field are at a rate that makes it harder to find internship sites and eventually jobs in the field. Our field has become a cancer that will not regulate its own growth, and that will, in the end, cause problems beyond belief. In metropolitan areas, the clamor for internship sites has produced free-for-all proportions, I am afraid, compounded by the fact that the competition for jobs is fierce. We do no service to our students or our own reputation if, at the end of a costly educational experience, many of them end up without jobs in their hard-won vocation.

Finally, agencies can move to an excellence of operation if they use community counseling skills. Don't reinvent the wheel, but find your niche and then search for partners to provide added value. Earlier in this book, I tell the story of several agencies that go the extra mile, collaborating with dentists, optometrists, and the like, to provide added service at minimal or no cost to their clients. It is this sort of additional forethought for clients' well-being that can set them heads and shoulders above the fray. In this day of limited funding, partner with other community agencies to provide much needed free or low cost continuing educational services, and find ways to provide those with the continuing educational credits that clinicians need to hold their licenses. The collaboration between agencies can produce a multiplier effect that could reduce costs, as well as increase staff competencies and keep them around in an era of job hopping. The training of new replacement staff, as well as the cost of rehire and staff loss, could be mitigated by providing more opportunity, engaging staff more in operations and creativity, and playing to their strengths. Our staff, as well as our leadership at every level, are our biggest resources, and we should do all we can do to maintain them. When one moves to a 360-degree model of development evaluation rather than one based on a single person's biased observations and changes the thinking that suggests there are three categories—superior, midlevel, and low–level employees—and commits to the work a J-curve entails, the field will grow stronger. We should focus on students' and employees' strengths rather than on their weaknesses, set collaborative attainable goals, and include them in the process of collaborative personal and organizational change. When you look for your destiny, know that changing to a strengths-based model will meet some resistance; therefore, become a trim tab and gather a group of like-minded people who are connectors, mavens, and salespersons and spread the word. In this way, the field will really begin to change. Then we can all watch us grow from a focus on numbers and quantity, to value and quality. You can do it.

My internship class in community mental health counseling ended with a circle where each of the interns was to write a capstone paper about their years in training and education, especially focused on how the internship experience had pulled several years of study together for them. As we each went around the circle talking (I took a turn also), we realized that three of the eight students were headed off to doctoral programs around the country, several had jobs already, and a few were still in the process of deciding what to do. I ended my talk with some information from my ongoing research for this book, particularly that envisioning is great, but taking the steps to make it come true is far more important. It is not enough to have insight or goals; it is the action of being acted upon, practiced, performed—all of the ending products of all of the strengths-based ideas—that makes the difference. One of the students said, "Ya know, my mother always says 'ain't nothin to it but to do it'" (L. Hayes, personal communication, June 23, 2010).

In the next chapter, I discuss session management, and in Chapter 8, there are real case situations with two widely diverse stakeholders that demonstrate how I use strengths-based clinical supervision to transform clinicians into competent, self-efficacious, and excellent stakeholders, capable of helping their own clients transform also. For surely, the point of clinical supervision, like clinical work itself, is not to evaluate and point out weaknesses, according to all of the strengths-based work, but to punctuate and amplify what is going well . . . going very well.

PART III

Faces of Strength: Putting My Currency Where My Mouth Is

7

SUPERVISION SESSIONS AND PERSONNEL MANAGEMENT

Vantage Point, Point of View, and Perspective

It's All in the Way You See It

Supervision based on social constructionism promotes multiple possibilities, an emphasis on meaning that is constructed through dialogue, and a view of the supervisory relationship as collaborative rather than hierarchical.

—Copeland, Dean, and Wladkowski (2011, p. 28)

Benjamin Kotkov (2005), an emeritus professor of psychology with as many letters after his name as a well-decorated four-star general, said that, "There are probably as many models of supervision as there are theories, and as many operating styles as there are supervisors" (p. 29). Well, we know that there are over 400 models of counseling and/or psychotherapy, and if Kotkov is correct, and I think he is, the field is as wide as the Mississippi River and as deep as the Pacific Ocean. That leaves a lot of room for variation, and not much to be certain of, regardless of all that has been written. I have also made the case that most of the models are based on a medial prototype that assesses for problems and seeks to correct those mistakes rather than look for what is going right, and it

encourages more of those behaviors and attitudes. But to be fair, at least at sometime during the course of supervision, the job of a supervisor is to help the supervisee become better as a clinician, *as well* as a person. To do that, one must have a vehicle to encourage growth and change. How the supervisor does that is through the process of encouragement and suggestion, all the while allowing the "youth" of the supervisee to explore and seek guidance when they think or feel they need it, to provide suggestions with an attitude that the supervisee has the right to find his or her own path. And that is the trick of being a strengths-based supervisor.

Throughout the preceding pages I have provided you with both the old and the new, at least as I understand and have practiced supervision over the past 40-plus years. I hope that you have come to understand, too, that there is a good reason to move from the old to the new. It is time, and it is being held back because of myth and money. Strengths-based work, especially when it comes to clinical supervision, is a far more empowering way of helping clinicians become a force for positive change. I must admit that I came to the strengths-based view quite by accident, as I was first supervised by several competent clinical supervisors from many different fields and models. All have been relatively helpful, and a few were hurtful in their attempts to make me competent in their own view. My journey of documenting and researching the strengths-based perspective began when Mei Chen and I first wrote an article back in 1999 in response to an article by Oppenheimer (1998). In Oppenheimer's article, she described an experience with supervision akin to the Lin-Chi Zen tradition, where students are beaten into submission in order to guide them on their journey. After reading this article and squaring it with my own experience after providing many workshops on clinical supervision, I came to the conclusion that both in the field and in academia, there are several reasons that propel one into the realm of being a supervisor—much of which does not make one competent. Much of our beliefs about being competent at supervision, either clinically or organizationally, come from both how we understand what can create change, as well as our own experience and education in supervision we received both early on and along our journey. In the field, one usually becomes a supervisor through attrition and years served. There is a belief that more years make one a better clinician and thus qualified to be a good supervisor. More experience does, in fact, make us more competent at what we do in own method (Gladwell, 2008). And along the way, we might change how and what we do to make it more simple as well as comfortable. Yet, as Miller et al. (2007) have shown, most clinical work is "enhanced" by looking for what the clinician and supervisor think has been going wrong—a problem-focused method—rather than looking for what works for each situation—a strengths-based method. So, many supervisors may have been trying to get their supervisees to do the same year after year, based on a problem-focused model. Chapter 1 is filled with models that demonstrate a problem-focused model. It is, after all, the common supervisory position emulating the model of more traditional clinical models. Many supervisors who came up this way, in my opinion, are still excellent supervisors. Nevertheless, it has been my experience that many of these folks have come to the position of being a supervisor because of their service and tenure, not because they have had course work or a record of effective work as a supervisor. In my 40-plus years in this field, I have known several well-educated and even well-authored supervisors who I would not want to supervise me or any of the students/colleagues in the field I care about. I have known early-in-the-field doctoral level supervisors, as well as old and seasoned supervisors, who practice what I consider to be an outdated, problem-focused, hierarchically oriented form of supervision as well as clinical care because they learned it early on and continue to believe it to work well. And it may do so, or they may just believe it to work. After all, as Johann Wolfgang von Goethe said, "A man sees in the world what he carries in his heart," (1828), or if you like a less intimidating view, remember that Einstein told us that our theory determines what it is we will see. I have gone at length to incriminate the more traditional medically oriented problem focus as the only way, so I needn't go any further.

In academia, as it is our capital for rank and privilege, there has also been an assumption that those who research, publish, and provide consultation and workshops on their subject are better at what they profess than those in the field; perhaps this is why there are so many jokes about the ivory towers. I have known many doctoral-level faculty who went straight through their master's and doctoral work skipping a solid base of clinical work, aside from their practicum and internship experiences, yet they ended up in faculty positions, supervising students' clinical experience. They may have advanced degrees, and even good solid knowledge of clinical work from a theoretical perspective, but they lack that fund of knowledge I spoke about earlier.

IMPLEMENTING STRENGTHS-BASED SUPERVISION STRATEGIES

I believe that all good supervisors have an ever changing plan that accompanies their journey with their supervisees, as well as an internal guidance system based on those executive skills I talked about in Chapter 2, which lead them through every session. These plans, or world views of supervision, may or may not be tailor made for the supervisee(s) the supervisor is seeing, but they should be. The refined personalized plan begins with the contracting of services to be provided by the supervisor and the expectations of the supervisee as well as their collaborative goals for the supervisory sessions. These inform the supervisors of what to say or do along the way, as they listen and interact with those whom they have this unique relationship. As they listen, watch, and think, how they respond is a function of this relationship and with what they see as important steps in helping them attain their goal of providing quality clinical work. Most beginning supervisors want to know what the cognitive process is, the thinking that goes on moment to moment during supervision. Over the rest of this chapter I provide several novel yet important ways in which I believe a strengths-based supervisor might use first personal operational changes and then systemic changes in order adopt a strengths-based bearing. I begin with a way to change how we view the colleagues we supervise using photographic techniques as a metaphor. This is followed by stages of the supervisory process, including contracting and evaluation, and ending with the 360-degree evaluation process instrumental in action research.

I have written quite a bit about worldview and how our mind has been enslaved (Siegel, 2007) by the narratives we have uploaded. Now I want to talk about several ways a supervisor can get around those preconceived ways of knowing—modify your epistemology if you will. I want to introduce you to some other new-to-supervision ideas that come from the arts and mindfulness.

Vantage Point, Point of View, and Perspective

One of the more interesting ideas is that of point of view and perspective. We toss these notions around like it matters because it does. But have you ever thought about what it means? How about perspective? How do you understand the concept of perspective, and how is it that two people have different perspectives and yet are viewing the same phenomena or scene? Our ways of thinking and understanding human interactions by understanding point of view, perspective, and vantage points are very real and provide a challenge to a singular point of view being correct. Even though I have thought about how I implement strengths-based supervision, I never actually thought of these different ways of understanding as clearly as I did until I began to take fine arts photography classes. As I became engrossed in how these different ways of seeing and understanding the same subject can be so different, as well as change what we are viewing, I could see the usefulness of them as applications to how we supervise. This is in line with the constructionist view and becomes relevant as we unpack the multiplicity they allow us with respect to what our own lens provides. For those of you who are adept at photography, I hope you will begin to see where I am going right away and forgive my beginner's mind at a field I love and continue to study. For those who do not, sit back and let this metaphor teach you something that may help you with both supervision as well as photography.

Photography, as well as supervision, are all about capturing information to illuminate a subject with richness and interest. While we might think that it is about truth, it is not. Renown photographer David Hurn has said that, "If truth implies factual accuracy and objectivity, then the connection is completely severed. The only factually correct aspect of photography is that it shows what something looked like—under a very particular set of circumstances" (Hurn & Jay, 2009, p. 39). We already know from the social constructionists that truth is something we create through our discourse. What is interesting to me is that both require dedicated and intentional thinking that effect the final outcome in a useful way. One can capture the same subject from multiple perspectives, points of view, and very different vantage points over time, intensity, and dimension. The final picture or outcome can be fuzzy, sharp, overexposed or underexposed. You have to have a plan, as well as follow that plan for each and every time you supervise or take a picture, if the outcome is to be remarkable, honest, and clear. One of my photography teachers, nationally know landscape photographer Willard Clay's mantra to us was, "You have to photograph like you mean it" (W. Clay, personal communication, June 18, 2011). What he means is that all of your being must be invested in having the best outcome. Neither good photography nor great supervision can be done without introspection. You have to know your equipment, study your subject, and take great care to ensure that the results produce the best possible outcome. As I studied the famous artistic photographers like Robert Frank, Henri Cartier-Bresson, and others, I realized that it was their ability to take an ordinary subject and make it exceptional that made them great. They are able to do that because they are intentional and introspective and look for the best in their subjects. It is that ability to translate what you do and make your work exceptional that I hope you are getting to understand as a supervisor, leader, or administrator.

I am intrigued by the fact that one begins to see what one has been taught or told to see. I took a nature photography class on the photographing of dragonflies, damselflies, and butterflies. These tiny little creatures, so illusive and fragile in the wild, became more obvious to me *because I was looking for them.* Our yard, a potpourri of wildflowers mostly filled with bees, became to my astonished eyes filled with Ruby Meadowhawk dragonflies. They were everywhere in our yard, literally, and illuminated to my wife and daughter also. One day, as my wife and I came upon a pond on the grounds where she works, we became focused on a tiny Bluet Damselfly, only a little over an inch long, as it flitted from one plant to another in the pond. Easily missed, we were now tuned in to see them. Because I was looking for them to photograph, they became almost too numerous to count. I am sure these very tiny creatures were always there, but we were now more aware of them, so we simply saw more of them. Einstein was correct when he said that our theory changes what and how we see. If we look for something, we will most likely see it. We become more aware of what was already there. Let us see how we might apply this to supervision.

Vantage point.

One's vantage point has to do with our own placement in space relative to the subject we are looking at. Photographers use vantage points all the time, as they climb up higher to see more of what they want to capture, or they back away from the subject to get a wider view, or they get closer to photograph a specific piece or part (see Photos 7.1 and 7.2). When I showed Photo 7.1 in my photography class and online at my Facebook page, many saw it as a mountain range in Scandinavia, until they saw a more complete part of the whole and could recognize it as a tree stump in water. Our eyes accept the signals and send them on to our brain, which interprets what we are seeing in an instant, sorting through many similar scenes and fixing on one, even though it is not the actual physical object. A lens, be it human, mechanical, or digital, has the ability to change the view of every object it is observing, depending on how we set the lens up, and because of a storehouse of preview experiences we fix to. Photographers use this to their advantage, for instance, in making part of the object being viewed appear closer to the eye, thus depth of field is used to their advantage. The object can also be manipulated by looking down on it, thus giving it a shorter and more compressed appearance as interpreted in the mind. TV and film camerapersons use this all the time in order to

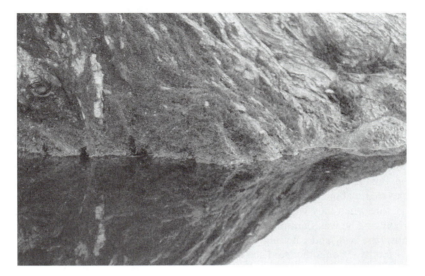

Photo 7.1

Photo 7.2

make someone tall appear shorter or someone short appear taller. Photographers can make a model look taller or shorter photographically by a slight elevation of the person's vantage point, looking down, thus compressing the subject ever so slightly. Vantage point and other visual effects can change how we see a subject.

When we talk about vantage point in supervision, it suggests that we have an opportunity to delay our response time to that "enslaved" view in our mind, if we become aware that every narrative has multiple points from where it can be told. Multiplicity of how something can be viewed is a fact of life, and like the example I gave of the witch Elphaba in the play *Wicked* back in Chapter 4, it depends a great deal on who is doing the telling. The story will change given the way the person doing the telling sees it and contextualizes it, and the story will vary again when someone else tells the same or similar story. Anyone who has siblings almost always will have competing versions of interesting family episodes that have been experienced by several different members of the family. When the president of the United States or a member of a political party does something that makes news, the members of the various party members will see it very differently. This is more than just "spin" but is informed by our ideologies, worldviews, and position in the family constellation. It is our own vantage point.

To me, vantage point in supervision is the theory we use. What is our "vantage point" or theory we use to understand the situation being talked about? Let me give you an example. I once heard a story from one of my supervisees regarding a mother and her son. The mother and son came to a clinical session, and the mother complained that the boy never listens to her. The mother gave an example about the boy's behavior from the week before when they were in a physicians' waiting room and he was slamming a small rubber ball against the wall and catching it over and over again—loudly. The mother said she told him to stop, then just sat there and turned her attention to the other two children she had with her, as he did it over and over again, ignoring her request. She was really mad, but she just waited him out by ignoring his behavior, much to the irritation of the other patients in the room.

Now some clinicians and supervisors would begin to think of this situation, hopefully with a bit more information, as a potential problem that might be oppositional defiant disorder or perhaps attention-deficit/hyperactivity disorder. Someone else would begin to ask questions about the sequences of behavior between mother and son, some would ask for further evidence that this behavior is typical, and some would ask about exceptions to this behavior in similar circumstances. When the mother told the clinician this story and how upsetting this was to her, the clinician asked the mother why she chose to respond to her son's behavior as she did. How did she make sense of her son's refusal to listen and her method of dealing with his behavior? Note that the clinician's question includes both parts of the interactional sequence, as well as an opening for historical content to be laid bare. The question inadvertently belies the clinician's belief and theory. During supervision, I asked the clinician to explain to me what theory she was using. Later, in the ending of this chapter, I present the form I ask clinicians to come prepared with that has a question about what model and theory they are using. Our theory selects what it is we will see and remember, and as a supervisor I want to be able to understand the supervisees' cases from their worldview, so that I might also present alternative views without stepping outright on their way of thinking. I then want to have the clinicians also present alternative meanings from the various theories or models they know. I want to help my supervisees see behavior from several different ways and from these begin to construct interactions with their clients that will come closer to being helpful to the family with their own views of their situation. White knuckle grips on a particular view of how to behave or the meaning ascribed to something limits our degrees of freedom and therefore our actions. Meaning shapes our view and our language, and as a constructionist, I understand behavior in the context of how language describes, thus creates, the reality we know.

Moving back to the case, this clinician was at a loss because both of her "theories" were based on the notion that the boy's behavior was a plea to get attention, and ignoring that inappropriate behavior was supposed to extinguish it with time and patience. It was a good theory perhaps, but it was not working in the way they both expected. Rather than repeating what was not working, I had the clinician think of alternative theories that might be appropriate and helpful. She recalled a discussion about systems therapy and metacommunication of positive and negative feedback loops she had during one of her classes a year or so before, and in fact she had used it in a varying form with some success in other cases. Metacommunication theory says that all behavior is communication, and in this case, ignoring the boy's inappropriate behavior could also be interpreted by him as positive feedback (what you're doing is not important to me), which means no change is required, and it is okay to continue the behavior.[1]

---

[1]Any of the several books on family therapy have sections on this unique cybernetic principle. It is difficult for beginners to comprehend but remarkable in its simplistic and on target way of understanding behavior from a different vantage point than the more common ones.

In this situation, in order for the change to be effective, the mother would have to repeat her effort to stop the boy, including imposing and following through with consequences if he does not cease and desist. The positive feedback (no change) would need to be changed to a negative feedback loop (make a change) that would be restated and implemented with consequences.

Going back to the supervision of this case, rather than providing the clinician with what the supervisor believes to be the correct or more correct clinical conditions, the supervisor engages the supervisee in the learning process, exploring for a different, more utilitarian outcome. Because I understand that there are multiple variations of this, we also need to explore other alternatives and have the clinician choose what he or she thinks would work best. I may make suggestions, and even tell stories of past failures and successes, but my sole job is to help empower this supervisor, while helping to provide several ideas, including my own strengths-based view. The supervisor gets to choose the idea, however.

Point of view.

Point of view is similar to a vantage point, but it is more of an internal process than simply changing your physical placement (theory) in relation to the subject. Focal length or the length and structure of the lens is something to be considered—is it a long lens made for seeing distances up close or a wide angle lens that takes in landscapes in great detail? The aperture, ISO setting (100, 200, etc., in film), and the speed of the shutter are all settings that once in place will effect the condition or final image. Any beginning photographer will tell what a struggle it is to find the right balance of these in order to produce a quality picture. If the aperture (size of the lens opening) is off, too much or too little light (information) will be allowed in, making the rendering overexposed or underexposed. So too, with the other settings and physicality of the camera, the quality of the picture will be affected. One can have a beautifully composed picture, only to have an overexposed one or limited viewing of the subject. Because supervision is all about the lenses we use to interpret and help make positive changes when

necessary as we dialogue with our supervisor, the same phenomena is apropos to what we are talking about. What are your settings with respect to supervision sessions? While I have said that vantage point is similar to theory, I believe that point of view is a more global setting. Do you believe that as a supervisor you have the best, and often the last, word on a supervisory session? Do you think that your point of view is more correct than your supervisee? Do you see your job as helping to correct your supervisees and instruct them in how to do clinical work your way? Would your supervisees talk one way with their clients and another with colleagues and supervisors? I am more inclined to believe that supervision is an open and collaborative process where my expertise is in how I help to open space for new and sometimes more useful ideas to come about.

In the original article, where Mei Whei Chen and I wrote about strength-based supervision (Edwards & Chen, 1999), my friend and colleague included a very unique idea that she used with her supervisees. She had them talk about their cases with an open chair set next to them, and she told them to visualize that their client was sitting in that chair. Now, as they talked about their cases and their clients, she had them talk about the case as if they were right next to them listening; she even had them talk to the empty chair containing the imaginary client. The force of this new physicality during supervision was amazing, and I began to use it during my own supervision sessions. The usual physicality is that we tend to talk in pathological and clinical terms when alone with our supervisors, but that language changes drastically when we need to account for what the clients might hear us saying about them. Our point of view is changed as we use different language. It often softens and opens up new possibilities for more direct work and less clinically oriented work—it becomes congruent, transparent, and open. A change occurs that makes the picture richer and more in focus, with just the right amount of light or insight.

Perspective.

According to the Encyclopedia Britannica, perspective is a "method of graphically depicting three-dimensional objects and spatial relationships on a two-dimensional plane or on a plane that is shallower than the original (for example, in flat relief)" (see http://www.britannica.com/ EBchecked/topic/453061/perspective). Perspective is a way of showing space and volume and making that which is being depicted in two dimensions full and rich, as if it were three dimensions (or four or five, if you are so inclined to include space and time).

When it comes to supervision, our job is to be as objective as we can and help the supervisees/ stakeholders make the rendering of their clinical work one that depicts it as richer, thicker, and more fruitful—to give it perspective. By providing a way to make a two-dimensional event (talking) into as close to a three- or more dimensional rendering as one can, we can give it depth both in terms of how the work is viewed and reported and also in terms of how we see our own relationship and behavior/work with our clients. Yes, it includes the clinician as a part of the system. As a supervisor, as well as a photographic artist, I use the shutter speed and aperture to increase or decrease the amount of information that comes into my focal plane to make an impression. If I let in too much at times, the image is overexposed, so to speak. Sometimes I only want a short burst of information, and other times I want to see the stars in the very dark night sky as the earth orbits through space. Metaphorically, it is the same in supervision as it is in photography. I can be a master of the technical, and my very sophisticated Cannon Camera has lots of bells and whistles to help me, but in the end, I am the master and artist of the composition I wish to help portray. If I want to show the motion of reeds as they sway gently, I can set the camera on a solid base or tripod and let the "shutter" open for a slightly longer time while stopping up or down the amount of light (information) coming in, thus giving the appearance of movement (three dimensional) on a two-dimensional plane, as well as brightness and clarity. If I want to have a clear and more exacting picture, I will open the aperture for more light and increase the speed of the shutter, catching the same subject without motion but with clarity and sharper focus on this two-dimensional plane. So it is with supervision, as we can slow our supervisee down and ask questions to expand the narrative subject, or we can ask for shallower yet faster broad panning questions and see more of the case's system.

One exceptionally fine way I have used is a Narrative Therapy questioning that I first learned about from the work of Narrative Therapy trainers Jill Freedman and Gene Combs (1996). What they have their "clients" do is take the issue or problem they might think they have, and instead of describing it as an adjective such as "hostile," or "irritable" where it defines the person, they make it into a noun, such as hostility, or irritability, making it far easier to do something about. If a supervisee describes himself or herself or a client as a noun, they can deal with it and make changes, or in narrative terms, fight off hostility when it "takes them over." By externalizing the "problem situation," supervisees can begin to see how they or their clients can have some control over the situation. This is rudimentary to any person skilled in Narrative Therapy.

The point, of course, is that you can use strengths-based techniques with your supervisors without the negative, pathology-finding techniques that are so much a part of traditional clinical work. Rather than being problem oriented, they become strength oriented. In this way, we also participate in their self-efficacy by pointing out their own strengths.

There are many strengths-based ideas that can be used in supervision that will increase your supervisee's perspective in a more strengths-oriented manner. Savoring past successes will help to place the supervisees into a success "set" in their mind, so that they might begin to take themselves into that way of thinking and viewing their work and that of their clients. Supervisees who have been trained in and believe in problem-oriented clinical models will begin to see their work, their clients, and the world from a strengths-based perspective, when you as the supervisor have them talk about their clients from multiple perspectives. This is really effective in group supervision when the members of the group are encouraged to explore their clients from multiple clinical models. Finally, having a supervisor who is upbeat, strengths-based, yet empathic to the difficulties the world gives those with whom we work with, be they clinical clients or supervisory clients, becomes that sunshine that keeps faces pointed in the bright direction. Being strengths-based does not mean to deny the fickleness of life. We live in a world that sometimes seems filled with violence, illness, and mean-spirited and self-centered people who, it seems, have power over others. Yet those who see the world realistically and optimistically tend to have better lives, less problems, and greater self-efficacy or self-determination. Like photographers, we have the ability to take what the subject is, and by applying different settings, make that subject brighter and more alive; then, depending on our skills with composition, we can make the ordinary into something exceptional. That is what this is all about, as far as I view this work.

WHAT IS CLINICAL SUPERVISION?

How we work with people, regardless if it is as a clinical site supervisor, university supervisor, university department chair, dean, provost or president, agency manager or executive, our work should involve the same basic ideology of human relationships as I have portrayed in this book. Our belief in people to do their best is the foremost importance of what we do. Yes, there are problems that occur, and yes, our job is also that of an evaluator of progress and performance, and yes, we are and should be gatekeepers of our professions. However, our overriding belief in people and their ability to figure out their work and lives regardless of where they came from, or how they are behaving today, is the absolute best measure of where they may end up if we believe and act toward them in ways that support rather than tear down. The Pygmalion effect is real. Our capacity as leaders means that it is our job to look for, capitalize on, and encourage their strengths

and abilities. As leaders we have the shadow of leadership radiating from us, and it is also real and will set the tone for those whom we lead. How we begin to understand our responsibilities will undoubtedly inform how we view both our work as well as the people we serve as leaders and supervisors. I hope that these photographic metaphors have brought life to what I intend you to take in and think about. Let us now look at how this might happen during the course of a single supervision session that parallels or is isomorphic to the longer course of a supervisory relationship.

Stages of Supervision

Like everything else we know, supervision of any kind has stages, and stages within those stages. Relationships that have meaning and last through any time-space continuum go through a process that can be looked at as stages. Supervising someone, or leading or administering to them in some way, also requires a relationship that has three primary parts: beginnings, a middle, and an ending or transitional part to a new understanding and relating within the relationship. The way that clinical language has been used to communicate this last piece is based on the older concept of termination—see someone for a specified period of time, and then never see them again in any capacity. Today that is hardly the case, and we should recognize it. Several former supervisees and I have Facebook relationships; we have gone out for lunch or coffee on occasion. Some of them are now supervisors in their own practice. One of these has graciously agreed to write the forward for this book. Thanks Kara. Those old rules about boundaries have become less rigid, and as social media and the world keep us in touch and closer, we need to rethink some of the notions we have had and hold on to. In any case, I have chosen to see the stages as being three simple distinctions in the grander scale, and, isomorphic over the course of the supervision—having similar stages (parts) within the grander scale, during the hour or so of each meeting. Once again, I think of them simply as beginnings, middles, and ends or transitions.

Beginning supervision is perhaps the most important part of this three-stage process as those to follow, unless we are to look at endings. Meeting for the first time has the usual chitchat, as both supervisee and supervisor begin to size each other up. It is fair to say that most supervisees already have impressions of who is their supervisor and what he or she represents in their life. Some would call this transference; I prefer to think of it as interface issues. It sounds less problematic to me. If this experience takes place in a training venue, like a university setting, even if it is attached to the university as a clinical site, the myth of the supervisor almost always has attachments from others who have had that supervisor last year or in years before. Some universities maintain books or lists of site supervisors, coded with past ratings by students who were with them in internships over the years. Coordinators who maintain records from years past will have information, or notes on site supervisors, and they will undoubtedly provide that to the student heading off to that site, if asked. Agency supervisors will have the same sort of information about their style or belief about clinical work; in fact, many may have been sought out because of that personal information. In Chicago and suburbs, agencies have notoriety and supervisors often have their own cult following. I am sure it is similar in all parts of our country. Students and new or even seasoned clinicians wanting to learn Cognitive Behavioral Therapy, Narrative or Solution-Focused Therapies, or the next big thing, will gravitate to sites where these people practice. Some agencies have seasoned clinicians just waiting for openings at these places so that they might also attach themselves to the glow of particular supervisors. I have no reason to believe it is different anywhere else in the country. Thus most often, the supervisor is already known by the supervisee prior to the actual supervision. Depending on that supervisor's reputation, the die is already cast for how the supervisee will start to view the supervisor. Remember, we are mainly enslaved by what we already "know." The supervisee will either be waiting for great things to happen or believing he or she is in for a rough ride. I usually ask new supervisors what they have heard about me and what they are expecting. In doing so, I am beginning the process of open and honest communication—trying to open spaces. I have done the same with them, prefacing that I understand that people talk, and rumor can be dangerous to our building an ongoing positive relationship. I still think it is important to have a conversation about what the discourse has been about each of us, both positive and negative, no matter how difficult it may be. I may even go so far as to tell them some of the things I have heard other people say about me—"He is to easy, too hard, not grounded in the right theories," and so forth.

As I have said, the supervisor may have privileged information about the supervisee, especially if they are at a university site. It is fairly typical and expected that faculty will engage in talk about particular students, those who are problematic, and those who are exceptional. I have actually heard faculty use diagnostic labels for some, and I have expressed my dismay at those who do so. On the other hand, there are those whose faculty have wonderful and glowing things to say about them, and again, this is based on personal opinions that are contextual. I am reminded of how teachers talk and put forth their own notions about problematic students like the telephone game we all used to play as kids. Information gains import depending on who says it and under what conditions. I am usually pleasantly surprised at how supposed problematic students become rational, solid people after I get to know them.

One of my favorite student-to-colleague transitions was Jennifer, a woman who had come from the substance abuse treatment community; she was fairly good at her job, I would think. But she knew a different set of techniques and ideas about clients than what was taught at our university and that I also hold about the substance abusing client. So she balked at a lot of what was taught, had an answer for everything, and made a nuisance of herself in classes where the professors were mostly more of a hierarchical nature. She did well with our chair at the time, a seasoned fellow with a real liking for the know-it-all students—probably like him at an early age I would bet. Anyway, I heard all the stories, listened to the tales and discussions during faculty meetings about what she did and how the department might get rid of her, and our chair reminded us all that her grades were almost straight A's. So I asked my favorite question when presented with such negativity: "So what do people like about her? What does she do well?" Asking a group of clinicians/academics such a question usually results in a quizzical look, followed by some indulgence to my supposed naiveté. But what can happen, with genuine questioning, is a reduction in their negative behavior and even a relanguaging and rearranging of the positive can come about. I ask this question in a sincere way, and it seems to get results from even the most tried and true problem-focused people.

My initial assessment of Jennifer was that she knew a great deal about counseling, but like many counselors who come from a practice of treating substance abusing clients, they most often have a larger stake in the process of treatment than their clients do. In any case, when Jennifer saw that I was firm about the basics, yet encouraging about those strengths she had, she began to lighten up a bit. I asked her input a lot on cases being presented during our group consultation, and others in the group began to see she had some real strengths. As an aside, every group, from classroom to agency, has had past experiences. Navigating these "set in stone" ideas can be difficult and yet, with patience and subtle persistence, they can be scaffolded and changed. A group can also be problem focused in its own development and makeup, and a supervisor's responsibility is to lead the group into a more positive dynamic.

In any case, within the first of three semesters in clinical experiences, Jennifer had taken her place as a solid and well-versed clinician that her colleague students could rely on for support and solid ideas.

An early assessment of the supervisee's strengths and areas for growth can be done collegially, by simply asking what the supervisee

expects to gain from this relationship. I ask this question in the very first session and mark it as a contractual agreement if we both agree. I ask this question as well at the beginning of each subsequent session. I want to understand what the supervisee knows and what models of clinical work he or she understands and uses most frequently. I want to know how the supervisee views our relationship and what he or she expects to gain during our time together. I have done this formally and informally, leaning more to the informal with perhaps a few notes to myself. Given that the relationship is going to last for awhile, I figure that the patterns of the supervisee's work will continue to show up as we work together. Some say they want lots of feedback, others might be interested in learning more about a strengths-based approach, and some at first just want their hours of supervision so that they can move on in their career. Regardless of their desires, I remember the notions my supervisor of my supervision, Dr. Tony Heath, believed: supervisees want to be treated as competent and collegial and will work better if they believe that their supervisor has something to offer them that will be useful (Heath & Storm, 1983). But my initial assessment is always conjoint, as we discuss together what the supervisee wants and what the supervisor can provide. Discussions are open and most often interesting, providing a place to be transparent, as well as a flexible and changeable relationship that fits us both.

With this as a base line, we can make an assessment together on how well we are progressing. I think it foolish to assume that a supervisee's disappointment in attaining his or her goals is one person's responsibility. Just as in couples counseling, the problem is in the relationship most of the time. Assessment and the feedback process is a two-way street, and it should be ongoing and regular, not an episodic event or occurring at the end of the supervision. I preface my remarks to supervisees with the notion that the work is theirs to do, that they know their clients better than I do, and that my ideas and feedback are just that—my ideas, and they are not set in stone. I understand that this makes some supervisees and supervisors queasy, but unless I am in the same room with the supervisees and their clients regularly, I am not living in their space and most often can only "get in that space" through our discussions. The more I help the supervisees expand their vision of *their* work with *their* clients, the closer we will come to a rendering that is squared with a better perspective. Remember that perspective is also a rendering that attempts to make a two-dimensional entity into a three- or more dimensional entity. It is never perfectly accurate or real, only an interpretation.

A LEARNING CASE

Jay was a brand new counselor in training. He had gone through all the classes in counseling, had done well in his skills classes, and was anxious to show the world how well he was going to do in his new occupation. Jay had been a retail manager in his previous life and had started out as a new college graduate working the floor and counters in a large downtown retail store for athletic and outdoor merchandise. Money was tight at the time; the recession had left little opportunity for jobs at higher levels, and he had taken this job because it had good working conditions, plenty of face time with the public, and an opportunity to advance, and most of all because it involved selling something he knew well. He also worked weekends, giving him a day off during the week to look for other jobs. But none came, and he grew accustomed to his duties, the people around him, and it was an excellent incentive to go to school via educational scholarships. After a year on the job, he was given an advancement to midlevel management and a raise that was very nice, plus job security. He decided to hedge his bets and entered into a clinical program on a part-time basis, and he found a fondness for the classes and other people who were working toward their advanced degrees. He had always been one of those people in high school and college that others gravitated toward to confide in and seek advice from, so as he began his skills classes, he learned very quickly that he had a special skill set—friendly and an open ear—that drew in his "clients." He got great grades and accolades from his instructors, but then came the internship.

On their first day in the internship class, I asked the students to get into dyads for 20 minutes and talk about their goals, what they have done well in their lives so far, and how much they thought their own mental attitude might contribute to their future success. I also told the story about my son as a best of the best, and I expected them to use that as a model (see Chapter 5). At the end of the 20 minutes, they each reported on their partner's views and thoughts on the topic while I wrote down what each person said regarding their goals and notes on interesting stories, taking care to draw links between those ideas that had some commonality. Most were awed by telling their best of the best story, often being more accustomed to talking about their problems. Several of the clinicians in training had been in the field before at lower-level jobs. There were two who were addictions counselors; one who had been employed at the state family and children's services organization, working to reunite children with their families; several who were right out of college after studying psychology; and Jay. Many talked about how they wanted to work independently in practice, and several believed that their skills were in their ability to "tell it like it is." They reported, almost to a one, that attitude had a great deal to do with their future success but that learning more about their clinical skills would make them really good at what they wanted to do. I asked Jay what he thought, and he looked like a deer in headlights. After all of his hard work, and the great feeling he had about his future, he had a few—actually more than a few—doubts. The rubber was finally going to meet the road, and here he was out of his element, faced with a group of peers who had been working the field or knew more about the theory and techniques than he did, and he was in internship. He stumbled a bit, and the professor interrupted to remind him of two of the elements of the question. "What have you done well in your life so far, Jay, and have you formulated any goals yet? You know you have nowhere to go without goals, and everyone has had successes they can lean on, so what do you think?"

Jay was able to scramble some thoughts together. He told us that he wanted to be a good counselor, that he is usually a good listener, and that people had opened up to him his whole life. It was enough to begin.

Jay's site supervisor reported that his work, although a bit hesitant, was solid entry-level work. When I asked if there was anything about Jay that seemed more than just average, he replied that Jay was always punctual and very well-groomed and dressed—he was professional in his manner. "Looking for his strengths?" he asked. And we had a conversation about a game plan to increase Jay's level of confidence by punctuating those behaviors each of us thought were above average. Now, this is not an inflated score. It is two people who agree that to be helpful to this young clinician in training, pointing out what he was doing well might lead to better outcomes—for the intern, for his clients, and for the agency and university. We had a game plan that they would work together to bring to Jay's attention to expected growth along the lines of better and better outcomes. Of course, he already had proven skills in the clinical area, as witnessed by excellent grades in those classes. He would not be in internship without them. And Jay flourished as did the rest of his group. His clients began reporting that they were seeing improvements, as Jay began to ask for their feedback, and his site supervisor continued to report growth in Jay's confidence and more importantly, his clients' growth became evident. Like the sunflower tracks the sun, positives began to track and follow more positives.

I believe that the issues that come with most beginning clinicians align in three themes: first is undervaluing their ability, the second is overvaluing their work, and the third is a wavering of efficacy (self-valuing). Each comes with its own territory and also can line up nicely with the developmental stages of clinicians (Stoltenberg, 1981; Stoltenberg & Delworth, 1987). Understanding and using the developmental perspective is something I advocate in Chapter 2 as an executive skill, for this precise reason.

Tag team clinical supervision.

Another way I make conjoint and solid assessments of supervisee's strengths and needs is through a game called Tag Team Counseling (Edwards & Chen, 1999). I have used this during group supervision in agencies as well as in clinical classes at university settings. Early in the relationship of the group, I have members role play a clinical situation, where one person is the client—perhaps emulating a difficult or stumping client from their caseload or a real situation from their life. We talk about the confidentiality that this form of multiple and unique supervision requires, and then I pick one person to also role play the clinician. They get in the center of a "fishbowl" made of the remaining members of the group including me, and then the game begins. They begin their work together, and at some point during the session, the clinician may "tap out" and pick someone from the group to carry on. The clinician may also be removed by the supervisor, or at a suggestion of one of the people from the group, or at the request of the client. This game can go on until it seems to be not useful any more, or until the class erupts in laughter, which usually happens. Processing the event, discussing what they liked about so and so's clinical work, or the dilemma presented, or the group process itself, are all fair game, with the caveat that to be helpful, comments must include what they liked, along with potential suggestions for even better work next time. Rejoinders are also allowed.

By the end of several weeks of this, and I must say that group members are leery and even shy about showing their wares in public sometimes, the group has seen multiple versions of clinical work, and members have discussed what works and what might have produced different outcomes. A sense that there are multiple ways to engage clients is always present.

I have explored using this model for both beginning sessions and ending sessions as specific points using a slightly revised model of this idea with good success, when supervisee(s) were stumbling with beginnings and endings.

Nevertheless, I have found this method to be a great way to assess and provide feedback to supervisees within a strengths-based model, all in a nonthreatening manner.

As a response to our original article, I have received a great deal of e-mail from others around the world as recently as 2011, asking for more information and providing positive feedback on the article even though it was published in 1999. I have been pleasantly surprised at people's reactions and interest.

Reflective team supervision.

I have gone at length in Chapter 4 to talk about the reflecting team model of supervision, and it is one of the primary parts of strengths-based work, as far as I am concerned. It provides clients and clinicians the opportunity to have a group of other clinicians watch an event, be it a live clinical session, a role play of a session, a discussion of a session either in a group or dyadic situation, or even a classroom event. More like the old fish bowl, the team happens when several people are designated as team members who watch and then reflect on what they saw and thought about during one of these events. The dialogue is mostly about what the event made the team members remember in their own lives or situations and how they began to make meaning of it, usually in a more positive way. Because I spent so much time discussing this in the previous chapter, I will not add content past what I have said, other than to reflect on a reflecting team situation I watched a few years ago.

Reflections of a reflection team.

One of the best ways to utilize this model of supervision is when a real live client and the clinician are available to work in front of a group of colleagues, and several of the clinicians in the group are willing to become the reflecting team. I know of many agencies where they use this model as a great peer supervision as well as a training for interns. Again, it provides multiple strengths-based views or at least alternative ways of thinking of the situation.

A LEARNING CASE

Jacquie was a clinician intern at a facility that primarily worked with HIV-infected and substance abusing men. She was glad to bring in a client, Andy, who she had worked with for several months and who had been sober for a good deal of that time. She reported that the main job of sobriety was going well and an aftercare plan for work and a halfway house was in place for a transition in a few weeks. Jacquie's agency supervisor also was invited and gladly accepted the invitation. As I met with the whole group including the agency supervisor, client, and clinician intern, I explained again what we expected to happen, including how the team would switch rooms with Jacquie and Andy after 40 minutes, reflect on what they had witnessed as well as thoughts they might have, and switch back again. This provides the client(s) with an opportunity to reflect on what team members had said during their time to reflect. I also provided a brief overview of the informed consent that Andy had signed and asked if there were any questions. There were none, so Jacquie and Andy went to an adjoining room while the rest of the group sat in front a large screen monitor to watch.

The actual session was fairly low-key, as Jacquie and Andy went over their progress and work that they had done together. Andy began talking about his two children who were living with his ex-wife, and he wondered how he would ever pay them back for all his past behavior. It seemed to be a small sticking point in the plan, and the issue of continued sobriety was discussed once again as the real problem in his life. Andy talked again of his children, and again Jacquie focused on the need to have continued sobriety. The 40 minutes were up, and I asked the team to go reflect and have Andy and Jacquie come into the monitor room with the group. There were small pleasantries on both sides after that switch, and then the team began to reflect. There were four members of this team, and each had good things to say about Andy's recovery, reflections about how happy he seemed, and the helpfulness of Jacquie in this process. It was a rather low-key reflection being an isomorph to the session they had just witnessed. One of the team members, Gary, who had experience as a son of an alcoholic, began to talk about his own life as a child, but then he stopped. There was a pregnant pause, as Gary began to look almost as if he was going to cry. And then he began to talk about how his father had worked really hard to make amends to his family. Gary was proud of his father for all the hard work he had done in a very similar situation to Andy's. He ended his reflection by saying that his father provided a legacy for his children that was an excellent model for them all. Not one of his siblings ever touched a drop of alcohol or used drugs, and they had been raised during the 1970s, when kids were using a great deal of the time. He ended his reflection by saying one more time that his father provided a legacy that could never be tarnished by any of his past behavior. There was dead silence in both rooms, and those in the monitor room later said that Andy was silently crying and wiping away the tears. A story about a team member's family, a reflection about his own experience brought on by what he had just witnessed, had hit home to more than one person.

(Continued)

(Continued)

After they switched places again, and Jacquie asked quietly what the team's reflection might have for him, he again fell silent, with tears falling. He had never thought about leaving a legacy or that after all he had put his family through he might even have the opportunity to do so. A few more things were discussed regarding the transition to aftercare, but the session was really over.

Jacquie had learned a lesson about the importance of family, her agency supervisor said much the same, she found the process useful for aftercare preparation, and the group learned a wonderful lesson about the work that can be done with a very complicated and potentially motivated substance abuse clientele. Would this same situation be different with different team members? Sure, but there is always something that can be found in what our clients and clinicians/supervisees present us with that can be gold for the mining.

Assessment to me, then, means that a supervisee describes what it is he or she wants to get out of a supervisory experience—goals, and we may add some more, with discussion and permission; then together we review the progress, make new goals or tweak the old, and go at it again. In many different ways, our job is to assess what they believe, how they work, what they want to learn, as well as how I as a supervisor can help them achieve those goals, by providing multiple variations of the scenarios they give us, without insisting on leaving too many of our own footprints on their way of thinking. Together we decide how well they have done obtaining their goals. Assessment also means that along the way, together we may come up with new goals. Goals can be personal, such as being more sure of themselves in clinical situations or listening more carefully to what our clients say they want out of life. Assessment is ongoing and ever changing at times. Assessment also means that I can tell supervisees how I see where they are going or why I think a different approach might be more helpful.

360-degree evaluations are, in my opinion, the best way of making an evaluation or assessing someone's worth, especially in clinical settings. If my original opinion, which I stated in Chapter 3, is correct, that what site supervisors want is not perfect clinicians but more than just well-trained people; they want clinicians who are of good quality, substance, integrity, and hold a positive attitude (Edwards & Pyskoty, 2004), then an evaluation that can show this more clearly is the 360-degree evaluation that I wrote about in Chapter 6; so I only touch on this here.

Think of this: What if the clients gave evaluations of their clinicians like Miller et al. (2007), who describe where the clients are always being asked, at the end of each session, if their clinician is on track with what they want from him or her? That feedback will continue to provide ongoing assessment regarding progress from one of the several parts of the circle. Then those ongoing goals and attainments, as defined by the client, can also be discussed between the clinician and the supervisor to see if the goals fit that way of thinking; teams can do the same thing during group supervision or through reflecting teams. What if the secretarial staff or other members of the agency or university were to provide ongoing feedback that help all know how they are perceived by others around them, thus providing a social voice of evaluation from those other than from a clinical perspective? And finally, what about the others like funding sources or anyone else that interfaces with the clinicians? Suppose they were to provide input for the evaluation?

Then, wouldn't there be a better multiple voice of evaluation of the person being evaluated?

Before you go off saying how difficult this would be, think about how it already happens. In every agency in which I have worked, that sort of evaluatory feedback is already provided by the referring agencies in both formal and informal ways. Supervisors and administrators get feedback both directly as well as indirectly in the form of referrals and comments regarding the work being done. Ask any secretary or the janitorial staff their opinion of the line staff, and if they believe it is really wanted and counts, you are more than likely to get straightforward responses. I knew where I stood with every Department of Children and Family Services worker and administrator, and most state organizations have an evaluative process. In Illinois, case review administrators provide solid feedback regarding the quality of services provided by the agency. I also knew how the janitorial services felt about me and about other clinicians in the agencies, as well as other staff. Why not institutionalize that informal evaluation so that it is part of the overall evaluation? A real 360-degree evaluation would get to that part site supervisors claim they really want—clinicians who are of solid good quality, with integrity and substance. Why do we make the evaluation solely on the clinician's clinical skills, and why are those skills assessed by the clinical supervisor, when the client and others would have an equal stake in the evaluation? I am suggesting that each of these factors are integral parts of a system, all that need be looked at to make a solid assessment of a clinician's work and being. It is better to have an evaluation from a multiple input source than a single input source. A multiple input always provides an evaluation that is closer to a robust, rich, and accurate outcome.

So, all of what I have said so far is part of beginnings, but it is also a part of the next two stages: middlings and endings. And yes, they are important in their own way, too. So I will spend a little time on each of these stages, presenting my own view on them and how they are useful to strengths-based work.

Middlings, according to Webster, means small of stature or not the best or worst of a food product. They are used as a filler for pet foods and extend the basics that have merit or worth. Today, where everything counts, the middlings are saved sooner than they used to, when they mostly ended up on the floor to be swept and discarded. I like this definition, as it fits how I think about the middle part of supervision from a strengths-based perspective. Middles of supervision are not necessarily the most robust part of a supervision experience, but they are extenders— they keep the conversation going, they pick up the smaller parts of the work, and they add substance to the real importance of what is happening. Back to the camera metaphor: What happens in the middle between learning how to shoot correctly like you mean it and producing exquisite pictures is the practice. Middlings are the practices and receiving feedback on one's goal attainments that increase the chance of having exquisite outcomes. When they measure the middlings of wheat and corn products, where the term middlings is used repeatedly, it turns out that they contain 96% of the energy value of barley and 91% of the energy value of corn. This is being seen as a cheap but potent biofuel. Middlings have potential beyond the output of beginnings and endings, in different, yet important ways. Middlings, where there may be difficulties because of supervisees' attempts to move away or be too independent too quickly from their supervisor, really have the potential for providing most of the energy and focus of a supervision session, if we are willing to let them have their heads more. Like adolescence, where they are attempting to go their own way, learn the ropes, and sometimes criticize adults (supervisors and trainers) who got them to where they are, they can be praised for their independent thinking and encouraged to learn more and practice and analyze their work in order to become even better. It is never too late to institute the action research model of analyze, include all stakeholders, reflect, design, implement, review outcome, analyze again for what has gone right and what would make it stronger, remake the plan, and implement again. It is a circle of a respectable way of doing most planning that gets results in the end, and it does not worry about making mistakes but on making ongoing small corrections along the way.

The middling phase is a useful segment of strengths-based work, and the major thrust of supervision at this point is providing supervisees with ways to evaluate themselves and their work by teaching them this way of thinking. The majority of the real efforts of clinical work come during this almost independence of practice, with a healthy dose of learning and practicing this reflective action research method. The goal, of course, is to make the supervisees almost self-sufficient and not afraid of asking for input for fear they will be disempowered in the process.

Another way to utilize the almost dreary middlings is to change the subject for a while from the issues the supervisees and their clients are working on and focus on both the supervisees' and their clients' cultural strengths (Smith, 2006). It can be most apparent that some of our students from cultures that have been marginalized have felt the pressure of being in graduate school and coming from families where they are the first to graduate college as well as the very first to go to graduate school. I have heard the story several times from different students how they feel like they now have to be role models for their younger siblings and cousins, and for some, even help support these younger family members when they are ready to go off to school. In Chapter 2 I tell the story of a supervisee who is gay and Latino, who is working with another gay man who is Asian. If you go back and read that story again, both my supervisee and I were stymied because, although we understood the gay culture well enough, the client's heritage was much different than either of ours. I encouraged my supervisee to change the discourse for a while to what strengths his culture had provided for him that he might use with his dilemmas. This small shift was enough to make a difference and bring them both out of the rut they were in and infuse a novel and useful new discussion. It also gave both my supervisee and myself a new point to begin understanding our own cultural perspectives, and we could talk about our own intentions to learn more, as well as be open to differences more than we thought we were.

Middlings are a perfect time to bring back our old friend savoring. I ask my supervisees/stakeholders/colleagues to think back to a few times when their work felt really good to them. I want them to remember the great moments—did it feel right, did they get great feedback from their client(s), did it seem like they were in the zone, or did a client report great progress? Anything that is about the relationship going well between their clients' goals and their work together is a time to remember and to spend time talking about why it was like that—what made it different and how they were a part of that experience. Remember my colleague Sue from Chapter 5 as she savored moments with her clients? I hadn't talked with her for some time, and she told me after we had that session that her clients told her she was the best clinician they had ever had. She had been worried because she didn't have much training in sexual therapy, and here her work had produced excellent results anyway. The key was focusing on what she knew, that their relationship had worked very well and they liked the results that had been produced. Savoring had also helped Sue begin to see herself in a stronger light. The angle of the lens produced a sharper image. Savoring helps us reexperience our best; it helps us come back to a place where we have confidence in our work, where self-efficacy—real self efficacy—can inform us of what we are capable of doing at our best.

So, middlings present us with the richness of self-evaluation and finding ways to keep your work—your clinical work—focused on looking at multiple ways of understanding the client/clinical system in order to have a richer and clearer view of what is going on and how to work within that system. I believe focusing on the positives and helping supervisees continue to look for what they do and can gain by staying focused on the positives will provide a better foundation for moving ahead.

Endings that are not really endings are what I believe we should aim for in strengths-based supervision. The concept of termination coming from the early days of psychoanalysis meant that the treatment was over, the patient was analyzed, and there was to be no further contact with the analysand. It was not only a breach of etiquette for analysts to have contact with their patients, it was problem enough that they could be sanctioned by the association to which they belonged. As psychoanalysis lost favor as the predominant method of treatment and training, new ways of thinking took over that seemed far more open to interpretation and context (Edwards & Pyskoty, 2004). Agency supervision could not abide by a standard where supervisors and supervisees who not only worked together but socialized as well could not have collegial and social time together. From the first days of my time working for the Department of Mental Health, our supervisors went out for drinks with us after work. Most of us in the Children's Day Treatment program got together on a regular basis, and when I was elevated to the status of unit supervisor, with a caseload of clients as well as colleagues I had to supervise, I was asked several times if I intended to cut off my relationships with friends I now had to supervise. I learned early on that it was fine with some, and some tried to take advantage of that previous relationship. I used my skills as a human being, I believe, rather than as a dictatorial manager, or even a clinician. It worked most often to be straight with those I supervised, to build, or try to build in some cases, an even stronger collegial relationship where I had a job to do, and at the same time had great respect for those I had to supervise. Yes, it adds another layer of potential conflict and risk, but as human beings, we are always coming up against those sorts of issues aren't we?

In graduate school, the best professors I had were those who were straightforward with me and yet were able to hold a relationship that had meaning. During my master's program, the head of our department had annual, and sometimes semiannual, parties at his house. Nothing got out of hand; we did not become bosom buddies, and when grades came out, they were done in a straightforward manner with a conference if there

were issues. I had one of these conferences early on in my master's program, when one of my professors, someone I respected and had gone out for drinks with in a group on a few occasions, took me aside and said, basically, that my work in class and in counseling labs was always spot on, but my written work was not up to graduate-level standards. "Jeff," he said, "if you are going to graduate from our program, you need to take the professional writing class here and not as an elective. Clearly in your case it is mandatory." I was thankful for his straightforwardness, and yes, I knew and recognized that I was not the best writer on the planet. Was I embarrassed? I was, but also I was relieved that someone did not worry that I would be upset or angry about what was said. And, in the end, it made me better, and yes, I still have to write and rewrite and so on and so forth. I use coping skills and have learned to rely on others most often, and today I am 100% better and have learned the lesson that we all have difficulties somewhere in our life, and it is those who do not recognize it or balk when someone gives them straight talk who have problems. This professor took the time to tell me that what I did at counseling was great, and that if I really wanted to be good, and respected, I would need to make some effort in changing something I was not as good at as others in my class. Good leaders are not afraid to give out praise and also be straight with those who may need something else to bring them up to speed. Is this a contradiction with anything I have said up to now? I don't think so. People in supervisory positions have to hold to some standards and that may mean that they have to point out areas where they believe work may need to be upgraded. It also means that they need to give out praises in great and worthwhile measure, more often than they give out suggestions, or in my case, an honest appraisal of what could get in my way of succeeding, from their point of view. It also means, as I have said right along, that being straight includes the caveat that these suggestions are from my personal viewpoint—my vantage point—that may see things from a different angle than others. I have some understanding of what might make a difference, and I can put it out there for them to observe, make note of, and choose an action around. When my professor gave me that suggestion, did it change the way we got along? Not at all, because my professor also gave me good solid praise as my writing got better. He was a colleague with more experience and knowledge about something I needed in order to succeed. And he was not one who pontificated about how much he knew or said he was better than me. He was someone I intended to be like, and I think I have made that mark because of our relationship.

Today, in graduate school and especially in doctoral preparation, if we are honest with ourselves, we all know that at some point, we may be working together in one capacity or another. It is up to us to build collegial relationships from the beginning, I think. I now am on boards and organizations with many of my former students. The relationships change, yet our humanity has never been different from those days in class or supervision.

Again, the point is that we need not be afraid of having honest quality relationships with people we are supervising or teaching. It can be likened to how I parented my child when she was an adolescent. I made lots of observations (evaluations to some) and she had the freedom to either go along with what I said, or try it out and see. There were times when she took a different path and it worked out okay, and sometimes it was less than perfect, but like our codes of ethics state, our clients (in this case supervisees) have the freedom to have their own opinions and actions, unless they are breaking the law or some ethical point. Then I have the mandate to help them change course and explain why I am insisting. If my daughter Zoe is driving my car with me in it, and she is speeding, I have the authority and the right to have her pull over and let me finish the ride. If it is an issue of difference of opinion, I let her have her way, and I still may give my opinion.

Endings in our supervisory relationships do not mean that we will not see each other again or have peer relationships in the future. And because of that, the way we end—or transition into—peer relationships is important. Our job as supervisors is to help prepare our supervisees to work more effectively, to be genuine and transparent in their work and life, and to begin the process of self-evaluation in order to be better clinicians. As I have pointed out throughout this book, our job is to prepare the total person to be responsible and continue growing in a self-efficacious manner. We want mature supervisees to become even more mature clinicians and that means being able to handle future relationships with their former supervisors as peers. Perhaps the next phase might be as a mentor, who also has supervisees and mentors of his or her own. Mentoring is a wonderful process that encourages and focuses our best efforts to be protégé-centered, strengths-based focused, ego-less in presence and self-need, and ripe in its producing good people. It is about providing what the protégé needs, while still being collegial in bearing by making suggestions and opening doors to future success. It can create great colleagues to follow us and be great leaders long after we are needed or are around. It is this ending point where supervisees have become their own person, taking on the call to add to our knowledge about clinical work, devising and trying out new and better ways to do the jobs we do now, with new energy and interest. Endings are important and should not be abrupt but have a natural transition, like most of us have with our children. They move on, become adults, have relationships of their own, and perhaps families, and the process recycles itself again and again. The idea of de-identification that has been used so well in understanding siblings' identification process from each other might be a nice way to end here. The process decreases rivalry among them and allows them to go off in their own direction. In this process, the de-identified mature former students or supervisees have an identity that is different from those who trained them, as it should be as they reach their own maturity in life. Endings are equally important and part of the three-stage journey of supervision. And if this is the ending point, it is equally important that the use of strengths-based supervision, focusing on their growth and personal agency—maturity—is an important part for me. We can all grow in our maturity and agency all the time, as far as I can see.

THE ADMINISTRATIVE PART: BUT FOR ALL WHO ARE INVESTED IN HELPING OTHERS

What is Administrative Supervision?

As I spent considerable time in Chapter 6 talking about leadership, organizations, and such, I will not rehash what I have said there. But I do want to cover some rather interesting information most clinical people would probably never read about in full. Two books that I think cover some of the most interesting and important information we should know about as people who have been charged with helping others in their daily tasks are Daniel Pink's (2009), *Drive: The Surprising Truth About What Motivates Us,* and Heidi Grant Halvorson's (2011), *Succeed: How We Can Reach Our Goals.*

I do not want to recap the entirety of either of these books, but I want to give you a brief idea of what each of them says about their subject as it applies well to our discussion of supervision— any kind of supervision.

Motivation

In Chapter 2, I mentioned the work of Florida and Goodnight (2005), who found that workers are no longer responsive to the carrot and stick motivation. It seems that their research, and that of Pink's (2009) book, agree on the subject, and Pink goes at length to show how the old world ways of trying to get the employees to engage and be involved with their work is not a real option these days. It was when workers were not well educated or they were in dire need of sustenance. But today our creature comforts are pretty much taken care of, allowing us to be closer to what Pink believes is the currency of the day. If this sounds familiar, it is. We are not in the Industrial Age, we are smack dab in the Knowledge Age and Information

Age, as Drucker (2005) told us. We are past the rewards of good work, because most workers are past the magical number researchers have found to be a pivot point. What is needed now, and managers and administrators should take notice, is a point when motivation is driven more by our desires to achieve mastery over problems. We are interested in intrinsic needs rather than extrinsic ones. We enjoy the challenge of learning more about something, finding new ways to improve a problem of concern, more than we need something from outside. Pats on the back or financial rewards are nice, but we long for the challenge of a puzzle. We like to have the satisfaction of knowing we accomplished something others have been puzzling about. Our motivation comes from within us, not from outside us. Pink (2009) cited the happenings of Wikipedia, the most used online encyclopedia ever, fully operated by volunteers, and the demise of Encarta, Microsoft's biggest failure, created by a workforce of some of the best history minds ever brought together. Yes, scholars may scoff that this group of rag tag (and polished professionals) made such a huge success as Wikipedia? How is it?

We keep on assuming that rewards from outside in the form of money or wall plaques are enough. What Pink tells us is that we need to change our game. It is not that we should abandon those old ways of recognition but that we need more—we need the challenge of our own conquest and making. I want to say that again, our own conquest and making—the central source of motivation today. The Sawyer effect is a big piece of the why or how. The pure enjoyment of the searching and finding becomes a form of a game. It is a central source of our delight, thus it is reward in itself. And it cannot be from outside—managers cannot suggest or force this on the workers; it has to come from the workers themselves. And here is the piece this book has been talking about all along. Our supervision, our collaborative efforts, our ability to work with those we are responsible for, require us to make an informed decision, as to if I tell them what to do, or let them do it the way they think is best, within parameters, and then stand by to make suggestions from an outside perspective, but only as a friendly editor or colleague.

Just today I was part of having this happen. The association that I am current president of, the Illinois Counselor Educators and Supervisors, is engaged at my request in finding and working toward, through action research, how we can go about changing the licensing law in Illinois from a 48-hour master's license to a 60-hour license. There are many parts to this, but briefly, I called together a team of 11 members I knew would work well together. I asked for a person to take responsibility of heading the research endeavor, and a good friend of mine stepped forward to take the challenge. It is a huge one, figuring out how we can convince a licensing board and many universities who are investing in a 48-hour license when change will mean more classes and more financial resources for students as well as universities. As an aside there is a split in the United States, where 68% of states require a 60-hour licensure or will have one within a few years and 32% require a 48-hour licensure. Anyway, the group began to debate online how we should go about our already settled upon plan, and my friend sent me a "help, this is getting out of control" e-mail. When I called, I used the metaphor of a group that is in the "storming stage" of development. My friend got it right away and figured out an e-mail to send the troops that settled them right down, provided them with direction again, and we were off and running. I did not want to take over for her; I wanted to collaboratively give her a different way of thinking about the dilemma at hand and let her run with it again. Her letter was far more endearing yet provided direction than I could have written. She was closer to it than I was, as the research guru and leader—it was her responsibility. Had I taken over I would have disempowered her authority and responsibility. I did not want or need that; I needed someone who was capable and a good leader, which she showed that she was, after a short consult from me as president. I know she likes doing this, and it is not for any financial gain. We are all volunteers wanting to do a good solid job, and she stepped up because

the next step—crafting and sending out a letter—was fun, I am sure. It was intrinsic motivation to do a job well, and one that she took on herself. The Sawyer effect, named after Mark Twain's book character Tom Sawyer, who was able to convince his friends that white-washing his aunt Polly's fence was great fun, is a sort of strange way of making this point, but the fact is that we do things because we convert them to fun things to do. It is far more productive of me to help myself know why writing this book is fun, rather than thinking about all the money I will not make for a book for academics and clinicians, many of whom I think will disagree with a great deal of what I have to say. And what about leadership? Why do people give away their time like it does not matter to be a leader of a professional organization that does not pay any money? It is a hoot, trying to fix issues and making things work well. That is why. Finally, it has to have creativity involved. What Pink and others go out of their way to show is that the new motivating factors are primarily about our human desire to be creative. With the new educational push around the country to parse down the creative arts and replace them with more math and science, one should wonder at educators' methods to focus more on math and science and remove the arts. We should have math and science instruction, yes, but not for extrinsic reasons. Math and science taught as interesting and creative endeavors that can be paired with the arts would make a far richer life and living for everyone involved, from the teachers who teach the teachers on down to the grade-school-level students. I write because I was a poor writer, was told I would never go to college, and yet here I am finding creativity and meaning in all that I do.

Pink shows how many organizations are allowing their employees to choose and work on interesting projects of their own, for at least 20% of their time at work. Suppose you were to set the standard, as a leader and administrator, that the employees could use a portion of their time to research new and creative ways to work with people in distress. If they picked their own special interest project, and went to work on it, their creativity and service could become a hallmark of your place of work. You could become a leader in new and innovated ways of helping communities, or families, or people who need more help. Your creative and flexible new way of helping employees find their own passion and creativity could infuse new energy and meaning into your work. Prevention programs or other social service projects could take off. Use teams to add interest, accountability, and collegiality in what they do together. Abandon those old ideas, and jump on the new. Read all you can about what real motivation is about, and use it to help your employees become successful.

Success: What is It All About Anyway?

Most of us in this field dream of being successful in one way or another. Clinicians want to be successful at helping their clients have better lives; supervisors want to assure that their supervisees become and continue to be good solid clinicians; managers, administrators, and senior management gather their own steam by assuring that what has been designated as theirs to run, runs well; and academics climb the ladder of success through the legacy they leave with their students and protégés, publications and service to community, college and leadership of associations, and other meaningful accomplishments. About my fourth or fifth year into my academic career, I came to a loggerhead with where I was professing in terms of potential movement toward my own success. I had published my share, had very good relationships with students, and sat on the numerous committees in all the right places, but I still felt stifled in my drive to success. My answer at the time was to respond to every call for jobs in my field all over the United States. My chair knew what I was up to and sat me down for a talk. What he said, basically, was that there are two ways to find success in our field. One is to become a small, but significant fish in a very big pond, and the other is to become a big fish in a smaller, but very significant pond. Of course, he

was talking about setting goals that were realistic. And looking back, it probably made all the difference in the world for me. To be a fish of any size means lots of work—publications, service, and face time, far more than I was currently doing and certainly more than I really carried to invest. I am a family guy, and even all the work I had already put in with school, writing, and service etched away time from those with whom I chose to put more investment. And so, success came back to what another good friend told me once, that you can either work like there is no tomorrow or you can lower your expectations to something more reasonable to who you really are. I am not unhappy with my lot in life as I look back. I have gone farther than I ever really dreamed I might and touched many lives along the way. I have been successful.

As a leader or supervisor, or whatever you are in this field, it is also your job to help those to whom you are responsible become more successful at not only their own jobs and aspirations but in life and as people too. It has to be holistic. It has to have balance. In order to talk about this second part of administrative supervision, or whatever you want to call it, I want to now discuss the second book I mentioned earlier (Grant Halvorson, 2011). I will not delve deep into Grant Halvorson's work, but I will provide you with a taste, like I did with Pink's work. Both are fun, interesting, and genuinely useful reads, that you should take time to enjoy and help inform your personage in this field.

Grant Halvorson (2011) began her study of success with a quote from one of the all-time successful people of our generation, Oprah Winfrey, as she commented on her continued struggle with her weight. She said, "My weight issue isn't about eating less or working harder. . . . It's about my life being out of balance . . . I let the well run dry" (xix). As you think about the folks you are responsible for and yourself, have you let the well run dry? Have you piled on too much for yourself and for those you are responsible for chasing the dream of the big pond? I know I did, and I am glad I had the sense and the good counsel of friends to help me set realistic goals for myself. I remember also the moment when I was cut off by the young man in his BMW, cell phone to ear making his next connection as I was doing the same—large practices and teaching at two universities was only getting me farther from balance. Spending that time with my family and young daughter would set the scale right. By the way, Grant Halvorson (2011) counseled her readers that Oprah's remark is "right on the money" (p. xix). In order to be successful, we need to set realistic goals and then work toward them. Our goals should be in balance with our lives. For Grant Halvorson, setting realistic goals is the first step to being successful. By this time, I hope you again understand that my discussion about being successful is not just about helping those you are in charge of—it is also about yourself too, just like all strengths-based ideas. Isomorphic properties, again, show that how you work will also affect those who you work with and for—the shadow of the leader is always present.

How many times have you given someone an assignment or request, followed by the command "do your best," as the person shakes his or her head in agreement? Well, apparently that is not the way to begin a wonderful outcome. Grant Halvorson said it is a bad way to motivate, as it has no specificity attached to it. And regardless of whether you are telling someone what you want, charting your own course of success at something, or collaboratively setting goals with someone you are responsible for, the more specific the plan, the better the results. It sets a bar as what will be considered successful, so that there will be no settling for less than the goal that has been established. Boy, does that make sense. After reading Grant Halvorson's statement, I began to think about all the times I could have done that with my own staff or students and supervisees. Make it clear (collaboratively) what we think is really successful. And it has to be like the three bears, not too hot, not too cold, but just right. If the goals are big pond goals, and it is not a fit for you or who you are working with, then the goals are not just right. If they are too cold, then they are not strong enough to motivate—do

your best. What is your best anyway, and how do you know what you or those you are working with are capable of unless they are challenged? "Difficult but possible is the key" (Grant Halvorson, 2011, p. 5). The interesting thing about this, and Grant Halvorson (2011) has lots of anecdotes as well as research to back it up, is that setting goals high is a great motivator. Remember the creative part of Pink's (2009) work? The goals of success and motivation dovetail very well here. If the goals are set realistically high, people feel challenged to be creative and succeed. They are motivated. But remember it has to be possible, contextually, for the situation and for the person. I think this is helpful in our thinking about evaluation also. In order for us to accurately and collaboratively evaluate someone's or our own outcomes, we first need to have set the bar for success accurately. Arbitrary outcome measures cannot be set without first checking to see if the goals are too high or not high enough. And setting those goals higher can have remarkable consequences, as it is far more interesting and rewarding to succeed at something difficult than something easy. We derive more satisfaction when we conquer something we might have believed was out of our reach. Grant Halvorson showed that setting goals appropriately higher than most expect of themselves leads to better work performance because of this intrinsic feeling of satisfaction when people become creative, facing difficult obstacles that are overcome and looking forward to the reward of self-satisfaction. It leads to better job satisfaction, as we talked about in the section earlier on motivation.

Success, also, and you will undoubtedly chuckle to yourself at this, has to do with how we language our goals. Yes, "Wanting to get an A on a math test can be thought of as wanting to 'get almost all of the answers correct' or 'master algebra'" (Grant Halvorson, 2011, p. 7). The goals you set up can have more effect on your motivation depending on how you state them—how the language you use is stipulated. One way of saying something will feel very different from the other, and this will make a big difference in motivation and also outcome. The goal, be it answering correctly or mastering algebra, will influence you in all sorts of important ways. The stating of a goal determines the strength of your motivation and whether you will continue on when the going gets tough.

I have two sons, both teachers in high school. One of them has two sons also. In our earlier days, when my sons were around 8 to 12, we used to go rock climbing a lot. One boy loved it and the other did it just to please me, sometimes lacking motivation to "finish the climb" when the going got tough. Of course, that set the tone for how I tried to motivate each child to make it to the top. Success! And I was not always successful. One would scamper right up the rock walls, enjoying the feeling of accomplishment; the other would struggle up the rock, stop halfway, and complain that he could not do it. I have pondered this many years, but last night at a local fair, I watched my two grandsons repeat the same pattern. Age placement is different, so I saw that it was not an issue of the older versus the younger. In fact, it was the younger one of my sons who would always race to the top, and this was reversed with my grandsons. Their temperament was different, and as one succeeded, and the other became defeated, the way they set their goals, the expectations their fathers had for each, became part of the way we thought about the rock climbing event. Our beliefs about ourselves are filled with how our collective minds have been imprinted into the narrative function of our brain/mind. One boy says to himself, this is going to be great. I can climb this, and either way, I win. If I make it, I have not lost face because it is part of the journey, not a defining moment, while the other has the opposite experience. Self-efficacy, or our belief in what we can do, is determined by the goals that are set

and the way they are languaged over and over again, into our zeitgeist as has been interpreted and reinterpreted during our life. Change the way the goal is stated and our eventual outcome. The way the goal is stated will "determine not only how strong your motivation is, but how long you'll persist when the going gets tough (Grant Halvorson, 2011, p. 56). Self-efficacy, our belief in our ability to be successful and to get back up again when we do not meet our goals, is determined by the language others use, as well as what we use, in setting up our goals for success. When we see our successes and failures as part of the journey, rather than as evaluations of our being, we set the context for future success. Or, as Grant Halvorson (2011) asked, do we see ourselves as being good or getting better? Our goal to be in process allows us to enjoy the ride, rather than to be supercritical and judgmental—thus hyper evaluative. It is the way the goals are set, not the eventual evaluation, that makes the difference. If we see the evaluation as only more information for future attempts rather than indictments, it is as Freedman and Combs (1996) did with their clients, instead of describing the situation as an adjective where it defines the person, they turned it into a noun, making it far easier to do something about that situation.

Goals and the way they are stated make a big difference about how people respond and succeed. As an administrator, supervisor, or leader of any kind, "the key to giving good feedback when someone is having difficulty is to keep her believing that success is still within her reach. Nothing saps motivation quite like self-doubt" (Grant Halvorson, 2011, p. 225). I hope that this short piece intended for administrators has been helpful to everyone who is responsible for the lives and living of others.

8

CASE EXAMPLES OF STRENGTHS-BASED SUPERVISION

A positive attitude may not solve all your problems, but it will annoy enough people to make it worth the effort.

—Herm Albright,
American writer (1876–1944)

You have brains in your head, you have feet in your shoes. You can steer yourself any direction you choose. You're on your own. And you know what you know. And you are the one who'll decide where to go.

—Dr. Seuss (1988, p. 2)

By this time you have read and understand about all of the strengths-based concepts I have presented. You also have a thorough, albeit brief, review of the more traditional supervision models used, along with a history of how they came about. Perhaps this is all new to you, or maybe you already are acquainted with these ideas. In any case, you have an idea how supervision has been done in the past, and I am hopeful, how it will be done in the future.

Supervision is a unique and important part of clinical work because it gives clinicians a second opinion regarding their work. For newer clinicians this can be a superb support system and a tool for learning more techniques. For those just learning, supervision is invaluable, and it can support and guide the clinician toward more successful directions. For those of you who have been practicing for some time, I encourage you to use this as a scaffold to what you already know and use, to additional, perhaps more helpful ways of supervising. Supervision is something that all clinicians should engage in regularly, regardless of their years as clinicians. However, supervision is only as useful as the fellow clinician that is providing that second opinion. All too often that work in the trenches is provided by a newer clinician who is still testing out and building his or her fund of skills. A supervisor who has been around the block a time or two will have a much larger fund of clinical experience to draw upon, as well as, one might hope, less of an ego involved in the process. In academia, again, it will always depend on the tenure of the supervisors, their experience in the field, as well as their own ego-less personality. Informed consent regarding what the supervisor will do during the session is essential, and a cooperative supervision contract is a must.

Many more times than I would like, I have found new supervisors in academia who have limited clinical experience. Yet, because of their status as a professor, they are allowed to supervise. There is nothing as galling to me as finding those who are responsible for the training and supervision of new members of our fields, who are so stuck on their own supposed abilities based solely on their degree and limited experience. We teach and supervise as we have been taught and supervised, modeling our ways after what we believed to have been helpful to us, or because of our admiration for those who helped us achieve standing in our field. This is only natural, as we teach what we "know" to be true, sometimes enslaved by the top-down narrative functions of our mind. Some are in love with the adoration that can come with the hierarchical position of being a supervisor. There is a natural transference phenomenon that occurs between supervisor and supervisee. Good supervisors are very aware of this and work steadily to give that power back to those for whom they work; and make no mistake, they are stakeholders in this process of supervision. Those who have worked in the trenches for any length of time understand how quickly clinical situations can change and how the process is really guided by the client— and how little we as clinicians have to do with an outcome based on an hour or two a week, if that. Yet, new up and coming clinicians can give adoration to pontificating more senior clinicians and supervisors, believing every word they say and following their every move, regardless of where it might take them. Then, when the work goes poorly, they will produce the most damning condemnations to their clients, with the proclamations that they were too ill, or not ready for therapy, rather than engaging in meaningful client-goaled work. And the same is at work during supervision.

Strengths-based supervision changes the usual version of this working process between clinician and supervisor and focuses on what the clinicians and their clients want from this supervisory experience. This does not mean that what the supervisor brings to the table is not important; on the contrary. Seasoned supervisors, like seasoned clinicians, have tons of experience upon which to base their work. This does not mean, however, that their experience and ideas will transfer to someone else's cases with the same wizardly effects. Human beings are unique, and every situation is different. The supervisees *are* the experts at knowing their own clients' situation, and it is our job to help them find spaces where they can move ahead, do more of the great work they are doing, or find alternatives. Our voice as a supervisor must be soft and subtle, and it should preface every suggestion we make or story we tell with something like, "I have an idea" or "This reminds me of another situation," followed up with, "Would you like to hear it?" or "How might what I said fit your case?" Ours must be a humble venture.

CASE PRESENTATIONS

The following two case vignettes are from real supervision situations that I videotaped, with informed permission, for a series of workshops I did on clinical supervision in order to demonstrate strengths-based work. They demonstrate my early ideas regarding strengths-based supervision. I also insert ideas from my current work into the cases as examples, so that you can see what I might do differently today. The first is a long session of Jane, who is dealing with her own countertransference issues and doubts of her work with a very difficult family. Take time to read the vignette through and think about what you might do as both a clinician and a supervisor. Think about why and how you might do either clinical work or supervision with the person in the vignette and what informs your decisions. These are the questions to ask: How did you come to your conclusions? Where did you learn the ideas you came up with? How might what you are thinking add or detract from the situation?

Next, Melody is a wonderful, long-time clinician from another field of mental health, who has a certain way of working but has added on a bunch of wonderful additions. Ask the same questions of yourself that you asked in the previous case. I am, as always, indebted to my stakeholder supervisors, who taught me so much.

JANE FACES HER SELF

The following is a peek at some early strengths-based clinical supervision I did with Jane, a college professor in a midlife career change, who is facing clients she never imagined could be so lovable, yet so rude, crude, and tattooed. Because of her mature, empathic, and straightforward outlook on counseling, Jane is well-liked by all of her clients, and she is quite successful. But then, one of her favorite family clients whom she had been working with for over 6 months, suddenly hit the wall. Jane, who did not see it coming, was amazed at the level of anger and hostility that could come about, from both her clients, as well as herself.

Jane: There's not very many people that I would do this for (being taped for the use of later demonstration).

Jeff: I know, and I appreciate that. I appreciate that you're willing to do it. What would you like to get out of supervision?

<This is my standard way of starting supervision. By asking what my supervisors want, I set the stage that this meeting is about what they want, not about me telling them how to do their work. Like clinical work, I believe that stakeholders need to feel and be a real part of the process. We are, hopefully, engaging in a coconstruction of ideas that will fit and be useful to them in their own work. In addition, I am working to increase their efficacy, their personal agency as a clinician, and in order to do that, they need to see their own competency in what they do, even in seeing and correcting their own mistakes. Meaning and meaning changes are created by the dialogic process, where there is a difference that makes a difference, not one that is

so jarringly different that their worldview rejects our discourse or corrects it by seeing my thoughts as greater than theirs. We have to do it together and agree for it to be accepted and be useful.>

Jane: Well I tell you tonight I had a day and a half!

Jeff: A day and a half?

Jane: Yes, well Susie and Susanna, our mother and daughter? . . . (gasp) . . . Susanna the mother had heart surgery and angioplasty or whatever they call it. And they found an aneurysm so they've done a balloon thing or whatever they call it. And now she's home and she is doing fine but is supposed to be taking it easy and not have any stress in her life. And she had made up her mind on Sunday that Susie was going to come home to live with her . . . she had been staying at her uncle and aunt's for a while, and I knew there was going to be problems. . . . I just knew there would be problems. Well, Susie came home on Sunday. And I figured, well let's give this until about Tuesday. And I was just about right. Anyway she (mom) called me this morning saying that she knew that when Susie got home from school she was certain that she knew what was going to happen . . . that there had been nothing but problems with Susie . . . screaming name-calling yelling and cursing. She is back to the same old thing and so is Susanna.

Jeff: What do you mean Susanna is too?

Jane: Mother is also. They have a way of relating to other, and each one knows how to push the other one's buttons in a heartbeat, and they do it all the time. Now I'm not saying it's on purpose, but it's unconscious. It's classic right out of the book.

<I have heard this sort of scenario before, and what I want to know is how it is playing out again. What are the behavioral sequences that set them back. Instead, I get a recapitulation of the case structure—a diagnostic assessment, if you will, of the family's patterns. Most often when clinicians are puzzled or upset about cases not going well, they will move back to talking about the client(s) history or pattern assessment. It is sort of like they are saying to me, "Look, I know a lot about this

client system." I know that they have a way of pushing each other's buttons; I want to know what is different now. This is what I think of as a saving-face operation by the clinician, in front of his or her supervisor. We all do it, and it is a normal way of moving away from how to create changes. Her statement that this family has not regressed to this state on purpose is right out of discussions we have had in the past, in group supervision, regarding patterns and pattern replication, rather than on conscious processes—or at least this is my construction of what has happened. I never got it confirmed, and I would not have asked. I want to lift her up, not be in her face or make her feel any worse than she already does. And so, I ask for her efforts in pattern interruptions: How was she a part of making helpful suggestions or behavior changes? I use the language of inference, assuming that she has done something already. I assume that she is competent and has engaged in some discussion regarding change, rather than just sitting on her hands going, "What am I to do? The sky is falling!">

Jeff: And what have you done to interrupt that?

Jane: Well first of all I suggested being apart for awhile, and that Susie might live at the uncle's place for awhile. So they could be apart and work things out in the future. Things go up and down, things were going really well for awhile and then there would be a dip, and that's the way it's been for the last three months. (sigh)

The aunt and uncle that Susie's been living with, I have met with, and he—they are brother and sister. They are sister and brother of mother Susanna. (Aside) This is a very intertwined dysfunctional family, all over the place but we won't go into any of that. Mom and sister really dislike each other very much. This is the sister that Susie has been living with. They have been at each other since they were in preschool, and they're still at it.

Jeff: Is this new information to you?

<Many times, interns especially, but supervisees in general, want you to know that they understand the dynamics of their client. So they begin a litany of case history and assessment. What I want to know, most of the time, is what they want from me and what they have done to begin a new process.>

Jane: No, I've known it for a while, but I didn't know it before Susie went there.

Jeff: You didn't know it before you suggested that?

Jane: No, right.

Jeff: So how did it come up?

Jane: Mom told me first.

Jeff: She went along with the suggestion?

Jane: Yeah, the brother was really coming to. . . . Remember there was a possibility that Susie was going to be hospitalized and mom's brother was against it. That said he really didn't want her to be hospitalized. Let, I think, it gets to stay with us. And they talked with me about it and I wanted of this a lot of Susie to stay with them and set it going to hospital. A good alternative for awhile . . . to let her cool down. And it worked for awhile.

Susie has done, personally, well. Mom has seemed to be better too. Mom has cooled down a bit. In the meantime, of course, boyfriend of mom's has moved in. And boyfriend and Susie don't get along. I have questioned her and the boyfriend has done nothing to make or hate him, she just doesn't want anybody to be with her mother. So she has admittedly . . . It is prejudging anybody that would come into the picture. She admits that. While mother on the other hand is lonely, needs to companionship, was a battered wife for years and years, before Susie's dad died. So she's used to playing victim. Susie has is grown up watching mom being abused, and doing the same thing. Susie has a real love-hate thing with mom. She wants limits, but verbally abuses her mother, and mom seems incapable of putting up any kind of structure, any limits for Susie. They just scream at each other and swear and name-calling that is . . . incredible.

<Once again, she has given me all the dynamics of the family. I want to focus her back on what she has done to be helpful. I can hear her complaints and empathize with her and still ask her to begin looking at the strengths of the family, as well as her strengths as a clinician. I want her to begin looking at what has happened that is leading to positives.>

Jeff: Now, okay so we know lots of the dynamics.

Jane: That's the background.

Jeff: And the things you've tried to do to change the . . . to change the patterns has been to remove Susie from the situation. And that worked for awhile.

Jane: It worked for a while. I've met with the aunt and uncle that she's been staying with. I met with Susie, I met with the mom many individually at times by herself and with and her boyfriend together . . .

Jeff: So you have done a yeoman's job of working with this family, the system.

Jane: The whole system! . . . and I have seen Susie alone every week, and seen Susie with her different people at times. It's been an up-and-down thing.

Jeff: What progress has been made with them that you think is at least satisfactory or that shows you that there's been some movement? What can you point to . . . that says there's some movement in a more positive direction or outcome?

<I am looking for positives, trying to steer the conversation in a direction that talks about positive outcomes that have come about during her work. What is great about her work with this family is that she has also stopped herself from an individual clinical perspective and is beginning to think about the family and her work with them from a systemic perspective. I could have taken this opportunity to point that out, but I didn't . . . oh, well.>

Jane: Well that's real hard. . . . this odd feeling I have . . . like a real failure right now, like king-size, I didn't tell you about today. Can I tell you about today?

Jeff: Sure.

Jane: Well, she called me today and she went on and on, and . . . and she was in tears. And she told me that the police were going to come today . . . she knows, because in Susie is going to act up and they were to put her in juvie (juvenile detention) and. So I pointed out to her I said they're not in a keep her in juvie, they are going to talk to her and

maybe keep her overnight and bring her right back . . . she hasn't done anything to be in juvie. And she said, "Well I can't contend with this, I can't live with this." So I said "You got to consider that she may become a ward of the state. If you go with DCF she might go into a foster home, and is that what you want?" And she said "no." So I said, "So Susanna, what are we to do?" And she said "I don't know."

So, I talked with her about things we talked about many times before . . . about not buying into the argument. About having space. She couldn't . . . she couldn't listen. So I suggested that she go and pick up Susie from school and come and . . . and see me. So I figured that's exactly what's going to happen tonight . . . that the police will get involved, and it's not going to be a good way to be . . . Well if it's going to go . . . then maybe it should go that way. And maybe with me there, they can talk about it in some calm. . . (wistful, dropping off while thinking). But I think that maybe they should at least know what the options are, what the possibilities are. Because we have reached the pinnacle. It seems to me. So I said to her, "When can you come in?" I'm thinking it might be tonight. And she said, "Be there in 15 minutes." And she was that kind of desperate she went to school, picked up Susie and she was there in 15 minutes.

It started very quickly, usually Susie's on good behavior during sessions with me present . . . whether alone or with her mom. But not today.

Jeff: She likes you!

Jane: Yes she does! Maybe not today. If she did like me, it was before today. Because she started in right away. Calling her mother names . . . was calling her a bitch. Calling her all kinds of things. Imitating her when she was warned about what she was saying. Pushing every button imaginable. *It was escalating and escalating and for the first time I've been there in six months* . . . I had the panic button out that was patched to the police station. The first time I have taken it out. But it got to the point where Susanna was up standing on her feet, saying, "I'll show you not . . . not to talk back to me . . . fuck you . . . I've had it, you want to talk about physical abuse?" Now at this point in time I am in between them physically. And I guess they wanted me to call the juvenile officer and have him come out. So I asked, and showed them the panic button. . . . And Susanna said "yes," and Susie said "I don't care." So I called the police right in front of them! And I told them what was gone on . . . that there was a mother/daughter confrontation and I would appreciate it if someone would come out as soon as possible. *And we had two policemen out there within 10 minutes.* The other counselor (at this agency) and I talked with Susie, while the policemen talked with mom.

And yeah, I feel like a big failure . . . because I couldn't do anything.

The policemen were really good, they talked with mom and said she is going to act, can act like an. . . . They were very calm, but they stood like the authority. And explain to Susie what the options were, and none of them were good. Going to the juvie (juvenile detention center) route or a foster home is not good. And she wasn't very cooperative, but she began to calm down and say that she would take it a day at a time. And she started to listen. And then they left. And just when we thought they had it settled and decided to go home. . . . That Susie was going to call me in the morning and reset an appointment . . . well, they didn't even make it to the corner. Susie started swearing and cursing, and mom got caught up in it. So they came back. And after a long while we finally got them to listen, and I told Susanna she shouldn't buy into it. . . . she shouldn't respond when Susie acted like that.

And we had a go through it all over again! And it was a mess . . . an absolute mess!

Jeff: (interested, sort of nervous laughter) So, you're feeling like a failure?

<With this last section, I chose to be quiet and listen respectfully, but I also challenged her negative connotations that the session was not at all helpful to the family or that as a clinician, she had done nothing useful. My voice tone has an air of respect but a very serious questioning tone.>

Jane: Yes! I am.

Jeff: Tell me about that.

<In retrospect, I think I am on shaky ground here, punctuating and asking for her feelings and thoughts about her feeling like a failure. Many will disagree with me here, but it is my perspective that asking for negative stuff only takes us in that direction. I wish I had said, "I think I can understand how you're feeling, and (not but) I had a different thought. I would be glad to share it with you, if you would like." However, it did lead us to a place where we could, together, look at her interface issues—that place where the clients' views and experiences and the therapist's views are different, yet intertwined. Of course, the isomorph is that the same thing is happening in the supervisor and supervisee/stakeholder views. My use of language sets the tone and the expectations of the direction of the clinical work. I have had students and workshop participants who have a very strict clinical view of a nondirective method question my willingness to, together with the client, set tone and direction. One must remember that all models of clinical work have equal outcomes, according to research. So, directive or not, clinical work seems to have good outcomes dependent on factors other than the model used (Miller, Duncan, & Hubble, 2005). Choosing a model of therapy is most likely done because of affiliation to a guild like psychologists (Cognitive Behavioral Therapy) or clinical counselors (person centered), and so forth, while simply asking what a client wants to work on and following through with that seems to work better. I suspect that is the same in clinical supervision, as well.>

Jane: Well I know it's a very complicated and enmeshed family and everything. And their family values are different. But I just feel like them for four or five months we should get further than this. . . . And I'm feeling bad about that I am. I am. I'm feeling bad.

<She, herself, has identified the key to her dilemma, a positive event in itself, as well as in the continuation of treatment. I could see it, but if I told her

and made it clear earlier, it would have not been as powerful. In fact, it would have disempowered her. Now, with her view of her clinical dilemma identified by her and made clearer for her, she has a better grasp on what to want out of supervision. So I reiterate the positives she has going with this family and begin to ask important questions regarding her outcome perspective.>

Jeff: So you have a very serious dysfunctional family where you have done some excellent crisis work, by providing some stopgap measures . . . things like that, and the family has progressed some degree, but you want to them to be fixed very quickly?

Jane: No, I know, but I would have liked a couple of baby steps.

Jeff: But they did take baby steps. As I'm hearing it.

Jane: Tell me about that.

Jeff: Well she finally drove her home. I mean . . .

<Sometimes clinicians are in the midst of the craziness and cannot see the forest for the trees. It is a part of the isomorph that supervisors need to be aware of most of the time. The clinician is as lost in not seeing alternatives or positives that he or she replicates what has been going on in the other part of the system, in the part of the system during the session. When the supervisor notices that, and does not replicate it, then the clinician can make changes. I saw the replicated isomorph and offered her a different view of the situation. Then Jane saw it and had a different, more helpful view.>

Jane: Okay . . . okay. She did do that.

Jeff: So I guess I'm . . .

Jane: Okay, she did . . . (comprehending and mulling over my words and her actions).

Jeff: I mean, it's taken her a long time to get there, but it's taken them a long time to get where they're at. So . . .

Jane: (sigh) I'm also having a hard time . . . I mean I am . . . I'm very fond of Susie, but the way she was talking to her mother I wanted to fly across the room and grab her. I don't think . . . any kid of mine would've ever talked to me that way. So I'm have a hard time with it too. And I'm not used to

mothers and daughters calling each other fucking bitches and whores and sluts and things like that. And idiots. It's not been part of my environment ever. Not that I haven't had some real rough stuff with my kids. But nothing like that . . . (quiet sigh) . . . so it's . . . it's hard for me. . . . It's hard for me not to identify with mom.

<The cruxes of her dilemma are her interface issues. At this point, I could have asked if she wanted to talk about this, but she was rolling, so I let it go, and just affirmed that I understood. This was tacit approval that we were going in the right direction. These days I might have made this point clearer.>

Jeff: Ummm, hmm.

Jane: It's very hard for me. But on the other hand I can see . . . I've stepped back enough to see that some of the stuff mom certainly has instigated. From a while back! And patterns have been set. And Susie's got away with everything. And . . .

<This is excellent insight, and I could have reiterated with an add-on such as, "You really do know this family well, *and* yourself in your work with them is coming along nicely.>

Jeff: So let's . . . can we take a look at some of the things you've done that have really been helpful?

Jane: Yeah . . . because I'm not seeing it right now.

<Here is the crack in the ice of her understanding that it is only a perception that might be a partial explanation, with room for alternative expanded views.>

Jeff: What . . . from the beginning, what are the strengths you have going with this family?

Jane: The strengths? (Incredulously)

Jeff: Yes, what kinds of things do you have going with this family that have been useful to you, helping you to be able to pull off some . . .

Jane: (eager, but a bit timidly) I know them all (the whole family system), I've met them all, and as different as they are from me, I like them all.

Jeff: Wow!

Jane: As individuals. And when I say all, I mean the uncle, the boyfriend, the whole bit . . . mom.

Jeff: Wow . . . wow. That's amazing to me, because I've known a lot of students . . . and even experienced therapists that haven't been able to pull that off . . . bringing in all parts of the system. And you seem to have been able to do that. And apparently they like you because they keep coming back. So if you say like, I would like you to come back, *and* they did . . . they come back? Yes?

Jane: Yeah!!

Jeff: So what is that tells you?

Jane: Well, part of me says that they're just desperate.

Jeff: (laughter), Well, that may be but . . .

<With my truthful discourse of contextualization comparing my experience with other clinicians, Jane's eyes have brightened, her mouth is beginning to turn up into a smile, and I can see the cloak of negativity begin to wither and fall off her, like a more confident and seasoned clinician might when discussing a case like this. She no longer seems defeated but is starting to put it all into a context of clinical work that takes some time and patience. Her narrative of this experience has thickened.>

Jane: I have to say, though, Jeff, that when Janine (the other counselor) came in and talked with Susie, and then the police came, they were saying the same sorts of things that I was saying . . . so I was saying to myself, "I'm not that much off or far afield" because . . . because, here are a bunch of people that have far more experience in this, and with this kind of situations than I do, and I was saying the same things. (long pause) But I want to help them help themselves. I don't want to step in and help them. I don't have a magic pill.

I tell them what I see, but I can't make the changes, only they can make the changes. I can provide the environment but them, but they get to do the work. And up until now I think they just have flat out not heard me. I don't think they've been doing the work . . . either one of them.

<I have been wondering about this piece all along, but again, I find it important that Jane sees it on her own. Now that she has said it, I can ask the question to punctuate her new thought and perhaps provide an answer to her question.>

Jeff: I was wondering about this piece. . . . Things get really hot for them and you seem to be always available for them. I wonder what you think about that . . . how you feel about that? (long pause) And I certainly don't have any recommendations at hand.

<Using both affective and cognitive avenues leaves openings for her conclusions, as well as the way she chooses to answer and make sense of my question and her answer. I want to leave space for her natural domain of activity.>

Jane: Now I know that. Well, I wondered that too, because this weekend I'm going to be gone teaching and I'm not available. I'm not available, oh, I'm really not available!

Jeff: I just got this image in my head of the little boy from Holland who had his finger in the dike. And what happened when he kept his finger in the dike?

Jane: I don't know, what happened?

Jeff: Well, he couldn't go anywhere, yet he had to stay with them.

Jane: Right! (Absorbing what I just metaphorically said)

Jeff: And it eventually cracked anyway—You are saying, "While I'm gone . . . while I'm gone, I am really gone . . . and how will they handle that?"

Jane: I'm gone, and I'm really not available and gone—Friday, Saturday, Sunday. You know what it's like when you teach, and I'm teaching all weekend. I'm really not available.

Jeff: I just wondered if you're just *too* available to them for crisis work.

Jane: I'm wondering that too. I just sassed (Department of Human Services Screening, Assessment and Support Services) them twice so far. And I asked mom about that this morning and she wanted nothing to do with it. They have seen psychologists, other counselors, and a psychiatrist who told her that there was nothing wrong with Susie. And the psychiatrist told them and told Mama it was all her fault . . .

Jeff: Let me get back to this because I'm just curious about all the things you've done well with his family.

<Again, the issue seems to wander a bit, so I want to, once again, bring it back to what this clinician has done well in the process. We, as clinicians, sometimes tend to see only the negatives in our own work. We really need to balance that out, and in fact, some of us need to self-correct to the other side a bit. It is clear that self-efficacy—personal agency if you will—is extremely important to becoming a good clinician.>

Jane: Okay, what do I do? (Thinking)

Jeff: What have you done that you've done well?

Jane: What I have done well?

Jeff: They keep coming . . . (Reiterating what we have covered already)

Jane: They keep coming, yes, and I built a relationship with Susie—it's a little cracked today. But I still believe I have a relationship with her. I may be the first woman . . . *ever* that Susanna—Mom—has trusted. She has no friends, no other friends. She's afraid of women . . . she is afraid.

Jeff: So you have a good relation too with the daughter *and* mother and the whole family.

Jane: Well that and a dollar will I get me a cuppa coffee . . . and you too . . . What good has it done? Other than that they know that someone is there. And they're not alone. And I'm not denigrating that I know that that's important. That's very important. But if they, I can't go on living like this. There would have been violence before the end of the day. There would have been violence in my office, if I let it escalate *one more* centimeter.

Jeff: But you didn't let it . . . what would have happened?

<I point out that she was a part of the de-escalating process, and I want to explore her catastrophic expectations that I do not believe. And like an excellent attorney, I try not to ask questions unless I already know the answers. Clinicians most likely get to this point a lot of times, and perhaps they even go farther, depending on their own internal systemic settings, but this time, in an enactment of their process, Jane's presence and actions modeled a change. They are most likely relieved of her sort of calm and very careful interactions and intervention into the violence.>

Jane: I don't know. I don't know. Mom was talking about "I should've had fucking heart attack" and daughter says, "I'll show you all . . . I'll make you sorry." You know this kind of stuff is going on. And "You can't make me do anything." And of course we all know that we can't make her it do anything . . .

Jeff: Do you think the daughter is afraid of her mother having a heart attack? That she might die?

Jane: Yes. Oh yeah. But she's won't let her mama know it. She's not going to show it. She actually said, "I wish you would've died. And then I could live my life." Oh yeah. Rotten terrible stuff they say to each other. *But I know inside she's just a little tiny kid that's just crying.*

Jeff: How do you know?

<I am looking for evidence that Jane already "knows" but has not used, which can inform and also perhaps validate for the family within sessions, that these family members have love and concern they do not act on when they are upset.>

Jane: Because I've seen it in my office, her and me together. I've seen it lots.

Jeff: So what do you say when she says those rotten, mean, awful things to her mother?

Jane: Usually I'm not there when she says that, but I hear about it from Susanna. It was there today, and I saw what happened. And I absolutely told her more than once to stop that kind of talk in my office, and that it was not acceptable kind of talk. In my office . . . it was not acceptable. I can understand anger and I can understand being upset but some things are just not acceptable to say.

Jeff: So do you think there's a possibility that you can link some of that knowledge that you have (about how she really feels) with the behavior you observed . . . the incongruity of it all?

Jane: Give me a hint.

Jeff: (shoulder shrug) (long pause)

Jane: I don't know . . . I don't know that I've ever felt quite as helpless as I did right before I called the police. It was icky. I don't know if you've ever been there . . . I didn't know what to do, Jeff. I just knew that something needed to be done. Rather quickly!

Jeff: And you did something!

Jane: Yes, I did something.

Jeff: But I think that's exactly what mom feels and the same thing the daughter feels. They get so engaged in their . . . cycle, that they don't know how to get out of it. They don't know what to do. They don't know what the safety valve is. And you provided it . . . you were the safety valve. You weren't inept . . . you did something!

You expected to be able to say some words and some kind of magic would change the system, but words sometimes are not enough.

<Famous couple therapist John Gottman (1999) talked about "bid turns": the action or voice of one person on another to get engaged again after a brief upsetting situation, to take another look at what happened and put the situation behind and move on. I took the opportunity here to have Jane look in depth at *what* she has done well.>

Jane: Not so much magically, but I thought that I might be able to get them to see a little . . . a little bit of reason . . . to begin to take to steps to meet each other half way.

Jeff: But they were way gone.

Jane: Oh, way gone. Way gone . . . and I saw that two minutes after they were in my office.

<Okay, it is now time to move again, from case consultation to looking for Jane's strengths and her meaning making of what happened in the clinical situation. She had data in front of her, and she did act, so how is she making the meaning of herself as a failure?>

Jeff: Okay, so why are you feeling so inept?

Jane: I don't know. (with great sorrow)

Jeff: Because it's the first time you've experienced it!!??

Jane: Yeah! Yeah . . . yeah!

Jeff: And it's foreign to you to have mothers and daughters cursing at each other and challenging each other.

Jane: To that extent. I mean I have two daughters, and oh yes, there were challenges and there was a lot of this (eye rolls) going on, but not like what Susie did. And I said it . . . said the Susie . . .

Jeff: This was uglier than you'd ever seen.

Jane: This was ugly! Ugly!!

Jeff: And you felt bad.

Jane: I felt bad. And mom is crying and the more she cried the nastier Susie got . . . it was almost like now I've gotcha. But she's not got a bad kid. So I know . . . Later on after the police had left, Susie and I went into the other room . . . and we talked a little bit. And I said, "You know Susie, what's going on between you and your mom is very natural and very normal between all mothers and daughters . . . except that it's gone over the line." And she looked at me and she said, "I know." She looked at me and she said, "I know!" And I said, "That can't continue."

Jeff: So . . . so in your best judgment what does mom need to do in order to not let it go on? And what do you need to do in order to help mom not let it over the line? What can you do? I mean, I think you've already presented her with some good options. Like when it gets out of control, call police.

<Now, it is time to move forward and begin taking what has been discussed and learned and put it into a possible plan for helping this family move forward, too. It is best to know when to give it back to the supervisee in order to begin to bolster his or her own agency. The fine line between giving our supervisees suggestions when they are really stuck, or giving them hints, or nothing at all, is tricky. We know from the research that clients do better when

they come up with the answers or solutions to their dilemmas, and I suspect that the same is true for supervisees. They follow through more and feel a sense of accomplishment, leading to their own efficacy and thus more successful behaviors.>

Jane: Yes . . . yes. And I also asked them to . . . I don't know if they will honor this, but I asked them and they said they would . . . that if things start to get heated and mom goes into her room and closes her door, that says to Susie don't knock at the door and you don't go in there . . . you have to let her be. And conversely when Susie gets upset and goes into her room mom needs to honor that too. I got them both agree to that. [see Milne, Edwards, and Murchie (2001) for a clearer understanding of how I train students to work with kids who exhibit oppositional defiant behavior.]

Jeff: That's a good agreement. What else?

Jane: Mom set out these rules, she made these rules up and she showed them to me . . . they're all reasonable. With one exception; I thought that the bedtime on weekends for Susie was too early, and I said I think that is too early and she agreed . . . she compromised.

Jeff: Really? She compromised?

Jane: O'ma gosh, yes, she did! That's right . . . that almost blew me away! [It is always amazing to me how much process information can be ignored or lost after a session.]

Jeff: So she's listening to you! She values your input.

Jane: Yes, she is??!!. I told mom that there has to be quiet consequences. If you said that this is the rule . . . that you can't go out or no TV until their homework is done . . . and there have to be consequences. So of course one of the things I want to do is work out some consequences with her. If Susie walked in and mom said, "You have to do your homework," Susie would scream at her and say, "I'm not going to do it!"

<I really wish that I had commented on the quiet consequences part. It provides a double description of what might be more useful ways of being for this

family, and it is an excellent example of how a clinician's fund of ideas can be usefully inputted into a client's fund. These days, I think I might have also said the following: "I have a thought and I am wondering if I might share it with you. Would you like to hear what I am thinking now?" And then I would tell her that I really liked the idea of quiet consequences, and I would be modeling another way to work—asking permission to share my ideas, as well as providing positive feedback on her idea.>

Jeff: So what keeps mom from following through?

Jane: She's been victimized for such a long time. She was victimized as a child. When she was married, and she stuck by her husband, she got beat by him.

Jeff: Sounds like she's standing up for herself more and more these days.

Jane: I guess she has, a little more and more.

Jeff: And you pointed that out to her?

Jane: Yes I have. Today on the porch before she left I asked her she if she was okay and she said, "Yes, I am a tough old broad." I said, "I understand you're a tough old broad, but you can do this, and you can get through the afternoon and into the evening." And she gave me a little smile and said, "Yes I can." So that's the best I thought I could do at that point. But it's hard, I mean I've never been in her situation, and it's hard to stop . . . and start standing up for yourself.

Jeff: And for you, with this case, what's the hardest part?

Jane: The hardest part? I think the hardest part is seeing mom feel the same feeling of helplessness that I felt when I was calling the police. I've seen her feel so helpless, so inadequate . . . so awful inside. And she does feel that way, and I want to help her feel better about herself. And when she does, then Susie will too.

<Jane now knows the isomorph and can be aware of it in the future, and she also can see that she was not a lump who did nothing during a session. This piece of work in our collaborative supervision session— seeing Jane as a stakeholder in the process of an

interconnected clinical session—made a difference in the way she works clinically, as well as then, how Susan will be a mom. I felt the pride, too, of helping someone who was feeling helpless, see the actions she took and her inner interface issues exposed, so that a clinician can work more successfully with a client.>

Jeff: So what did you do different today, than what mom usually does?

Jane: Well, I took control. I took control. (sigh).

Jeff: Yeah, you took control . . . you call the police . . . you modeled for mom a good tough old broad way of doing things.

Jane: I also told Susie that I wasn't going to have that kind of talk in my office.

Period!

Jeff: You drew a boundary, and yes, it doesn't sound like a bad session to me at all. It sounds like a scary session . . . but a good one.

Jane: It was scary.

<Being a big believer in metaphor and storytelling, I could have told—as I am sure any seasoned clinicians who have worked with multiproblemed families could—stories of scary and difficult cases. It just didn't seem to be the time. But I believe in sharing my own times of difficulties with clients, if it seems appropriate, and with the permission of the clinician with whom I am working. Again, I offer alternative multiple views and respectfully add them to our shared socially constructed narrative of clinical work, if the clinician would like to hear about my situations. Nine times out of ten, the clinician listens with rapt attention to my tales of mistakes, normalizing the difficulty of the work we do.>

Jeff: Sounds like an out-of-control session with two out-of-control people. But it doesn't sound like a bad therapeutic session . . . sounds like a fairly decent therapeutic session.

Jane: You don't know how many fractions milliseconds . . . I was saying, "What would Jeff do . . . what would Jeff do?"

Jeff: I would probably do the same thing but not as quick as you did. I mean you did a really good job. Why you look at me like that? You look at me like you don't believe me?

Jane: I don't know.

Jeff: I think the problem is that you have gone through all of these horrible, horrendous times with these clients . . . I mean, like this is a very goofy family. They had years to practice their silliness, and they're disempowered and you demonstrated that you can take control. They did their crazy stuff in front of you, which is neat . . . I mean they trusted you enough to let you see what shit was going on. That was the first time you've ever done it, but it was also the first time you ever have a family like this act bizarre in front of you. You took control.

Jane: Yeah, it really is.

Jeff: I mean you took control!

Jane: I guess I did.

Jeff: So when you think about it like that, I mean what do you think about yourself?

<This is an agency (personal agency) question, meant to have her assess her growth and personal agency. Another way to ask it is, "How were you able to do that?" Both questions are meant to provide an internal assessment of capability.>

Jane: I don't know.

Jeff: Maybe you're not there yet.

Jane: I'm not there yet.

Jeff: Can you process the way that says to yourself this is a first-time event and I handled it even though I thought I was stuck in a situation that was nerve-racking? And that you handled it decently?

Jane: (long thoughtful pause) Well, maybe I could.

Jeff: Could you really?

Jane: Then maybe I really could.

Jeff: Can you incorporate that in your own internal tapes about how you do your counseling?

Jane: Yeah, I could . . . I mean I was sort of pleased with the way I help them to leave. I said I know, what you guys, what I need a break, and if I don't get a break soon under you, homicidal. And it was enough to make them stop and was a piece of levity.

Jeff: Sounds like a good session today.

Jane: Does it really?

Jeff: Yeah.

Jane: Okay, thank you.

The rest of the session was more about the mechanics of how she might handle the next couple of clinical sessions. I believe we should all go into sessions with a game plan and then stand ready to abandon our plan, to be where the clients are, but basically this supervision session was over. Jane had gone through a very trying and difficult session with a very difficult family. She had weathered the session and in fact had made some decent therapeutic moves. The biggest improvement, however, was that Jane was beginning to see that she is capable of handling difficult, highly emotional, and potentially out-of-control sessions. She is in the process of her own experience of families in conflict and the fact that they could not be used as a model for how others might behave. Some people would come to call it countertransference; I prefer to see it as interface issues that every therapist has along the way. The more we practice, the more things we see that are disturbing, the better we get in handling. It is a major part of her supervision on this day to process how she sees herself and to begin to experience herself as a capable and still-learning clinician.

MELODY'S STRENGTHS SING

Too many people overvalue what they are not and undervalue what they are.

—Malcolm Forbes,
American publisher (1919–1990)

This next vignette presents a seasoned, nationally known music therapist who went back to graduate school to gain the "clinical training" that state licensure requires, and she received *and* gave back a whole lot more. She first attended a traditionally oriented doctoral program in clinical psychology and was bashed publicly for the skills she already had. She was told that what she already knew were not "real" clinical skills and that the faculty at the clinical psychology program would teach her to be a real clinician. How arrogant a statement this is to someone who already knows a great deal!

Not one to give up, Melody decided to quit the doctoral program and try our master's degree counseling program, which is noted for its emphasis on strengths. She was prepared to be scolded once again for lack of "clinical skills" and was pleasantly surprised to find that I would rather work with what she already had and increase the skills that she might need in her internship sites. Call it strengths-based, or call it scaffolding; she was an excellent student, and she is an excellent colleague and clinician now. I must say that in my estimation, Melody far surpassed what many clinicians have in their tool bag, which includes great empathy and experience.

In the beginning, as I do with all my students and supervisees, I ask Melody what goals she had for the coming year. She had already thought about this and stated that she knew how to do music therapy well, had loved the classes on clinical skills she had taken so far, and wanted to increase her ability to use talk therapy as a single modality. My comment to her was that she should think of talk therapy as an adjunct to what she already knew. The look of relief on her face was incredible. She said, "You mean I can still use music therapy as part of my internship?" To which I replied, "I would hope that you would use the skills you already have and increase in practice those skills you don't feel you have mastered yet. Why would you not want to use good clinical skills you already know? Besides, if you've passed our individual counseling skills class, I'm quite sure you know what to do." Again, the look of relief was evident; her anxiety level lessoned, and her smile told me she was ready to begin. From this point on, Melody came in ready to be supervised, and she was always prepared with a case to discuss. Her eagerness to learn, to practice, and to ask for feedback, was first rate. Students learn better, and share more willingly their questions, when they know that we are both stakeholders in this process and that my job is not to prove to them how much better I know how to counsel than they do. The reverse is also true. Those students who are afraid I am going to tell them what they are doing wrong are most often the most difficult to work with at first. Their anxiety and their need to save face tend to shut them down. Language systems therapists have always known that the words you use, along with the attitude you have toward them, can either open them up to conversation or shut them down. My goal is always to open them up for collegial dialogue and possible acceptance of my suggestions, as well as the cocreation of new possibilities. Multiple perspectives on clinical process are always an important part of collaborative strengths-based work.

The following is a truncated transcript of our final session together. What always amazes me during our final session is that students are surprised at how quickly the year has gone by and how enjoyable our time has been. Without exception, I can always agree. Melody is acting as a music therapist and clinician in a hospital, so she continues to use music as an excellent way to engage clients.

Jeff: So what is it that you would like to talk about?

Melody: This is a . . . this guy Robin is 44 years old and I worked with him over . . . over Christmas. He came in last fall and I worked with him during his chemotherapy, and only during chemo sessions until maybe March, when he finished his treatment. And then I didn't see him any more for a while. And recently he called and asked to see me, and I said yes and I saw him yesterday. And he opened up to me in a way he had not done before. Most of time it was like, "HEY, play me Greensleeves on your guitar," and I would do that. He never really got into anything much, he didn't take the invitation to work more, so we just worked on a level of his response. And just to back up a little bit, there was a 21-year-old in

the hospital who was dying and his name was Jake . . . actually he'd brought in his girlfriend and an aunt married by pastoral counselors . . . so he died. So, Robin comes in for treatment this time, and he was really upset and he said that one of the boys who he had in Boy Scouts had died . . . it was this Jake. And I said, "I know about this Jake." You know . . . so we talked. And he was grief stricken. I was thinking it was about his own . . . his own unintended grief and that he couldn't work during the time he was undergoing his chemotherapy . . . must have been too much. Anyway he comes in yesterday. As I said before, I had told him he could come in and talk to me anytime you want to . . . and he said, "I wasn't completely truthful with you during the last session. And I found out some really bad news the same day that I had found out about Jake. I found out that my wife was having an affair." She had been having an affair for 13 years. And he spent most of the session unloading . . . just pouring it out.

Jeff: Sadness? Anger?

<I wanted to get it clear whether this person was feeling anything or was just numb (which is a feeling). Anger is a great cover-up for sadness, and some people see sadness as clinical depression, so I wanted to see what Melody was making of this. What I could have done is congratulated her on making a good enough relationship with him that he sought her out for continued work. I could have also had her remember some important and positive work she might have done with him and to take a moment to savor it.>

Melody: He doesn't go there, he's not real emotional. He is very sweet, but he does have his emotions there. I did ask him . . . I said, "It sounds like you are really angry!?" And he said, "I am really angry, but I want to help her! I want to help her." He had found out that every Friday night she would go out to the bar and then come home drunk. She was his second wife. His first marriage ended because his wife was unfaithful.

Jeff: He is too sweet of a guy!

Melody: He is too sweet of a guy and they started couples counseling last week and the counselor said to him, "I'm surprised you're still here." He has just gone through major cancer treatment and he'd got back to work . . . is having difficulty getting back fully because he is still a little bit too sick. So he also has grief about not being able to go back to work. So when he confronted her about the affair—he knows the guy she was sleeping with—she admitted that her father had continually sexually abused her, and . . . and she feels like that's something that caused all as in all this. So he wants to help her.

Jeff: So that's the forgiveness factor.

Melody: Yes, the forgiveness factor. He feels sorry for her . . . she says that she is stopping seeing this guy, but he doesn't believe that. She brought the guy home to their own . . . to their bed, and that's really painful for them. And he thinks that she's probably seeing lots of other guys too. So he has grief about this cancer, grief about not being able to work yet, and grief about his marriage.

Anyway, so in my time working as an intern I have never had someone come in for issues of infidelity. I have spent a lot of time with stress reduction work and some grief issues. I told him that he really needs to have his own counselor. And he said his marriage counselor said she really wants to see him alone. But she's on vacation for two weeks. He's in crisis, this guy. And I wasn't exactly sure how to approach this. I told him that he can come in and talk to me but he can't do it and indefinitely . . . not in treatment here, because it's not my focus while he's there. I did support what he was saying, and give him feedback and all that stuff. But my heart goes out to them because it's just not a good time for them to be dealing with this, especially without a therapist.

So what'll I do next week when he comes in?

Jeff: Well what do *you* think you should do? Let's talk about that and get a sense of your thinking.

Melody: He hasn't told anybody . . . but his doctor knows and his nurse knows, and now I know. And his blood pressure is really up.

Jeff: I guess it is.

Melody: And they wonder what the hell's going on, so I'm the next person who he decided to tell. So . . . you think he should get his own therapist?

<Initially, there is little talk about what she is thinking. She is looking for ideas from someone she believes might have more information and answers than she does, not confirmation of her own thinking, and she asks me a direct question: "What should I do when he comes in next week?" I thought the respectful thing to do was both answer her, as well as enlarge the question/answer focus in order to be collaborative.>

Jeff: Yeah, I think that would be a good thing for him to do. What is the likelihood that he is going to do that?

Melody: Whew. . . . I don't know; he's just at that savior place where he says, "I want to help her." And I said to him, "It would be good for you to examine, what's this about that you want to save these two women . . . ? What's the pattern? You know he admitted that there is a pattern.

Jeff: Well, I think it's a good thing you said . . . that there is a pattern.

Melody: And I *said* do you see a pattern here . . . can you?

Jeff: Well, what did he say to that?

Melody: He said that "yes I do, but I want to help her." And at the end I said, "I think you should focus on you. You have been through an enormous treatment." And he did, he started to think about what it would be like to leave her. They're still being intimate. And she likes that.

<Here is a long-time clinician who has never experienced a situation like this, and she has no roadmap.

Unless a graduate student has the opportunity to take a class on working with couples that includes how to work with infidelity or even sexuality, most students will beat a loss. Her work in hospitals and hospice as a music therapist had never brought her to a place where she has experienced this sort of dilemma with a client. She has new learning to take in and incorporate into her fund of knowledge, and she is open to hearing from her supervisor about what to do. The task, then, is to help Melody think about what she might do with this young man, while also providing my input, as a way of helping her think about how she might work with this situation—not as a blueprint, but as a way of scaffolding her own thoughts and knowledge. I want to help her incorporate some of my experience in with hers; we are coconstructing and collaborating meaning that will become hers in her own way of work.>

Jeff: I think she likes it too much (the intimacy).

<I could have asked some more questions regarding the contractual part of their marriage, in retrospect. There are lots of folks who have different ideas about marital relationships and monogamy than I do. I believe I come off a bit judgmental.>

Melody: She clearly does. And her definition of a relationship is strange.

Jeff: As you talk about this situation at this moment, there are a number of thoughts that run through my head. Would you like to hear them?

Melody: (nodding her head affirmatively)

Jeff: They are as follows: Number one, I think you're right on target. So why does he feels like he needs to help these people, rather than deal with his own needs? Presented with this sort of scenario, there are a number of things that people might do. People might go through a rage, get violent—we're glad that he didn't but . . . and some in his place might hunker down and say, "I need to take care of myself, not everyone else," or some might use all of this as a distraction for his own issues and medical problems. I'm sure that there are lots more, too.

<I am teaching the idea of multiple causes, outcomes, and potential interventions here. This is the training part of Bernard's discrimination model (1979, 1997) that I include in the executive skills section in Chapter 2 of this book. I also believe that what I am doing is like a single-person reflecting team, providing multiple perspectives in an isomorphic forwarding process, as Melody might also do as a way of accessing multiple outcome potentials for *her* clients (see Stinchfield, Hill, & Kleist, 2007).>

Melody: I know his wife . . . she sat with us in during his cancer treatment a number of times.

Jeff: So my question to him and to you would be why does he choose this path as opposed to being upset, leaving, rage, taking better care of himself . . . ?

Melody: He has some victim mentality, and after his diagnosis of and cancer treatment he is . . . if you can . . . (pause).

Jeff: So how is it that he keeps himself from being really angry? Or taking care of himself, etc.?

Melody: And I asked that, I said, "How is it that you are not so angry?" And he said, "I think I am angry. And I was getting pissed." But he wants to help her get through this because she's been abused. And I think that he thinks that she can't help herself. And he wants to save their marriage. But he's not sure that they can go on after this. But I think that he's really beginning to understand the depth of what's been going on these last past years.

Jeff: This has been part of the relationship quite a long time. What has the affair meant to him?

Melody: Well, that would be a good question to ask. I'm not sure that I asked him that.

Jeff: Well you know there's been a lot of this been written about affairs; affairs are puzzling to me. You know I know my own feelings about affairs and what happens if my significant other was involved in an affair, and they aren't pretty.

Some people have written books about that . . . some believe that affairs can be helpful to the marriage because it brings spice to the marriage or wakes them up. One of the psychiatrists at Northwestern who trained me used to talk about how affairs could be seen in the same light . . . communicating that they dare to want more spice in a relationship. People do it because they like to get back involved with their spouse; some people do it because they're angry with their spouse.

Melody: . . . she's continued this through his cancer!

Jeff: You're feeling pissed at her?

<As I reread this vignette, I wondered when I would get around to the interface issues. I spend a great deal of time giving her multiple reasons why people have affairs and have self-disclosed a part of my own internal constraints, but I have not asked her about her own interface issues, her own feelings, beliefs, and thoughts. And almost right after this, I talk about my own clinical experience, which surprises her. I ask myself and answer my own question in my head: "What would you have done, and why?">

Melody: Yeah, I am, and I mean he's a sweet guy and he doesn't deserve this, especially with his cancer. So I was glad that at the end we could talk about what this pattern meant for him. What's his part in this?

Jeff: Yeah, infidelity is hard . . . I think I have only treated about four couples that presented for an affair . . .

Melody: Really?

Jeff: That I know of. The first one I really flubbed up terribly. Because it was sort like this one, in that the guy was not angry at all. And he was like, "I just went to go through this and you are supposed to make it better." And I can feel my own feelings starting to surface. And that's not useful either as you want to find some middle ground and recognize your own anger and deal with it.

Melody: I almost said, "I'm getting pissed at her."

Jeff: So what stopped you?

Melody: I don't know . . . I did not want to put my feelings on him. I want to find out where he was at. I suppose I could have. I just didn't say that. It was hard to get a word in edgewise; he was just pouring out. No tears, but it could have happened at any time.

Jeff: So maybe he's really in touch with it more than you think with. You know they say that anger is a good cover-up for sadness. So it was really sad. And you know . . . some believe that most of us guys don't deal with the sadness . . . it is either rage, or. . . .

Melody: He went into a whole lot of things about how he was afraid that he would be a jealous spouse now and that he wouldn't be able to make it. And he's a man and worried about the money piece more.

Jeff: Well I don't know. So what has been useful about what we've talked about so far?

<As I have talked about in previous chapters, the work of Miller et al. (2005) continues to inform my thinking that the best work is that which is useful to the clients, be they clinical clients or supervisees. If what I am providing is not useful, then I am not being effective.>

Melody: Yeah, I don't know that it would be good for him to get a therapist. Because I just said, "You know I'm just a music therapist and I'm not a licensed counselor yet. And I would like to see you get somebody specifically for yourself."

<I suppose I could have dealt with her insecurities of being "just" a music therapist, but a full year of working with her had demonstrated to me over and over again that she is a great clinician who is able to work from multiple angles, and she is gifted at what she does, no matter which modality she has been using with her clients. There are many times when I suggest to new or experienced clinicians that they change their venue, work with art or music or play as a way of integration and access to their clients' needs. Why should Melody be any different, only more gifted and talented in music than most clinicians?>

Jeff: I think that's good advice. Professionally for him. And I think you are as good as they get for someone like him.

Melody: Well I've never done this (marital infidelity clinical work).

Jeff: Well, clinically it has nothing to do with your experience or your ability to deal with them. It's just you are not licensed yet.

<The literature is fairly clear about what keeps people coming back and working on their own issues. And in the end, the relationship between client and clinician seems to mean more than some sophisticated technical information about this or that, although we all work as if it does. My guess is that a good congruent, transparent, respectful relationship between Melody and her client will go far. But, as I have said about clinicians in their middle stages, they all want to learn techniques as if they are a great big magic wand.>

Melody: Yeah. And I would have to read a bunch of books beforehand.

Jeff: The other thing that really is curious to me is why he says that her having been sexual abused would let her off the hook for doing this.

<I am purposely distracting her here and going back to a part that I think we both have been wondering about. This gives her a bit more confidence that she knows something more about the case than she thinks she does.>

Melody: Yeah, thank you. Thank you.

Jeff: And just because a person's been through a bad experience, that doesn't let them off the hook. If you're in a committed monogamous relationship, you can't use that as an excuse.

Melody: Yeah, and that's really interesting point because now you're grown up and in a committed relationship, and you can't use those kinds of things that happened for an excuse anymore.

Jeff: Well, anything else you want know?

Melody: No, that was enough. I'm just interested in anything you have to say, because I've never been in this situation before.

Jeff: Why I guess what I'm telling you is that even though I've had more training and a bit more experience than you, when it comes to this I'm no better than you are because you have the relationship.

Melody: (Shaking head, but not totally sold on what I am saying).

Jeff: Can I ask you a just another question?

Melody: (Nodding head affirmatively).

Jeff: You can answer this on whatever level you like . . . this is our last session. When you think about the supervision that you and I have had, and the supervision you have had at your site, what's the difference and what are the similarities? What's this been like for you?

Melody: The supervision with you has been fabulous. I just have brought in all kinds of stuff and some ethical stuff. And it's been really helpful that you could see me as a music therapist . . . and you've validated me in what I know already. So like what I was doing, you validate me. In the hospital, my supervisor, she is my supervisor there. And she really helps me with the ethical stuff. And by the way, she had a different take on what I should have done with that one situation than you did. But you both agreed that I should've asked the client before she died. So I guess what a lot of my supervision has been is supporting my gut and what's going on and validating that I know what I'm doing. With both of you.

Jeff: So, are there differences between your supervisor and me, did you notice?

Melody: She's more go by the book ethically in the hospital.

Jeff: Anything else and questions?

Melody: Now I should get a supervisor as soon as I can do this sort to work toward my LCPC.

Jeff: I think that is a great idea.

<As I read these last few paragraphs during the final editing process, I could not stop from smiling.

Melody said, "So I guess what a lot of my supervision has been is supporting my gut and what's going on and validating that I know what I'm doing. With both of you."

I could not help but think that is almost the main point of this book, so I am really pleased that she got it. She is also, in a backhanded way, asking if I would continue to supervise her, which I decline on my own principles. I did not supervise anyone outside of the university setting for personal reasons. I did not want to work anymore than I already did at the university. Several years ago, I decided that I wanted to spend less time working and more time with my family. I did the university gig and independent practice too, and I learned of the importance of balance, which has become one of my standard messages. I almost always get a blank stare from my upper middle class professional clientele when I suggest that they might do better as a family if they cut back on their jobs and made, say, $300,000 instead of $500,000. Many of them just don't get it that part of their kids' problems is related to the parents' own need to make more, do more, and buy more, rather than take more time with their children. I live in one of the most affluent counties in the United States, and we have a plethora of kids with social and substance abuse problems. So I just decided to practice what I preached and never looked back. This is not for everyone, but it has worked well for me in a culture where money, prestige, and social standing can overwhelm people and give them a false sense of security, while leaving their children without good role models for living a happy life. On their deathbed or at retirement, I do not think anyone ever says, "I sure wish I had spent more time at the office.">

Melody: The supervision with you has been really very real; I appreciate that.

Jeff: What do you mean by that?

Melody: Well, you're not into formalities, so that relaxes me so that I can talk about things that I need to. We can laugh about things.

Jeff: It's important to laugh! Many times at ourselves. And on that I guess we'll end.

This rather long piece of supervision again represents how I typically work. I try to be chatty and engage in a two-way dialogue. But when there are issues that seem to go beyond where my supervisees have been, I present a context that I hope indicates to them that they did as well as they could, sometimes better than expected. As I have mentioned throughout this book, strengths-based supervision in any form, be it clinical or administrative, is more than techniques; it is a philosophy, a way of being, and an attitude about the people with whom we work and their ability to succeed, sometimes with our help. It has been my experience that just like the children who were helped by teachers and instructors in the research which led to the Pygmalion effect, our supervisees can learn and perform at the top of the J-curve, if we believe in them and are willing to work with their strengths, rather than focusing on their deficits and problems.

9

LESSONS LEARNED AND
WHERE TO FROM HERE?

The mortal wound of psychotherapy occurred when it made objects-to-be-fixed of the people it was trying to help.

Gerald May (1990, p. 62)

Some of it's magic, some of it's tragic, but I had a good life all the way.

—Jimmy Buffett (1973, side A, track 3)

I began my career in mental health back in 1967 as an activity therapist at one of the new community mental health facilities in Illinois. The mandate to begin deinstitutionalization of the large mental health hospitals, where patients of all sorts were housed, was part of President John Kennedy's attempt to make life better for those who need society's help, provided in a more humane manner (Community Mental Health Act, 1963). Pollack and Feldman (2003) said that this one act "was a turning point in the history of mental health policy and services in the United States (p. 377). The plan was to have more open spaces and access to real-world life, as well as to place patients in closer proximity to where they had come from, rather than parceling them off and out of sight. It also provided for the training of mental health professionals, of which I was a part. The new facility where I began to work had lots of safety

glass windows for outdoor viewing. Most living quarters were unlocked pavilions rather than warehouse-like wards, and there was access to the outside, both accompanied and sometimes unaccompanied by appropriate staff. I still think of this as the golden age of mental health, when relationships with clients and their family and staff were the treatment of the day rather than heavy dosing of medications—mostly Thorazine (Chlorpromazine) and Stelazine (Trifluoperazine) used for psychosis, schizophrenia, and severe chronic anxiety in those days. Although medication was used back then, the thrust of the 1970s, as I remember it, was to use relationship and milieu in our efforts to help—counseling skills were used more than psychopharmaceuticals. The Day Treatment Center where I was assistant director, one of the first of its kind, patterned itself after the Orthogenic School that Bruno Bettelheim (1974) directed, and two of his key staff consulted with us in our work. Later Chuck Kramer's Family Institute of Chicago, eventually claimed as its own by Northwestern University, became a prime consultation factor for our program. Finally, Gerald May's (1990) call convinced me that we are not here to fix others but to help them become better at being who they already are: "Simply be how you are, completely. Better yet, just realize that you *are* being who you are, right now, completely" (p. 103). This is completely different than the remediation and problem-focused ideas we have been indoctrinated from the medical model that the pharmaceutical companies and the medical association have used in their marginalization of strengths-based clinical work.

One day as I came onto the campus of the large, modern mental health facility where I worked, I saw a young woman running along one of the many winding paths, directly toward me. This was not very strange, except that immediately behind her, by about 25 yards, were three men running and shouting. One was in a uniform, and the other two were dressed in the usual casual civilian clothing of the day at this facility; they were yelling at the young woman, and then they started yelling at me. "Stop her! Grab her! She is running away!" they shouted at me. For some reason, tackling a young woman, who by now I recognized as a patient, did not seem the prudent course of action. Instead, I turned myself in the direction she was running and started to match her stride until we were both running side by side. "Where are we going?" I asked. "I don't know" she said, "away from them." "Nice day to be outside running," I said, and after a few more yards, I started to take a fork in the walkway that led back to the pavilions. "Let's go this way," I said, and as I suspected and hoped, she followed my lead running side by side toward her temporary place of residence. As we got closer I said, "I'm tired and thirsty; would you like something to drink?" Well, to all the staff's surprise, a young, inexperienced mental health worker had done what others thought impossible. Without a fight or tackling her, I used the young woman's current strengths—her ability to run—and I matched her

and offered an alternative that worked out better for all concerned. What a nice beginning that was for my career.

To be competent in supervision or clinical work, one must not only know theory and models but be ready to engage our clients—be they clinical or supervisory—with creativity, respect, and the eco-psychological wisdom of leaving less footprints. One can be nondirective *and* directive, according to the needs that are presented, and still be respectful of the client, if the aim is focused in an agentic in outcome. Had I let this woman run off the campus, she might have ended up in greater troubles, and that would not have been helpful to anyone involved.

Wrapping Up

Philosophy

I have advocated and taught the concepts of strengths-based work over the past decade. During this time, there have been quite a few people who have contested my ideas, as well as those who have asked serious questions. Here are comments from a former student:

> The Seligman quote, "I do not believe you should devote overly much effort to correcting your weaknesses" troubles me. A favorite author, Barbara Ehrenreich, would have problems with this quote, especially with such events as the recent financial crisis, Bill Gates' work at multiple problems in Africa, and Al Gore's rants on global warming, and would disagree with doing little to correct weaknesses. There is even a new movie about King George working on his stuttering. (student unnamed, personal communication, December 12, 2010).

Rather than get into a rant myself about Ehrenreich, who has a large following of people and who chooses to bash anything that has to do with promoting positives, I responded thus:

> There is a quantitative and qualitative difference between the problems in the physical world (natural science) and that of a human's internal world.

I would agree with Gates' assessment of Africa or even Ehrenreich's view of our financial crisis, but there are so many variables of what constitutes "mind" (see Bateson or Siegel). Because we are bio-socio-psychological-spiritual-family-of-origin and cultural creatures—locally, nationally, and politically—our worldviews are unique. With such natural diverseness among people, who then has the right to make determinations of what is correct and what is not, thus deviant, pathological, or weak? By what collective authority have those who make these consensus opinions been awarded? The royal road to health most often has to be in an individual's worldview, which can be co-constructed, or re-storied if you will, with a gentle kind affirming person who offers alternative views that are, as Bateson say, a difference that makes a difference . . . enough of difference, but within their preset worldviews.

By the way, if you are interested, David Cooperrider from Case Western, and others from Benedictine University, have been using a likeminded version of Strengths-Based thought for Organizational Development, Leadership Development, and Management called Appreciative Inquiry (AI), that is simply amazing. They change organizations using the same strengths-based principles. Dr. Marty Seligman just contracted with Cooperrider and his folks to teach the components of Positive Psychology that have to do with Positive Organizations at Penn State. Leadership of the Illinois Counseling Association (ICA) used their principles and hired a consultant two years ago to do the initial training of prospective leaders, with huge success. Thirty-five new emerging leaders are beginning to take over the ICA with new, wonderful results. (J. Edwards, return e-mail, December 12, 2010).

Making the jump from the material world to that of what our mind thus our reality, creates for us, is something that does not necessarily transfer well universally and can place limitations on how we view, thus behave, in the material world. How we choose to act or behave in the real world comes from our language-constructed worldview (mind) and affects our behavior. Our check on reality of how positive people are (including ourselves) is severely skewed toward the negative. Optimistic people, those who have

self-efficacy/personal agency, live better lives, as has been demonstrated and written about by Seligman (2002), yet our own beliefs regarding happiness and depression are greatly tilted toward the negative percent. Americans believe "that the lifetime prevalence of clinical depression is 49 percent (it is actually between 8 and 18 percent), that only 56 percent of Americans report positive life satisfaction (it is actually 83 percent)" (Seligman, 2002, p. 50). We have the media blitz, a pervasive collective unconscious focused by advertisements of pharmaceutical companies, which insist that a pill will cure our ills, and a competitive nature that accepts as true the split between winners and losers. This zeitgeist that informs us how our "entitled" world inflates the grades or accomplishments of some in order to mollycoddle our young, rather than to face the "fact" that some people win and many must lose, plays a huge part in who we are. These beliefs are indelibly written on the Western code of thinking negatively. When we transfer these to the world of mental health, we have to notice that the world of the psychiatrist these days has been co-opted by the insurance companies who have moved from talk therapy to prescribing medications, after a brief consultation. What most of us know already and decry and do nothing about, is that the field of mental health "is rapidly changing in the United States from a cottage industry to one dominated by large hospital groups and corporations" and that "psychiatric hospitals that once offered patients months of talk therapy now discharge them within days with only pills" (Harris, 2011). But I have put forth many examples of how the world in which we practice and supervise has changed, our ideologies and fundamentals shifted, and with that, our optimism dampened. We are under siege from the very same venues that have been trying to change the middle class structures for years. There is no evidence that medications are more helpful than talk therapy; in fact, the opposite is more accurate. There is no evidence that all folks who have complaints and want some help get better by focusing on their problems rather than by looking at their strengths. Again, the evidence is piling up in the direction of some combination of the two. And for some, focusing on their problems brings about additional iatrogenic problems, while focusing on their strengths is a blessed relief (Boisvert & Faust, 2002). As you continue to see in this last chapter, our forefathers, and a ton of those practicing today, are content and pleased with the results of strengths-based work. If you are one who believes in the strengths-based approach, or if you are beginning to see the light of this method, then I have some ideas for you that will help. But enough of this, as I could fill another book with these ideas and research.

Application

Our supervisees and employees watch carefully to see what we are doing. We are models for their behavior in the end, and it behooves us to model good behavior to all. They also take in what they see us doing, compare it with their own experiences, and make their own meaning from it, as a way of increasing their own repertoire and fund of behaviors and attitudes. In 1970, a doctoral student in business and organization, Larry Senn was studying leadership in business organization culture when he found a phenomenon that he termed "shadow of the leader." What this relates to is that those at the top become models for their subordinates and their behaviors, likes and dislikes, preferences, and most importantly for our concern, the way they treat those under them. How those at the top behave and treat those beneath them is replicated in how subordinates treat folks under them. In our field we have called it parallelism, or more precisely, an isomorph. A great example of this is provided by Steven Covey (2004), as he discussed a consultation he made with a large bank, at the request of its CEO. He reported that his work with the bank seemed to go nowhere, until he discovered by accident that the CEO, a married man, was having an affair with one of the bank employees, and everyone knew it. The employees, who were being blamed for their own lack of commitment and productivity, were all affected by the CEO's obvious lack for trust his not-so-private

life was demonstrating. His leadership shadow was casting a pall over every employee, which affected their work and ethic. What we as supervisors, managers, or directors show our "reports" has an enormous effect on them, as well as where we work and practice our skills.

Collegiality versus top-down hierarchy.

Bernard and Goodyear's (2006) book, *Fundamentals of Clinical Supervision,* cites my colleague Mei Whei Chen and my work with a not-so-complimentary commentary. They made their point clear; they believe supervision is and has to be hierarchical and evaluative: "This has seemed problematic to some (e.g., Edwards & Chen, 1999; Porter & Vasquez, 1997) who have suggested the term covision as an alternative to supervision and to signal a more collaborative relationship" (p. 12).

Bernard and Goodyear (2006) went on to say that what makes supervision supervision is the hierarchical relationship and the power to evaluate. In fact, they even called supervision an intervention that takes it out of what I consider a helpful collegial relationship. The word "intervention," by definition in its most radical sense, is considered to be a "coup d'état," while other, milder meanings are "to occur, fall, or come between points of time or events"; "to enter or appear as an irrelevant or extraneous feature or circumstance"; and last, "to come in or between by way of hindrance or modification" (see http://www.britannica.com/bps/search?query=intervention). I seriously hope that is not what they mean.

Bernard and Goodyear's (2008) *Fundamentals of Clinical Supervision* is an excellent source for beginning doctoral students who wish to know about the history and rudiments of supervision in complete detail, and it is a great resource for research. Their book title is apropos, as it denotes the "foundation or base on which something is built," or more appropriately as a synonym, "rudimentary" (see http://library.neiu.edu/index.html), as in biology meaning, "that which is incomplete" (see http://library.neiu.edu/index.html). However, it is stuck in the roots of older worldview ideas, insistent that supervisors *always* know more about the clinical work of their supervisees and that hierarchy is not only important but mandatory to supervision.

Two points regarding their work are necessary for me to complete my critique of their critique. First, as I have suggested—no, insisted—the majority of literature on clinical supervision has been for doctoral students, or at the very least for graduate students in training to be supervisors. It is not for those masses of clinical supervisors who are in the trenches. Yes, it is true that when doctoral and master's students come into programs they are there to learn about their chosen craft. However, it is also true, probably more so for doctoral students, that many if not most of them have already had a wealth of information and experience. The form of education in most programs I know is pedagogical philosophically, based on the educational progress and preparation for children, by definition. One can see this practice perhaps from the one-up position some use in teaching, but even there, alternative methods of collaborative instruction informed by postmodern and social constructivist thought have claimed a legitimacy in education (Beck, 1993). Second, that supervision is always hierarchical and evaluative is troubling to me. I have made my case elsewhere in this book that supervision does not have to be hierarchical to be effective and evaluative means that one person is making comments and comparing them with what he or she knows; thus, this is not always correct for every situation encountered. In triadic supervision other students give suggestions, make comments, and so forth, all without the stigma of a hierarchical "I know more than you" implied by this comment. It is not necessary to provide corrective feedback that is meant to point out what has gone wrong, when suggestions and strengths will gain similar results.

Strengths-Based and agentic focused.

As the beginning of Chapter 3 shows, our roots as mental health clinicians, no matter what your field of study, have a solid strengths-based philosophy behind them. Abraham Maslow, 1971; Carl Rogers, 1961; Rollo May, 1967; and Gerald May (1977) all disavowed the ideas of pathological thinking and looked for strengths within those for whom they worked. We should add to this list the names of Alfred Adler, George Albee, Harlene Anderson, Roberto Assagioli, Virginia Axline, Insoo Kim Berg, Murray Bowen, Gene Combs, Mihaly Csikszentmihalyi, Steve de Shazer, David Epston, Milton Erickson, Victor Frankl, Jill Freedmen, Ken Gergen, Carl Jung, George Kelly, R. D. Laing, Shane J. Lopez, James E. Maddux, Ann S. Masten, M. Scott Peck, Fritz Perls, Christopher Peterson, Martin Seligman, C. R. Snyder, Thomas Szasz, Froma Walsh, Paul Watzlawick, Carl Whitaker, John Weakland, Michael White, and many others who challenge the medical model that marginalizes the founders' voices and the people with whom they work. Elsewhere in these pages, I have repeated Seligman's (2002) history lesson regarding the transformational results that the ending of World War II had on clinicians and academics in our field. Money from the government for research and working with returning GIs became the change agent that moved us into a period of time where pathology is king. Albee and Ryan-Finn (1993) corroborated this with their work showing how the "organic-medical orientation" took hold and a rise in DSM categories become suspect with how "mental health professionals could be paid only for treating conditions in the manual" (p. 17); this is strongly supported by the manufacturers of pharmaceuticals who pay large sums to lobby the politicians (Barlett & Steele, 2004). But aside from that, one must also consider that the research that has been conducted on strengths-based avenues, although in its infancy, has shown that it has the same power to heal as any other model, but with far less stigma. And Positive Psychology has been moving in fast to show excellent results with depression and hopeful results toward other problems at higher rates than medication (Seligman, 2005; Seligman et al., 2006). The problem, as stated by several authors over the years (see, e.g., Edwards & Heath, 2007), is the methodology of expressing outcome.

Some treatment methods are just not amenable to being converted statistically, when outcomes are more than simple better or worse expressions. The mystic of quantitative research, while qualitative methods have usually taken a back seat to what is considered appropriate, is too broad of a topic to cover here, but for those interested, the commentaries are numerous (Denzin, & Lincoln, 2005; Flick, 2006; Guba & Lincoln, 2005; Lincoln & Guba, 1985; Lindlof & Taylor, 2002; Loseke & Cahil, 2007; Marshall & Rossman, 1998; Silverman & Marvasti, 2008; Strauss & Corbin, 1998). But the debate really centers on the issue of whether clinical work is a medical "hard" science or a social science. And to muddle the matter in our favor even more, medical science has been infiltrated by qualitative methods in its subfield of public health studies that find better uses for qualitative methods in epidemiology research than in the mythic, quantitative research. Remember Bertrand Russell's (1953) notion on causality, that there is no such thing, that the point on which most quantitative research pitches its trust melts away? As Stringer (2007) has said, "It ought to be apparent by now that generalized, one-size-fits-all solutions do not work" (p. xi). He believes, as do I, that "without intimate knowledge of local context, one cannot hope to devise solutions to local problems" (p. xi). We must face facts that like politics, every problem we take on is local sociologically as well as contextual at the larger level.

The point is that empowering clients, be they clinical or supervisory, has always seemed to be a far better approach to working than pointing out what *we see* as mistakes of problems and insisting that they work our way. Helping our supervisees develop their personal agency along with the correlate of self-efficacy is extremely important to the development or any skill and set of activities, as Bandura (1997, 2001) has taught us. Again, from Chapter 3, Zimmerman and Cleary (2006) are quite careful to point out that, "Personal agency refers to one's capability to originate and direct actions for given purposes. It is influenced by the belief in one's effectiveness in performing specific tasks, which is termed self-efficacy, as well as by one's actual skill" (p. 45).

I used to believe that I knew better than my supervisees, until one day a student in one of my family counseling classes asked me if I corrected my internship students after listening to their tapes. She followed this up by saying that she did not understand how a supervisor could listen to a tape recording of her work with a client and then give what she claimed were pronouncements regarding what she should have reflected on or said during the session. "She is not in the room with me; she doesn't know my clients like I do. How can she pretend to know my clients better than I based on her doctorate only?" Of course, I knew the professor/supervisor she was speaking of and that her fund of clinical work was based entirely on her own one-year internship experience under strict methodological conditions in a university counseling center. This supervisor did not have long-time experience in the field, where clients are like butterflies sometimes, hard to catch and fragile to hold. She was going with some formulaic means to work with clients—fine, but every clinical situation is different, and armchair quarterbacking is most often without any solid knowledge of where to go or what to do. Atkinson and Heath (1990), while discussing the limitations of conscious thought, suggested that even if one supposes that "controlled observations could yield certain information about the world (a premise that is rejected by second-order cyberneticians), it is unlikely that we could ever observe broadly and rapidly enough to be able to safely predict the consequences of our actions at all systemic levels" (p. 146). Once again the works of cybernetics, and those who followed Bateson's (1972) thinking and the ideas of brain science (Siegel, 2007), where we understand that our thoughts are limited by preconceived top-down enslavements, come together nicely. Not only can we not know all the possible consequences of our actions in a multiverse of interconnected systems, but our preconceived ideas are so embedded and a part of our inner landscape as to make complete understanding of another and therefore provide anything but mere suggestions, rather than pronouncements of fact.

Again, I have found it far more useful to offer ideas, engage in helping the clinicians find their own ways that work, and talk about ways they can get better feedback from their clients, rather than giving cookie cutter phrases that seem to fit a specific method. We should be informed by our methods not caged by them. In the end, our work should be to shoulder the provision of helping supervisees see and believe in their ability to be open and real, while believing in their own ability to work with clients in the real world. We do this, like good clinicians, by praising their respectable work and offering thoughts and suggestions on those we are unsure of in an open and dialectic manor. I tend to have faith in what Atkinson (1993) suggested when he said this about his own work: "It is my responsibility to be clear that my observations are primarily information about myself. If I imply that my observations say more about my clients than about me, I assume that I am abusing my position of influence" (p. 168).

Strengths-Based leadership and appreciative organizations.

Several months into this chapter, two things happened that equally propelled me along the path less traveled again. The first was a series of quips that happened on one of the educators' electronic mailing lists of which I am a part. Mostly a lurker, someone asked the question regarding clinicians practicing privately prior to their obtaining a license and without the support of supervision or consultation—a risky undertaking, from my point of view. I posted back, mentioning the work of Malcom Gladwell (2008) and his book *Outliers,* where he uses the work of many respectable researchers to reconstruct and establish his ideas, specifically the need to put in many, many hours of practice before one can become accomplished. Within minutes, this *New York Times* best seller book and three-time *New York Times* best-selling author was railed against by one of the mailing list community's senior members,

saying that Gladwell took liberties and used others' research to make his points. The post went on and on and on, with a warning that perhaps this was a post some might find too academic. The poster was correct (how positive of me), but I was struck with how finicky the poster was by making such a comment. Do academics have some sort of matter-of-factness with our critics? Are we so shallow that we put down anyone who is not an academic, shunning how interesting and potentially useful their ideas might be—without statistical analysis? In any case, it led me to wander in my wondering to the idea of subjectivness and the enslavements we place on our ideas, especially regarding information exchange. Our own enslaved ideas about leadership and management are full of top-down ways of managing other people, leftover from the days of the Industrial Revolution. People who work for these types of people have not been aware of how interactions in our world are recursive and can come back to haunt them. As I am typing these words, the Democrats and Republicans in Congress are engaged in a huge battle to see who is the most powerful. Filled with the competitive spirit that believes it is okay to do whatever one wants in order to get one's way, both parties seem completely unaware of the fact that one's actions, over time, will circle back on one's self, creating more power struggles. Circular outcome is the true nature of human beings, yet we all believe in a simplistic linear process. What goes around does comes around. How you treat others will come back to haunt you, later on. We need to change the ways we lead, converse, and manage, if we are to succeed in an information age. If some can villify the notion that teachers and mental health care workers attempt to have quality pay, while corporate executives and even middle management have the right to be paid huge sums of money, all the while being bailed out with large sums of our dollars, we are certainly doomed forever as a country. Language does count; it will come back on us and we need to lead in such a way as to show the consequences of our words and actions.

When I worked for a state social services agency as an administrator, I had two fantastic bosses. They were well aware of the many pitfalls that could happen in a state-run government agency where political appointees ran the organization with limited understanding of social policy or human behavior that is needed to work effectivly with some of the most disturbed and disturbing segments of the population. In pockets of poverty, disenfranchisment can cause people to do things way beyond the norm of usual social mores. "Repeatedly, epidemiological studies have shown that very poor people are at the highest risk for many pathological conditions, including mental disorders" (Albee & Ryan-Finn, 1993, p. 115). Whenever something went wrong on a caseworker's caseload, the person could be in huge trouble if he or she had not managed correctly the hundreds of multiproblemed family situations that were shepherded. That would then trickle down to the administrators who were responsible for making sure everything was all according to Hoyle. These two savvy directors would head off any problems by direct communication with their workers and excellent relationship skills and analytic abilities with their bosses. People cannot control others these days; they can only make rational suggestions and work collaborativly to make things better. They seemed to be the only ones who had read the following words of Albee and Ryan-Finn (1993): "Somehow this compelling evidence that social class, irrespective of racial and ethnic background, is associated with higher and then subsequently average rates of mental disorders has failed to permeate the consciousness of those who control the explanatory models"(p. 115). They were my first examples of what I would come to know as strengths-based or appreciative informed leaders. And I continued to use them as examples later as I directed programs.

As I have put forth in Chapter 5, leadership, to be effective, should be about providing support as well as relational collegial direction, rather than top-down mandates or edicts. Whitney, Trosten-Bloom, and Rager (2010), in describing the philosophy of appreciative leadership, called it "the relational capacity to mobilize creative potential and turn it into positive power—to set in motion postive ripples of confidence, energy, ethusiasm, and performance" (p. 7). As with our describing other aspects of strengths-based work, they say it is a way of being. Strengths-based ideas permeate the very essence of those who embody it, but this is not without a conscious effort and work toward it as a self-goal every day and almost every moment of one's life. We live, after all, in a world that is problem saturated and infected by those who see the glass as half empty most of the time.

I have found that many great ideas have never been scrutinized by quantitative methods. The information that the Gallup poll uses (Rath & Conchie, 2008) and synthesizes into useful nuggets is an excellent source for direction as a leader or supervisor or agency director. To determine what types of people you are supervising or leading and then construct your work with them to engage their strengths is far more effective than to expect that everyone works the same way or learns at the same rate. I love how Rath and Conchie (2008) suggest that leaders must be mindful of how they structure their leadership to be aware of potential problems that might go along with attempts to influence: "You may decide to post the performance records of all your staff, but remember that only your competitive people will get a charge out of public comparison" (p. 137). Again, the circularity of actions can be problematic if you fail to understand the potential consequences of even the best of intentions in regard to their long-range and multiple effects. We live in a circular, multicausal world. I would hope that supervisors or directors would not do so, but I told the story in Chapter 1 about a director of an organization who gave out awards for employees who had the best records of productivity as measured by the number of clinical interviews and paperwork completed. This leadership style, although intended to motivate, did not take into consideration the strengths styles of individual employees, and it sure gave me the creeps.

Great leaders as well as supervisors are empathic and sensitive of those whom they have as reports. Great leaders are protective of their people and work steadily to provide for them and help them grow. They are servant leaders, opening the door for their employees to succeed, for the organization's sake, as well as for their own. Providing for your reports' success can only make you look good.

In organizations looking for positive change, AI (see, e.g., Anderson et al., 2008; Cooperrider & Srivastva, 1987; Cooperrider et al., 2008; Srivastva, & Cooperrider, 1990) is the best method for helping organizations empower and create change within the workforce. The multiple buy-in and feeling of collaborative work creates a situation right out of erroneously maligned Tom Peters and coauthor Robert H. Waterman's (1982) *In Search of Excellence*. Two of the major principles from their eight themes—having productivity through treating rank-and-file employees as a source of quality and learning from those you serve (needs assessments)—are core principles of AI, and they are certainly in line with Drucker's (2001) concept of a workforce that is part of the Information Age. Yet, managers, supervisors, and directors of mental health agencies may not have a clue regarding operating from strengths-based positions. It is more likely that they use the more typical top-down hierarchical management and supervisory philosophy. Our field is filled with a problem-focused mentality, yet it is evident that there is a better way. Certainly, we must understand at some basic level that leadership and organizations that empower their employees reach out and ask for their ideas at the ground level and utilize their deep understanding of the organization's needs to succeed better than a top-down hierarchy.

Empowering instruction.

I have saved the best for last; however, I made a great attempt to introduce it in Chapter 1. Without great adult-centered education, none of what we do would work well. When I entered graduate school, I experienced occasionally the sort of educational processes that motivated and inspired. Many of the professors I had were strengths-based, but I doubt that they would have called it that back then. Those professors who went the extra mile to let me know what capabilities I had, and to cross those imaginary boundary lines to include me in their work, were the ones who inspired my deep love of my profession. I had professors who set the bar by giving choices to their students: "If you want an A, do so much work; if you are content with a B, and really it's a good grade, do this much." I heard this over and over again. Dr. Mary Farnum told us we were the ones who would change the world and our field, if we wanted. And when our faces belied our lack of belief, she would say, "Well, if not you, then who? Why shouldn't it be you? Do you really want to sit by and let someone less qualified set the standards?" It was these empowering professors and instructors who, when in passing, would say something like, "You know I just finished reading the latest book by Ken Gergen and . . . ," and so off I would go to buy the book. Or there were instructors who said, "You know, with a little work, you might turn this paper into an article for publication!" So, it was no surprise to me that when I began my own teaching, I emulated those who inspired me. And I watched with excitement and tears in my eyes, movies about great teachers: Robin Williams in *Dead Poets Society,* or Richard Dreyfuss in *Mr. Holland's Opus,* or even Yoda in *Star Wars.* My students noticed the difference and would report to me, "You're not like other teachers. We can tell you want us to succeed." Now, I must confess, that close to the end of my full-time career, I slacked a bit, as I was overwhelmed by multiple commitments, angst over retirement from a place where I loved to teach, and an awareness—first at a for-profit university where I taught part time and then at a state university—that many students I came in contact with had an entitlement attitude. But I never forgot or misplaced my belief that empowering students to be their best by pointing out their potential was the best part of my job. Today, I have tons of

Facebook friends who are former students, now colleagues. It is to this end that I place the idea of andragogy center stage.

First, however, I must situate what I have to say by telling you that Beck (1993), in critiquing his own teachers, said the following: "If we believe in a democratic approach to inquiry we should model it ourselves, so that our students understand what we mean and are given the opportunity to develop a democratic pedagogy which they can in turn employ." As I mentioned in Chapter 3, B. F. Skinner made the point that to teach in a college or university setting, one most probably would have never had course work or supervised experience about how to teach; this applies to some degree with how to supervise. Counselor educators might be the exception, but other disciples may have never had any formal experience with current educational practices as applied to adult learners, unless they have sought it out themselves. Even among those who have had course work or teaching experience over a long period of time may still adhere, in their teaching and supervision style, to this archaic perspective. We teach and give back only what we know. Our epistemology limits us and enslaves us from knowing numerous other options that might fit those whom we wish to help. One very rigid, former academic colleague of mine was just sure that students needed to take the lecture notes they wrote, type them out, and return them the next class period for a grade. I am talking about graduate students here. I know it is common practice in some undergraduate classes to show films, ask the students to take notes and then return them at the end of the film to be sure they were paying attention. Negative mindsets of instructors like these contradict everything we know about teacher expectations, as researched by Rosenthal (2002). Yet, there is another way.

Andragogy.

Andragogy, as conceived and developed, first by Alexander Kapp way back in the early 1800s and later by Knowles (1950, 1968, 1980) and other adult education scholars (Chickering & Gamson, 1999; Keeton, 2004; Shea, Pickett, & Pelz, 2003), has suggested that improvements over the typical educational system should include what Chickering and Gamson (1999) called the seven principles of good practice. These time-tested practices have now been brought out as a vehicle to promote better teaching and adult learning in our asynchronous world of education. The seven principles follow:

1. Encourages contacts between students and faculty.

2. Develops reciprocity and cooperation among students.

3. Uses active learning techniques.

4. Gives prompt feedback.

5. Emphasizes time on task.

6. Communicates high expectations.

7. Respects diverse talent and ways of learning. (Chickering & Gamson, 1987, p. 2)

All of these concepts consist of learning strategies focused on adults. They respect the knowledge and skills that the students already have, expecting that they will add their own take on what it is they are learning. They make it clear that adults learn more from active learning processes, doing and making their own evaluations in collaboration with their instructors. The instructors frame what and how they speak to their stakeholder students with positive evaluations that are quickly followed up by a few suggestions regarding what might be helpful, giving choice and credit to them for what they know and can do well. Doesn't this sound pretty much like what I have been advocating as strengths-based work from as far back as that delightful tale that Jeff Zeig (1987) told about Mary Goulding's work? (If you forgot, go back to Chapter 3, page 75, for a refresher.) Also, unlike a great deal of the education today, where the student has the sole responsibility of learning what is spit out as gospel by the instructor, it allows for knowledge and experiences from the student to be part of a dialectic process between adult learner and instructor, who together coconstruct new tailored understandings, relying on multiple perspectives of people—worldviews—that fit the situation and the learner as well as add new understanding for the instructor. This sounds like social construction and solution-focused and narrative ideas combined. In any case, it also does not mean that one can throw the baby out with the bathwater. Instead, there is an admission that the old ideas (the baby, if you will) do not fit every case, every situation, every cultural context, every combination of supervisor/clinician/client system, either.

The J-curve that I talked about in Chapter 5, although relatively new, is a game changer for education in any form. The own-ness for success is changed from the more traditional bell-shaped curve, where a percentage of students are expected to succeed at the highest level, and some are expected to fail, while the majority fall somewhere in the middle statistically, to one where the numbers of success increase exponentially. This increase is not left to chance, as might normally occur if events were random, but it is advanced to the higher ground due to the increased involvement of teacher to student ratio of interaction and instruction to start. Interestingly, every one of those writings about andragogy place student to teacher ratios high on the list of successful instruction. Teaching can no longer assume the pedagogical stance of static learning, followed by absorption and memorization, followed by examination, to assure total absorption of what the instructor has put forth. Active involvement, commitment on all parts, and intentional learning communities where stakeholders are considered strong and capable, are seen as most important for adults of any level to succeed in the abundance for the J-curve to be effective.

And so, I argue that given the fragmented and multimodeled field of counseling, the democratic constructivist process should also occur in the supervision arena. In fact, I think education and success of any sort need to reevaluate how success is accrued and facilitated. I do not know about others' supervisees or supervisors

in training, but it has been my experience that supervisees are creative, highly educated people who have been trained in counseling skills and who are all too aware of the many different models available to them. This has been true for students as well as postgraduates, who obtain my supervision services for licensure. In my opinion, hierarchy should be left for last, when it is also the supervisors' responsibility to act as a gatekeeper for the field. Even then, I would use it judiciously. Gatekeeping activities should be done in a collaborative, multisystemic way, using the 360-degree procedure I described in Chapter 5: above board and transparent, with great empathy and understanding for what the one leaving by the back gate is feeling, thinking, and experiencing.

Parenthetically, it has been my contention throughout this book that the paradigm has changed, and some have just failed to get on board. As I discussed in Chapter 1, there are many reasons to move past the old status quo that has informed our field. Covey (2004) stated the following: "If you want to make *minor,* incremental changes and improvements, work on practices, behaviors or attitude. But if you want to make significant, quantum improvement, work on paradigms" (p. 19). Pedagogy and supervision, therefore, come to mean the act of mutual inquiry. I think it is time for a change!

MOVING FORWARD

An editor friend of mine looked over Chapter 3 of this book and made the comment that she thought I beat the idea of strengths-based work to death. She learned her clinical skills about the same time as I did but has stayed static, practicing the same way, looking at life from the same half-empty/half-full balancing act most of us have done along the way. However, I hope that I have made the strengths-based point without killing your enthusiasm, having shown solid evidence and supporting documentation to validate (although I hate that word and all it implies about truth) that the use of strengths in clinical and supervisor work—as a matter of course in any human endeavor—is not only adequate and efficacious but most often a more appropriate means of helping. If I have beat it so much that you are tired and bored, then I have gone too far. I feel an urgency to promote my thoughts about strengths-based methods as being better than the medical model. There is lots of other evidence that the marginalization of strengths-based ideas and methods is done for monetary gain, as the insurance companies promote a medical model of medications over less dangerous but longer-term treatments. In another of my books (Edwards & Heath, 2007), it was shown that millions of dollars are used to lobby for such medical pharmacutical treatments, over safer talk therapy that includes strengths-based treatments. Economics and politics push the broom that wants to sweep anything but the medical model under the rug and out the back door.

Where to From Here?

I believe there will be an ever expanding movement toward using strengths-based ideas in our field. The time is slowly marching on, but there are enough people who love the idea of working with people's strengths, rather than being psychic voyeurs. Like the growing power imbalance of those who want to have fair and transparent government all across the world today, including in our own states, many of us are already practicing and using our voice to object to the coercive means that try to tell us what to believe and how to practice. We have to see it all in the larger picture. What is happening across this planet is the same that has been happening in our field of mental health, of which clinical supervision is a part. Many of us are tired of the power and financial success, which insist that big pharma and its dystopian view of life are correct. We know that this quick and easy way of working with people it proffers is for financial gain and funded by the huge coffers to all the lawmakers (Barlett & Steele, 2004; Edwards & Heath, 2007). Big pharma wants us to see problems rather than facilitate strengths.

Things to Remember and Things You Can Do

Remember from the very heart of Chapter 4 that what makes therapy work is not just the cognition or the "aha!" moments in life—it is the performance, repeated performance. Often when I talk to classes about strengths-based work, and I get to the part about performance and behavior, the students' eyes gloss over. For some, behaviorism is a bad word. Performance is the heart and soul of change. Practice makes perfect, and you cannot do the change if you are not willing to put in the time to practice it. Just like going to the gym, you have to do it over and over again. It has to be a change in lifestyle to be effective, and for that you need to have a plan, to be active in your practice, and mostly to enlist the help and support of others. Strengths-based work does not come easy. Many forces are out to get us. But in the end, it is always a kinder, more gentle, longer lasting and fulfilling way to work and live. When you fall off that horse and begin to diagnosis and make excuses, get back on again as soon as you can. That is also the meat and potatoes of this work, because we are changing a whole world-view that has deep, deep pockets and beliefs.

Look at the truth.

If you have not read Seligman's works, at least read *Authentic Happiness* (Seligman, 2002). He documented the benefits of being happy and content, regardless of the criticism of a few discontented naysayers. There are specific activities and attitudes that successfully contented persons engage in every day. Happy people live longer statistically, and contentment is not about wealth or power but about an internal process. There are many activities you can suggest to clients and supervisees that will increase their quotient of happiness and their ability to succeed in life in general. The more I use these ideas, the more I see the results, the more I refine my practices, the more I believe them to work, the more I trust them, the more I use them, ad infinitum. But read the material critically and with an open, unenslaved mind, if you can. As Louis Pasteur (1854) said once, "In the field of observation, chance favors the prepared mind." Make use of the ideas of others, as much as you can. Strengths-based ideas have been around for a long time in our field, but never have so many with such vigor used and researched them. Be part of this process, if you believe; work with strenghths, observe, and document. Be a part of the efforts to show the success of this growing field of work with people from many fields. Remember my former doctoral advisor Mary Farnum's words, "If not you, then who?" They have rung true for me and a generation of folks that believed her, and like me, they have passed that optimism forward. Pay it forward.

Take time as often as you can to use these concepts on yourself. There is no better model for others than your own success and optimistic attitudes. Do not succumb to those naysayers, but also do not be a thorn in their sides. Remember my Grandmother Bea who said, "A fly is caught more with honey that with vinegar." Solid facts and knowing what you are talking about, complete with references and your positive non-Pollyannaish attitude, make more converts. Think about what sort of legacy you want to leave, and then goal it and work toward it.

During my master's program in counseling psychology, I was interested in what processes were involved with helping kids move from a residential treatment facility to adoptive placement (Edwards, 1987). I was also doing the real work of placements from the center where I worked and vowed to write and publish my first article about something that perplexed me. I also wrote down as a goal that I would publish at least two articles in my career, and I just kept moving after that.

Goaling works, as does enlisting the help of others to achieve your goals. I began the process of developing what I call "intentional learning communities" when I was teaching practicum and internship classes. I encouraged the students to begin their collaborative process of working together, supporting each other and all of the regular events that transpire during this time.

They had to pass a departmental proficiency exam, and they started there with small groups designed to study for this final pass-out exam; this carried over to groups that still network with each other 15 years later. I had friends at a local family counseling center that were committed to providing services, internships, and scholarship at a higher level. They became the model for others and contributed to the literature in the field many times over—legacy through intentional learning communities. There is strength in numbers, and this is so strengths enhancing for those who are part of the community.

Be a trim tab.

Covey (2004) used a nautical piece of equipment to metaphorically describe what can happen in any organization. The trim tab is a small, movable part on the rudder of a large ship that can move through the water easier than the large rudder. As the trim tab moves, it gives impetus for the large rudder to begin the movement. That this metaphor is directed at the very cumbersome components of large organizations or group of thinkers in order to promote and cause change is important to note. Small, significant changes can create and effect larger, almost immovable parts that are responsible for the group's direction. This has first-order change implications, and we all can be trim tabs, helping change to occur. Use strengths-based ideas, and talk about them with others or in an intentional learning group. Keep a log of all sessions, record your impressions and your stakeholders' impressions of your work together, and then use that material to write an article about your experiences. Remember, if not you, then who? Enlist your stakeholders in the writing process, have them validate what you are writing and make corrections when they can as a form of content validity.

Be an encourager.

Boy, I don't know about you, but during my 45 years of working in this field, I have met all kinds. The ones I have learned to avoid are those who are always negative. I had a colleague a long time ago who always had an attitude—a real bad attitude about everything. She was super smart, but she looked at the world as a quarter empty all the time. When she did her own internship, she was vocal about her desire to see (and correct, of course) real pathology. She would talk openly about her clients, complaining about their lack of motivation. I wondered how her clients survived her. One day, I stopped her in her tracks and asked this: "So, what do you like about your client?" She had never thought about this question before, so I helped by talking about some mythical client of mine who had a long-suffering problem that he was working hard to defeat. This simply amazed and dumbfounded her.

What kinds of people do you like to be with? I can almost bet on your answer. If you are reading this book, you are someone who likes to be uplifted and to uplift others. Work to be an uplifter, not someone who always looks for the problems in life. By this, I do not mean that when confronted, you should just drop it or make light of it. No. Take it on with gusto, and do what you can to defeat it, or it will take you over. Be a winner, but be realistic too. This weekend my wife and daughter were coming back from my in-laws' house and talking about our future. Daughter Zoe is getting ready to graduate from high school and go off to college, and money is tight. My wife Betsy said, "I've been thinking about going back to horseback riding." After a brief pause, I said to her that I think that is a great idea, and that she should pursue her dreams. We have always worked at uplifting each other, finding ways to succeed in our own goals and have our own time, as well as collective time. Betsy smiled and I am sure began to formulate ways she could accomplish all of our goals, including her own of returning to a hobby she once loved. Today, after grading papers, making lists of what I need when we go grocery shopping, and working—almost finishing this book, I remembered that my friend and colleague, Andy, was putting on a free concert two towns over. Andy plays a mean hammered dulcimer, and I have never heard him play live. Now I wanted to finish this last chapter and help my wife shop, but I mentioned Andy's

performance that afternoon. She said, "Go ahead, hon. Zoe and I like to shop together anyway. You've been working hard; take a break." She lifted me up, and she supported me. Now this does not happen all the time; in fact, we both have good voice and can say what we want and need. But my point is, that like a good marriage, any relationship needs to have uplifting times. Work at your half-full attitude, and maybe it will even become three-quarters full a great deal of the time. (My valedictorian engineer brother-in-law tells me that the problem resides with the size of the glass, not whether it is half full or half empty, and I am getting to the point where I like bigger glasses metaphorically.)

Elicit your stakeholders' participation in the process.

Somewhere in at least two of the chapters, I mentioned my friend Scott Miller and his colleague's (Hubble et al., 1999; Miller et al., 2007) efforts on what makes for good clinical work. To paraphrase, you should ask your clients and supervisees what they want, what they think has been working, and generally include them in the process. I have found this to be a wonderful way of supervising. If done right off the bat, it seems to set the tone that allows for greater freedom on the part of both parties to be open and have voice. When taking this less than hierarchical stance, it also says to our clients that we trust them and want them to trust us in this venture together. Great relationships (the therapeutic relationship) have a wonderful give and take to their process, and the trust can withstand the difficulties that sometimes go along with clinical work. My supervisees have gotten used to me asking, at the end of each supervision session, how things went from their perspective and what else we could have done to fulfill their needs and expectations. That simple request, slow going at first, becomes a major focus of how supervision transpires. Note that it is an adult to adult facilitation of coconstruction of the session, complete with input and negotiation from both sides. It is all based on a lowered hierarchical relationship.

Evaluation and appraisal.

Evaluation and appraisal are really the valuing or calculating of something with a statement of value. The actual definition of evaluation is this: "The action of evaluating or determining the value of (a mathematical expression, a physical quantity, etc.), or of estimating the force of (probabilities, evidence, etc.) something" (see http://library.neiu.edu/index.html). Any action can be described in both negative or positive valence, and as we have spent pages on, strengths-based work prefers to begin and accentuate the positives, and instead of spending time on what our perception is of any negative, to give suggestions, lots of suggestions, instead of punctuating our perception of a negative. In addition to providing an evaluation of supervisees' skill sets that I think are useful, and feedback of what I believe might be additional or alternative ways of doing something, I also believe it is our job to do more than educate or help them be better clinicians. It is important to make our stakeholders better and more fulfilled individuals, just like we should be doing with our clinical clients. I continue to think about the national and state surveys I did and the glaring statements that led me to believe that site supervisors want more than skilled clinicians; they want clinicians who have maturity and good character (Edwards & Pyskoty, 2004). To me, this means modeling character and introducing and inducting them to a profession of ethical practices, as well as being involved with the various associations that provide context and networking.

Agentic means.

Remember that the main reason for strengths-based work is the development of personal agency. The practice of empowerment and agency facilitating dialogue is presented in order to help supervisees use their own voice and strengths. Personal agency and self-efficacy are the springboards for empowering supervisees into positive change collaborators. It is empowering twice, when you help others find their agency and voice—they benefit as do you. Management and leadership may use different words, but the ideas are the same. All require helping the people we work with find their own voice. The voice and agency we strive to give our stakeholder supervisees mean that we must work to see their strengths and to point them out. Our view, as well as theirs, require a change in the way we think. Earlier in this book, I told you the story of a young boy who came to the United States from Spain and was labeled "at risk" in school because he could not read English (a disability). His most powerful statement to the audience at the ACA that day was that one day he decided to see himself as "at potential" rather than "at risk" (Bermeo, 2009). I worry about how we broaden the scope of disability and make it stigmatized. It is funny, too, that language and coconstructed language create the problem we then believe as real. When I start seeing the people I work with as at potential, it is like the road less traveled—it makes all the difference. How different would it be if we all saw each other as "at potential," rather than as having a disability? I challenge you all to go out, be a trim tab where you can, and promote strengths-based ideas to everyone. It is time to change the way we see and work with our clients and supervisees; they are all stakeholders in our process, even if they have yet to discover it. You can help!

Thanks for taking the time to read my book.

10

EPILOGUE

Thanks to Officer Blackwell, Mr. Jones, Coach Canino, and All the Rest

I get by with a little help from my friends.

—Paul McCartney and
John Lennon (1967, side 1, track 2)

Great hopes make great men.

—Thomas Fuller,
English historian (1608–1661; 1759, p. 67)

When I was about 4 or 5 years old, my eyes began to turn inward; the medical term for what I had is strabismus—crossed eyes—the result of a series of very high fevers, I was told. When I got to grade school, I had problems academically and was unable to read until the fourth grade, after having corrective surgery. I was in the bluebirds reading group, but our whole group knew what that meant, as did the rest of the class; special education was not around in the 1950s. The stress of being a kid who could not even catch the kick ball or move along at the same academic pace as the others took its toll, despite parents who tried their level best to provide me with good medical care, love, and reassurance. My grade school days were no picnic. By the time I reached eighth grade, I was hopelessly behind, and on the last day of the year I was humiliated in two classes by very insensitive teachers, both of whom responded to questions from the other children regarding who among their classmates might not have passed on to high school. I can still hear my shop teacher Mr. Doughty's voice and feel the insensitive cold stare of my eighth-grade math teacher whose name I am glad to have forgotten: "Everyone but Edwards passed." The children's heads began spinning around to see me face down on my desk crying.

Well, the next year was no picnic either, as my parents sent me off to military school where I was supposed to learn better from smaller, supervised classroom experiences—what a laugh. I had so many demerits that I was always walking for hours in a circle on the guard path carrying a heavy M1 military rifle for having ill-prepared lessons. This was supposed to be a better experience?

A year behind my classmates, my high school career began with my father taking me for freshman registration and pleading with me to take Latin so I could study to be a doctor. What an incongruent incomprehensible statement for a youngster who had just repeated eighth grade to understand. Doctor? Not me! Hinsdale High School, one of the best in Illinois, boasted a 95% rate of graduates who went on to college, and my counselors were no help as they *knew* from the start that I was going to be a curve breaker . . . and in my case, that was not good.

But I was graced with some very kind and ardent adults in my life, all whom were determined to let me know I could be whatever I wanted to be. For a while, I strayed along the path of many at-risk teens, but I was lucky. In addition to my sometimes too sympathetic but encouraging parents, there was Officer Art Blackwell, the police youth officer in my town. I had gotten into some minor scrapes with the law with some friends, yet Art always took the time to tell me that he thought I was quite capable. He praised me for the electronics work I had done on my 1951 Ford. I beamed and was lifted up. I was told by my sophomore English teacher, Mr. Jones, that I too could go to college, and that even he, the highest level of academic I could think of at the time, had received less than stellar grades. He said, "It doesn't matter what you have done before, Jeff; it's what you do from this point on that counts. And you can do better and go to college if you try." My papers and reading got progressively better, and the praises from teachers did too. Isn't it funny how we all like to be praised? Then there was Coach Tony Canino, my gymnastics team coach. A Korean War veteran paratrooper with a bullet hole scar in his leg to prove it, Coach C caught me and some of my hoodlum friends smoking during my freshman year—in front of his house, no less. Duh! As he took the smokes, pack and all, and crushed them under his boot, he said, "You are off the team for the rest of the year, Edwards, but you're too

damn good not to come back next year. So you better show up . . . and stop smoking!" Well, I earned my varsity letter two years in a row, and looking back as a graduate of Hinsdale High School class of 1964, those years were some of the best days I ever had—until now.

College was not much to speak of; I got married and went part time, graduating with an average grade point while working at a state mental health hospital, and after a few years I was even supervising others. Graduate school, once I got in, became a safe haven, as several professors took a liking to me, mentoring me as they included me in writing journal articles, encouraging me to write my own, and inviting me into important professional organizational leadership positions. At the suggestion of one of my professors, I took a writing course to strengthen that what professors are supposed to do well, but it is a struggle sometimes as I write and rewrite my publications. I have learned that practice makes me better, as does asking for suggestions and help. Strengths beget strengths, and I learned of my own personal agency and capabilities. I was not at risk, but at potential. Unlike the weather forecasts, I had a 70% chance of success, rather than 30% chance of failure. If I did not make it the first time, I went back and tried again. My publication list is longer than any other professor in my department, and my first book won an award for best publication of the year.

Positives beget positives, and I have learned to pay it forward. There was the time in 1979 when I was working at a residential treatment center for disturbed children, and I was the therapist for a very unhappy 12-year-old girl. We had just come back from a home visit with her mother that had gone very poorly. On our third attempt to meet with her mom, she finally came to the front door drunk and naked from the top up. My small client was devastated, and we left without having the visit. Later, after returning back to the center, one of the other therapists who heard what happened commented to me that this girl was going to have to spend a lot of time going into her past to deal with the problems that she would have from her experiences. Somehow, that did not fit for me, and I remember retorting, "No, I think we will need to redouble our efforts to help her move forward and develop her own strengths." I was an early learner of the power of strengths-based work.

Have the strengths-based experiences I had been bestowed by good, understanding people during my teen years set the stage for how I would change all the pathological thinking I had been taught? Is that how I came to a place where my interests are more in the direction of looking for more positive treatment? The field again began to change in the late 1980s, as Narrative and Solution-Focused Therapy helped me amplify what I did well, and as another of my mentors and supervisors, Dr. Froma Walsh, taught me to look for and use my resilient nature in my own life as well as my clinical work. I was drawn to the various theories and methods, sometimes to the consternation of colleagues who "just knew" that the royal road to mental health relied on good diagnosis of the problem along with all the causes and then a hardy effort to remediate and bring up the past. No way!

As I began to teach and supervise, I found this new way to work with my supervisees, where I thought of them as stakeholders (supervisees) and looked for their strengths rather than behaviors that are deficits based. This was quiet different from most of my own supervision. I have been practicing as well as teaching and training this strengths-based method for many years now.

I began to pass it forward with my own daughter Zoe, with what we now call the monkey bars incident. One day many years ago, Zoe came home from kindergarten upset because she could not, on her first attempt, do the hand over hand procedure that monkey bars required.

Our family motto from that point on became "practice makes perfect," and our family creed has become one of perseverance in all we do. Every day as she arrived home, she would tell me that she had added an additional bar to her monkey bar training, until finally she was able to do the complete length. Together we learned of her personal agency in life. Today she is a straight A senior in high school, reading like a champ, playing piano, and spending time as a leader in her youth group. She has large-dollar Presidential Scholarship offers from all of the colleges she has applied to, and I am confident of her road to adulthood success. She has mastered her own personal agency.

As I look out over the landscape of what has been my life's work in the field of mental *health* practice, I see that I could have personally and professionally been involved with what former APA president and inventor of Positive Psychology, Marty Seligman, aptly and sarcastically said we should call the National Institute for Mental Illness. Without the strong encouragement of the many people who could see me as at potential rather than at risk, I would have never begun the process of changing my self-efficacy and agency, as Bandura calls it. I am pleased that I have learned the lesson well and believe that our culture and the fields of both clinical practice and clinical supervision should begin to see our field with a new prediction for a 70% chance of staying dry, rather than a 30% chance of showers. I hope that you will consider adapting this model to your own, or if you are already practicing this way, that you will add to the literature with new and novel methods of using strengths-based supervision. The world is ready and waiting for a better way.

REFERENCES

Adair, J. (1987). *Effective teambuilding: How to make a winning team* (rev. ed.). London, UK: Pan Books.

Adair, J. (1996). *Effective motivation.* London, UK: Pan Books.

Adair, J. (2003). *Effective strategic leadership: An essential path to success guided by the world's great leaders.* London, UK: Pan Books.

Adair, J. (2005). *The inspirational leader: How to motivate, encourage and achieve success.* London, UK: Kogan Page.

Adair, J. (2007). *Leadership and motivation: The fifty-fifty rule and the eight key principles of motivating others.* London, UK: Kogan Pag.

Adams, D. (1991). *Dirk Gently's holistic detective agency.* New York, NY: Pocket Books.

Akhurst, J., & Kelly, K. (2006). Peer group supervision as an adjunct to individual supervision: Optimizing learning processes during psychologists' training. *Psychology Teaching Review, 12*(1), 3–15.

Albee, G. W., & Ryan-Finn, K. D. (1993). An overview of primary prevention. *Journal of Counseling and Development, 72,* 115–123.

Allen, D. W. (1967). *Micro-Teaching: A description.* Retrieved from ERIC database. (ED019244)

Allen, D. W., & Eve, A. W. (1968). Microteaching. *Theory into Practice, 7*(5), 181–185.

Allport, G. (1983). *Becoming: Basic considerations for a psychology of personality.* New Haven, CT: Yale University.

American Association for Marriage and Family Therapy. (2007). *Approved supervisor designation standards and responsibilities handbook.* Retrieved from http://www.aamft.org/imis15/Documents/Approved_Supervisor_handbook.pdf

American Psychiatric Association. (2000). *Diagnostic and statistical manual of mental health disorders: DSM-IV-TR* (4th ed., text rev.). Washington DC: Author.

American Psychological Association. (2002, August). *Guidelines on multicultural education, training, research, practice, and organizational change for psychologists.* Retrieved from http://www.apa.org/pi/oema/resources/policy/multicultural-guidelines.aspx.

Andersen, T. (1987). The reflecting team: Dialogue and meta-dialogue in clinical work. *Family Process, 26*(4), 415–428.

Andersen, T. (1991). *The reflecting team: Dialogues and dialogues about the dialogues.* New York, NY: W. W. Norton.

Andersen, T. (1992a). Relationship, language and pre-understanding in the reflecting process. *The Australian and New Zealand Journal of Family Therapy, 13*(2), 87–91.

Andersen, T. (1992b). Reflections on reflecting with families. In S. McNamme & K. Gergen (Eds.), *Therapy as social construction* (pp. 55–68). Newbury Park, CA: Sage.

Andersen, T. (2001). Ethics before ontology: A few words. *Journal of Systemic Therapies, 20*(4), 11–13.

Anderson, C. E. (2000). Supervision of substance abuse counselors using the integrated developmental model. *The Clinical Supervisor, 19*(2), 185–195.

Anderson, H., Cooperrider, D., Gergen, K. J., Gergen, M., McNamee, S., Magruder Watkins, J., & Whitney, D. (2008). *The appreciative organization.* Chagrin Falls, OH: Taos Institute Publications.

Anderson, H., & Goolishian, H. (1988). Human systems as linguistic systems: Preliminary and evolving ideas about the implications for clinical theory. *Family Process, 27,* 371–393.

Anderson, H., & Goolishian, H. (1992). The client is the expert: A not-knowing approach to therapy. In S. McNammee & K. Gergen (Eds.), *Therapy as social construction* (pp. 25–39). Newbury Park, CA: Sage.

Aponte, H. J. (1991). Training on the person of the therapist for work with the poor and minorities. *Journal of Independent Social Work, 5,* 23–39.

Aronson, E. (2010). *Not by chance alone: My life as a social psychologist.* New York, NY: Basic Books.

Ashby, W. R. (1952). *Design for a brain.* London, UK: Chapman & Hall.

Ashby, W. R. (1956). *An introduction to cybernetics.* London, UK: Chapman & Hall.

Asy, T. P., & Lambert, M. J. (2001). The empirical case for the common factors in therapy. In M. Hubble, B. Duncan, & S. Miller (Eds.), *The heart and soul of change: What works in therapy* (p. 40). Washington, DC: American Psychological Association.

Atkinson, B. J. (1993). Commentary: Hierarchy: The risk of imbalance. *Family Process, 32,* 167–170.

Atkinson, B. J., & Heath, A. W. (1990). Further thoughts on second order family therapy; this time it's personal. *Family Process, 29,* 145–156.

Baker, K. D., & Neimeyer, R. A. (1999). Professional and paraprofessional group treatments for depression. A comparison of cognitive–behavioral and mutual support interventions. *Journal of Consulting and Clinical Psychology, 67*(4), 491–501.

Bandura, A. (1977a). *Social learning theory.* Englewood Cliffs, NJ: Prentice Hall.

Bandura, A. (1977b). Self-efficacy: Toward a unifying theory of behavioral change. *Psychological Review, 84,* 191–215.

Bandura, A. (1986). *Social foundations of thought and action: A social cognitive theory.* Englewood Cliffs, NJ: Prentice Hall.

Bandura, A. (1997). *Self-efficacy: The exercise of control.* New York, NY: Freeman.

Bandura, A. (2001). Social cognitive theory: An agentic perspective. *Annual Review of Psychology, 52,* 26. doi:10.1146/annurev.psych.52.1.1

Barlett, D. L., & Steele, J. B. (2004). *Critical condition: How health care in America became big business—and bad medicine.* New York, NY: Broadway Books.

Barnard, C. P., & Miller, B. (1987). Cotherapy: A means of training with the family. *Australian and New Zealand Journal of Family Therapy, 8*(3), 137–142.

Barrett, F., & Cooperrider, D. L. (2002). Generative metaphor intervention: A new approach for working with systems divided by conflict and caught in defensive perception. In R. Fry, F. Barrett, J. Seiling, & D. Whitney (Eds.), *Appreciative inquiry and organizational transformation: Reports from the field* (pp. 121–145). Westport, CT: Quorum Books/Greenwood Publishing.

Barrick, M. R., & Mount, M. K. (1991). The big five personality dimensions and job performance: A meta-analysis. *Personal Psychology, 44,* 1–26.

Barthe, H. J. (1985). Processes in the course of team supervision: Constructive and destructive effects. *Praxis der Kinderpsychologie und Kinderpsychiatrie, 34*(4), 142–148.

Bateson, G. (1972). *Steps to an ecology of mind: Collected essays in anthropology, psychiatry, evolution, and epistemology.* Chicago, IL: The University of Chicago Press.

Bateson, G. (1979). *Mind and nature: A necessary unity (advances in systems theory, complexity, and the human sciences).* New York, NY: Hampton Press.

Bateson, G., & Bateson, M. C. (1988). *Angels fear: Towards an epistemology of the sacred.* Chicago, IL: The University of Chicago Press.

Bateson, G., Jackson, D. D., Haley, J., & Weakland, J. (1956). Toward a theory of schizophrenia. *Behavioral Science, 1,* 251–264.

Beck, C. (1993). *Postmodernism, pedagogy, and philosophy of education.* Retrieved from http://www.ed.uiuc.edu/eps/PES-Yearbook/93_docs/BECK.HTM

Becvar, D. S., & Becvar, R. J. (2008). *Family therapy: A systemic integration* (7th ed.). Boston, MA: Allyn & Bacon.

Behan, C. P. (2003). Some ground to stand on: Narrative supervision. *Journal of Systemic Therapies, 22*(4), 29–42.

Benard, B. (1991, August). *Fostering resiliency in kids: Protective factors in the family, school, and community.* San Francisco, CA: Far West Laboratory for Educational Research and Development. Retrieved from http://www.cce.umn.edu/pdfs/NRRC/Fostering_Resilience_012804.pdf

Benshoff, J. M. (1993). Peer supervision in counselor training. *The Clinical Supervisor, 11*(2), 89–102.

Berg, I. K. (1994). *Family based services: A solution-focused approach.* New York, NY: W. W. Norton.

Berger, M., & Dammann, C. (1982). Live supervision as context, treatment, and training. *Family Process, 21*(3), 337–344.

Berman, J. S., & Norton, N. C. (1985). Does professional training make a therapist more effective? *Psychological Bulletin, 98,* 401–407.

Bermeo, C. A., (2009, March). *Developing a climate of access, equity and excellence in education for all students.* Paper presented at the meeting of the American Counseling Association, Charlotte, NC.

Bernard, J. M. (1979). Supervisor training: The discrimination model. *Counselor Education and Supervision, 19*(1), 60–68.

Bernard, J. M. (1981). Inservice training for clinical supervisors. *Professional Psychology, 12*(6), 740–748.

Bernard, J. M. (1989). Training supervisors to examine relationship variables using IPR. *The Clinical Supervisor, 7*(1), 103–112.

Bernard, J. M. (1992). Training master's level counseling students in the fundamentals of clinical supervision. *The Clinical Supervisor, 10*(1), 133–143.

Bernard, J. M. (1997). The discrimination model. In E. Watkins (Ed.), *Handbook of psychotherapy supervision* (pp. 310–327). New York, NY: Wiley.

Bernard, J. M. (2005). Tracing the development of clinical supervision. *The Clinical Supervisor, 24*(1–2), 3–21.

Bernard, J. M., & Goodyear, R. K. (2004). *Fundamentals of clinical supervision* (3rd ed.). Boston, MA: Allyn & Bacon.

Bernard, J., & Goodyear, R. K. (2006). *Fundamentals of clinical supervision.* Boston, MA: Allyn & Bacon.

Bernard, J., & Goodyear, R. K. (2008). *Fundamentals of clinical supervision* (4th ed.). Boston, MA: Allyn & Bacon.

Bettelheim, B. (1974). *A home for the heart.* New York, NY: Knopf.

Biggs, D. A. (1988). The case presentation approach in clinical supervision. *Counselor Education and Supervision, 27*(3), 240–248.

Birchler, G. R. (1975). Live supervision and instant feedback in marriage and family therapy. *Journal of Marital and Family Therapy, 1*(4), 331–342.

Bird, N., Merrill, T., Mohan, H., Summers, S., & Woodward, A. (1999). Staying alive in our work: A group's experience in peer supervision. *Canadian Journal of Music Therapy, 6*(2), 51–67.

Bishop, A. (2000). *Becoming an ally: Breaking the cycle of oppression* (2nd ed.). Boston, MA: Allyn & Bacon.

Blocher, D. H. (1983). *Developmental counseling.* New York, NY: Ronald Press.

Block, P. (2000). *Flawless consulting* (2nd ed.). San Francisco, CA: Jossey-Bass/Pfeiffer.

Boisvert, C., & Faust, D. (2002). Iatrogenic symptoms in psychotherapy: A theoretical exploration of the potential impact of labels, language, and belief systems. *American Journal of Psychotherapy, 56*(2), 244–259.

Bonanno, G. A. (2004). Loss, trauma, and human resilience: Have we underestimated the human capacity to thrive after extremely aversive events? *American Psychologist, 59*(1), 20–28.

Boscolo, L., Cecchin, G., Hoffman, L., & Penn, P. (1987). *Milan systemic family therapy.* New York, NY: Basic Books.

Bowen, M. (1966). The use of family theory in clinical practice. *Comprehensive Psychiatry, 7,* 345–374.

Bowen, M. (1974). Toward the differentiation of self in one's family of origin. In E. Andres & J. Lorio (Eds.), *Georgetown family symposium* (Vol. 1, n.p.). Washington, DC: Department of Psychiatry, Georgetown University Medical Center.

Bowen, M. (1976). Theory in the practice of psychotherapy. In P. J. Guerin (Ed.), *Family therapy: Theory and practice* (pp. 42–90). New York, NY: Gardner.

Bowen, M. (1978). *Family therapy in clinical practice.* Northvale, NJ: Jason Aronson Inc.

Boylston, W. H. & Tuma, J. M. (1972). Training of mental health professionals through the use of the "bug in the ear." *American Journal of Psychiatry, 129,* 92–95.

Braun, S. A., & Cox, J. A. (2005). Managed mental health care: Intentional misdiagnosis of mental disorders. *Journal of Counseling & Development, 83*(4), 425–433.

Breggin, P. (1991). *Toxic psychiatry.* New York, NY: St. Martin's.

Brownlee, J. V., & McKenna, A. (2009). Review of the reflecting team process: Strengths, challenges, and clinical implications. *The Family Journal, 17,* 139–145.

Bryant, F. B. (2003). Savoring beliefs inventory (SBI): A scale for measuring beliefs about savouring. *Journal of Mental Health, 12*(2), 175–196.

Bubenzer, D. L. (1991). Use of live supervision in counselor preparation. *Counselor Education and Supervision, 30*(4), 301–308.

Buffett, J. (1973). He went to Paris. On *A White Sport Coat and a Pink Carnation* [CD]. Nashville, TN: Dunhill.

Burke, E. (1774). *The orator, a treasury of English eloquence* (p. 6). Retrieved from Google Books website: http://books.google.com/books?id=1JD pHQM5PqEC&pg=PA6&dq

Butler-Byrd, N. (2010). An African American supervisor's reflections of multicultural supervision. *Training and Education in Professional Psychology, 4*(1), 11–15.

Carlson, T. D., & Erickson, M. J. (2001). Honoring and privileging persona experience and knowledge: Ideas for a narrative therapy approach to the training and supervision of new therapists. *Contemporary Family Therapy, 23*(2), 199–220.

The Carroll-Keller Group. (n.d.). *Conflict resolution.* Retrieved from http://www.c-kg.com/ Cashwell, C. S. (1994). *Interpersonal process recall.* Retrieved from ERIC database. (ED372342)

Champe, J., & Kleist, D. M. (2003). Live supervision: A review of the research. *The Family Journal, 11*(3), 268–275.

Chemers, M. M. (2002). Efficacy and effectiveness: Integrating models of leadership and intelligence. In R. E. Riggio, S. E. Murphy, & F. J. Pirozzolo (Eds.), *Multiple intelligences and leadership* (pp. 139–160). Mahwah, NJ: Lawrence Erlbaum.

Chen, M., Froehle, T., & Morran, K. (1997). Deconstructing dispositional bias in clinical inference: Two interventions. *Journal of Counseling and Development, 76,* 74–81.

Chen, M., & Noosbond, J. P. (1997a). The reflecting team in group work: "Un-sticking" a stuck system. *Together, 25,* 10.

Chen, M., & Noosbond, J. P. (1997b). From deficit toward competency: Discourse and language in clinical practice. *The Humanistic Psychologists, 25*(3), 287–308.

Chen, M., & Noosbond, J. (1997c). *Group process illuminated: Facilitating the here-and-now through the reflecting team.* Retrieved from ERIC database. (ED407366)

Chen, M., & Noosbond, J. (1999). Un-sticking the stuck group system: Process illumination and the reflecting team. *Journal of Systemic Therapists, 8,* 23–36.

Chen, M., Noosbond, J. P., & Bruce, M. (1998). Therapeutic document in group counseling:

An active change agent. *Journal of Counseling and Development, 76,* 404–411.

Chen, M., & Rybak, C. J. (2003). *Group leadership skills: Interpersonal process in group counseling and therapy.* Florence, KY: Wadsworth.

Chickering, A., & Gamson, Z. (1987). Seven principles of good practice in undergraduate education. *AAHE Bulletin, 39,* 3–7.

Chickering, A. W., & Gamson, Z. F. (1999). Development and adaptations of the seven principles for good practice in undergraduate education. *New Directions for Teaching and Learning, 80,* 75–81. doi:10.1002/tl.8006

Christensen, T. M., & Kline, W. B. (2001). The qualitative exploration of process-sensitive peer group supervision. *Journal for Specialists in Group Work, 26*(1), 81–99.

Church, A. H., & Bracken, D. W. (1997). Advancing the state of the art of 360-degree feedback: Guest editors' comments on the research and practice of multirater assessment methods. *Group & Organization Management, 22*(2), 149–161.

Clipson, C. R. (2005). Misuse of psychologist influence: Multiple relationships. *Journal of Aggression, Maltreatment & Trauma, 11,* 169–203.

Cohen, B. Z. (1999). Intervention and supervision in strengths-based social work practice. *Families in Society, 80,* 460–466.

Cohen, N. A., & Rhodes, G. B. (1978). Social work supervision: A view toward leadership style and job orientation in education and practice. *Administration in Social Work, 1*(3), 281–291.

Coleman, P. T., & Deutsch, M. (2006). Some guidelines for developing a creative approach to conflict. In M. Duetsch, P. T. Coleman, & E. C. Marcus (Eds.), *The handbook of conflict resolution: Theory and practice* (pp. 402–413). San Francisco, CA: Wiley.

Community Mental Health Act, U.S. Public Law 88–164 (1963).

Constantine, M. G. (1997). Facilitating multicultural competencies in counseling supervision: Operationalizing a practical framework. In D. B. Pope-Davis & H. L. K. Coleman (Eds.), *Multicultural counseling competencies: Assessment, education and training, and supervision* (pp. 290–209). Thousand Oaks, CA: Sage.

Conklin, T. A. (2009) Creating classrooms of preference: An exercise in appreciative inquiry. *Journal of Management Education, 33*(6), 772–792.

Coontz, S. (2000). *The way we never were: American families and the nostalgia trap.* New York, NY: Basic Books.

Cooperrider, D., Barrett, F., & Srivastva, S. (1995). Social construction and appreciative inquiry: A journey in organizational theory. In D. M. Hosking, H. P. Dachler, & K. J. Gergen (Eds.), *Management and organization: Relational alternatives to individualism* (pp. 157–200). Brookfield, VT: Avebury/Ashgate.

Cooperrider, D. L. (2000). Positive image, positive action: The affirmative basis of organization. In D. L. Cooperrider, P. Sorensen, D. Whitney, & T. Yaeger (Eds.), *Appreciative inquiry: Rethinking human organization toward a positive theory of change* (pp. 29–54). Champaign, IL: Stipes.

Cooperrider, D. L., & Dutton, J. E. (Eds.). (1999). *Organizational dimensions of global change: No limits to cooperation.* Thousand Oaks, CA: Sage.

Cooperrider, D. L., & Sekerka, L. E. (2006). Toward a theory of positive organizational change. In J. Gallos (Ed.), *Organization development* (pp. 223–238). San Francisco, CA: Jossey-Bass.

Cooperrider, D. L., & Srivastva, S. (1987). Appreciative inquiry in organizational life. In W. Pasmore & R. Woodman (Eds.), *Research in organizational change and development* (Vol. 1, pp. 129–169). Greenwich, CT: JAI.

Cooperrider, D. L., & Whitney, D. (2000). A positive revolution in change: Appreciative inquiry. In D. Cooperrider, P. Sorensen, D. Whitney, & T. Yager (Eds.), *Appreciative inquiry: Rethinking human organization toward a positive theory of change* (pp. 3–28). Champaign, IL: Stipes.

Cooperrider, D. L., Whitney, D., & Stavros, J. M. (2008). *Appreciative inquiry handbook: For leaders of change* (2nd ed.). San Francisco, CA: Berrett-Koehler.

Copeland, P., Dean, R. G., & Wladkowski, S. P. (2011). The power dynamics of supervision: Ethical dilemmas. *Smith College Studies in Social Work, 81*(1), 26–40.

Copello, A., & Tobin, D. (2007). Clinical team supervision for practitioners treating co-existing mental health and drug and alcohol problems. In A. Baker & R. Velleman (Eds.), *Clinical handbook of co-existing mental health and drug and alcohol problems* (pp. 371–387). New York, NY: Routledge/Taylor & Francis Group.

Corey, G. (2008). *Theory and practice of counseling and psychotherapy* (8th ed.). Belmont, CA: Thompson Brooks/Cole.

Covey, S. (2004). *The 8th habit: From effectiveness to excellence.* New York, NY: Free Press.

Cox, J. A., Banez, L., Haley, L. D., & Mostade, J. (2003). Use of the reflecting team in the training of group workers. *Journal for the Specialists in Group Work, 28*(2), 89–105.

Crawford, R. W. (1994). Bug-in-the-ear revisited: Type of supervision directives, trainee CPI personality dimensions, and ratings of supervision effectiveness. *Dissertation Abstracts International Section A: Humanities and Social Sciences, 54*(12-A), 4359.

Csikszentmihalyi, M. (2008). *Flow: The psychology of optimal experience.* New York, NY: Harper Perennial Modern Classics.

Culbreth, J. R. (1999). Clinical supervision of substance abuse counselors: Current and preferred practices. *Journal of Addictions & Offender Counseling, 20*(1), 15–25.

Dale, R. (1988, September/October). The constructivists are coming. *The Family Therapy Networker, 12*(5), cover.

D'Andrea, M. (2000). Postmodernism, constructivism, and multiculturalism: Three forces reshaping and expanding our thoughts about counseling. *Journal of Mental Health Counseling, 22,* 1–16.

D'Andrea, M., & Daniels, J. (1997). Multicultural counseling supervision: Central issues, theoretical considerations, and practical strategies. In D. B. Pope-Davis & H. L. K. Coleman (Eds.), *Multicultural counseling competencies: Assessment, education and training and supervision* (pp. 290–309). Thousand Oaks, CA: Sage.

Daniels, J. A., & Larson, L. M. (2001). The impact of performance feedback on counseling self-efficacy and counselor anxiety. *Counselor Education and Supervision, 41,* 120–130.

Denzin, N. K., & Lincoln, Y. S. (Eds.). (2005). *The Sage handbook of qualitative research* (3rd ed.). Thousand Oaks, CA: Sage.

de Shazer, S. (1984). The death of resistance. *Family Process, 1,* 11–17.

de Shazer, S. (1988). *Clues; investigating solutions in brief therapy.* New York, NY: W. W. Norton.

de Shazer, S. (1994). *Words were originally magic.* New York, NY: W. W. Norton.

Digman, J. M. (1990). Personality structure: Emergence of the five-factor model. *Annual Review of Psychology, 41,* 417–440.

Dressel, J. L., Consoli, A. J., Kim, B. S. K., & Atkinson, D. R. (2007). Successful and unsuccessful multicultural supervisory behaviors: A delphi poll. *Multicultural Counseling and Development, 36,* 51–64.

Dossey, L. (1990). Personal health and the environment. In J. Rifkin (Ed.), *The green lifestyle handbook: 1001 ways to heal the earth* (pp. 79–83). New York, NY: Henry Holt.

Drucker, P. F. (1968). *The age of discontinuity: Guidelines to our changing society.* Piscataway, NJ: Transaction Publishers.

Drucker, P. F. (1985, May–June). The discipline of innovation. *Harvard Business Review, 63*(3), 67–72.

Drucker, P. F. (1990). *Managing the non-profit organization: Practices and principles.* New York, NY: Collins.

Drucker, P. F. (1998). *Peter Drucker on the profession of management.* Boston, MA: Harvard Business Press.

Drucker, P. F. (2001). *The essential Drucker: In one volume the best of sixty years of Peter Drucker's essential writings on management.* New York, NY: HarperBusiness.

Drucker, P. F. (2004, June). What makes an effective executive. *Harvard Business Review, 82*(6), 58–63, 136.

Drucker, P. F. (2005). *The effective executive in action.* New York, NY: Collins.

Dugo, J. M., & Beck, A. P. (1997). Significance and complexity of early phases in the development of the co-therapy relationship. *Group Dynamics: Theory, Research, and Practice, 1*(4), 294–305.

Eastwood, C., McCreary, L., Lorenz, R., Neufeld, M., & Freeman, M. (Producers), & Eastwood, C. (Director). (2009). *Invictus* [Motion Picture]. United States: Spyglass, Warner Brothers.

Edwards, J. K. (1987). Continuity and orchestration of after care services to disturbed children: From residential treatment to adoptive home. *Journal of Residential Treatment for Children and Youth, 4*(4), 53–67.

Edwards, J. K. (2001). *An investigation into the state of the art and current needs for the clinical training of behavioral health care professionals in the United States across disciplines and within clinical training sites* (final report). Northeastern Illinois University Committee on Research Grants, Chicago.

Edwards, J. K. (2011). *Strengths-Based supervision in clinical settings.* Thousand Oaks, CA: Sage.

Edwards, J. K., & Chen, M. W. (1999). Strength-Based supervision: Frameworks, current practice, and future directions. *The Family Journal, 7,* 349–357.

Edwards, J. K., Chen, M. W., White, L., & Bradley, D. (2001). *Narrative/Postmodern psychotherapy in a managed-care world: An electronic qualitative Delphi study* (final report). Northeastern Illinois University Committee on Research Grants, Chicago.

Edwards, J. K., & Heath, A. W. (2007). *A consumer's guide to mental health services: Unveiling the mysteries and secrets of psychotherapy.* Binghamton, NY: Haworth Press, Inc.

Edwards, J. K., Heath, A. W., & Todd, T. C. (1993). The relationship of family therapy to inpatient psychiatric care. In M. Squire, C. Stout, & D. H. Ruben (Eds.), *Current advances in inpatient psychiatric care: A handbook* (pp. 83–97). Westport, CT: Greenwood Press.

Edwards, J. K., & Kleist, D. (2007). *Family counseling since then.* Paper presented at the annual conference of the Illinois Counseling Association, Tinley Park.

Edwards, J. K., & Pyskoty, C. (2004). Clinical training needs of Illinois counselors: A survey of internship sites. *Illinois Counseling Association Journal, 152*(1), 3–14.

Efran, J. S., Lukens, R. J, & Lukens, M. D. (1988, September/October). Constructivism: What's in it for you? *Family Therapy Networker, 12*(5), 27–35.

Eliot, T. S. (1943). *Four quartets.* New York, NY: Harcourt Brace.

Enbysk, M. (2006). *Bosses: 7 communication tips.* Retrieved from http://www.microsoft.com/middle east/atwork/smallbusiness/bosses_7_commu nication_tips.aspx

Evans, D. R., & Hearn, M. T. (1997). Sexual and non-sexual dual relationships: Managing the boundaries. In D. R. Evans (Ed.), *The law, standards of practice, and ethics in the practice of psychology* (pp. 53–83). Toronto, Ontario, Canada: Emond Montgomery.

Fatzer, G. (1986). Team supervision as organizational development. *Gruppendynamik, 17*(1), 49–57.

Fenell, D. L., & Hovestadt, A. J. (1986). Family therapy as a profession or professional specialty: Implications for training. *Journal of Psychotherapy & the Family, 1*(4), 25–40.

Field, L. D., & Chavez-Korell, S. (2010). No hay rosas sin espinas: Conceptualizing Latina-Latina supervision from a multicultural developmental supervisory model. *Training and Education in Professional Psychology, 4*(1), 47–54.

Fine, M. (2003). Reflections on the intersection of power and competition in reflecting teams as applied to academic settings. *Journal of Marital Family Therapy, 29*(3), 339–351.

Finley, N. E. (1994). Leadership: The collaborative process. *Journal of Leadership and Organizational Studies, 1,* 57–66.

Fisk, D. (2009, December 21). Re: Delete my Facebook account, leadership and boundaries. [Electronic mailing list message]. Retrieved from https://list serv.kent.edu/cgi-bin/wa.exe?A2=CESNET-L;W99vmg;200912211707000600C

Fitz-enz, J. (2001). *How to measure human resource management* (3rd ed.). New York, NY: McGraw-Hill.

Flick, U. (2006). *An introduction to qualitative research.* Thousands Oaks, CA: Sage.

Florida, R., & Goodnight, J. (2005, July/August). Managing for creativity. *Harvard Business Review, 83*(7), 124–131, 193.

Fong, M. L., & Lease, S. H. (1997). Cross-cultural supervision: Issues for the white supervisor. In D. B. Pope-Davis & H. L. K. Coleman (Eds.), *Multicultural counseling competencies: assessment, education and training, and supervision* (pp. 387–405). Thousand Oaks, CA: Sage.

Forrest, S. P., & Peterson, T. O. (2006). It's called andragogy. *Academy of Management Learning & Education, 5*(1), 113–122.

Fox, M. J. (n.d.). Michael J. Fox quotes. Retrieved from http://www.brainyquote.com/quotes/authors/m/michael_j_fox.html

Freedman, J., & Combs, G. (1996). *Narrative therapy: The social construction of preferred realities.* New York, NY: W. W. Norton.

Friedlander, M. L., Siegel, S. M., & Brenock, K. (1989). Parallel processes in counseling and supervision: A case study. *Journal of Counseling Psychology, 36*(2), 149–157.

Friedman, T. L. (2005). *The world is flat: A brief history of the twenty-first century.* New York, NY: Farrar, Straus & Giroux.

Frost, R. (1916). *The road less traveled. Mountain interval.* New York, NY: Henry Holt.

Fuller, T. (Ed.). (2010). *Gnomologia, adagies and proverbs, wise sentences and witty sayings, ancient and modern, foreign and British.* White Fish, MT: Kessinger Publishing. (Original publication 1759)

Furman, B., & Ahola, T. (1988). The return of the question "why": Advantages of exploring pre-existing explanations. *Family Process, 27*(4), 395–410.

Gallant, J. P., & Thyer, B. A. (1989). The bug-in-the-ear in clinical supervision: A review. *The Clinical Supervisor, 7*(2–3), 43–58.

Garmezy, N. (1991). Resiliency and vulnerability to adverse developmental outcomes associated with poverty. *American Behavioral Scientist, 34*(4), 416–430.

Geisel, T. S. (1988). *Oh, the places you'll go!* New York, NY: Random House.

Gergen, K. J. (1991). *The saturated self.* New York, NY: Basic Books.

Gergen, K. J. (1994). *Realities and relationships, soundings in social construction.* Cambridge, MA: Harvard University Press.

Gergen, K. J. (2001a). *The saturated self: Dilemmas of identity in contemporary life* (2nd ed.). New York, NY: Basic Books.

Gergen, K. J. (2001b). *Social construction in context.* Thousand Oaks, CA: Sage.

Gergen, K. J. (2006). *Therapeutic realities, collaboration, oppression and relational flow.* Chagrin Falls, OH: Taos Institute.

Gergen, K. J. (2009a). *An invitation to social construction* (2nd ed.). London, UK: Sage.

Gergen, K. J. (2009b). *Relational being.* New York, NY: Oxford University Press.

Gershenson, J., & Cohen, M. S. (1978). Through the looking glass: The experiences of two family therapy trainees with live supervision. *Family Process, 17*(2), 225–230.

Gill, V. (2003). *Next big thing* [CD]. Nashville, TN: MCA Records.

Glosoff, H. L., Corey, G., & Herlihy, B. (1996). Dual relationships. In B. Herlihy & G. Corey (Eds.), *ACA ethical standards casebook* (5th ed., pp. 251–266). Alexandria, VA: American Counseling Association.

Goodyear, R. K., & Bernard, J. M. (1998). Lessons from the literature. *Counselor Education and Supervision, 38*(1), 6–22.

Gottman, J. (1999). *The seven principles for making marriage work.* New York, NY: Crown Publishing.

Gottman, J. M., & Silver, N. (2000). *The seven principles for making marriage work: A practical guide from the country's foremost relationship expert.* Lemon Cove, CA: Three Rivers Press.

Guterman, J. T. (1994). A social constructionist position for mental health counseling. *Journal of Mental Health Counseling, 16,* 226–244.

Gutheil, T. G., & Gabbard, G. O. (1993). The concept of boundaries in clinical practice: Theoretical and risk-management dimensions. *American Journal of Psychiatry,150,* 188–196.

Gladwell, M. (2000). *The tipping point: How little things can make a big difference.* New York, NY: Back Bay Books/Little, Brown.

Gladwell, M. (2008). *Outliers: The story of success.* New York, NY: Little, Brown.

Gonzalez, R. C. (1997). Postmodern supervision: A multicultural perspective. In D. B. Pope-Davis & H. L. K. Coleman (Eds.), *Multicultural counseling competencies: Assessment, education and training, and supervision* (pp. 350–386). Thousand Oaks, CA: Sage.

Goodrich, T. J., Rampage, C., Ellman, B., & Halstead, K. (1988). *Feminist family therapy: A casebook.* New York, NY: W. W. Norton.

Goolishian, H. A. (1990). Family therapy: An evolving story. *Contemporary Family Therapy, 12,* 173–180.

Grant Halvorson, H. (2011). *Succeed: How we can reach our goals.* New York, NY: Hudson Street Press.

Greenleaf, R. K. (2002). *Servant leadership: A journey into the nature of legitimate power and greatness.* Mahwah, NJ: Paulist Press.

Griffith, J. L., Griffith, M. E., Krejmas, N., McLain, M., Mittal, D., Rains J., & Tingle, C. (1992). Reflecting team consultations and their impact upon family therapy for somatic symptoms as coded by structural analysis of social behavior. *Journal of Systemic Medicine, 10,* 53–58.

Grönfeldt, S., & Strother, J. (2006). *Service leadership.* Thousand Oaks, CA: Sage.

Guba, E. G., & Lincoln, Y. S. (2005). Paradigmatic controversies, contradictions, and emerging influences. In N. K. Denzin & Y. S. Lincoln (Eds.), *The Sage handbook of qualitative research* (3rd ed., pp. 191–215). Thousand Oaks, CA: Sage

Hardcastle, D. A. (1991). Toward a model for supervision: A peer supervision pilot project. *The Clinical Supervisor, 9*(2), 63–76.

Hardy, K. V. (1993). Live supervision in the postmodern era of family therapy: Issues, reflections, and questions. *Contemporary Family Therapy, 15*(1), 9–20.

Harkness, D., & Hensley, H. (1991). Changing the focus of social work supervision: Effects on client satisfaction and generalized contentment. *Social Work, 36*(6), 506–512.

Hale, J. R., & Fields, D. L. (2007). Exploring servant leadership across cultures: A study of followers in Ghana and the USA. *Leadership, 3,* 397–417.

Hall, J., & Hammond, S. (1998). *What is appreciative inquiry?* Bend, OR: Thin Book Publishing.

Hansen, J. T. (2010). Consequences of the postmodernist vision: Diversity as the guiding value for the counseling profession. *Journal of Counseling and Development, 88*(1), 101–107.

Harris, G. (2011, March 5). *Talk doesn't pay, so psychiatry turns instead to drug therapy.* Retrieved from http://www.nytimes.com/2011/03/06/health/policy/06doctors.html?_r=1&ref=health

Hatcher, T. G., & Cutler-White, C. (2009). Editorial—Catching up to our past: Vocational education, andragogy, and real work. *Human Resource Development Quarterly, 20*(3), 231–235.

Hazucha, J. F., Hezlett, S. A., & Schneider, R. J. (2006). The impact of 360-degree feedback on management skills development [Special issue]. *Human Resource Management, 32,* 325–351.

Heath, A., & Tharp, L. (1991). November. *What therapists say about supervision.* Paper presented at the annual conference of the American Association for Marriage and Family Therapy, Dallas, TX.

Heath, A. W., & Storm, C. L. (1983). Answering the call: A manual for beginning supervisors. *The Family Therapy Networker, 7,* 36–37, 66.

Heath, A. W., & Storm, C. L. (1985). From the institute to the ivory tower: The live supervision stage approach for teaching supervision in academic settings. *The American Journal of Family Therapy, 13*(3), 27–36.

Henderson, P. G. (2009). *The new handbook of administrative supervision in counseling.* Alexandria, VA: American Counseling Association.

Hendrix, C. C., Fournier, D. G., & Briggs, K. (2001). Impact of co-therapy teams on client outcomes and therapist training in marriage and family therapy. *Contemporary Family Therapy: An International Journal, 23*(1), 63–82.

Henley, W. E. (1891). *Invictus, a book of verses* (3rd ed.). New York, NY: Scribner & Welford.

Heppner, P. P., & Kivlighan, D. M. (1994). Dimensions that characterize supervisor interventions delivered in the context of live supervision of practicum counselors. *Journal of Counseling Psychology, 41*(2), 227–235.

Herlihy, B., & Corey, G. (1997). *Boundary issues in counseling: Multiple roles and responsibilities.* Alexandria, VA: American Counseling Association.

Hess, A. K. (Ed.). (1980). *Psychotherapy supervision: Theory, research, and practice.* New York, NY: Wiley.

Hess, A. K. (2008a). Ethical and legal considerations in psychotherapy supervision. In A. K. Hess, K. D. Hess, & T. H. Hess (Eds.), *Psychotherapy supervision: Theory, research and practice* (pp. 521–536). New York, NY: Wiley.

Hess, A. K. (2008b). Psychotherapy supervision: A conceptual review. In A. K. Hess, K. D. Hess, & T. H. Hess (Eds.), *Psychotherapy supervision: Theory, research, and practice* (2nd ed., pp. 3–24). New York, NY: Wiley.

Hess, A. K., Hess K. D., & Hess, T. H. (Eds.). (2008). *Psychotherapy supervision: Theory, research and practice.* Hoboken, NJ: John Wiley & Sons.

Heuer, G. (2009). "Spooky action at a distance": Parallel processes in Jungian analysis and supervision. In D. Mathers (Ed.), *Vision and supervision: Jungian and post-Jungian perspectives* (pp. 164–182). New York, NY: Routledge/Taylor & Francis Group.

Heylighen, F., & Joslyn, C. (2001). Cybernetics and second-order cybernetics. In R. A. Meyers (Ed.), *Encyclopedia of physical science & technology* (3rd ed., pp. 1–24), New York, NY: Academic Press.

Hogan, R. A. (1964). Issues and approaches in supervision. *Psychotherapy: Theory, Research and Practice, 1,* 139–141.

Holloway, E. L. (1995). *Clinical supervision: A systems approach.* Thousand Oaks, CA: Sage.

Holloway, E. L., & Neufeldt, S. A. (1995). Supervision: Its contributions to treatment efficacy. *Journal of Consulting and Clinical Psychology, 63,* 207–213.

Hubble, M. A., Duncan, B. L., & Miller, S. D. (1999). *The heart and soul of change: What works in therapy.* Washington, DC: American Psychological Association.

Hunt, D. E. (1971). *Matching models in education: the coordinating of teaching methods with student characteristics.* Toronto, Ontario, Canada: Ontario Institute for Studies in Education.

Hurn, D., in conversation with Jay, B. (2009). *On being a photographer: A practical guide.* Anacortes, WA: Lens Works Publishing.

Inman, A. G. (2006). Supervisor multicultural competence and its relation to supervisor process and outcome. *Journal of Marital and Family Therapy, 32*(1), 75–85.

Jackson, L., Junior, V., & Mahoney, D. (2007, October 13). *An inquiry into conflict resolution process in the clinical supervisory system.* Poster session presented at the conference of the Association for Counselor Education and Supervisors, Columbus, OH.

Jang, K., Livesley, W. J., & Vernon, P. A. (1996). Heritability of the big five personality dimensions and their facets: A twin study. *Journal of Personality, 64,* 577–591.

Janis, I. (1972). *Victims of groupthink; a psychological study of foreign-policy decisions and fiascoes.* Boston, MA: Houghton, Mifflin.

Janowsky, Z. M., Dickerson, V. C., & Zimmerman, J. L. (1995). Through Susan's eyes: Reflections on a reflecting team experience. In S. Friedman (Ed.), *The reflecting team in action: Collaborative practice in family therapy* (pp. 167–183). New York, NY: Guilford Press.

Jones, T. S. (2005). Editors introduction—The emperor's "knew" clothes: What we don't know will hurt us. *Conflict Resolution Quarterly, 23*(2), 129–139.

Juhnke, G. A. (1996). Solution-focused supervision: Promoting supervisee skills and confidence through successful solutions. *Counselor Education and Supervision, 36,* 48–57.

Jung, C. (1933). *Modern man in search of a soul.* New York, NY: Routledge.

Kabat-Zinn, J. (2009). *Full catastrophe living: Using the wisdom of your body and mind to face stress, pain, and illness* (15th anniversary ed.). Surrey, UK: Delta Publishing.

Kadushin, A. (1992). What's wrong, what's right with social work supervision. *The Clinical Supervisor, 10*(1), 3–19.

Kadushin, A., & Harkness, D. (1976). *Supervision in social work.* New York, NY: Columbia University Press.

Kadushin, A., & Harkness, D. (2002). *Supervision in social work* (4th ed.). New York, NY: Columbia University Press.

Kagan, N. (1972). *Influencing human interaction.* Retrieved from ERIC database. (ED065793)

Kagan, N., Schauble, P., & Resnikoff, S. J. (1969). Interpersonal process recall. *The Journal of Nervous and Mental Disease, 148*(4), 301–457.

Kahn, E. M. (1979). The parallel process in social work treatment and supervision. *Social Casework, 60,* 520–528.

Kassan, L. D. (2010). *Peer supervision groups: How they work and why you need one.* Lanham, MD: Jason Aronson.

Keeney, B. (1983). *Aesthetics of change.* New York, NY: Guilford Press.

Keeton, M. T. (2004). Best online instructional practices: Report of phase I of an ongoing study. *Journal of Asynchronous Learning Networks, 8*(2), 75–100.

Keim, J. (1998). Strategic family therapy. In F. Dattilio (Ed.), *Case studies in couple and family therapy* (pp. 132–157). New York, NY: Guilford Press.

Keller, J. F., Protinsky, H. O., Lichtman, M., & Allen, K. (1996). The process of clinical supervision: Direct observation research. *Clinical Supervisor, 1,* 51–64.

Kellum, K. E. H. (2010). Structured reflecting teams in group supervision: A qualitative study with school counseling interns. *Dissertation Abstracts International Section A: Humanities and Social Sciences, 70*(8-A), 2902.

Kerr, M. E., & Bowen, M. (1988). *Family evaluation: An approach based on Bowen theory.* New York, NY: W. W. Norton.

Keys, C. L. M., & Lopez, S. J. (2005). Toward a science of mental health: Positive directions in diagnosis and interventions. In C. R. Snyder & S. J. Lopez (Eds.), *Handbook of positive psychology* (pp. 45–62). Oxford, UK: Oxford University Press.

Kirsch, I. (2009). *The emperor's new drugs: Exploding the antidepressant myth.* London, UK: The Bodley Head.

Kirsch, I., & Moncrieff, J. (2007). Clinical trials and the response rate illusion. *Contemporary Clinical Trials, 28*(4), 348–351.

Kivlighan, D. M. (1991). Live supervision in individual psychotherapy: Effects on therapist's intention use and client's evaluation of session effect and working alliance. *Professional Psychology: Research and Practice, 22*(6), 489–495.

Klages, M. (2007). *Literary theory: A guide for the perplexed.* London, UK: Continuum International.

Klein, C. R. (2009). What do we know about interpersonal skills? A meta-analytic examination of antecedents, outcomes, and the efficacy of training. *Dissertation Abstracts International: Section B: The Sciences and Engineering, 70*(5-B), 3213.

Klitzke, M. J., & Lombardo, T. W. (1991). A bug-in-the-eye can be better than a bug-in-the-ear: A teleprompter technique for on-line therapy skills training. *Behavior Modification, 15*(1), 113–117.

Knowles, M., Holton, E. F., & Swanson, R. A. (2005). *The adult learner: The definitive classic in adult education and human resource development* (6th ed.). Burlington, MA: Elsevier.

Knowles, M. S. (1950). *Informal adult education: A guide for administrators, leaders, and teachers.* New York, NY: Association Press.

Knowles, M. S. (1968). Andragogy, not pedagogy. *Adult Leadership, 16*(10), 350–352, 386.

Knowles, M. S. (1980). *The modern practice of adult education: From pedagogy to andragogy.* Englewood Cliffs, NJ: Prentice Hall/Cambridge.

Kolb, D. A. (1984). *Experiential learning: Experience as the a source of learning and development.* Englewood Cliffs, NJ: Prentice Hall.

Koob, Jeffrey J. (2002). The effects of solution-focused supervision on the perceived self-efficacy of therapists in training. *The Clinical Supervisor, 21*(2), 161–183.

Korinek, A. W., & Kimball, T. G. (2003). Managing and resolving conflict in the supervisory system. *Contemporary Family Therapy, 25,* 295–310.

Korzybski, A. (1933). *Science and sanity: An introduction to Non-Aristotelian systems and general semantics.* Laxeville, CT: International Non-Aristotelian Library.

Kottler, J. A., & Shepard, D. S. (2008). *Introduction to counseling: Voices from the field.* Belmont, CA: Thomson, Brooks/Cole.

Kotkov, B. (2005). The perils of supervision and teaching in the psychotherapy setting. *Annals of the American Psychotherapy Association, 8*(2), 28–34.

Kouzes, J., & Posner, B. (2007). *The leadership challenge.* San Francisco, CA: Jossey-Bass.

Krauth, L. D. (1995). Strength-Based therapies. *Family Therapy News, 26,* 24.

Kuenzli-Monard, F., & Kuenzli, A. (1999). Does a difference make the difference? The reflecting team as an integral part of a psychotherapeutic process. *Therapie Familiale: Revue Internationale en Approche Systemique, 20*(1), 23–37.

Kuhn, T. (1970). *The structure of scientific revolutions* (3rd ed.). Chicago, IL: The University of Chicago Press.

Lamb, D. H., Catanzaro, S. J., & Moorman, A. S. (2004). A preliminary look at how psychologists identify, evaluate, and proceed when faced with possible multiple relationship dilemmas. *Professional Psychology: Research and Practice, 35,* 248–254.

Lamb, D. H., Catanzaro, S. J., & Moorman, A. S. (2008). A preliminary look at how psychologists identify, evaluate, and proceed when faced with possible multiple relationship dilemmas. In D. N. Bersoff (Ed.), *Ethical conflicts in psychology*

(4th ed., pp. 217–221). Washington, DC: American Psychological Association.

Lambert, M. J., & Bergin, A. (1994). The effectiveness of psychotherapy. In A. Bergin & S. L. Garfield (Eds.), *Handbook of psychotherapy and behavior change* (4th ed., pp. 143–189). Chichester, UK: John Wiley & Sons.

Lantz, J. E. (1978). Cotherapy approach in family therapy. *Social Work, 23*(2), 156–158.

Larson, L., & Daniels, J. (1998). Review of the counseling self-efficacy literature. *The Counseling Psychologist, 26*(2), 179–218.

Lassiter, P. S., Napolitano, L., Culbreth, J. R., & Ng, K. M. (2008). Developing multicultural competence using the structured peer group supervision model. *Counselor Education and Supervision, 47,* 164–178.

Lax, W. D. (1992). Postmodern thinking in a clinical practice. In S. McNamee & K. Gergen (Eds.), *Therapy as social construction* (pp. 69–85). Newbury Park, CA: Sage

Lax, W. D. (1995). Offering reflections: Some theoretical and practical considerations. In S. Friedman (Ed.), *The reflecting team in action: Collaborative practice in family therapy* (pp. 167–183). New York: Guilford Press.

Lebensohn-Chialvo, P., Crago, M., & Shisslak, M. (2000). The reflecting team: An innovative approach for teaching clinical skills to family practice residents. *Family Medicine, 32*(8), 556–560.

Leddick, G. R. (1994). *Models of clinical supervision.* Retrieved from ERIC database. (ED372340)

Leddick, G. R., & Bernard, J. M. (1980). The history of supervision: A critical review. *Counselor Education and Supervision, 19*(3), 186–196.

Lee, R. E., & Everett, C. A. (2004). *The integrative family therapy supervisor: A primer.* New York, NY: Routledge.

Lever, H., & Gmeiner, A. (2000). Families leaving therapy after one or two sessions: A multiple descriptive case study. *Contemporary Family Therapy: An International Journal, 22,* 39–65.

Lewis, J. A., Lewis, M. D., Daniels, J. A., & D'Andrea, M. J. (2010). *Community counseling: Empowerment strategies* (4th ed.). Belmont, CA: Thomson, Brooks/Cole.

Liddle, H. A., Breunlin, D. C., & Schwartz, R. C. (Eds.). (1988a). *Handbook of family therapy training and supervision.* New York, NY: Guilford Press.

Liddle, H. A., Breunlin, D. C., & Schwartz, R. C. (1988b). Family therapy training and supervision; an introduction. In H. A. Liddle, D. C. Breunlin, & R. C. Schwartz (Eds.), *Handbook of family therapy training and supervision* (pp. 3–10). New York, NY: Guilford Press.

Liddle, H. A., & Saba, G. W. (1983). On context replication: The isomorphic relationship of training and therapy. *Journal of Strategic & Systemic Therapies, 2*(2), 3–11.

Liddle, H. A., & Saba, G. W. (1985). The isomorphic nature of training and therapy: Epistemologic foundation for a structural-strategic training paradigm. In J. Schwartzman (Ed.), *Families and other systems: The macrosystemic context of family therapy* (pp. 27–47). New York, NY: Guilford Press.

Liddle, H. A., & Schwartz, R. C. (1983). Live supervision/consultation: Conceptual and pragmatic guidelines for family therapy trainers. *Family Process, 22*(4), 477–490.

Lincoln, Y. S., & Guba, E. G. (1985). *Naturalist inquiry.* Newbury Park, CA: Sage.

Lindlof, T. R., & Taylor, B. C. (2002). *Qualitative communication research methods* (2nd ed.). Thousand Oaks, CA: Sage.

Littrell, J. M., Lee-Borden, N., & Lorenz, J. A. (1979). A developmental framework for counseling supervision. *Counselor Education and Supervision, 19,* 129–136.

London, M., & Beatty, R. W. (1995). 360-Degree feedback as a competitive edge. In R. W. Beatty, L. S. Baird, C. E. Schneier, & D. G. Shaw (Eds.), *Performance, measurement, management, and appraisal sourcebook* (pp. 208–220). Batavia, NY: HRD Press.

London, P., Wohlers, A. J., & Gallager, P. (1991). 360 degree surveys: A source of feedback to guide management development. *Journal of Management Development, 9,* 17–31.

Loseke, D. R., & Cahil, S. E. (2007). Publishing qualitative manuscripts: Lessons learned. In C. Seale, G. Gobo, J. F. Gubrium, & D. Silverman (Eds.), *Qualitative research practice* (pp. 491–506). Thousand Oaks, CA: Sage.

Luborsky, L., McLellan, A. T., Woody, G. W., O'Brien, C. P., & Auerbach, A. (1985). Therapist success and its determinants. *Archives of General Psychiatry, 42,* 602–611.

Luborsky, L., Singer, B., & Luborsky, L. (1975). Comparative studies of psychotherapies: Is it true that "everyone has won and all must have prizes"? *Archives of General Psychiatry, 32*(8), 995–1008.

Maclennan, B. W. (1965). Co-therapy. *International Journal of Group Psychotherapy, 15*(2), 154–166.

Maddux, J. E. (2005). Stop the "madness"; Positive psychology and the deconstruction of the illness ideology and the DSM. In C. R. Snyder & S. J. Lopez (Eds.), *Handbook of positive psychology* (pp. 13–25). Oxford, UK: Oxford University Press.

Mahoney, M. J. (2005). Constructivism and positive psychology. In C. R. Snyder & S. J. Lopez (Eds.), *Handbook of positive psychology* (pp. 745–750). Oxford, UK: Oxford University Press.

Man, J. (2009). *The leadership secrets of Genghis Kahn: 21 lessons from history's most successful conqueror.* London, UK: Transworld Publishers.

Marek, L. I., Sandifer, D. M., Beach, A., Coward, R. L., & Protinsky, H. O. (1994). Supervision without the problem: A model of solution-focused supervision. *Journal of Family Psychotherapy, 5*(2), 57–64.

Marshall, C., & Rossman, G. B. (1998). *Designing qualitative research.* Thousand Oaks, CA: Sage.

Martinez, R. P., & Holloway, E. L. (1997). The supervision relationship in multicultural training. In D. B. Pope-Davis & H. L. K. Coleman (Eds.), *Multicultural counseling competencies: assessment, education and training, and supervision (multicultural aspects of counseling and psychotherapy* (pp. 325–349). Thousand Oaks, CA: Sage.

Masten, A. S. (2001). Ordinary magic: Resilience processes in development. *American Psychologist, 56*(3), 227–238.

Masten, A. S., & Curtis, W. J. (2000). Integrating competence and psychopathology: Pathways toward a comprehensive science of adaptation in development. *Development and Psychopathology, 12,* 529–550.

Maslow, A. (1971). *The farther reaches of human nature.* New York, NY: Viking Press.

Mauzey, E. D. (1998). Live supervision with novice counselors-in-training: The effect of delayed, phone-in, and bug-in-the-ear supervision interventions on trainee anxiety, anger, and speech behavior. *Dissertation Abstracts International Section A: Humanities and Social Sciences, 58*(8-A), 3021.

May, G. (1993). *Simply sane: The spirituality of mental health.* Danvers MA: The Crossroad Publishing Company.

May, G. (1990). *Simply sane: The spirituality of mental health.* New York, NY: Crossroads.

May, R. (1967). *Psychology and the human dilemma.* New York, NY: W. W. Norton.

McAdama, E., & Mirza, K. A. H. (2009). Drugs, hopes and dreams: Appreciative inquiry with marginalized young people using drugs and alcohol. *Journal of Family Therapy, 31*(2), 175–193.

McCartney, P., & Lennon, J. (1967). With a little help from my friends. On *Sgt. Pepper's Lonely Hearts Club Band* [CD]. London, UK: EMI Studios.

McCauley, C. D., & Hezlett, S. A. (2002). Individual development in the workplace. In D. Z. Ones, N. Anderson, & H. K. Sinangil (Eds.), *Handbook of industrial, work and organizational psychology: Personnel psychology* (Vol. 1, pp. 313–335). Thousand Oaks, CA: Sage.

McNamee, S., & Gergen, K. J. (Eds.). (1991). *Therapy as social construction.* Newbury Park, CA: Sage.

McNeil, B. W., & Worthen, V. (1989). The parallel process in psychotherapy supervision. *Professional Psychology: Research and Practice, 20*(5), 329–333.

Meidinger, H. (1991). School-based supervision as an example of systems-oriented counseling in the school. *Psychologie in Erziehung und Unterricht, 38*(4), 292–297.

Merriam, B. M., Caffarella, R. S., & Baumgartner, L. A. (2006). *Learning in adulthood: A comprehensive guide.* San Francisco, CA: Jossey-Bass.

Merriam, S. B. (2001). Andragogy and self-directed learning: Pillars of adult learning theory. *New Directions for Adult and Continuing Education, 21*(89), 3–14.

Meynckens-Fourez, M. (1993). Team supervision. *TherapieFamiliale: Revue Internationale en ApprocheSystemique, 14*(3), 277–289.

Mikels, L., & Sartori, T. (2009). *Apply a j-curve to achieve success, not perpetuate excuses.* Retrieved from ASQ website: http: www.ASQ.org

Miller, S. D., Duncan, B. L, & Hubble, M. A. (2005). Outcome-informed clinical work. In J. Norcross & M. Goldfried (Eds.), *Handbook of psychotherapy integration* (2nd ed., pp. 84–104). New York, NY: Oxford University Press.

Miller, S. D., Hubble, M., & Duncan, B. L. (1996). *Handbook of solution-focused brief therapy.* San Francisco, CA: Jossey-Bass.

Miller, S. D., Hubble, M. A., & Duncan, B. L. (2007, November/December). Supershrinks. *Psychotherapy Networker, 14*(4), 27–35, 56.

Milne, J. M., Edwards, J. K., & Murchie, J. C. (2001). Family treatment of oppositional defiant disorder: Changing views and strength-based approaches. *The Family Journal, 9*(1), 17–28.

Minuchin, S. (1974). *Families and family therapy.* Oxford, UK: Harvard University Press.

Minuchin, S. (Ed.). (1997). The leap to complexity supervision in family therapy. In J. Zeig (Ed.), *The evolution of psychotherapy: The third conference* (pp. 271–281). Philadelphia, PA: Brunner/Mazel.

Moleski, S. M., & Kiselica, M. S. (2005). Dual relationships: A continuum ranging from the destructive to the therapeutic. *Journal of Counseling & Development, 83,* 3–11.

Monk, J., & Winsland, J. (2000). *The use of reflecting teams in counselor education and supervision.* Paper presented at the annual meeting of the Western Association for Counselor Education and Supervision, Gatos, CA.

Montalvo, B. (1973). Aspects of live supervision. *Family Process, 12*(4), 343–359.

Moran, A., Brownlee, K., Gallant, P., Meyers, L., Farmer, F, & Taylor, S. (1995). The effectiveness of reflecting team supervision: A client's experience of receiving feedback from a distance. *Family Therapy, 22*(1), 31–47.

Morrissey, J., & Tribe, R. (2001). Parallel process in supervision. *Counselling Psychology Quarterly, 14*(2), 103–110.

Moskowitz, S. A., & Rupert, P. A. (1983) Conflict resolution within the supervisory relationship. *Professional Psychology: Research and Practice, 14*(5), 632–641.

Munson C. E. (1979). *Social work supervision: Classic statements and critical issues.* New York, NY: Free Press.

National Association for Social Workers. (2005). *Human rights practice update: Multiculturalism.* Retrieved from http://www.socialworkers.org/practice/equity/multiculturalism-PU0505.pdf

Neal, J. H. (1996). Narrative therapy training and supervision. *Journal of Systemic Therapies, 15,* 63–77.

Nelson, M. L., & Friedlander, M. L. (2001). A close look at conflictual supervisory relationships: The trainee's perspective. *Journal of Counseling Psychology, 48*(4), 384–395.

Nelson, M. L., Gizara, S., Hope, A. C., Phelps, R., Steward, R., & Weitzman, L. (2006). A feminist multicultural perspective on supervision. *Multicultural Counseling and Development, 34,* 105–115.

Neufeldt, S. A. (1997). A social constructivist approach to counseling supervision. In T. Sexton & B. L. Griffin (Eds.), *Constructivist thinking in counseling practice, research, and training* (pp. 191–210). New York, NY: Teachers College Press.

Neukrug, E. (2003). *The world of the counselor: An introduction to the counseling profession* (2nd ed.). Pacific Grove, CA: Thomson, Brooks/Cole.

Neukrug, E. S. (2011). *Counseling theories and practice.* Belmont, CA: Thomson, Brooks/Cole.

Nichols, M. P. (2009). *The essentials of family therapy* (4th ed.). Boston, MA: Allyn & Bacon.

Nichols, M. P., & Schwartz, R. (2001). *The essentials of family therapy.* Boston, MA: Allyn & Bacon.

Nylund, D., & Corsiglia, V. (1994). Being solution-focused forced in brief therapy: Remembering something important we already knew. *Journal of Systemic Therapies, 13*(1), 5–12.

Ober, A. M., Granello, D. H., & Henfield, M. S. (2009). A synergistic model to enhance multicultural competence in supervision. *Counselor Education and Supervision, 48,* 204–221.

Online Research Methods Knowledge Base, Evaluation. (2009). Retrieved from http://www.socialresearchmethods.net/kb/intreval.htm

Onyett, S. (2009). Working appreciatively to improve services for children and families. *Clinical Child Psychology and Psychiatry, 14*(4), 495–507.

Oppenheimer, M. (1998). Zen and the art of supervision. *The Family Journal, 6,* 61–63.

Overholser, J. C., & Ricciardi, A. M. (1992). Clinical supervision of substance abuse therapy. In J. Levitt, D. Ruben, & C. E. Stout (Eds.), *Handbook for assessing and treating addictive disorders* (pp. 325–338). Westport, CT: Greenwood Press.

Pasteur, L. (1854, December 7). Retrieved from http://en.wikiquote.org/wiki/Louis_Pasteur

Pearson, B., & Piazza, N. (1997). Classification of dual relationships in the helping professions. *Counselor Education and Supervision, 37,* 89–99.

Perloiro, M. F., Neto, L. M., & Marujo, H. A. (2010). We will be laughing again: Restoring relationships with positive couples therapy. In G. W. Burns (Ed.), *Happiness, healing, enhancement: Your casebook collection for applying positive psychology in therapy* (pp. 15–28). New York, NY: Wiley.

Peters, T., & Waterman, R. H. (1982). *In search of excellence.* New York, NY: HarperCollins.

Peterson, C. (2006). *A primer in positive psychology.* New York, NY: Oxford University Press.

Peterson, C., & Seligman, M. (2004). *Character strengths and virtues: A handbook and classification.* New York, NY: Oxford University Press.

Philp, K., Guy, G., & Lowe, R. (2007). Social constructionist supervision or supervision as social construction? Some dilemmas. *Journal of Systemic Therapies, 26,* 51–62.

Pichot, T., & Dolan, Y. M. (2003). *Solution-focused brief therapy: Its effective use in agency settings.* Binghamton, NY: Haworth Clinical Practice Press.

Piercy, F. P. (1986). *Family therapy education and supervision.* Binghamton, NY: Haworth Press.

Piercy, F. P., & Sprinkle, D. H. (1986). Family therapy theory building: An integrative training approach. In F. P. Piercy (Ed.), *Family therapy education and supervision* (pp. 5–14). Binghamton, NY: Haworth Press.

Pink, D. H. (2009). *Drive: The surprising truth about what motivates us.* New York, NY: Riverhead Books.

Pinsof, W. M. (1995). *Integrative problem-centered therapy: A synthesis of biological, individual, and family therapy.* New York, NY: Basic Books.

Pollack, D., & Feldman, J. M. (2003). Introduction to the special issue of Community Mental Health Journal commemorating the 40th anniversary of the Community Mental Health Centers Act of 1963. *Community Mental Health Journal, 39*(5), 377–379.

Polloio, D. E., & Macgowan, M. J. (2010). The andragogy of evidence-based group work: An integrated educational model. *Social Work with Groups, 33,* 195–209.

Powell, D. J., & Brodsky, A. (2004). *Clinical supervision in alcohol and drug abuse counseling: Principles, models, methods.* San Francisco, CA: Jossey-Bass.

Powers, W. T. (1973). *Behavior: The control of perception.* New York, NY: Aldine de Gruyter.

Presbury, J., Echterling, L. G., & McKee, J. E. (1999). Supervision for inner vision: Solution-focused strategies. *Counselor Education and Supervision, 39*(2), 146–155.

Prigogine, I. (1997). *The end of certainty.* New York, NY: Free Press.

Protinsky, H. (2003). Dismounting the tiger: Using tape in supervision. In T. C. Todd & C. L. Storm (Ed.), *The complete systemic supervisor: Context, philosophy, and pragmatics* (pp. 298–307). Bloomington, IN: IUniverse.

Puig, A., & Fukuyama, M. (2008). A qualitative investigation of multicultural expressions of spirituality:

Preliminary findings. *Counselling and Spirituality, 27*(2), 11–37.

Quaintance, J. L., Arnold, L., & Thompson, G. S. (2010). What students learn about professionalism from faculty stories: An "appreciative inquiry" approach. *Academic Medicine, 85*(1), 124–133.

Quinn, R. E. (2005, July 1). *Moments of greatness: Entering the fundamental state of leadership.* Retrieved from http://hbr.org/2005/07/moments-of-greatness-entering-the-fundamental-state-of-leadership/ar/1

Quinn, W. H., Atkinson, B. J., & Hood, C. J. (1985). The stuck-case clinic as a group supervision model. *Journal of Marital and Family Therapy, 11*(1), 67–73.

Ralph, N. B. (1980). Learning psychotherapy: A developmental perspective. *Psychiatry, 43,* 243–250.

Rath, T., & Conchie, B. (2008). *Strengths based leadership. Great leaders, teams and why people follow.* New York, NY: Gallup Press.

Reynolds, V. (2002). Weaving threads of belonging: Cultural witnessing groups. *Journal of Child and Youth Care, 15*(3), 89–105.

Rinella, V. J., & Gerstein, A. I. (1994). The development of dual relationships: Power and professional responsibility. *International Journal of Law and Psychiatry, 17,* 225–237.

Robinson, G. E. (2006). Supervision of boundary issues. In J. H. Gold (Ed.), *Psychotherapy supervision and consultation in clinical practice* (pp. 83–106). Lanham, MD: Jason Aronson.

Rodriguez, C. I., Cabaniss, D. L., Arbuckle, M. R., & Oquendo, M. A. (2008). The role of culture in psychodynamic psychotherapy: Parallel process resulting from cultural similarities between patient and the therapist. *The American Journal of Psychiatry, 165*(11), 1402–1406.

Rogers, C. R. (1951). *Client-Centered therapy; its current practice, implications, and theory.* Oxford, UK: Houghton Mifflin.

Rogers, C. R. (1961). *On becoming a person: A therapist's view of psychotherapy.* London, UK: Constable.

Roller, B., & Nelson, V. (1991). *The art of co-therapy: How therapists work together.* New York, NY: Guilford Press.

Rønnestad, M. H., & Skovholt, T. M. (1993). Supervision of beginning and advanced graduate students of counseling and psychotherapy. *Journal of Counseling and Development, 71,* 396–405.

Rønnestad, M. H., & Skovholt, T. M. (2003). The journey of the counselor and therapist: Research findings and perspectives on professional development. *Journal of Career Development, 30,* 5–44.

Rosenthal, R. (2002). The Pygmalion effect and its mediating mechanisms. In J. Aronson (Ed.), *Improving academic achievement: Impact of psychological factors on education* (pp. 26–35). Waltham, MA: Academic Press.

Rosenthal, R., & Rubin, D. B. (1978). Interpersonal expectancy effects: The first 345 studies. *Behavioral and Brain Sciences, 3,* 377–386.

Russell, B. (1953). On the notion of cause, with applications to the free-will problem. In H. Feigl & M. Brodbeck (Eds.), *Readings in the philosophy of science* (p. 387). New York, NY: Appleton.

Rutter, M. (1979). Protective factors in children's responses to stress and disadvantage. In M. W. Kent & J. E. Rolf (Eds.), *Primary prevention of psychopathology; social competence in children* (Vol. 3, pp. 49–74). Hanover, NH: University Press of New England.

Rutter, M. (1990). Psychosocial resilience and protective mechanisms. In J. Rolf, A. S. Masten, D. Cicchetti, K. H. Nuechterlein, & S. Weintraub (Eds.), *Risk and protective factors in the development of psychopathology* (pp. 181–214). New York, NY: Cambridge University Press.

Schott, M. (2007). Team supervision in forensic psychiatry—Protection from outside. *Psychiatrie, 25*(1), 25–29.

Schwartz, S. (2003). What is this feeling. On *Wicked* [CD]. New York, NY: Decca Broadway, Universal Classics Group, a division of UMG Recordings.

Schwarzbaum, S. (2009). Interview with Jill Freedman: A conversation about having conversations. *The Family Journal, 17,* 160–167.

Schwarzbaum, S. E., & Jones Thomas, A. (2008). *Dimensions of multicultural counseling: A life story approach.* Thousand Oaks, CA: Sage.

Scott, K. J., Ingram, K. M., Vitanza, S. A., & Smith, N. G. (2000). Training in supervision: A survey of current practices. *The Counseling Psychologist, 28*(3), 403–422.

Senn, L. E. (1970). *Organizational character as a tool in the analysis of business organizations* (Unpublished doctoral dissertation). University of Southern California, Los Angeles.

Senn, L. E., & Hart, J. (2006). *Winning teams—Winning cultures.* Los Angeles, CA: The Leadership Press.

Selekman, M. D., & Todd, T. C. (1995). Co-creating a context for change in the supervisory system: The solution-focused supervision model. *Journal of Systemic Therapies, 14*(3), 21–33.

Seligman, M. E. P. (1975). *Helplessness: On depression, development, and death.* San Francisco, CA: W. H. Freeman.

Seligman, M. E. P. (1991). *Learned optimism: How to change your mind and your life.* New York, NY: Knopf.

Seligman, M. E. P. (1996). *The optimistic child: Proven program to safeguard children from depression & build lifelong resilience.* New York, NY: Houghton Mifflin.

Seligman, M. E. P. (1998). *Learned optimism: How to change your mind and your life.* New York, NY: Knopf.

Seligman, M. E. P. (2001). Comment on "priorities for prevention research at NIMH." *Prevention and Treatment, 4,* 24.

Seligman, M. E. P. (2002). *Authentic happiness: Using the new positive psychology to realize your potential for lasting fulfillment.* New York, NY: Free Press.

Seligman, M. E. P. (2005). Positive psychology, positive prevention, and positive therapy. In C. R Snyder & S. J. Lopez (Eds.), *Handbook of positive psychology* (pp. 3–12). Oxford, UK: Oxford University Press.

Seligman, M. E. P., & Csikszentmihalyi, M. (2000). Positive psychology: An introduction. *American Psychologist, 55*(1), 5–14.

Seligman, M. E. P., Parks, A. C., & Steen, T. (2004). A balanced psychology and a full life. *Philosophical Transactions of the Royal Society of B: Biological Sciences, 359*(1449), 1379–1381.

Seligman, M. E. P., Rashid, T., & Parks, A. C. (2006). Positive psychotherapy. *American Psychologist, 6*(8), 774–788.

Selvini, M., & Selvini Palazzoli, M. (1991). Team consultation: An indispensable tool for the progress of knowledge. Ways of fostering and promoting its creative potential. *Journal of Family Therapy, 13,* 31–52.

Selvini Palazzoli, M. (1986). Towards a general model of psychotic games. *Journal of Marital and Family Therapy, 12,* 339–349.

Selvini Palazzoli, M., Boscolo, L., Cecchin, G., & Prata, G. (1978). *Paradox and counter paradox.* New York, NY: Jason Aronson.

Shamai, M. (1998). Therapist in distress: Team-supervision of social workers and family therapists who work and live under political uncertainty. *Family Process, 37*(2), 245–259.

Shamai, M. (2004). Therapist in distress: Team-supervision of social workers and family therapists who work and live under political uncertainty. *Family Process, 37*(2), 245–259.

Shapiro, F. (2001). *Eye movement desensitization and reprocessing: Basic principles, protocols, and procedures* (2nd ed.). New York, NY: Guilford Press.

Shavit, N. (2005a). Sexual contact between psychologists and patients. *Journal of Aggression, Maltreatment & Trauma, 11,* 205–239.

Shavit, N. (2005b). Sexual contact between psychologists and patients. In S. F. Bucky, J. E. Callan, & G. Stricker (Eds.), *Ethical and legal issues for mental health professionals: A comprehensive handbook of principles and standards* (pp. 205–239). Binghamton, NY: Haworth Maltreatment and Trauma Press.

Shea, P. J., Pickett, A. M., & Pelz, W. E. (2003). A follow-up investigation of "teaching presence" in the SUNY learning network. *Journal of Asynchronous Learning Networks, 7*(2), 61–80.

Siegel, D. J. (2007). *The mindful brain: Reflections and attunement in the cultivation of well-being.* New York, NY: W. W. Norton.

Silverman, D., & Marvasti, A. (2008). *Doing qualitative research: A comprehensive guide.* Thousand Oaks, CA: Sage.

Silverthorn, B. D., Bartie-Haring, S., Meyer, K., & Toviessi, P. (2009). Does live supervision make a difference? A multilevel analysis. *Journal of Marital and Family Therapy, 35*(4), 406–414.

Singh, A., & Chun, K. Y. S. (2010). From the margins to the center: Moving towards a resilience-based model of supervision for queer people of color supervisors. *Training and Education in Professional Psychology, 4*(1), 36–46.

Siporin, M. (1975). *Introduction to social work practice.* New York, NY: Macmillian. Siporin, M. (1980). Ecological systems theory in social work. *Journal of Sociology and Social Welfare, 7*(4), 507–532.

Skinner, B. F. (1984). The shame of American education. *American Psychologist, 39*(9), 947–954.

Skovholt, T. M., & Rønnestad, M. H. (1992). Themes in therapist and counselor development. *Journal of Counseling and Development, 70,* 505–515.

Skovholt, T. M., & Rønnestad, M. H. (1995). *The evolving professional self: Stages and themes in therapist and counselor development.* Chichester, UK: John Wiley & Sons.

Smith, D., & Kingston, P. (1980). Live supervision without a one-way screen. *Journal of Family Therapy, 2*(3), 379–387. Smith, E. J. (2006). The

strength based counseling model. *The Counseling Psychologist, 34*(1), 13–79.

Smith, M. L., Glass, G. W., & Miller, T. I. (1986). *The benefits of psychotherapy.* Baltimore, MD: Johns Hopkins University Press.

Smith, R. C., Mead, D. E., & Kinsella, J. A. (1998). Direct supervision: Adding computer-assisted feedback and data capture to live supervision. *Journal of Marital and Family Therapy, 24*(1), 113–125.

Smith, T. E., Jenkins, D., & Sells, S. (1995). Reflecting teams: Voices of diversity. *Journal of Family Psychotherapy, 6,* 49–70.

Snyder, C. R., & Lopez, S. J. (Eds.). (2005). *Handbook of positive psychology.* Oxford, UK: Oxford University Press.

Sokal, A., & Bricmont, J. (1999). *Fashionable nonsense: Postmodern intellectuals' abuse of science.* New York, NY: Picador.

Speedy, J. (2000). Consulting with gargoyles: Applying narrative ideas and practices in counselling supervision. *European Journal of Psychotherapy & Counselling, 3,* 3.

Spiess, W., & Stahli, L. (1990). Group/team supervision in special education institutions: Facts and reflections. *Vierteljahresschrift fur Heilpadagogik und ihreNachbargebiete, 59*(4), 452–465.

Srivastva, S., & Cooperrider, D. L. (Eds.). (1990). *Appreciative management and leadership.* San Francisco, CA: Jossey-Bass.

Starhawk. (1987). *Truth or dare: Encounters with power, authority, and mystery.* New York: Harper & Row.

Stiles, W. B., Shapiro, D. A., & Elliot, R. (1986). Are all psychotherapies equivalent? *American Psychologist, 41,* 165–180.

Stinchfield, T. A., Hill, N. R., & Kleist, D. M. (2007). The reflective model of triadic supervision: Defining an emerging modality. *Counselor Education & Supervision, 46,* 172–183.

Stoltenberg, C. D. (1981). Approaching supervision from a developmental perspective: The counselor complexity model. *Journal of Counseling Psychology, 28,* 59–65.

Stoltenberg, C. D. (2005). Enhancing professional competence through developmental approaches to supervision. *American Psychologist, 60*(8), 857–864.

Stoltenberg, C. D., & Delworth, U. (1987). *Supervising counselors and therapists: A developmental approach.* San Francisco, CA: Jossey-Bass.

Stoltenberg, C. D., & McNeill, B. W. (2009). *IDM supervision: An integrative developmental model for supervising counselors and therapists* (3rd ed.). New York, NY: Routledge.

Stone, G. L. (1997). Multiculturalism as a context for supervision: Perspectives, limitations, and implications. In D. B. Pope-Davis & H. L. K. Coleman (Eds.), *Multicultural counseling competencies: Assessment, education and training, and supervision* (pp. 263–289). Thousand Oaks, CA: Sage.

Storm, C. L., Todd, T. C., Sprenkle, D. H., & Morgan, M. M. (2001). Gaps between MFT supervision assumptions and common practice: Suggested best practices. *Journal of Marital and Family Therapy, 27,* 227–239.

Strauss, A., & Corbin, J. (1998). *Basics of qualitative research: Techniques and procedures for developing grounded theory.* Thousand Oaks, CA: Sage.

Stringer, E. T. (2007). *Action research* (3rd ed.). Thousand Oaks, CA: Sage.

Sumerel, M., & ERIC Clearinghouse on Counseling and Student Services. (1994). *Parallel process in supervision.* Retrieved from ERIC database. (EDCG9415)

Thomas, A., & Schwarzbaum, S. E. (2005). *Culture and identity: Life stories for counselors and therapists.* Thousand Oaks, CA: Sage.

Thomas, F. N. (1991). Solution-Focused supervision: The coaxing of expertise. In S. D. Miller (Eds.), *Handbook of solution-focused brief therapy* (pp. 128–151). San Francisco, CA: Jossey-Bass.

Thomasgard, M., Warfield, J., & Williams, R. (2004). Improving communication between health and infant mental health professionals utilizing ongoing collaborating peer supervision groups. *Infant Mental Health Journal, 25*(3), 194–218.

Todd, T. C., & Heath, A. W. (1992). Supervision of substance abuse counselors. In J. Levitt, D. Ruben, & C. E. Stout (Eds.), *Handbook for assessing and treating addictive disorders* (pp. 313–323). Westport, CT: Greenwood Press.

Todd, T. C., & Storm, C. L. (Eds.). (2002). *The complete systemic supervisor: Context, philosophy, and pragmatics* (pp. 298–307). Bloomington, IN: IUniverse.

Tomm, K. M., & Wright, L. M. (2004). Training in family therapy: Perceptual, conceptual, and executive skills. *Family Process, 18*(3), 227–250.

Trenhaile, J. D. (2005). Solution-Focused supervision: Returning the focus to client goals. *Journal of Family Psychotherapy, 16*(1–2), 223–228.

Trepal, H. C., Granello, D. H., & Smith, C. (2008). Duty to protect: Whose session is it anyway? In L. E. Tyson, J. R. Culbreth, & J. A. Harrington (Eds.), *Critical incidents in clinical supervision: Addictions, community, and school counseling* (pp. 149–154). Alexandria, VA: American Counseling Association.

Triantafillou, N. (1997). A solution-focused approach to mental health supervision. *Journal of Systemic Therapies, 16*(4), 305–328.

Tsui, M. (1997). The roots of social work supervision: An historical review. *The Clinical Supervisior, 15*(2), 191–198.

Tsui, M. (2005). *Social work supervision: Contexts and concepts.* Thousand Oaks, CA: Sage.

Turner, J., & Fine, M. (1995). Postmodern evaluation in family therapy supervision. *Journal of Systemic Therapies, 14*(2), 57–69.

Twain, M. (1869). *The innocents abroad, or the new pilgrims' progress.* Bloomington, MN: American Publishing.

von Foerster, H. (1949). *Cybernetics: Transactions of the sixth conference.* New York, NY: Josiah Macy Jr. Foundation.

von Foerster, H. (2002). *Understanding understanding: A volume of von Foerster's papers.* New York, NY: Springer-Verlag.

von Goethe, J. W. (1828). *Faust.* Paris, France: Gérard de Nerval.

Vygotsky, L. S. (1987). Thinking and speech. In R. Rieber & A. Carton (Eds.) & N. Minick (Trans.), *In L. S. Vygotsky, collected works* (Vol. 1, pp. 39–285). New York, NY: Plenum. (Original work published 1934, 1960)

Walsh, F. (1996). Family resiliency: A concept and its application. *Family Process, 35*(3), 261–282.

Walsh, F. (1998). *Strengthening family resilience.* New York, NY: Guilford Press.

Walsh, F. (2003a). Clinical views of family normality, health, and dysfunction: From deficit to strengths perspective. In F. Walsh (Ed.), *Normal family process: Growing diversity and complexity* (pp. 27–57). New York, NY: Guilford Press

Walsh, F. (2003b). Family resilience: A framework for clinical practice. *Family Process, 42,* 1–18.

Walsh, F. (2006). *Strengthening family resiliency* (2nd ed.). New York, NY: Guilford Press.

Walter, J. L., & Peller, J. E. (1992). *Becoming solution-focused in brief therapy.* New York, NY: Brunner/Mazel.

Walumbwa, F. O., Hartnell, C. A., & Oke, A. (2010). Servant leadership, procedural justice climate, service climate, employee attitudes, and organizational citizenship behavior: A cross-level investigation. *Journal of Applied Psychology, 95*(3), 517–529.

Ward, P. (1997). *360 degree feedback.* London, UK: Charter House.

Watkins, C. E. (1997). *Handbook of psychotherapy supervision.* New York, NY: Wiley.

Watkins, J. M., & Cooperrider, D. (1996). Organizational inquiry model for global social change organizations. *Organization Development Journal, 14*(4), 97–112.

Watson, M. F. (2005). Supervising the person of the therapist: Issues, challenges and dilemmas. *Contemporary Family Therapy, 15*(1), 21–31.

Watzlawick, P. A., Beavin, J. H., & Jackson, D. D. (1969). *Pragmatics of human communications.* New York, NY: W. W. Norton.

Werner, E. E. (1995). Resilience in development: Current directions. *Psychological Science, 4,* 81–82.

Werner, E. E., & Smith, R. S. (1982). *Vulnerable but invincible: A longitudinal study of resilient children and youth.* New York, NY: McGraw-Hill.

West Russo, J. K., Edwards, J. K., & Mahoney, D. M. (2011). Competencies in the supervision of mental health counselor interns: A Delphi study. *Journal of Counseling in Illinois, 1*(2), 5–15.

Wetchler, J. L. (1990). Solution-Focused supervision. *Family Therapy, 17*(2), 129–138.

Wheeler, J. (2007). Solution-Focused supervision. In T. Nelson & F .N. Thomas (Eds.), *Handbook of solution-focused brief therapy: Clinical applications* (pp. 343–370). New York, NY: Haworth Press.

Whitaker, C., & Garfield, R. (1987). On teaching psychotherapy via consultation and cotherapy. *Contemporary Family Therapy: An International Journal, 9*(1–2), 106–115.

White, M. (1984). Pseudo-Encopresis: From avalanche to victory, from vicious to virtuous cycles. *Journal of Family Systems Medicine, 2,* 150–160.

White, M. (2007). *Maps of narrative practice.* New York: NY: W. W. Norton.

White, M., & Epston, D. (1990). *Narrative means to therapeutic ends.* New York, NY: W. W. Norton.

White, M. B., & Russell, C. S. (1997). Examining the multifaceted notion of isomorphism in marriage and family therapy supervision: A quest for conceptual clarity. *Journal of Marital and Family Therapy, 23*(3), 315–333.

Whiting, J. B. (2007). Authors, artists, and social constructionism: A case study of narrative supervision. *The American Journal of Family Therapy, 35,* 139–150.

Whitney, D., Cooperrider, D. L., Garrison, M., & Moore, J. (2002). Appreciative inquiry and culture change at GTE: Launching a positive revolution. In R. Fry, F. Barrett, J. Seiling, & D. Whitney (Eds.), *Appreciative inquiry and organizational transformation: Reports from the field* (pp. 165–180). Westport, CT: Quorum Books/Greenwood Publishing Group.

Whitney, D., & Trosten-Bloom, A. (2010). *The power of appreciative inquiry: A practical guide to positive change* (2nd ed.). San Francisco, CA: Berrett-Koehler.

Whitney, D., Trosten-Bloom, A., & Rager, K. (2010). Leading positive performance: A conversation about appreciative leadership. *Performance Improvement Journal, 49*(3), 5–10.

Wiener, N. (1948). *Cybernetics: Or control and communication in the animal and the machine.* Paris, France: Librairie Hermann & Cie.

Wilkerson, K. (2006). Peer supervision for the professional development of school counselors: Toward an understanding of terms and findings. *Counselor Education and Supervision, 46*(1), 59–67.

Willoughby, G., & Samuels, N. (2009). *Brilliant: The Heathside story: Appreciative inquiry in whole school transformation.* Chichester, West Sussex, UK: Kingsham Press.

Worrall, J. M., & Fruzzetti, A. E. (2009). Improving peer supervisor ratings of therapist performance in dialectical behavior therapy: An internet-based training system. *Psychotherapy Theory, Research, Practice, Training, 46*(4), 476–479.

Wright, B. A., & Lopez, S. J. (2005). Widening the diagnostic focus: A case for including human strengths and environmental resources. In C. R. Snyder & S. J. Lopez (Eds.), *Handbook of positive psychology* (pp. 26–44). Oxford, UK: Oxford University Press.

Wright, L. M. (1986). An analysis of live supervision "phone-ins" in family therapy. *Journal of Marital and Family Therapy, 12*(2), 187–190.

Worthen, V., & McNeil, B. W. (1996). A phenomenological investigation of "good" supervision events. *Journal of Counseling Psychology, 43,* 25–34.

Yogev, S. (1982). An eclectic model of supervision: A developmental sequence for beginning psychotherapy students. *Professional Psychology, 13,* 236–243.

Young, J., Saunders, F., Prentice, G., Macri-Risely, D., Fitch, R., & Pati-Tasca, D. (1997). Three journeys toward the reflecting team. *Australian and New Zealand Journal of Family Therapy, 18,* 27–37.

Zeig , J. K. (Ed.). (1987) *The evolution of psychotherapy.* New York, NY: Brunner/Mazel.

Zimmerman, B. J., & Cleary, T. J. (2006). Adolescents' development of personal agency: The role of self-efficacy beliefs and self-regulatory skill. In F. Pajares & T. Urdan (Eds.), *Self-Efficacy beliefs of adolescents* (pp. 45–69). Charlotte, NC: Information Age Publishing.

INDEX

Ackerman, Nat, 19
Action-centered leadership, 129
Adler, Alfred, 91, 199
Adlerian model, 79*t*
Administrative supervision:
Appreciative Inquiry (AI), 84, 138–141
  defined, 128
  educational practices, 127–128
  organizational development, 84, 138–141
  session management, 169–173
  supervisory paradigm shift, 84
  See also Strengths-based leadership;
    Strengths-based management
Adult learning, 76–78, 204–205
Advancing Together: Centralizing Feminism and
    Multiculturalism in Counseling Psychology
    Conference (1998), 31
Agreeableness, 58
Ahola, Tapani, 20–21
Albee, George, 199
Allport, Gordon, 80
American Association for Marriage and Family
    Therapy (AAMFT):
Approved Supervisor Designation (ASD), 20, 106
  competency boundaries, 44
  supervision legitimacy, 9
American Counseling Association (ACA):
  competency boundaries, 44
  social work supervision, 5–6
American Personnel and Guidance Association
    (APGA), 5–6

American Psychiatric Association, 12, 72, 111
American Psychological Association, 32
American Psychologist, 109, 111
Anderson, Harlene, 199
Anderson, Tom, 20–21, 104
Andragogy, 76–78, 204–205
Appreciative Inquiry (AI):
  defined, 84
  designing phase, 140
  destiny phase, 140
  discovery phase, 139
  dreaming phase, 139–140
  strengths-based leadership, 138–141, 197
  supervisory paradigm shift, 84
Assagioli, Roberto, 199
Association for Counselor Education and
    Supervisors (CES), 5–6
Association for Multicultural Counseling and
    Development (AMCD):
  client worldview, 34*f*
  counselor self-reflection, 33*f*
  intervention strategies, 34–36*f*
  multicultural competencies, 32, 33–36*f*
Atkinson, Brent, 20
Audiotaped supervision, 16–17
Authentic Happiness (Seligman), 110, 206
Axline, Virginia, 199

Bandura, Albert, 12, 80, 109
Bateson, Gregory, 19–20
Behavioral model, 79*t*

Bell-curve evaluation, 135–136

Berg, Insoo Kim, 96, 199

Bernard, J., 7–8, 198–199

Best-practices model, 73

Bettelheim, Bruno, 195–196

Big Five personality domains:
agreeableness, 58
conscientiousness, 58
extraversion, 58
interpersonal relationship skills, 57–58
neuroticism, 58
openness, 58

Blackwell, Art, 212

Bowen, Murray, 143, 199

Brackett, J., 4

Breunlin, D., 8, 9

Brief Strategic model, 79*t*

Bug-in-the-ear format, 18–19

Burke, E., 127

Canino, Tony, 212

Case examples:
conflict resolution skills, 62
isomorphs, 50–51
Narrative Therapy, 102–103
personal agency, 29
Positive Psychotherapy, 116, 117–118
problem-focused model, 106–108
psychology model, 116, 117–118, 122
reflecting teams, 105
resiliency model, 122
session management, 160–161, 163–164
Solution-Focused Therapy, 99
strengths-based supervisory skills, 29, 42, 50–51, 53–54, 62

Case presentations:
clinical supervision formats, 16
"Jane," 177–187
"Melody," 187–193
research introduction, 175–176

Case Western Reserve University, 138

Character Strengths and Virtues (Peterson and Seligman), 111, 112*t,* 117

Charismatic leadership, 129

Chavez-Korell, S., 32

Chen, Mei, 20, 28, 150, 155, 198

Chicago Institute for Psychoanalysis, 43

Chlorpromazine, 195

Chrysler Corporation, 129

Chun, K. Y. S., 32

Clay, Willard, 152

Client Centered model, 79*t*

Clinical depression, 110

Clinical supervision boundaries:
competency boundaries, 43–44
supervisory boundaries, 52–57

Clinical supervision configurations:
contracts, 22
group supervision, 24
individual supervision, 22
informed consent, 22
peer group supervision, 24–25
person-of-the-therapist supervision, 22, 43
traditional perspective, 22–26
training contexts, 25–26
triadic supervision, 22–24

Clinical supervision domain skills, 37–43
case example, 42
conceptualization skills, 38–39
consultation skills, 40–41
counseling skills, 41–43
personalization skills, 39
process skills, 38
training skills, 39–40
See also Strengths-based supervisory skills

Clinical supervision formats:
audiotaped supervision, 16–17
bug-in-the-ear, 18–19
case presentations, 16
cotherapy, 18
feedback, 15–22
hierarchical model, 16
Interpersonal Process Recall (IPR), 16, 17
live supervision, 19
phone-in supervision, 19
problem-focused model, 15
reflecting teams, 20–22
team breaks, 19–20
traditional perspective, 4, 15–22
videotaped supervision, 17–18

Clinical supervision models:
 developmental supervision model, 4, 12–15
 integrated supervision model, 4, 12, 13–15
 model defined, 4
 orientation supervision model, 4, 11–12
 traditional perspective, 11–15
 See also Supervisory paradigm shift;
  specific model
Clinical supervision stages:
 beginning stage, 158–165
 middle stage, 165–166
 session management, 157–169
 transitional stage, 162, 166–169
Clinical supervision tradition:
 client defined, 4
 family therapy supervision, 8–9
 literature review, 4–8
 psychotherapy supervision, 5, 7, 8, 11
 research introduction, 3–4
 social work supervision, 4–5, 6–7
 substance abuse counseling supervision,
  10–11
 supervision configurations, 22–26
 supervision formats, 4, 15–22
 supervision models, 4, 11–15
Clinical Supervisor, The, 6
Clinician attributes, 78–80
Clinician developmental stages:
 beginning stage, 45
 challenge/growth stage, 47–48
 strengths-based supervisory skills, 44–48
 trials/tribulations stage, 45–47
Clinician empowerment:
 psychology model, 124–125
 session management, 150
Clinician motivation, 169–171
Cognitive model, 79*t*
Coles, Catherine, 144
Collaborative language-based therapy, 75–76
Collaborative languaging systems, 81, 94–96
 model premises, 94–95
 supervisory concepts, 95–96
Combs, Gene, 156, 199
Community Mental Health Act (1963), 195
Conceptualization skills, 38–39

Conchie, B., 76, 84
Confidentiality, 43–44
Conflict resolution skills:
 case example, 62
 conflict prevention, 61–62
 hierarchical model, 59–60
 resolution strategies, 60–61
 scaffolding, 61
 strengths-based supervisory skills, 59–62
Conscientiousness, 58
Consultation skills, 40–41
Contracts:
 clinical supervision configurations, 22
 informed consent, 22, 43
Control theory, 91–92
Coontz, S., 121
Cooperrider, David, 84, 138, 142, 144, 197
Cotherapy, 18
Council for Accreditation of Counseling and
  Related Educational Programs (CACREP), 22
Counseling Psychologist, The, 88
Counseling self-efficacy (CSE), 62–63
Counseling skills, 41–43
 See also Strengths-based supervisory skills
Counselor complexity model, 12–13
*Counselor Education and Supervision
 Journal,* 5–6
Covey, Stephen, 144–145, 198
Cross-cultural competency:
 defined, 29
 psychology model, 123
 strengths-based supervisory skills, 29–30
 supervisory paradigm shift, 81
 See also Multicultural competency
Csikszentmihalyi, Mihaly, 199
Cultural sensitivity, 30
Cybernetics:
 defined, 91
 Narrative Therapy, 100
 second-order cybernetics, 64, 91–92, 100
 self-efficacy, 64
 social constructivism, 91–93

Dead Poets Society, 203
Death of Resistance, The (de Shazer), 96

Deficit model. *See* Problem-focused model
de Shazer, Steven, 96
Developmental supervision model:
    counselor complexity model, 12–13
    defined, 12
    discrimination model, 12, 15
    success criteria, 12–13
    traditional perspective, 4, 12–15
Diagnostic and Statistical Manual of Mental Health Disorders-IV, 12, 73, 110, 111
Dialectical Behavior Therapy, 25
Discrimination model, 12, 15
Dreyfuss, Richard, 203
Drive (Pink), 169
Drucker, Peter, 84–85, 203

Educational practices:
    administrative supervision, 127–128
    adult learning, 76–78, 204–205
    andragogy, 76–78, 204–206
    democratic pedagogy, 204
    instructional empowerment, 203–204
    supervisory paradigm shift, 76–78
Epston, David, 100
Ethics:
    client confidentiality, 43–44
    competency boundaries, 43–44
    informed consent, 43
    sexual misconduct, 43, 52
    strengths-based supervisory skills, 43–44
Evaluation process:
    bell-curve evaluation, 135–136
    defined, 134
    J-curve evaluation, 136–137
    problem-focused model, 133
    strengths-based leadership, 132–137
    strengths-based supervision, 209
    360-degree evaluation, 134–135, 137
    See also Session management
Evidence-based practice, 28–29, 39
Evidence Validated Therapy (EVT), 71
Evolution of Psychotherapy, The (Zeig), 75
Extraversion, 58
Eye Movement Desensitization and Reprocessing (EMDR), 72

Family Institute of Chicago (Northwestern University), 106, 121, 196
Family Therapy Education and Supervision (Piercy), 8–9
Family Therapy Networker, 81
Family therapy supervision:
    isomorphs, 49, 50
    live supervision format, 19
    model usage rates, 79*t*
    multicultural competency, 9
    reflecting teams, 20
    resiliency model, 118–119, 120–121
    team breaks, 19–20
    traditional perspective, 8–9
Farnum, Mary, 203, 207
Feedback:
    clinical supervision formats, 15–22
    self-efficacy, 64
Field, L. D., 32
Financial concerns, 70
Frankl, Victor, 199
Freedman, Jill, 156, 199
Friedman, T., 124
From the Margins to the Center (Singh and Chun), 32
Fundamentals of Clinical Supervision (Bernard and Goodyear), 7–8, 198–199
Furman, Ben, 20–21

Genentech, 130–131
Gergen, Ken, 199
Gladwell, M., 12–13, 74, 138, 141, 201
Goodyear, R., 7–8, 198–199
Goolishian, Harry, 143
Goulding, Mary, 75, 204
Group Leadership Skills (Chen and Rybak), 28
Group supervision, 24
Groupthink, 94

Haley, Jay, 143
Grant Halvorson, H., 169
Handbook of Family Therapy Training and Supervision (Liddle, Breunlin, and Schwartz), 8, 9
Handbook of Psychotherapy Supervision (Watkins), 7, 8

Happiness:
  authentic happiness, 206–207
  Positive Psychology, 110–111
Harkness, D., 4
Heath, Tony, 20, 159
Henderson, P., 84
Hess, A., 5, 7
Heuristic Model of Non-Oppressive Interpersonal
    Development (HMNID), 36–37
Hierarchical model:
  clinical supervision formats, 16
  conflict resolution skills, 59–60
  integrated supervision model, 14–15
  orientation supervision model, 11–12
  psychology model, 124–125
  strengths-based supervision, 198–199
  supervisory boundaries, 52, 55–57
  supervisory paradigm shift, 71, 74
Hurn, David, 151–152

Iacocca, Lee, 129
Illinois Counseling Association, 140–141, 197
Illinois Counselor Educators and
    Supervisors, 170
Illinois Department of Mental Health, 22
Individual supervision, 22
Industrial-Age workers, 70–71, 80, 84–85
Information-Age workers:
  session management, 169
  strengths-based leadership, 131, 145
  supervisory paradigm shift, 70–71,
      76–77, 80, 85
Informed consent, 22, 43
In Search of Excellence (Peters
    and Waterman), 203
Integrated developmental model (IDM), 13
Integrated supervision model:
  defined, 13–14, 15
  hierarchical model, 14–15
  integrated developmental model (IDM), 13
  integrative family therapy, 13–15
  strengths-based supervision, 13–14
  traditional perspective, 4, 12, 13–15
Integrative family therapy:
  basic principles, 14*t*

strengths-based supervision, 13–14
traditional perspective, 13–15
Internet resources:
  peer group supervision, 24–25
  Positive Psychology, 111
Interpersonal Process Recall (IPR), 16, 17
Interpersonal relationship skills:
  Big Five personality domains, 57–58
  conflict resolution, 59–62
  strengths-based supervisory skills, 57–65
Intervention skills, 38
Invictus, 140
Isomorphs:
  case example, 50–51
  defined, 48
  family therapy supervision, 49, 50
  isomorphic structure, 49*f*
  problem-focused model, 51–52
  strengths-based supervisory skills, 48–52

J-curve evaluation, 136–137
Jewish Family Services, 19
Journal of Family Medicine, 100
Jung, Carl, 199
Jungian model, 79*t*

Kadushin, A., 4
Kapp, Alexander, 204
Keith, Alan, 130–131
Kelling, George, 144
Kelly, George, 91, 199
Kennedy, John F., 129, 195
Kleist, David, 82
Knowledge-Age workers, 70–71, 76, 85
Kramer, Chuck, 196
Kuhn, T., 72

Laing, R. D., 199
Language:
  collaborative language-based therapy, 75–76
  collaborative languaging systems, 81, 94–96
  Narrative Therapy, 100
  social constructivism, 93–94, 100
Law of the few:
  connectors, 142

mavens, 142
salesmen, 142
strengths-based leadership, 142–144
Leadership Secrets of Genghis Khan, The (Man), 129
Leading-edge practices:
    strengths-based leadership, 131
    supervisory paradigm shift, 73, 74
Licensed Clinical Professional Counselor (LCPC),
        11, 40
Licensed Clinical Social Worker (LCSW), 40
Licensed Marriage and Family Therapist (LMFT), 11
Liddle, H., 8, 9
Live supervision, 19
Lopez, Shane J., 199

Maddux, James E., 199
Man, J., 129
Mandela, Nelson, 140
Maps of Narrative Practice (White), 82
Maslow, Abraham, 80, 109, 199
Masten, Ann S., 199
May, Gerald, 196, 199
Medical model. *See* Problem-focused model
Medications, 195–196
Mental Research Institute, 96
Milan team (Italy), 19–21
Miller, Scott, 143, 208
Mr. Holland's Opus, 203
Multicultural competency:
    client worldview, 34*f*
    cultural sensitivity, 30
    defined, 30
    family therapy supervision, 9
    Heuristic Model of Non-Oppressive Interpersonal
        Development (HMNID), 36–37
    intervention strategies, 34–36*f*
    postmodernism, 30–31
    power and privilege, 31
    psychology model, 123
    resiliency model, 32
    self-reflection, 31–32, 33*f*
    social constructivism, 30–31
    strengths-based supervisory skills, 29–37
    structured peer group supervision (SPGS), 36
    supervisory paradigm shift, 81
    synergistic model, 36–37

Multiple Impact Therapy (MIT), 19
Munson, C. E., 4
Myers, Richard, 124

Narrative Therapy:
    case example, 102–103
    model premises, 100–101
    session management, 156
    supervisory concepts, 101–104
    supervisory paradigm shift, 75–76, 82
    usage rates, 79*t*
National Advisory Mental Health Council, 110
National Association for Social Workers (NASW), 32
National Institute for Mental Health, 143
Neuroscience, 92–93
Neuroticism, 58
New York Times, 201
No Hay Rosas Sin Espinas (Field and Chavez-
        Korell), 32
Normal Family Process (Walsh), 87

Openness, 58
Organizational development:
    administrative supervision, 84, 138–141
    supervisory paradigm shift, 84
Orientation supervision model:
    hierarchical model, 11–12
    problem-focused model, 11–12
    psychotherapy supervision, 11
    self-efficacy, 12
    traditional perspective, 4, 11–12
Outliers (Gladwell), 12–13, 74, 201

Parallel process:
    defined, 49
    problem-focused model, 51–52
    psychotherapy supervision, 49–50
    strengths-based supervisory skills, 49–50
Peck, M. Scott, 199
Peer group supervision:
    clinical supervision configurations, 24–25
    multicultural competency, 36
Peller, Jane, 143
Perls, Fritz, 199
Personal agency:
    case example, 29

defined, 62
psychology model, 122
strengths-based supervision, 199–201, 209
strengths-based supervisory skills, 29, 62–64
supervisory paradigm shift, 75
Personalization skills, 39
Person-of-the-therapist supervision, 22, 43
Perspective, 151–152, 155–157
Peters, T., 203
Peterson, Christopher, 83, 109, 111, 112*t*, 117, 199
Phone-in supervision, 19
Piaget, Jean, 91
Pienaar, Francois, 140
Piercy, F., 8–9
Pink, D., 169
Point of view, 151–152, 155
Positive Psychology, 109–111, 112*t*
    character strengths/virtues, 111, 112*t*
    clinical depression, 110
    contextual factor, 143–144
    happiness, 110–111
    Internet resources, 111
    premises of, 109–111
    process skills, 38
    social constructivism, 115
    stickiness factor, 143, 144
    strengths-based leadership, 132, 142–144, 197
    supervisory paradigm shift, 72, 75–76, 83
Positive Psychotherapy, 111, 113–118
    case examples, 116, 117–118
    ideal therapy sessions, 113–115*t*
    premises of, 111, 115
    savoring, 117–118
    signature strengths, 118
    supervisory concepts, 115–118
Postmodernism:
    characteristics of, 89–91, 93, 106, 108
    collaborative languaging systems, 94–96
    multicultural competency, 30–31
    Narrative Therapy, 100–104
    problem-focused model, 106–108
    reflecting teams, 20, 104–105
    research introduction, 87–89
    Solution-Focused Therapy, 96–99
    supervisory paradigm shift, 81–82

Prevention and Treatment, 110
Problem-focused model:
    case example, 106–108
    clinical supervision formats, 15
    evaluation process, 133
    isomorphs, 51–52
    orientation supervision model, 11–12
    parallel process, 51–52
    session management, 150
    strengths-based supervision, 196–198
    supervisory paradigm shift, 71, 74–75, 78, 80–85
Process skills, 38
Professional Clinical Counseling, 9
Professional education. *See* Educational practices
Psychodynamic model, 79*t*
Psychology model:
    case examples, 116, 117–118, 122
    clinician empowerment, 124–125
    cross-cultural competency, 123
    forced practice methods, 125
    guiding principles, 125–126
    hierarchical model, 124–125
    multicultural competency, 123
    personal agency, 122
    Positive Psychology, 109–111, 112*t*
    Positive Psychotherapy, 111, 113–118
    resiliency, 118–122
    self-efficacy, 122
    strengths-based supervision, 122–126
    supervisory paradigm shift, 72, 75–76, 79*t*, 80–81, 82–83
    technological advancements, 124
Psychopharmaceuticals, 195–196
Psychotherapy supervision:
    audiotaped supervision, 16–17
    counseling skills, 41
    models of, 79*t*
    orientation supervision model, 11
    parallel process, 49–50
    session management, 167
    traditional perspective, 5, 7, 8, 11
Psychotherapy Supervision (Hess), 5, 7
Pulp Fiction, 89
Pygmalion effect:
    Appreciative Inquiry (AI), 140

conceptualization skills, 39
Narrative Therapy, 102
strengths-based supervision, 193

Rath, T., 76, 84
Reality model, 79*t*
Reflecting Model of Triadic Supervision
  (RMTS), 23–24
Reflecting teams:
  case examples, 105
  clinical supervision formats, 20–22
  family therapy supervision, 20
  model premises, 104–105
  postmodernism, 20
  session management, 162, 164–169
  social constructivism, 20, 21–22
  supervisory concepts, 105
  supervisory paradigm shift, 82
Resiliency model:
  at-risk youth, 119
  case example, 122
  defined, 83
  family therapy supervision, 118–119, 120–121
  model premises, 118–121
  multicultural competency, 32
  social constructivism, 120–121
  supervisory concepts, 121–122
  supervisory paradigm shift, 75–76, 83–84
Rogers, Carl, 16–17, 80, 109, 199
Rybak, C. J., 28

Samuels, Neil, 140–141
Savoring, 117–118
Sawyer effect, 169–170
Scaffolding, 61
Schaumburg Family Counseling Center
  (Illinois), 136–137
Schwartz, R., 8, 9
Schwarzbaum, Sara, 29–30
Second-order cybernetics, 64, 91–92, 100
Self-efficacy:
  counseling self-efficacy (CSE), 62–63
  defined, 62
  feedback, 64
  orientation supervision model, 12

psychology model, 122
second-order cybernetics, 64
session management, 173
strengths-based supervision, 200
strengths-based supervisory skills, 62–64
supervisory paradigm shift, 75
Seligman, Martin, 83, 87, 109, 110, 111, 112*t*,
  117, 142, 144, 197, 199, 206, 213
Senn, Larry, 198
Servant leadership, 129–130
Service leadership, 130–131
Session management:
  administrative supervision, 169–173
  beginning supervision stage, 158–165
  case example, 160–161, 163–164
  clinical supervision stages, 157–169
  clinician empowerment, 150
  clinician motivation, 169–171
  Information-Age workers, 169
  middle supervision stage, 165–166
  Narrative Therapy, 156
  perspective, 151–152, 155–157
  photographic metaphors, 151–153, 155, 156
  point of view, 151–152, 155
  problem-focused model, 150
  psychotherapy supervision, 167
  reflecting teams, 162, 164–169
  research introduction, 149–151
  Sawyer effect, 169–170
  self-efficacy, 173
  social constructivism, 151–152
  strategy implementation, 151–157
  strengths-based supervisory skills, 64–65
  success criteria, 171–173
  Tag Team Counseling, 162
  360-degree evaluation, 164–165
  transitional supervision stage, 162, 166–169
  vantage point, 152–155
Sexual misconduct, 43, 52
Shapiro, Francine, 72
Signature strengths:
  Positive Psychotherapy, 118
  strengths-based leadership, 132
Singh, A., 32
Skinner, B. F., 204

Snyder, C. R., 199
Social constructivism:
  characteristics of, 90–95, 106, 108
  collaborative languaging systems, 94–96
  conceptualization skills, 39
  control theory, 91–92
  cybernetics, 91–93
  language, 93–94, 100
  multicultural competency, 30–31
  Narrative Therapy, 100–104
  neuroscience, 92–93
  Positive Psychology, 115
  problem-focused model, 106–108
  reflecting teams, 20, 21–22, 104–105
  research introduction, 87–89
  resiliency model, 120–121
  session management, 151–152
  Solution-Focused Therapy, 96–99
  strengths-based leadership, 130, 144
  supervisory paradigm shift, 75–76, 81–82
Social work supervision:
  defined, 6
  models of, 79t
  supervisory paradigm shift, 79t
  traditional perspective, 4–5, 6–7
Social Work Supervision (Munson), 4
Solution-Focused Supervision (SFS), 97–98
Solution-Focused Therapy:
  case examples, 99
  model premises, 96–98
  strengths-based leadership, 143
  supervisory concepts, 98–99
  supervisory paradigm shift, 75–76, 81–82
  usage rates, 79t
Srivastva, Suresh, 138
Star Wars, 203
Stelazine, 195
Strengths Based Leadership, 76
Strengths-based leadership:
  action-centered leadership, 129
  application of, 201–203
  Appreciative Inquiry (AI), 138–141, 197
  charismatic leadership, 129
  defined, 127, 128–129
  evaluation process, 132–137

Information-Age workers, 131, 145
Knowledge-Age workers, 131
law of the few, 142–144
leading-edge practices, 131
Positive Psychology, 132, 142–144, 197
postmodernism, 144
qualities of, 131–132
research introduction, 127–129
servant leadership, 129–130
service leadership, 130–131
signature strengths, 132
social constructivism, 130, 144
Solution-Focused Therapy, 143
supervisory paradigm shift, 84, 138, 141–146
tipping-point of change, 138, 141–144
Strengths-based management:
  defined, 128
  supervisory paradigm shift, 70–71, 84–85
Strengths-based supervision:
  application of, 198–205
  authentic happiness, 206–207
  case presentations, 176–193
  encouragement, 207–208
  evaluation process, 209
  future directions, 205–207
  hierarchical model, 198–199
  integrative family therapy, 13–14
  mental health treatment, 195–196
  paradigm movement, 206
  personal agency, 199–201, 209
  personal experiences, 211–213
  philosophy of, 196–198
  problem-focused model, 196–198
  self-efficacy, 200
  stakeholder participation, 208
  supervisory paradigm shift, 69–70, 73–76,
    80–85
  supervisory performance, 206
  trim-tab metaphor, 207
  See also Psychology model; Postmodernism;
    Session management; Social constructivism;
    Supervisory paradigm shift
Strengths-based supervisory skills:
  case examples, 29, 42, 50–51, 53–54, 62
  clinician developmental stages, 44–48

conceptualization skills, 38–39
conflict resolution skills, 59–62
consultation skills, 40–41
counseling skills, 41–43
cross-cultural competency, 29–30
ethics, 43–44
evidence-based practice, 28–29, 39
interpersonal relationship skills, 57–65
isomorphs, 48–52
multicultural competency, 29–37
parallel process, 49–50
personal agency, 29, 62–64
personalization skills, 39
process skills, 38
research introduction, 27–29
self-efficacy, 62–64
session management, 64–65
supervisory boundaries, 52–57
supervisory domain areas, 37–43
training skills, 39–40
StrengthsFinder 2.0, 76
Structural model, 79t
Structured peer group supervision (SPGS), 36
Structure of Scientific Revolutions, The (Kuhn), 72
Substance abuse counseling supervision, 10–11
Succeed (Grant Halvorson), 169
Success criteria:
developmental supervision model, 12–13
session management, 171–173
Supervision and Education in Charity (Brackett), 4
Supervision in Social Work (Kadushin and
Harkness), 4
Supervisory paradigm shift:
administrative supervision, 84
Appreciative Inquiry (AI), 84
best-practices model, 73
clinical work, 81–85
clinician attributes, 78–80
collaborative language-based therapy, 75–76
collaborative languaging systems, 81
cross-cultural competency, 81
educational practices, 76–78
Evidence Validated Therapy (EVT), 71
field contradictions, 71–73
financial concerns, 70

hierarchical model, 71, 74
Industrial-Age workers, 70–71, 80, 84–85
Information-Age workers, 70–71, 76–77, 80, 85
Knowledge-Age workers, 70–71, 76, 85
leading-edge practices, 73, 74
multicultural competency, 81
Narrative Therapy, 75–76, 82
organizational development, 84
personal agency, 75
Positive Psychology, 72, 75–76, 83
postmodernism, 81–82
problem-focused model, 71, 74–75, 78, 80–85
psychology model, 72, 75–76, 79t, 80–81,
82–83
psychotherapy supervision, 75, 79t
reflecting teams, 82
research introduction, 69–71
resiliency model, 75–76, 83–84
self-efficacy, 75
social constructivism, 75–76, 81–82
social work supervision, 79t
solidifying change, 144–146
Solution-Focused Therapy, 75–76, 81–82
strengths-based leadership, 84
strengths-based management, 70–71, 84–85
strengths-based supervision, 69–70, 73–76,
80–85
tipping-point of change, 138, 141–144
Synergistic multicultural model, 36–37
Szasz, Thomas, 199

Tag Team Counseling, 162
Tarantino, Quentin, 89
Team breaks, 19–20
Technological advancements, 124
Thomas, Anita, 29–30
Thorazine, 195
360-degree evaluation:
evaluation process, 134–135, 137
session management, 164–165
Tipping Point, The (Gladwell), 138, 141
Tipping-point of change, 138, 141–144
Top-down metacognition, 64
Training skills, 39–40
Transactional Analysis, 75

Triadic supervision, 22–24
    Reflecting Model of Triadic Supervision
        (RMTS), 23–24
Trifluoperazine, 195

U.S. Army, 124–125
U.S. Department of Defense, 72
U.S. Department of Veterans
        Affairs, 72

Vantage point, 152–155
Veterans Administration Act (1946), 80
Videotaped supervision, 17–18

Wal-Mart, 129
Walsh, Froma, 87, 199
Walter, John, 143

Walton, Sam, 129
Waterman, R. H., 203
Watkins, C. E., 7, 8
Watzlawick, Paul, 199
Way We Never Were, The (Coontz), 121
Weakland, John, 199
Whitaker, Carl, 199
White, Michael, 82, 100, 143, 199
Wicked, 90, 153
Williams, Robin, 203
Winfrey, Oprah, 171
World is Flat, The (Friedman), 124

Young, Andy, 82, 106

Zeig, J., 75, 204
Zinn, Earl, 16–17

ABOUT THE AUTHOR

Dr. Jeffrey K. Edwards is professor emeritus from the Department of Counselor Education, the Family Counseling Program at Northeastern Illinois University, and a contributing faculty at Walden University in the College of Social and Behavioral Sciences, the Mental Health Counseling Program. Dr. Edwards has been a clinical supervisor since 1970 and has trained many supervisors along the way. He is a past president of the Illinois Counseling Association and current president of the Illinois Counselor Educators and Supervisors Association. Edwards has published and presented on many subjects in the field, including on supervision. His first book, with Anthony Heath, was *A Consumers Guide to Mental Health Services: Unveiling the Mysteries of Psychotherapy,* a Haworth Series in Clinical Psychotherapy book.

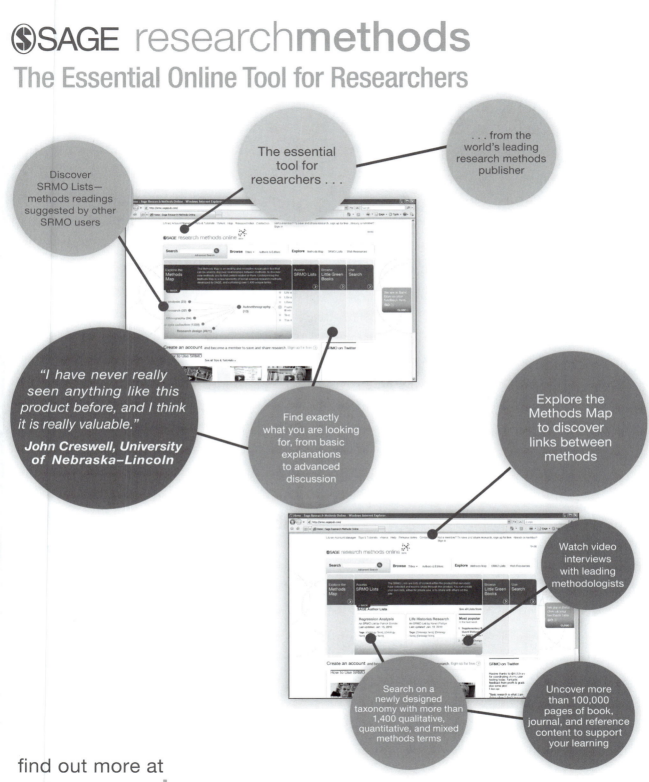

SAGE researchmethods

The Essential Online Tool for Researchers

The essential tool for researchers . . .

. . . from the world's leading research methods publisher

Discover SRMO Lists—methods readings suggested by other SRMO users

"I have never really seen anything like this product before, and I think it is really valuable."

John Creswell, University of Nebraska–Lincoln

Find exactly what you are looking for, from basic explanations to advanced discussion

Explore the Methods Map to discover links between methods

Watch video interviews with leading methodologists

Search on a newly designed taxonomy with more than 1,400 qualitative, quantitative, and mixed methods terms

Uncover more than 100,000 pages of book, journal, and reference content to support your learning

find out more at
srmo.sagepub.com